JUL 2011

IF YOU ASK ME

IF YOU ASK ME

(And of Course You Won't)

Betty White

G. P. PUTNAM'S SONS

New York

PUTNAM

G. P. PUTNAM'S SONS
Publishers Since 1838
Published by the Penguin Group
Penguin Group (USA) Inc., 375 Hudson Street, New York, New York 10014, USA •
Penguin Group (Canada), 90 Eglinton Avenue East, Suite 700, Toronto,
Ontario M4P 2Y3, Canada (a division of Pearson Penguin Canada Inc.) •
Penguin Books Ltd, 80 Strand, London WC2R 0RL, England •
Penguin Ireland, 25 St Stephen's Green, Dublin 2, Ireland
(a division of Penguin Books Ltd) • Penguin Group (Australia),
250 Camberwell Road, Camberwell, Victoria 3124, Australia
(a division of Pearson Australia Group Pty Ltd) • Penguin Books India Pvt Ltd,
11 Community Centre, Panchsheel Park, New Delhi–110 017, India •
Penguin Group (NZ), 67 Apollo Drive, Rosedale, North Shore 0632, New Zealand
(a division of Pearson New Zealand Ltd) • Penguin Books (South Africa) (Pty) Ltd,
24 Sturdee Avenue, Rosebank, Johannesburg 2196, South Africa

Penguin Books Ltd, Registered Offices: 80 Strand, London WC2R 0RL, England

Library of Congress Cataloging-in-Publication Data

White, Betty, date.
If you ask me: (and of course you won't)/Betty White.
p.   cm.
ISBN 978-0-399-15753-0
1. White, Betty, date.   2. Television actors and actresses—United States—Biography.   I. Title.
PN2287.W4577A3 2011   2011007358
791.4502'8082—dc22
[B]

Printed in the United States of America
1   3   5   7   9   10   8   6   4   2

Book design by Meighan Cavanaugh

While the author has made every effort to provide accurate telephone numbers and
Internet addresses at the time of publication, neither the publisher nor the author
assumes any responsibility for errors or for changes that occur after publication.
Further, the publisher does not have any control over and does not assume
any responsibility for author or third-party websites or their content.

Penguin is committed to publishing works of quality and integrity.
In that spirit, we are proud to offer this book to our readers;
however, the story, the experiences, and the words
are the author's alone.

Gratefully Dedicated

to

Loretta

Marysue

and

Bruce

Contents

LETTERS

STAGECRAFT

LOVE AND FRIENDSHIP

ANIMAL KINGDOM

STATE OF AFFAIRS

SINCE YOU ASKED . . .

Foreword

One time I remember hearing someone ask my friend, George Burns, if he had read a certain book, current at the time.

George said, "I can't read a book cuz I'm writing one."

We all laughed — George could make anything sound funny — but he was absolutely right. Whatever else you may be involved in, writing a book takes precedence. There is that inexorable due date staring you in the face.

By my sixth book you'd think I would know better, yet once again I was thrilled when they asked me to do another one.

I simply love the process. And not just because I can do it sitting on the couch with my shoes off and my dog by my side.

Writing is my favorite thing.

Betty White
2/14/11

BODY AND MIND

© Bettmann/Corbis

GROWING OLDER

*O*ld age isn't for sissies."

"I can't believe I'm getting old."

"Why do people ever say 'Happy Birthday'?"

And the list goes on—we've heard them all. However, if one is lucky enough to be blessed with good health, growing older shouldn't be something to complain about. It's not a surprise, we knew it was coming—make the most of it. So you may not be as fast on your feet, and the image in your mirror may be a little disappointing, but if you are still functioning and not in pain, gratitude should be the name of the game.

Actually—and don't laugh—there may even be some upsides to aging. People treat you more gently. They may even think your years of experience make you wiser than you are. And <u>somebody</u> always finds you a place to sit down, whether you want it or not.

Somewhere along the line there is a breaking point, where you go from not discussing how old you are to bragging about it. I have never lied about my age, but these days I seem to work it into the conversation at the drop of a hat. Please stop me before I get to the point of, "Hi, I'm Betty White—I'm eighty-nine years old!" There's nothing to brag about—I didn't accomplish that age, it sneaked up on me.

There is even a funny side to aging, if one has a warped sense of humor.

If one has no sense of humor, one is in trouble.

I joined the American Women's Voluntary Services
when World War II broke out.

ON
REFLECTION

*I*n show business, the mirror obviously plays a big part in one's life, but early on—long before I started working—my beloved mother taught me another role the mirror plays. I can still hear her:

"Bets, you can lie to anyone in the world and even get away with it, perhaps, but when you are alone and look into your own eyes in the mirror, you can't sidestep the truth. Always be sure you can meet those eyes directly. Otherwise, it's big trouble, my girl."

It may sound like a cliché, I realize, but oh, it's so

true. On rare occasions I have tried to prove my mom wrong. I stare back at my reflection and try to rationalize my way out of something, but it never works. Those eyes in the looking glass take on a life of their own.

It still works, Mom. Even after all these years.

My beloved mom—Tess White.

Animal lover that I am, I am often handed animals by pet owners at events and appearances, like this cute little devil.

HEALTH

As the years add up, I am so grateful for the good health I have been blessed with, and I don't ever take it for granted for a second. I make it a point to never let my weight vary more than five pounds in either direction; I wear glasses to read or to drive; I have a two-story house and a bad memory, so all those trips up and down the stairs take care of my exercise.

I had my eyes done in 1976 and have let nature take its course ever since. As for my hair, I have no idea what color it really is, and I never intend to find out. My mother's hair never went gray, it just went mousy. So when mine started going that way, I just started tinting it and haven't stopped. And I never will!

In terms of my weight, I weigh myself every morning. And if I go up one pound, I take it off the next day. It's easy to take a pound off, you just skip something. But if it goes to three pounds, it becomes more difficult and one of them usually just stays there. Or five pounds—even worse—sometimes those just stay. I watched it happen with my mother. So I figure it's easy to just take them off immediately, and it's not too much of a sacrifice.

I don't have a sweet tooth, but I do have a cocktail before dinner. I also love french fries and hot dogs. The famous Pink's hot dog company in California actually named a hot dog after me, and since I eat mine plain with no condiments, it's the Betty White "Naked" Dog. So if my weight goes up a pound or so, it's easy to find something to cut out to bring it back down.

My obsessive addiction to crossword puzzles I chalk off as mental gymnastics. I love games and puzzles. On the set of *The Lost Valentine*, a Hallmark movie, Jennifer Love Hewitt and her boyfriend, Alex Beh, and I played Scrabble during every lunch break. And I always have a book of crosswords or acrostics in my purse wherever I go. Whenever I've had a puppy, I've put newspaper down for him, but if I put down a piece of the paper and there's a crossword in there, I'll snatch it right up and say, "No, you can't go on that!"

I subscribe to the Crosswords Club and the Puzzle Club and get a new set of puzzles every month. They were given to me as a gift, and I renew them all the time. I have stacks piling up. I won't live long enough to do all these puzzles, but it's a comfort zone for me.

And no, you can't use a dictionary or an encyclopedia—that's a cheat.

I'm not a big pill-taker, and almost never have a headache. But I once read an article about Dr. Linus Pauling, who took vitamin C every day to stave off colds. I thought, If it's good enough for Linus Pauling, it's good enough for me—why not? I asked my doctor, and my doctor said that's rubbish, vitamin C has nothing to do with the common cold. But I wasn't taking any other vitamins, so I started taking vitamin C every morning. I haven't had a cold in twenty years.

I attribute my generous supply of energy to DNA— my father was so filled with energy, my mom used to call him "Horace the Hummingbird." She'd say, "Honey, could you light long enough to sit down?"

I'm grateful to have inherited that gene. But in the end, the energy is also very much due to enjoying what

I am so lucky to do for a living. Show business. If all this sounds too "Little Mary Sunshine," please put up with me while I celebrate it.

Human nature being what it is, I'm ashamed to say that even with all the good stuff, there are still days when the misgivings move in. Maybe when I'm overtired or overloaded—or over_something_. In spite of myself, I find it harder to roll with the punches. I get irritated inside and begin to feel that I'll never catch up. When this happens, I try desperately to resist indulging those ungrateful moods, and I try to attack any one of the many things that need doing, but it just doesn't work and I don't accomplish a damned thing. It might take a little while to shake those doldrums.

It's been widely reported that I prefer the company of animals to humans. As a matter of fact, Barbara Walters asked me that direct question in an interview at one point. With Barbara, you don't hedge.

I said, "Yes, that's true!" Now, here with you I want to be on the level: It _is_ true.

Can you blame me? Animals don't lie. Animals don't criticize. If animals have moody days, they handle them better than humans do.

Next time I'm feeling overwhelmed, I think I'm going to start channeling my dog Ponti.

I moved to Chappaqua, New York,
for a spell after marrying Allen Ludden.

SENSES

S ooner or later, some of our senses lose a little of their efficiency. (What do I mean "some"?! What do I mean "a little"?!) Eyesight, for example.

It sneaks up on you.

Reading and needlepoint have been passions for me since I was a child, and as middle age approached, I tried not to notice the fact that my eyes were gradually changing—things weren't quite as sharp. I'm not sure how long I could have gotten away with ignoring it if it weren't for my husband, Allen Ludden.

AWARDS

I know it sounds like a cliché, and I've discussed it in my interviews and other books, but it's the truth— I truly believe a nomination in and of itself is the greatest honor one can receive for one's work.

When you're nominated, you get it all sorted out in your mind—not <u>who's</u> going to win, but that you yourself are <u>not</u>. And that's not being coy—that's being realistic.

At the Screen Actors Guild Awards in 2011, I was nominated for Outstanding Performance by a Female

Actor in a Comedy Series, and the actors with whom I was nominated were simply extraordinary—Tina Fey of *30 Rock*, Jane Lynch of *Glee*, Edie Falco of *Nurse Jackie*, Sofía Vergara of *Modern Family*, and me for *Hot in Cleveland*. When I saw the competition, it took all the nervousness away. I thought, *This is great, but I'm never going to win!*

So when my name was announced, I was simply stunned. I'd nearly forgotten I was nominated. And if you think I was in shock, you should have seen Jeff Witjas. He looked at me, and the color just drained from his face. Meanwhile, the girls from *Hot in Cleveland* were jumping up and down with excitement—they were, if possible, more delighted than I was!

As with the instances when I've won previous awards, it all happened so fast. There's always a striking and sudden contrast: one minute, you're sitting at the table, wherever that may be, and the next you're onstage. You've been sitting in the audience long enough that you know your environment around your table, you know who's seated nearby, but you get up those steps and turn around, and suddenly you see the whole overview of the audience. And that's overwhelming, because you haven't thought of all those people in that great big auditorium. You've thought only about the tables nearby.

When you turn around, the impact of what you see scares anything out of your head that was ever there!

I've never, in all the instances I've been nominated for an award, prepared a speech. I've known whom I would thank, but I've never actually written a speech. And this occasion was no different. And as in times past, I opened my mouth and words came, and God knows what they were. But it is such an exciting feeling.

When I picked up the SAG statue itself, which presenter Jon Hamm had left on the podium for me, it felt like it weighed twenty-five pounds. All I could think about was that it was the heaviest award I'd ever held.

Allen's always there when I win an award, or when anything special happens, because nobody would celebrate it like he did. So he was right up there with me.

Ever wonder what happens to an actor after they accept an award and leave the stage?

After you win, someone escorts you backstage to a room filled with press. They all ask you questions and take photos. Then, if it's early enough in the program—which it was, at the SAGs—they'll take you back to the table. That was great, because the girls were just so excited. I think Valerie was still jumping up and down, bless her.

We had also been nominated for the show itself, for Outstanding Performance by an Ensemble in a Comedy Series. That was the one I wish we had won rather than the individual, but my castmates didn't seem to care one bit.

My beloved castmates couldn't have celebrated more.

Actors tend to take the bows for their performances and forget to share the credit with those who put the words on the page. Where would we be without them? To be blessed with good writing is such a privilege, and I have been so lucky. Shows like *The Mary Tyler Moore Show* and *The Golden Girls* have lasted over time thanks to some of the best writing in the business, and I am ever grateful.

The morning after the SAG Awards, we had a table read for *Hot in Cleveland*. Suzanne Martin, the creator of the show, who does a lot of the writing, walked in and said, "Welcome to the <u>award</u>-winning *Hot in Cleveland!*"

It was a great moment.

Completely stunned at the
2011 Screen Actors Guild Awards!

NAME-DROPPING

At the 2010 SAG Awards, I was honored with the Life Achievement Award.

I got up from the table, and once again I had that moment of sudden contrast—when I got up to the podium, I turned around, and here's this enormous Shrine Auditorium audience. It's just overwhelming.

When I gained my composure, I tried to explain that being in show business is like living in a small town.

Your paths really cross and cross again through the years.

Even if you've not seen someone in a long time, all of a sudden you're working with him or her again.

I talked about how two show-business people who encounter each other might not <u>know</u> each other, but they're automatically in the same club, and they greet each other like friends.

And I talked about how I've <u>never</u> gotten used to running across a celebrity. I'm always impressed. I've never outgrown it. I still remember the thrill I had the day I came home and there was a message that Fred Astaire had called. <u>Fred Astaire!</u>

So I said to the audience . . .

"I look out here and everybody is famous. And I've had the privilege of knowing many of you and working with some of you—I've even <u>had</u> a few of you! You know who you are."

Afterward, as I was led back to my table, George Clooney was at the podium. He saw me walking across the room and said, "And while I'm here, I'd like to thank Betty White for her discretion."

At the 2010 Screen Actors Guild Awards.
My friend Sandra Bullock presented me with
the Life Achievement Award.
KEVIN WINTER/GETTY IMAGES

TURNING
DOWN ROLES

I'm often asked if there are roles I was offered that I regret turning down.

The answer is <u>No</u>.

Sure, I've turned down parts in movies that went on to be successful.

One was *As Good as It Gets*.

But in that movie, there was a scene in which a character throws a dog down a laundry chute. When I read the part, I told the director, James Brooks, who is amazingly talented, "I just can't do that!" I know it's for laughs, but given my feelings about animals and my work for animal welfare, I just didn't find it funny. I didn't think it would be a good example to people who might try it in real life.

I was hoping that Jim would change it! But Jim had fallen in love with the scene and wouldn't change it. So I said, "Sorry, I can't do it. But thank you very much!"

Another script was sent to me, and it started with a truly disgusting scene in which a drunken Santa Claus is vomiting all over a stack of toys. I didn't find that funny, either. The scriptwriters were these really talented guys, but I said, "Thank you but no thanks!"

So the answer is, more than regretting <u>not</u> taking a role, I feel good that I've turned down roles for the right reasons.

With Leslie Nielsen in Chance of a Lifetime.

OLD FRIENDS, NEW STORIES

*I*t's always a joy to know your castmates.

I've known Carl Reiner for years. Lately, he's been appearing on *Hot in Cleveland* as a guest star in a recurring role—my character's boyfriend, no less.

Carl Reiner and Allen were in the Army together in World War II in the Pacific. I met Carl one night years later, when Allen had all the guys from his outfit over to our house. There was Mort Lindsey and Howie Morris and Harry David and Carl. No wives were invited. So I fixed a couple of big casseroles for the fellas and took the dogs upstairs to the bedroom. I wasn't allowed downstairs—it was one of those guys' nights out.

Carl recently told me, "I wouldn't have a career without Captain Ludden."

I had no idea what he was talking about, and said so.

Carl told me about this entertainment group Allen was in, called the Army Entertainment Section. Carl had written some material and stood up one night in front of the guys and read it.

Allen said, "You've got to do more of that."

Maurice Evans was also in the outfit, so Allen got Maurice to take the material to a producer, and Carl was off and running. He continued to be a writer but also went on to become one of our great comedians. It took a Shakespearean actor and a game-show host to make it happen in the beginning, but Carl took it from there.

Today, every so often, Carl will say to me, "Wouldn't Allen get a kick out of this if he were here—seeing us working together?"

I don't tell Carl, but I think Allen _is_ getting a kick out of it, because he's never very far from me. Ever.

With Carl Reiner on the set of Hot in Cleveland.

THE
RED CARPET

Several times throughout this opus, I mention how much I love this business I'm in. And I mean every word of it.

But for all the things I enjoy about it, if ever I'm asked if there's something I <u>don't</u> like, the answer is a resounding <u>Yes</u>.

Red-carpet events.

Don't get me wrong. When I'm at home watching television, I love seeing who's there and what they're wearing. But when you're the walkee, it can be an absolute nightmare.

In real life, you step out of the car and immediately you're struck blind and deaf as you're greeted by a line of photographers armed with flash cameras and microphone-wielding television reporters, three deep, all shouting at you.

Betty!

Betty!

Over here!

Betty, look here!

Look up, Betty!

Mrs. Ludden! (They know that will get my attention!)

With all the flashing lights and the noise, you tend to lose your balance. All of a sudden, you're staggering and you're sure people are thinking, *Oh, she's had a few!*

The lights are glaring and the noise is horrendous, but you try to be as polite as possible, because these aren't villains, they're just people trying to do their jobs.

Sometimes the function has somebody who takes you down the carpet. For instance, TV Land will send someone if the four of us are doing the event. But always, I also have Jeff walking behind me, at the edge of the media zone, off the red carpet. Riding shotgun, which I need.

Historically, premieres have always had these red-carpet events. But the process has taken on new proportions of late. Every event has a system of protocol, and the number of stars and reporters and photographers and media outlets just seems to grow and grow.

It feels like everyone's there with a microphone. And I know a lot of them—we do interviews all through the year. So as you're stumbling around, you're trying to talk to all sorts of different people. Usually a representative from the project (whatever project it may be) guides you to various reporters along the way—likely, they mix and match us along the way, to be fair to all the outlets. But you can't really hear what they're saying, given all the noise, so you just keep talking and hope you're making some kind of sense. It's all seat-of-the-pants.

You can't resent it—it's a necessary evil to promote a project. It's a hazard one just has to get over.

It's not my favorite part of my job. Have you noticed?

I would rather go to the dentist for a root canal.

*The TV Land folks threw me an eighty-ninth
birthday party. Here I am with the girls
from* Hot in Cleveland. . . . *The red
carpet is a lot better with friends!*

D Dipasupil/FilmMagic.com

With Malin Akerman, Ryan Reynolds, Sandra Bullock,
Anne Fletcher, and Mary Steenburgen
on the set of The Proposal.

THE PROPOSAL

*D*oing movies is different but interesting.

One thing in particular struck me about being on the set of *The Proposal*—what a joy it was to work with Sandra Bullock.

Here's this big movie star, and there wasn't anything "movie star" about her at all. She was just as down-to-earth as she could be. We became great and dear friends. Still are. The same goes for Ryan Reynolds.

Anne Fletcher, the movie's wonderful director, had been a choreographer originally. We all got relaxed and silly with one another, so she wouldn't just walk onto the set—she'd do a ballet leap onto the set, saying, "The director is here!"

In one of the scenes in the movie, Sandra and I are dancing around a bonfire.

On that day of filming, we'd been working all day, but we had to finish that night, because we were moving locations the next day. It was three o'clock in the morning, and I had to sing this blinking Eskimo song in order to shoot the scene.

First I had to learn it. And Eskimo makes no sense. I don't know how Eskimos communicate! But I learned it. God knows what I was really saying.

And then it came time to dance around the fire.

Anne just turned us loose—told us to do whatever we felt like doing. And Sandra's such a good sport. So just about the time we started moving around . . .

Drip.

Drip.

Drip.

The rain started, and it kept getting harder and harder.

Now, we had to finish this scene! We were leaving the site the next day. So they put up a canvas on four big poles to keep us dry. But the rain continued—harder and harder.

I've said before I love my profession, and I do. At three o'clock in the morning in the rain, you'd better love it a <u>lot</u>.

With Sandra—a scene in The Proposal.

THE LOST
VALENTINE

For the Hallmark movie *The Lost Valentine* with Jennifer Love Hewitt, we shot in this pretty little house in Atlanta in a lovely neighborhood. Across the street was a low wall, and behind it was this big grassy lawn.

All the neighbors knew that I was working there, so they all brought their dogs.

We'd look across the street from the set, and they'd all be lined up—owners and dogs, sitting on the wall.

Between scenes, I'd go across the street to say hello and get to know all the dogs.

There was this young man, Mitch, hired to escort me around the set, who would go over with me. One day he came in and said, "Betty, there's a Newfoundland out there."

The way he tells it, at the word "Newfoundland," I <u>shot</u> out of my chair like a bullet! Why not? I don't get to smooch with a Newfie that often.

So I got my dog fix every day.

Now, that's a happy set.

With Jennifer Love Hewitt on the set of the
Hallmark movie The Lost Valentine.

LETTERS

INTERVIEWS
(REDFORD)

*I*t is a real privilege to have been working in this business for so long, but there are a few built-in hazards—some of which can't be avoided. Interviews, for example. There is no way to even estimate the number of them I have done over the years—we must be in the millions by now. This means I have answered the same questions, told the same anecdotes, wheezed on and on ad infinitum, again and again. The interviewers know the material better than I do, going in—and it's tough to put a fresh spin on it.

A few years ago I was asked one of the standard questions for probably the umpteenth time: "Is there anything you haven't done in your career that you would still like to do?"

Well, I had just seen Meryl Streep and Robert Redford in *Out of Africa* for the third time, so the answer was automatic: "Yes, Robert Redford." And I was surprised to suddenly find it was true! Ever since, I have realized that that answer fits a variety of situations, and I have used it accordingly.

I have never met him. I never want to meet him (I'd be too embarrassed after taking his name in vain so many times). However, what began as a crush on a movie star soon grew into genuine admiration. I became aware of his concern for the environment, his love of and respect for nature, his involvement with The Wilderness Society, and I maintain that the Robert Redford answer works for me in almost any department.

Fast-forward to January 2010. A few days after I had received an unbelievable honor from the Screen Actors Guild, I brought the mail in one morning, as usual, and found the following letter.

Dear Mrs. Ludden:

Robert Redford has asked that I forward his congratulatory note to you on receiving the

Lifetime Achievement Award from the Screen Actors Guild.

   Cheers to you!

            Sincerely,

            Donna Kail

            Assistant to Robert Redford

More than a note, the congratulation consisted of a delightful, <u>funny</u> six-stanza poem that began with "Dear Betty" and ended with "Congratulations, Robert."

By now I don't have to tell you how my mind was blown. Of course, my first reaction was that someone was putting me on, but the stationery was authentic, and on looking further, I found a great picture of himself, signed "Guess who? Robert Redford."

Finally, I found the courage to write him a thank-you and said I couldn't promise to stop using his name—unless he didn't find it funny.

I can only say that Robert Redford is one class act.

P.S. I know you would love to hear the poem. Sorry.

With Bandit, Dancer, and Stormy.

ZUMA Press/Newscom

WRITER'S
BLOCK

*C*ertain common clichés maintain that most men love hardware stores, just as women dote on shoe stores. I have no idea how accurate that is, because, personally, I am strange for stationery stores. Not for the fancy writing paper—it's those tablets and packs of lined three-hole notebook pages and those packs of typing paper that turn me on. I even buy those things when I go to the grocery store, whether I need them or not.

Let's say I am in the middle of a writing project and have, perhaps, hit a slow spot. Bringing in this stuff can recharge the battery. Or, if I am <u>not</u> in the middle of a writing project, it can often cause me to start one.

Why? I have no idea, but it has been that way all my life—even back to my school days. A fresh pack of paper was the best incentive in the world for me to tackle my homework.

As weird as all this sounds, I am not alone. I can remember once being told by an author—who was rather well known at the time—that on the rare occasions when he hit a stubborn writer's block, there was only one specific brand of green-lined paper that could get him started again. He called it his "paper laxative." As soon as he'd bring in a pack, the ideas would start again.

Okay, so I'm weird. At least I am in good company.

John Steinbeck, who was Allen's and my good friend, did his writing standing up at a drafting table—in longhand, his white bull terrier, Angel, lying across his feet. People always seem amazed that I write in longhand. Well, if it's good enough for Steinbeck, it's good enough for me! I really can't communicate to a machine—the thoughts want to go from my brain down my arm to my hand to the page. After I've written that first draft, I copy it over again onto another page. That's when the most changes are made, as I polish and rewrite the original—once again, in longhand.

My mother had beautiful handwriting her entire life. As a little kid, I loved the times with her when I would make her write something so I could see how closely I could copy it. It wasn't a learning chore, which I probably would have resisted. It was a game.

Somewhere in those fun sessions she managed to make a point that has stuck: handwriting is a means of communication. Why not make it as easy to read as possible?

I still remember those lovely times with my mother when I would try to copy her handwriting. Maybe it isn't only John Steinbeck's influence after all.

With our computers today, we have a whole new population who will find all of this totally academic, since they write by hand as little as possible. Even signing their names seems to have gone by the boards.

Computers can't take all the blame. Both my business manager and my doctor have handwriting that is practically unreadable. Whenever I get fan mail in which the handwriting is absolutely illegible, I wonder if they've taken writing lessons from my business manager!

Ironically, when I grew up and entered into show business, I found many people who actually practiced diligently to make their autographs as eye-catching, illegible, and uncopyable as possible!

On *Hot in Cleveland*, Valerie Bertinelli, Wendie Malick, Jane Leeves, and I sign scripts each week to be used as charity auction items. I am always so grateful that I know their names, because I wouldn't have a clue from their signatures, which are as distinctive and interesting as they are. You can't imagine how dull my readable but boring "Betty White" looks on that script cover in that distinguished company.

I must practice.

to do it from then on. But just try to repeat it—you can't get it back to save your soul from perdition. Now and then, that "good line reading" doesn't happen until you're driving home after the show. But, of course, the party's over by then.

I've heard some of the best actors say the same.

It's a strange craft!

With James Lipton on Inside the Actors Studio.

BRAVO/PHOTOFEST

TELEVISION

Over time, I've turned down three Broadway shows. I love summer stock. But with summer stock, there's a beginning and an end to the production. Maybe a week's rehearsal and three or four weeks playing the show, then you're free.

If you get into a Broadway show and it doesn't work, you're a failure. And if it does work, you may be stuck for who knows how long. It just doesn't sound great to me!

My theatrical friends think I'm a Neanderthal.

"It's <u>THEATER</u>," they protest.

"I know," I say, "but I'm <u>television</u>!"

I was there when television first started. We grew up together.

When I graduated from high school, television had just begun in New York, but it hadn't yet started in California.

I had done our senior play and was asked to do an experimental television show downtown. Our senior class president and I did a scene from *The Merry Widow* up on the fifth floor of the Packard Automobile building. And it was broadcast all the way to the bottom floor. My parents had to stand in front of a tiny little monitor on the first floor to see me! But it was the beginning of television in Los Angeles.

Then I actually got paid (a little) to do a role as the girl behind the hotel desk on a show called *Tom, Dick, and Harry*. Never do a show with three comics who have a broom. But it was fun.

Al Jarvis had seen me on that, and he called and asked if I would be his Girl Friday on a TV show he was going to do. Al had had a marathon radio show, and now he was going to be on for five hours, five days a week. They soon upped it to five and a half hours a day and added Saturday. That was *Hollywood on Television.* I'd been getting paid $5 by the local station.

When Al called, I thought, *Maybe I'll get another $5!*

Instead, Al offered me $50 a week! I was shocked. Even more so when they gave me $200 per week when they extended the airtime.

For two and a half years we worked together on that program. And then, Al went over to ABC, and I inherited *H.O.T.*

You talk about experience—it was like going to television college.

One of the things I realized from the first time I ever did television was the intimacy of the audience. There are never more than two or three people watching a television program—if there are more than three people in a room, they're usually talking among themselves, not listening to you! So as a television actress, I knew my audience was always very narrow. Later, when I did movie roles, however, it was for this great big audience. And I didn't know that audience's content at all. You don't have that feeling of reaching an individual. And you <u>don't</u> look at the camera!

No matter how television has grown, you're still really just talking to those two or three people.

People greet me on the street as a friend, not a celebrity. "Hi, Betty!"

I was walking down the street the last time I was in New York, and a guy drove by and rolled down his window and hollered, "I love *Hot in Cleveland*, Betty!" Had I been a film star, he wouldn't have done that.

There's a remoteness to film stars. As an accessible television performer, you have to be careful walking down the street—you might pick up a hundred new best friends. It's so unlike film stars, it's a different genetic makeup.

Television and I discovered each other together. It was a very short window to get in, timing-wise.

I was blessed with that timing, because we were inventing as we went along in those first days of television. And I joined the parade.

On Boston Legal *with James Spader.*

LOVE AND

FRIENDSHIP

Our wedding day—June 6, 1963.

GLOBE PHOTOS

FULL CIRCLE

*L*ife does have a way of coming full circle.

As of this writing, I have just finished shooting a movie (*You Again*) starring three great gals—Jamie Lee Curtis, Kristen Bell, and Sigourney Weaver. I thoroughly enjoyed working with all three but got a special kick out of getting to know Sigourney. It was her father, Pat Weaver, who was at the time the president of NBC, where I got my first network job (*The Betty White Show*) more than half a century ago.

After several years of doing local television, going

"national" was a major turning point in my career, and it was a dream come true.

At the time, I was working five and a half hours a day, six days a week, with Al Jarvis in a live broadcast. No script—all ad-libbed—on KLAC's Channel Thirteen in the local Los Angeles area. The show was called *Hollywood on Television.*

After two years, Al left and I inherited the show and worked solo for two and a half years. Every Thursday night I was also doing a one-hour variety show that was something like a small-scale *American Idol* (like they say, there's nothing entirely "new" in this world!). It was all local. People would come on the Thursday-night show and sing, and whoever won the variety show, whoever got voted the best performer, would have a week appearing on our daytime show. Here I should mention that I would sing, too—and I don't know how they could tell me from the amateurs!

So after the five-and-a-half-hour daily broadcast on KLAC, we would hold auditions to screen the candidates for the variety show. They'd sing for us, and some you wouldn't believe—you just didn't know where to look. You'd think, *This is the longest song that was ever sung!* And you felt so sorry for these people. . . . But sometimes we'd get lucky. The most memorable winner was a young Gogi Grant, who went on to achieve a great career.

On *Hollywood on Television*, we finally got music—a guitar player named Roc Hillman. I would sing three songs each day to his accompaniment.

Then came Pat Weaver's job offer, which was a godsend. Pat warned me what it would entail:

"Do you think you can handle doing a half-hour show every day, five days a week?"

Well, after five and a half hours a day, six days a week, I wondered what I would do with all the time off! I would also have a five-piece band, led by well-known music man Frank De Vol. Roc Hillman, of course, was still on guitar.

Pat Weaver was a real mover and shaker in the television business, and many of his innovations are still extant today. It was Pat, I believe, who first divided television time into segments like on the *Today* show and *The Tonight Show*.

Little did I dream that all these years later I would be working with his star of a daughter. Sigourney wasn't even a gleam in her father's eye at that time.

Nice as he was, I was in total awe of Pat when I

worked for him back then. I must admit, at first I felt a bit of the same when I started working with Sigourney, since I have been a devout fan of hers, especially her fine performance as Dian Fossey in *Gorillas in the Mist*.

I am delighted to say that we have grown into warm and loving friends. You can't imagine how thrilled I was when I came offstage after *Saturday Night Live* to find her waiting to say hello in my dressing room. She and Victor Garber (also in *You Again*) had come over to surprise and support me. These are moments I absolutely cherish.

But it doesn't stop there.

The day before the SAG Awards in 2011, I was at an event and a gentleman approached me and introduced himself. He said, "I'm Roc Hillman's son! My dad's still alive!"

I said, "You've got to be kidding me!"

He said, "No, he's one hundred and four, and he's still going!"

Like I said, life sure does have a way of coming full circle.

On the set of You Again *with Sigourney Weaver,*
Odette Yustman, Kristen Bell, and Jamie Lee Curtis.
ZUMA Press/Newscom

DATING DU JOUR

At this moment in time, it seems somewhat current and choice for women to pair up with younger men. These gals are called "cougars."

Well, animal lover that I am, a cougar I am not. All my life, even as a kid, I have preferred men older than I am.

Unfortunately, today I don't think there <u>is</u> anyone older than I am!

Even at this age, once in a while I meet a man who seems a trifle more interesting than usual. Nothing untoward—just someone who might be fun to know a little better. I've even thought (<u>to myself</u>) that it might be nice if he asked me to lunch or dinner, perhaps. Then reality kicks in and it cracks me up. This guy is probably a much younger man—maybe only eighty—and not about to even look my way.

So I don't worry very much about whether I'm going to be asked to lunch. I know I had a rare thing in my relationship with Allen. In fact, my castmates on *Hot in Cleveland* seemed so curious about him—and asked so many questions about him!—that I finally had to wonder out loud, "Why do you always ask me about Allen?"

The answer was simple: "We love the look you get on your face when you talk about him."

ABC Photo Archives/ABC via Getty Images

LOSS

*A*llen is always with me.

The other night, a dear friend, Mark Alexander, called me to say he had seen the Hallmark Hall of Fame movie I did, *The Lost Valentine*.

He said he was surprised to see me doing something dramatic.

"At one point, when you were crying so hard, you glanced up and it stopped me cold. I knew who was in your mind."

I think the toughest thing about loss, and the hardest

challenge, is the isolation you feel in its aftermath. You spent so much time sharing your life with someone, talking through issues, even disagreeing about things, and all of a sudden there's a hole. There's nobody there and you think, *Well, who's in charge?*

My God, it's me. I have to make the decisions. I can't share the decisions any longer.

And that's tough because you don't fully trust your own judgment.

That's why it's great to have people like Jeff Witjas in my life. And why it was so great to have Jerry Martin, whom I lost just a few weeks ago. Jerry and I would talk to each other around dinnertime almost every night. I could get things off my chest that I couldn't necessarily air to anyone else.

The older you get, the fewer of those there are.

I always thought I would be the one who would go— particularly with the Golden Girls, because I was the oldest. But then we lost all of them, and I'm the only one left and I'm still functioning. I think, *How did that happen?*

MARIO ROMO/GLOBE PHOTOS

On Mama's Family *with Vicki Lawrence
and Rue McClanahan.*

FRIENDSHIPS

There are all kinds of different friendships.

With a new friend, you start to tell an anecdote and there's a whole explanation that needs to go with it so they'll understand.

But with old friends, you don't have to do the backstory, because you talk so often that they know what's going on in your life—or maybe they were there at the time.

Then there are the business friends—whose job it is to tell you where you're wrong, whereas your other friends may just agree with you.

Friendship takes time and energy if it's going to work. You can luck into something great, but it doesn't last if you don't give it proper appreciation. Friendship can be so comfortable, but nurture it—don't take it for granted.

My closest friends have always been boys or men. As a kid, I wasn't interested particularly in what the girls were talking about. I had to watch myself. I didn't want to get a reputation that I don't like women, because that's not true at all. I just like guys best.

That's not politically correct these days. But it's still fun.

With Mary.

AGENT JEFF

Jeff Witjas and I met at the William Morris Agency when I was a client. He wasn't my agent, but I knew him from the company. When William Morris began to disintegrate, Jeff moved over to APA and set up shop there.

My long-term agent, whom I adore, and who is still one of my dearest friends, Tony Fantozzi, was one of the partners at William Morris, but then he retired. So I inherited a new representative with whom I wasn't really connecting.

I kept getting calls from APA: Would I come in and take a meeting?

They weren't from Jeff, but I knew where they were generated from.

Tony, who was no longer with William Morris, said in his inimitable tough-guy Italian accent, "Why don't you take the meeting?"

So I went down to APA, and I went into this boardroom for a meeting with all their executives seated around the table. I didn't have to explain my work or what I'd done or my background. They'd all done their homework. I was really impressed by that, and very gratified. So we talked quite a bit, and then they made the formal request: Would I consider coming to the agency?

I said, "Let me think it over."

After the meeting, Tony picked me up and we went back to the Beverly Hills Hotel and had a beer and talked about it. I explained to him that I was really impressed at how they had worked at being informed about my career to date.

Tony said, "Why don't you go with them?"

And so Jeff became my representative at APA, and I haven't stopped working since.

We're a great team. He never lets me go on a trip— for instance, to New York—without accompanying me. Not just as a protector but as an arranger—he takes care of all the appearances and sets everything up while we're in town. He's a delightful travel companion, because he never lets me get overloaded but he still gives me the freedom to do things that are important to me.

On one occasion, we were spending three nights in New York. We're both fans of Chinese food, so that first night we found this wonderful Chinese restaurant and were as happy as could be. As you know, there are <u>many</u> good restaurants in New York City. So on the second night we were trying to decide where to go to eat and somehow decided to go back to the same place.

The third night, we didn't even discuss it—we just went right back to the Chinese place. And the next time we were to go to New York, he called in advance from California and set up a reservation.

It's obvious how well we get along.

When we get home, I call his wife and daughter and thank them for loaning him to me.

We have a lot in common, and I rely on him implicitly.

I trust his judgment more than I trust my own!

With my agent, Jeff Witjas, and Ann Moore, then the CEO of Time, Inc.

ANIMAL

KINGDOM

BUTTERSCOTCH

*L*et me share another animal-related episode that I revisit in my mind from time to time, like a mental DVD.

BraveHearts Therapeutic Riding & Educational Center is a fine therapeutic riding school in Chicago dedicated to giving disabled children a new perspective, and I was invited to host their annual fund-raiser. I was familiar with BraveHearts because the former chairman of Morris Animal Foundation, Dan Marsh, and his wife, Dayle, are on the board. A few years earlier, they had enlisted my help on behalf of a beautiful young horse named Butterscotch who had terribly crippled hooves—a result of flounder, followed by a bad case of pneumonia. There wasn't money for the necessary medical procedures at the time, but Dan and Dayle made such a case for him, I couldn't resist getting involved. I underwrote the surgery and he made a complete recovery. When the invitation came to host the benefit, my first thought was *I'll get to meet Butterscotch!!* and off I went.

I arrived in Chicago the day of the fund-raiser and that afternoon was taken to the ranch for a tour of the school.

Riding therapy enables children who have spent time looking up from a hospital bed to get an entirely different view of the world, looking down from the back of a horse. They are led around a corral by a young person walking alongside. Instead of boring exercises in a bleak hospital environment, they receive the same benefits in an exciting and stimulating setting.

As the tour ended, I headed straight for the stables to find my friend, Butterscotch. They had warned me that he had a tendency to nip, but when I walked up to his stall he put that velvet nose in my hands and seemed to appreciate the kisses.

so many older dogs that need homes desperately. So that's where I'll look, and we can grow older together.

And then there are cats. Cats are not remote. People who think cats are that way may never have lived with a cat. My Bob, for instance. If my knee was bent, he was on my lap or on my shoulder in a flash. He followed me around the house like a dog. In bed at night, I'd reach over to turn the light out and he'd be there. For eleven years I fell asleep with that purr on my shoulder. Cats love you very much—they are just more subtle about it.

You're never too old to adopt a pet if you look ahead and make arrangements for their future. Then relax and enjoy each other.

With another "planted" pet.

STATE OF

AFFAIRS

NAMES

Having spent so many years memorizing lines, I am pretty good at remembering names. ("Pretty good" is probably a euphemism.)

My problem is <u>faces</u>. They just don't seem to register. I have no memory for faces at all. Consequently, at those gatherings where you are introduced to several people at the same time, I wind up with a bunch of names I can remember but I don't know where to put them. I try to make silent notes in my head: JohnSmithbluetie. JaneJonespearlearrings. Sometimes those notes can carry you through a whole evening before they evaporate.

That game may work with total strangers but not with someone you've met before and should remember but don't. You are off to a bad start when you say, "It's nice meeting you." And they respond with, "Yes, it's nice seeing you <u>again</u>."

An added hazard in my line of work is when the name you can't come up with happens to be that of a celebrity. Everyone else in the room knows that name—except you! As the celebrity approaches, it's too late to ask someone nearby for help. You can't ask the celeb or you'll hurt his ego. Just pray you don't have to make any introductions.

There are too many examples in real life to mention—that awkward moment when I just don't know someone's name happens all the time!

People approach you out of context—people you've not seen in years. Or they approach in groups. Or they've aged or changed their hair color or put on weight—making recognition even more difficult. I still will introduce myself in these situations—"Hi, I'm Betty White"—in the hopes they'll do the same. Invariably, they not only don't reciprocate, they look at me as if I'm out of my mind.

The 2011 SAG Awards was a classic example. There I was, in a room filled with actors from popular movies and shows all across television. They're celebrities. And I don't know who they are! You feel like you're on the edge of a cliff the entire night.

And in this industry, our business makes for an instant familiarity. All night, people approached me and said, "Oh, hello, Betty—I loved you in *Saturday Night Live*" or "*Hot in Cleveland* is great," and so on. And I don't know the person from Adam—though I most probably should.

You can't cover all the bases, but you wish you could cover a few.

The worst part is, a lot of people don't take kindly to your not remembering. But you're fighting as hard as you can. You've used up all of the clichéd ways of avoiding the situation, but you still can't grasp the name in question.

One time I tried what I thought was a great way to learn that elusive moniker. I asked, "How do you spell your last name?"

The answer came back, "With an i."

Great.

Whatever memory trick you employ, it is well worth the effort. People are often surprised and pleased when you call them by name—especially in a crowd.

One more complication is added for me as my hearing dims: I may not hear the name clearly in the initial introduction, and the only thing worse than forgetting a name is calling someone by the wrong one.

You are probably thinking that if I let a big party be all that work, why don't I just stay home? <u>Great idea!</u> And I usually do.

The operative word here is "big." I thoroughly enjoy a small group of friends—six, or maybe even eight. You can get into stimulating conversation, laugh together, disagree on occasion, and, if you're not careful, even learn something.

And you don't have to bother with all those name games.

See—I'm not quite as antisocial as I sound. Not quite.

With George Burns—a face and a name
you could never forget.

DINING ROOM TABLE

My desk, and what was originally intended to be my office, is located in a spare bedroom upstairs. The fax machine lives there, as well as my stuffed animals and piles and piles of books people send me in the hopes I'll take a look at them for endorsement or out of curiosity or for pleasure. I'm too busy to read much of anything lately, but it's against my religion to throw out a book, so they keep stacking up and stacking up. It's gotten to the point that whenever Donna needs to fax something, I find myself saying, "No, no, let me do that!" so she doesn't have to see the messy room.

As that room filled up, I found that I kept bringing my work downstairs to the dining room table at the end of the living room. It sits by a big window looking out to the garden, and Donna and I find it a most pleasant workplace. Unfortunately, the table keeps getting piled higher and higher with leftover works in progress that have become virtually permanent. The dining room table has become an echo of the upstairs spare bedroom!

At four a.m., which seems to be my witching hour, I wake up not in a panic about memorizing my lines or what the day on the set might bring. No, I wake up haunted by that mess in that office—and the growing mess on my dining room table!

I think to myself, *Betty, you <u>must</u> clean this mess before you die.* God forbid someone else has to rifle through what's piled on there. I fantasize about bringing in giant garbage bags and just tossing everything out—but I can't bring myself to do it.

What about my potential dinner guests? With no place to serve them, we wind up with cocktails and hors d'oeuvres in the den, then we go out to eat. I am not what might be called one of the world's greatest hostesses.

One of my New Year's resolutions will be to finally clear that table.

But not this year.

Ironically, I could hear very well back then.

ENTOURAGE

So many stars have staff, and I'm often asked about mine.

I have a wonderful housekeeper, Edna, who's been with me for almost twenty-five years. She's been with me so long I couldn't possibly ask her to retire. But she's slowing down like we all are. So a few years ago I hired her a cleaning lady named Anita.

If I have to do anything on the weekend, like attend a poker game, which means driving down to Newport

Beach, Anita will come in and feed Ponti and help me out. It's a very comfortable situation.

When it's not comfortable is when something happens like what happened the other morning. I woke up early, as usual, to go to the *Hot in Cleveland* table read. I made Ponti his dish of food and stepped outside to put it down for him. Just then the wind picked up and slammed the door shut behind me, locking me out. I have an elaborate system of keys hidden to get me back into the house, but when I went to find the final key, it was missing. Luckily, I'd gotten far enough inside that there was a phone in the room. So I had to call Glenn Kaplan, my business manager, who lives nearby. Glenn has an extra set of my house keys, and fortunately he was still home. But his copies of my keys were in his office so he had to drive there to get them and bring them back up to me.

By the time he got to me, I'd been almost exclusively outside for forty-five minutes in nothing but my bathrobe. And you can imagine how glamorous I looked when he arrived!

My dear friend Jerry Martin used to have a set of keys to my house, too, and he used to take care to visit Ponti when I was on set. In fact, I'd never have been able to film *The Proposal* without Jerry's assistance.

When I was first called about the role, I was told the filming was supposed to take ten weeks in Boston. I said I couldn't possibly leave for that long. But then the schedule was cut down to six weeks, and Jerry volunteered to visit Ponti every day. I managed to make it back a couple of times on weekends, so between the two of us, along with Edna and Anita, I felt that Ponti was covered as he adores them all.

Sadly, we lost Jerry very suddenly a few weeks ago.

I not only miss him deeply but on a morning like the one when I locked myself out, I start wondering about the wisdom of my staffing situation! Should I have more help? But I so enjoy being alone.

That said, the other downside to my system is that I slip behind a little all the time. I <u>never</u> finish a day and think, *I'm all caught up.*

Then what am I doing writing a book? I needed to write a book at this time in my life like I needed another hole in my head.

But I couldn't turn it down, it was such a temptation.

I told you up front that writing is my favorite thing.

POKER

I'm not a great poker player but I love to play.

Bob Stewart of Goodson/Todman, who created game shows like *Password*, *$25,000 Pyramid*, and more, hosts a poker game that he's run for more than fifty years. Bob and I have been friends for almost that long, and about fifteen years ago he invited me to deal in. Our group plays at the Newport Beach house of Ann Cullen, whose late husband, Bill Cullen, was also a great game-show host. We all giggle and scratch and have a wonderful time.

We don't play for big money, but we play for <u>blood</u>.

It's dealer's choice, and each hand is high/low. We don't play a lot of wild games. Screw Thy Neighbor (it's really Screw Your Neighbor, but we call it Screw <u>Thy</u> Neighbor, to class it up) is my favorite. You get a chance to keep a card or pass it along.

I think the only reason they let me into the game is that I usually leave about $13 on the table. We have a brass cup engraved with "Pico Poker Club," and whoever comes out ahead at the end of the night takes this cup home. The winner can enjoy the cup until the next game, but God forbid you don't return it then. The penalty for that offense is $2,000 or death, whichever is most appropriate.

One day, Henry Pollick, who lives in the Valley, was almost to Ann's and realized he'd forgotten the cup. He turned around and must have done some creative driving to get home to pick it up and make it back in time for the game.

Just as we were wondering where Henry was, he raced in, breathless. "I can't afford the penalty!" he said, and we all burst out laughing.

I love to play cards and rarely have anybody to play with anymore.

So these games are precious.

On Match Game—*I've always loved a great game.*

MODERN
TECHNOLOGY

(Thoroughly Modern Betty?)

*E*very time you begin to think you're such a contemporary and you don't feel your age, you realize you don't own a computer!—and intend to keep it that way.

There are a few reasons for this.

I get a lot of mail, as I've mentioned before. Donna does most of the fan mail, but the volume of my personal mail, too, is enormous! I come in with an armful every day and sort it into different stacks. I may push one stack aside, but before I do, I at least have an idea of what's <u>in</u> that stack. If I had a computer and clicked a button to "store" something, I wouldn't sleep at night! I'd wonder what was stored in there, did I answer this or that or the other? That scares me. I think of it as the computer equivalent of my upstairs office and dining room table.

And many people use computers to write. They talk about how efficient it is, how fast. But I can't create with a machine. As I said in "Writer's Block," there's a connection from my brain to the paper through my longhand writing that just works for me.

When my agent and publisher and I got together to work on this book, my publisher worked with an amazing instrument I had never seen—a computerized pen that recorded audio and plugged into the computer. A <u>talking</u> pen? I named it Bruce.

It's a far cry from that first book I ever wrote when I was a kid, which was one hundred pages in longhand, written with a pen you dipped in ink!

Thank you, Bruce. I don't deserve you.

ADRIAN SANCHEZ-GONZALES/LANDOV

CHILDREN

When I was a little girl, my mother loved baby dolls. She collected them.

But my toys were always animals.

I would spend all my lunch money on little blown-glass animal families at the toy store, which I later had to spend a lot of time dusting.

Barbara Walters once asked me if I ever had desired to have a child.

The answer is, I never did think about it.

I know there are many career girls today who would

disagree, but I'm not a big believer in being able to do both. I think somebody takes the short end of the stick.

I had such a wonderful rapport with my folks, but my mother didn't work. She was home with me.

It's an individual choice. I didn't think I could do justice to both career and motherhood, maybe because I had the mother I did. It's <u>such</u> an individual choice.

And I'm a stepmother. I have the best stepchildren in the world.

When Allen and I first married, I became the stepmother of teenagers. Never having had children, I was suddenly the mother of teens! But we got along great. So great, they called me "Dragon Lady," lovingly.

Even after all these years, we love each other dearly, and I am most proud of the children this career girl inherited. A major blessing—yet again.

SINCE YOU

ASKED . . .

Holding the 2011 Screen Actors Guild
Award for Outstanding Performance by a
Female Actor in a Comedy Series.

INTEGRITY

*I*t's important to maintain as level a head as possible in this exciting business over the years.

The toughest time is when you're on a roll . . . when everything is going phenomenally well, like it is for me right now.

That's when you have to remember that image in the mirror and not let success get to you. It is important that you not believe your own publicity. Be grateful for whatever praise you receive, but take it with a grain of salt.

PART
I

BEFORE THE GODS ARRIVED
December 30, 1500–March 26, 1519

1

There are those who call me *La Chingada,* who say I was a whore. They lie. A whore sells her body, but I gave mine, and gave my heart and gave my mind until the bitter last. There are those who call me traitoress. Liars. I betrayed no one. I was betrayed. Monstrously betrayed, cruelly betrayed. But from the very hour of my birth I seemed marked for a strange destiny.

I was born at midnight, to the crash of thunder and the flicker of lightning. That I was born at all was due to the bold intervention of my grandmother, Ix Chan. After hard labor lasting from long before sundown, my mother's strength gave out and she sagged, half-unconscious, dangling from the straps around her wrists that supported her in a squatting position between two stone wall brackets in which torches flamed. The old midwife poked and prodded and exhorted, in vain. My mother had no more strength. I was doomed to die in her womb. But my grandmother had one of her visions and saw the solution. She ran for my father, who was waiting with the clan heads and priests in the main hall of the stone palace, and told him what he must do.

He undid the supporting straps, laid my mother supine on a straw mat and, kneeling above her head like a woman grinding corn, he shoved down hard on the bulging abdomen that writhed with futile muscular spasms. Shoving again and again and shouting to her to help him, he finally shoved me out of her body and into this world.

The high priest came in then and the midwife held me up to him and he sprinkled water over me from his sacred staff tipped with seven rattlesnake tails. Chanting a prayer to the goddess of childbirth and eater of dead babies, he shaped on the soft center of my skull a patty of white maize paste. Invoking the benign influence of Ixchel, the

3

moon goddess, he tied around my waist a belt of snakeskin from which dangled a scalloped seashell of gold, symbol of purity, with which he covered my genitals. I would wear this until adulthood, if I lived. My birth merited these attentions from the high priest himself, for I was the first child of the ruler of Paynala.

My grandmother told me all this, and how the wind that night seemed ready to tear the steep thatch roof off, and how it made the torch flames dance wildly, casting peculiar shadows across the tattooed face of the high priest as he stared down at me from underneath his mass of tangled hair, in which blood-red feathers were knotted. And she told me that when my mother learned she had a daughter, she turned her dazed face to the wall and slept, or pretended to. So my grandmother's arms were the first to enfold me with love. "Your mother wanted a son," she said, "but I wanted a granddaughter to warm my old age." My father, having reassured himself that my mother was only asleep and not dead, came over then and looked down at me and wiped blood from my head quite tenderly. It was he who gave me the name by which I came to be known, the name of a great snow-capped mountain to the north: Malinche.

My grandmother was a small, thin widow of fifty, but power burned in her like a secret flame. She had ruled in Paynala until her consort died, and at times still sat with the clan heads and war chiefs in the council house. They were in awe of her because she had the gift of prophecy, and great wisdom. She always wore a long, loose tunic the green of jungle shadows, and there were small bright ornaments in her high-coiled hair—a gold butterfly, a tortoise of jade, a silver skull. Her earrings were dark jade plugs set in rims of silver like round eyes staring from her slit earlobes. Her own eyes were dark and deep, with fans of tiny lines at the outer corners. She had no doubt of the importance of the town of Paynala. "We have been favored by many of the gods," she told me, "because our ancestors scorned to obey evil priests who dishonored sacred symbols." I had no idea at the time what this meant, but it conveyed to me that we were a chosen people.

And so when my father Taxumal had taken as wife the daughter of the chieftain of a little town in the highlands far to the west it had upset everyone, for he had thus spurned several eligible young women of Paynalan clans other than his own, any one of whom Ix Chan would have preferred as a daughter-in-law to my mother, Chituche.

My grandmother conceded that Chituche had been very beautiful at eighteen, with large slanted eyes and a full, rather sullen mouth.

She was adept at weaving and at featherwork, very skillful at trapping and catching wild jungle birds for their plumage. She had refused several men who wanted to marry her, and her parents did not press her to get a mate. There were four older brothers to grind maize and weave clothes for, but more compelling than this practical fact was Chituche's stony inner strength. When anyone tried to get her to do what she did not want, she never showed anger or sulked or wept; she disappeared. She had secret hiding places in the jungle and always took with her an obsidian knife. But when my mother set eyes on my father she changed overnight. She washed her blue-black hair with soap bark and put on a new skirt of her own weaving. Kneeling opposite him at the supper mat, she looked up and sent out the strong wish that he would want her. He was instantly drawn to the beautiful, silent girl whose feather tapestry, half finished on the loom, glowed with ancient motifs passed down over centuries from the Old Ones to the south. He believed she must have depths beyond the average.

Handsome, noble, tall, my father was not a man to leap into the tying of the mantles only because of a woman's physical beauty. Political astuteness played a part in his decision to wed a stranger; after the marriage, her town became a satellite of Paynala and several other villages to the west followed suit, which meant that Paynala could count on them for extra warriors if peril threatened. Thus far Paynala had stayed free of Aztec domination; their capital was far to the northwest. But he knew of their recent conquests on the coast; Paynala was only a short distance inland.

And so my mother came to Paynala and at a ceremony held at the foot of the great gray stone pyramid in the plaza, the high priest tied their mantles together—and their lives. To my mother this must have been a dazzling occasion as flutes shrilled and drums thudded and people threw bright flowers. "To Chituche you owe your physical beauty," my grandmother once conceded. "Although it took long enough to conceive you, as the Goddess of the Moon well knows."

My first real memory is of the day the traveling traders came to Paynala in my fourth year. I can still see that small procession filing across the square in the blaze of mid-morning sun, toward the shade of the great ceiba tree by the palace steps where I sat. In the lead were two forbidding men in long, dark capes the color of dung and dried blood, tied on one shoulder. They wore tall black hats with rounded crowns. They were *pochtecas* from the distant capital of the Aztecs— shrewd, hard men who down several centuries had made of trade so

5

honored a calling that a few had even attained the rank of lower Aztec nobles. They boasted that they never lied, never cheated, never spied for their ruler. Traveling vast distances from sea to sea and from the deserts of the north down to Yucatán, they spoke many dialects and effected the exchange of exotic goods, slaves, and news. They were always followed by a file of nearly naked *tamanes,* human beasts of burden bearing heavy loads held onto bent backs by leather straps around their foreheads.

On that day I remember so well, the traders had with them several slaves roped by their necks to a long pole. One was a child. When I asked my mother why those people were tied like that she said they were for sale, and if they were recalcitrant they would end as sacrifices at some temple. Human sacrifice was not practiced in Paynala, so I was unsure what this meant. She said that to the north the priests cut out the victim's heart with a stone knife. To the south the victims were drowned in deep, dark sacred wells. The roped figures took on a tragic aspect and I did not look at them any more, but fixed my attention on some small wares which the *pochtecas,* chatting with my father, spread out on the palace steps. Among them was a curious golden pendant shaped like a coiled snake with a human face, a plume sweeping back from its head. It charmed me.

I had been many times to market day, when people from far away arrived with produce and merchandise, and I understood the principle of barter. So I ran to the rear garden to pick some flowers, then I got the attention of the shorter trader and offered the bouquet for the little snake man. When he turned his head to look down at me, I saw the deep new crescent scar on one cheek that drew up that corner of his mouth in a leer. "The pendant is worth more than a bunch of flowers," he said. "But maybe your father will buy it for you." It was worth a cotton mantle, he said, and I was overjoyed when my father nodded. The trader with the scar put the pendant on my palm and added a thin braided cord, pointing to the hole in the pendant through which it was to be threaded. He called my father's attention to this generosity and remarked that the journey had been long and that he was hungry and thirsty.

I followed them into the palace and knelt on the floormat with my father, my grandmother, and the traders, to whom my mother brought a clay jug of sweetened maize water, which they all sipped formally from small clay cups. I managed to thread my pendant and to put it on, but then I could not see it, so I took it off and laid it on the mat before me, studying my little snake man with delight.

The news the traders brought that day was unusual indeed. First they told us that the year before the Aztec ruler Ahuitzotl the Cruel had died and had been succeeded by one of his nephews, Moctezuma the Second. To us, this was something like learning that one star in the sky had been replaced by another just like it. But their second piece of news was truly astounding.

A short time before Moctezuma's coronation, bizarre strangers had come floating over the sea to the shore of Yucatán, far to the south. They had arrived in several great houses that rode on the water and had atop poles as tall as trees which held aloft great cloth canopies that swelled out with the wind and made the vessels move. A brave Yucatán chieftain who had himself rowed out in a long canoe to the largest of them said that the pale strangers had bearded faces and spoke no language he could understand. He got the impression they did not know where they were; their leader kept pointing landward and repeating the word *India*. The chieftain kept replying *Yucatán*. At last the ships turned and sailed eastward, leaving him puzzled, a little frightened, and glad it was not his land they apparently sought. The description of the alien mariners fascinated me. Indians do not grow beards, so the words were "pale men with long hair on their faces."

"If they *are* men," the older *pochteca* said with a significant glance at my father, "and not, as some suspect, supernatural beings."

Just then I held up my snake man and set it swinging back and forth, fascinated by the way it gleamed in the light from the doorway.

"Look at Malinche!" It was my grandmother's voice, and I saw her finger pointing to my pendant. Everyone was staring at it, so I set it swinging faster. Then someone gave a nervous laugh and my mother commanded me to stop.

My snake man was a representation of the god Kukulcan, the great Feathered Serpent of ancient legend. Centuries ago he had taken human form as a tall white-skinned man with a dark beard. Kind and wise, he had come across the sea from the distant east to teach people many things, particularly to abandon human sacrifice. After many years he had sailed east again but promised his weeping followers that someday he or his descendants would return, to judge how well his precepts had been followed and to punish the wicked who had disobeyed his commands.

My swinging the pendant depicting this deity had affected Ix Chan because it seemed to her uncanny. Why had I set it in motion at the instant the strange visitors were described? Had it been an omen, suggesting that the bearded strangers might next visit the shore not far

7

to the east of Paynala? Using a little child's hand, had a god whimsically confirmed his imminent presence? "I am troubled," she confessed. "Never in all my years on earth has there been any hint of the god's return. This is the first."

The older *pochteca* nodded. "I can see that you are intelligent people here, so I will tell you that when Moctezuma's couriers brought him the same news, he did not take it lightly either. A priest at the temple of our war god told me Moctezuma spent long hours consulting the stars in order to learn if those strangers were divine beings."

"And what did the stars tell him?" my father demanded.

"I do not know. I only mean that the possibility worried him, as it should any thoughtful ruler." He nodded respectfully to my father, from whom he hoped to make a pleasant profit before the day was done.

The *pochteca*'s news brought about a clash of wills between my father and the old high priest. Ah Tok argued that extreme measures should be taken to propitiate our gods. Those bearded strangers might reappear on the shore just to the east of Paynala or the new Aztec ruler might decide on further conquests to extend his wide domain and provide fodder for his war god. A slave must be bought and sacrificed so we could offer our deities that strongest proof of abject devotion, a human heart.

At the council meeting where Ah Tok tried to alarm and sway the clan heads, my father opposed him. His grandfather had long ago convinced even the priests that human sacrifice must be abandoned. To my father, the very idea of a blood-stained altar was repugnant. If hearts and blood bought the favor of the gods, he said, then such sacrifice was useless to protect us against the Aztecs, since we could never offer as many hearts as they. As for the mysterious strangers, what if they had indeed been emissaries from Kukulcan, who had said that only fruit and flowers should be laid on his altar? We must continue to obey this gentle deity, as we had for many decades of peace and plenty. My father's view prevailed. Ah Tok was forced to forget his desperate remedy.

Although the cruel sacrifice he had desired would not have prevented it, a few months later three frightened refugees arrived from the north to gasp the news that an Aztec army had just swept into their town. Resistance had proved futile; their warriors were dead or captured. The Aztecs might continue southward, to us.

My father had all the women, children, and old men leave for the Black Cave in the hills just to the west of town. Its mouth was cleverly hidden by shrubs and stones and could be reached only by a narrow rope bridge suspended over a deep, swift stream. Nearly four thousand of us filed into the great cave, carrying food, firewood, and blankets. Beyond it were other caves, in one a pool of crystal water in which swam pale eyeless fish. The torches showed gray stalactites from which hideous faces seemed to scowl down at me. My fear vanished after my grandmother told me that centuries ago a little band of our ancestors had taken refuge here after a long journey from an ancient city in the land of the Mayas to the south, a city which gods and people had at last abandoned. Greedy priests had long before taken to selling replicas of holy objects to people in the distant highlands to the west for certain products they wanted. In time those sacred artifacts lost their value, for the barbarians learned to make reproductions of them. The gods became cold; there were earthquakes, disease, and drought. The water supply became scant, receding deeper and deeper in the great *cenotes*. At last a young rebel nobleman exhorted people to follow him from the dying city to a new place. A young priest joined him, and so did several hundred courageous common folk, weary of laboring in fields and quarries to sustain priests and rulers so decadent. "After a long journey they came to the river that flows near our town and found this great cave," my grandmother said. "And here our ancestors camped during the season of rains until the jungle could be cleared and houses built. We will be safe here, too."

The days we spent in the cave were unhappy ones, because we knew we might emerge at last to find our men all killed or captured and our life as a people over and done. At last we heard a familiar voice calling us. The Aztecs had come and gone. Paynala's ruler was now a mere vassal of Moctezuma after a victory both brief and bloodless.

My father had used an old strategy—to leave the town empty, the

9

BEFORE THE GODS ARRIVED

warriors bivouacking in the heavy jungle nearby. From a tall tree on a hill he had watched the Aztecs enter Paynala from the river road. They were like ants, filling the whole town square and the lanes leading off from it, and still they came up from the seacoast, thousands and thousands, with helmets shaped like eagle heads, or jaguars'. Their drums pounded to the rhythm of one beating heart, and their bone flutes sounded like human screams. Our nine hundred warriors could not hope to prevail against them.

Without his sword or shield or black-and-red war paint but wearing his feather headdress to show his status, my father marched alone into the town and across the square past ranks of Aztec soldiers to the steps of the pyramid where the banner of the Aztecs' war chief was held aloft. He knew only a few words of their language, enough to say "Taxumal bows to the might of Moctezuma." He had to kneel and touch earth and bring that hand to his forehead in humble reverence. He was told that from this day forward to the end of time, Paynala would be visited each year by Moctezuma's tax collectors, to whom we would give whatever portion of maize, cocoa beans, cotton mantles, and other local products they might demand. Failure to do this would end in the extermination of all Paynalans. Luckily for us, the maize crop was only half-grown and unripe. After devouring nearly everything else, the Aztecs took themselves off, leaving in my father's heart and so in mine an overwhelming sense of loss. Our independence was gone forever.

But there was little time to brood, for the immediate problem was to find enough to eat to stay alive until the maize was ripe. Hunters killed deer, hares, and iguanas; our conquered neighbors in Coetzacoalcos on the coast let us catch fish to help feed ourselves. Everyone but the tiny children and the old and feeble worked to clear new fields from the jungle. Fortunately for our survival, our soil was rich and provided two crops of maize a year. Working on his milpa only a few hours a day, a man could feed a family of five. Now he worked longer and harder to produce a surplus for Moctezuma. The easygoing times were over.

It was my grandmother who decided it would be to Paynala's advantage if its ruler could speak the language of our conquerors fluently enough to negotiate with the tax collectors. We all knew a few words of this Nahuatl tongue, but we spoke a dialect of the Mayan language. The two were nothing alike, having been originated in ages past by two very different peoples. The speakers of Nahuatl had come from a region far, far to the northwest, while our Mayan ancestors, legend said, had crossed the sea to the east in a flotilla of small ships from a distant, mysterious island called Aztlán.

When the *pochtecas* visited us a month or so after our conquest by the Aztecs, my father told them we wished to buy a slave who spoke Nahuatl. They had with them two, a young female Toltec who had worked as cook for a noble family in the Aztec-dominated city called Texcoco and her little daughter, who was my age. My father was curious as to why they had been sold. The older *pochteca* said, with a sly look, that he thought the master had become enamored of the pretty slave and the mistress jealous. "I won't charge you much for the child," he said. "I'm being generous because I know your community is somewhat depleted of resources." But he asked the usual two hundred cocoa beans, claiming he could have got much more from a certain rich old cacique of Tabasco who had a penchant for women from distant parts.

The slave woman was named Xochitl, a common Aztec name meaning flower. Plucked rudely from her former life, she feared the same fate again, and was abject and eager to please my mother. The little girl's name was Atotlotl, which means ibis. I shortened it to Ato. My father and grandmother spent many hours with Xochitl until they had a quite large Nahuatl vocabulary, and they made a habit of conversing together in this tongue, which annoyed my mother, causing Xochitl to tremble. I learned Nahuatl with less effort. At first little Ato was shy and silent, but soon we were babbling away happily, each in her own language. Ato was slow to learn mine and I was eager to learn hers, and before many months had passed my father laughed and said I had casually learned more Nahuatl than he for all his application.

Ato was pretty like her mother, having the same almond-shaped eyes with little folds at the inner corners. From her I learned that the bloodthirsty Aztecs surprisingly included in their pantheon of deities the kindly god who hated blood, for one day Ato pointed to my pendant and insisted that god was named Quetzalcoatl. Ix Chan confirmed that the god indeed had two names. Ato was somewhat bloodthirsty herself, and one day confided a dream she had had, that my mother died and my father married her mother, and we became sisters.

As yet I had no sister or brother, but one day when I was five, my mother said, "You are going to have a baby brother before too long." She had become quite cheerful of late. But time passed and no brother appeared, so I asked when he might be expected. By now the bright gleam was gone from her eyes. She replied sharply that there would be no brother, and when I asked what had happened to him she sent me away.

Crushed, I wandered into the central room of the palace and heard my father and grandmother talking of this very mystery. It was dusk and they did not see me in the shadows by the doorway.

"Chituche has conceived four children since Malinche was born and has lost all of them," Ix Chan said. "Your blood and hers are now enemies. I have seen this happen before. She will not bear you another living child. And so Malinche must be educated to become ruler of Paynala. She must study at the young priest's school with the boys and I will endeavor to teach her what I know. Weaving and featherwork, however exquisite, will not enable her to deal with tax collectors, drought, earthquakes, and Ah Tok."

"But what of my younger brother?"

"Dak Cho is not a leader and knows it. So do the clan heads and everyone in Paynala."

"But what about Ah Tok? He doesn't like women."

"The final decision is not his, but yours. You are evading my suggestion because you still hope that Chituche will bear you a son."

"Ah Tok says she will. He cast the sacred stones of prophecy at her feet only a week ago." My father sounded hopeful.

"As a prophet he is not renowned. Hope must have some basis in reality. Your hope for a son does not." She lowered her voice. "As for prophecies, on the night Chituche miscarried for the first time, I had a strong vision. I saw Malinche, grown to womanhood, addressing our people as the new ruler of Paynala. It troubled me deeply, for I thought it meant your early death. But now I know it meant that you would never have a son to take your place."

A solemn sense of my own importance had stolen over me as I eavesdropped in the shadows by the inner doorway. I saw myself as Ix Chan had envisioned me, and saw the faces of my people looking up as I spoke to them.

My father said, "Certainly no harm can be done if Malinche attends the priest's school."

I walked toward them. "When I rule Paynala, will you both help me?" I wanted a denial of that troubling remark about my father's death.

Startled, they glanced at each sadly. My grandmother said, "A worthy husband will be chosen for you by the clan heads. But a ruler can expect help only from the gods, and sometimes even they will offer none.''

When I told my mother of my destiny, she was unimpressed. ''Women are made for other purposes than to rule a town.'' Her mouth was bitter and she slammed down the crossbeam of her big loom very hard, crushing down the rising band of woven cotton as if she were also crushing down her deep resentment. But she had not given up her dream of having a son. This I was soon to learn in a way that overwhelmed us both.

I suppose it was natural that my mother preferred to believe that the goddess of childbirth would relent, the moon goddess smile at last. She continued to turn abjectly to the high priest for encouragement, bringing many offerings to the foot of the sacred pyramid, which women were not permitted to ascend. Ah Tok encouraged her to hope and had her eat peyotl and brew infusions from strange herbs he gave her. He burned woodpecker feathers under her nose and mixed the ashes with dog milk and a fermented maize drink called balche, which made her vomit. The peyotl gave her visions that frightened her. My father told her not to take any more of the high priest's remedies but I think she did so secretly.

It was fortunate that the slave Xochitl was a cook, for my mother spent most of the daylight hours working on a huge feather wall tapestry depicting the goddess Cioacoatl, whose hideousness awed me. Her head and body were formed of two thick serpents twined face to face, their eyes huge and round. Over her dangling breasts hung necklaces of skulls, severed hands, and hearts. I wondered why the deity responsible for the birth of babies should look so fearsome. The loom was in my parents' sleeping alcove, and when I entered one day I found my mother kneeling at an open chest near it. She was holding up a small loincloth she had woven, of a size to fit a boy of four or five, and she stared at the garment with a forlorn expression. I felt very sorry for her and went and knelt beside her, for even if she had no son, she had me.

She turned her head and gazed blankly, then forced a smile that changed to a childish and mischievous grin. "Let's see how you would look as a boy!"

There was something strange about the idea of putting on a male's garment, even in fun, and I took a step backward, suspended between compliance and uneasiness.

"Look, Malinche, I have gilded sandals, too, and a turquoise necklace." She took these new lures out of the basket and displayed them like a vendor. "And a feather headdress!" It was a miniature of the panache of green quetzal feathers my father wore on state occasions. I had always admired it; women were allowed no such headdress, only the small ornaments they pinned into the braided crown of their own hair. Could there be any harm in my mother's little game? Eyeing the little green panache I took off my skirt.

With cold hands my mother quickly dressed me in the garments made for a son. The loincloth's long front panel reached well above my ankles. I felt that I looked not only like a boy, but like one who had outgrown his clothes. But my mother clapped her hands together and burst into shrill laughter while tears flooded her too-bright eyes. "What a tall son I have!" she cried, and clasped around my neck the turquoises set in silver. "And now the noble headdress!" Smiling, she put it on my head, leaned back to stare. "But the hair is wrong," my mother said, frowning. "Come over here to me."

I obeyed, uneasy again. She reached out to the loom beside her and picked up the small sharp knife of black obsidian she used to cut cotton threads to the length she desired. Swift as a striking snake she reached out for one of my braids.

I could not move or speak. The knife came up to my braid. I heard and felt the tiny snicking sounds as some of the hairs were severed. I screamed and tried to step away from her.

"Stand still!" she commanded and jerked me forward by my braid. She wasn't smiling any more.

"I don't want hair like a boy's!" I began to cry, not only for the hair I seemed about to part with, but because my mother had turned into a threatening stranger.

"Stop!" My father was in the doorway and for a confused instant I thought he meant that I should stop crying and let my mother have her way.

14

His voice arrested her arm in its frantic sawing motion. She let go of my braid and sank back on her heels and looked stupidly down at the knife in her hand. Then he threw it to the floor, where it clattered on the stone, the blade pointing to my feet. She buried her face in her hands and began to sob.

My father came to me, snatched the feather headdress off, tossed it aside and smiled down into my eyes. "Your mother is sorry she frightened you."

"It was only a game," I squeaked.

"I know a better one." He caught me around the waist and swooped me high above his head, laughing up at me. "Fly, little eagle-girl! Flap your wings and fly to the sun!" This always delighted me, and I flapped and flew, smiling down into his eyes. He let me down to the floor with an exciting swing. "Now go to Ix Chan's house. But first put on your own clothes."

As I dressed, my mother's harsh sobs ceased. Still kneeling she looked up at my father who frowned down as though at a puzzling stranger. "What was I going to do?" she whispered. "What am I going to do?"

His words dropped on her like stones. "Stop listening to Ah Tok. Throw out his medicines. Thank the gods for our daughter. Give away these toys." He pointed to the boy's trappings strewn on the floor.

My mother stood up slowly and wearily, and as I backed out the doorway she bent and began to gather up the husks of the dream she must now abandon.

Ix Chan's house was a stone annex built at the rear of the palace after my father had married Chituche. Ix Chan said she considered it ill luck if the husband's mother and his wife shared the same roof, but I think the truth was that she had been shocked when my father brought home a rustic stranger and had taken that means of avoiding her. To an inner room for sleeping was attached an anteroom with a thatch roof and lattice sides up which green vines had been trained. I loved this bower with its moving leaf shadows, its sweet garden smells.

"Why are you so sad?" Ix Chan asked me as soon as we were kneeling companionably on the floormat. Before I could tell her, a mellow voice called Ix Chan's name, and into the bower trundled a fat smiling neighbor holding out a basket piled high with mangoes and ripe cactus pears. "Here is the mother of Na Chel Cuy to bring you a few humble fruits and news of the day," she beamed. She always referred to herself as "the mother of Na Chel Cuy." After bearing two puny daughters, she had produced an enormous, beautiful boy who became the focal point of her life.

"Perhaps concerning your son?" Ix Chan asked.

"How did you know?" Reaching for a cactus fruit, the mother of the miracle stared in surprise.

"A wild guess," my grandmother said drily.

The proud mother told us then that Na Chel Cuy, though barely ten, had that day speared in the jungle a large ocelot, had won two games in the ball court, and had found time to scrape the ocelot hide, a lustrous one in perfect condition. "This boy of mine will make some lucky girl the best of husbands," she simpered, and reached forward to pat me on the head, glancing meaningfully at Ix Chan. She was always fawningly sweet to me, always curried favor with Ix Chan and my parents, clearly in the wistful hope of betrothing her son to Taxumal's daughter.

"I fear you have spoiled your son for any wife," Ix Chan said, for his garments were always of the finest, his food the best. His arrogance made other children dislike and fear him.

Denying that she had spoiled her son, the doting mother devoured fruit and regaled us with descriptions of several more of his recent exploits and at last took her sated bulk cheerily out the doorway. My grandmother pointed to the nearly empty basket and we began to laugh. Ix Chan did not question me about my earlier sadness, seeing me apparently happy again. But I doubt that it would have made any difference if Ix Chan had known the truth about the intensity of my mother's obsession. In the loom of time a fatal pattern had barely begun to take shape; some of the threads that would form it were not yet off the spindle.

My father had not lost the respect of our people in bowing to the might of Moctezuma, but rather had gained even more esteem. The Paynalans, sensible folk, agreed with the sentiment he had expressed when he first addressed the populace after the Aztec warriors left and we all returned from the cave. "Survival is preferable to death and slavery. Tribute to Moctezuma is the price of our survival. Working harder to pay that tribute is better than repose in a burial urn. To work!"

Aware that the Aztec tax collectors might prove rapacious, my father decided to hide away a portion of our nonperishable products in the Great Cave in order to build up a reserve that would see us through a drought or some other calamity. He had a secondary motive: our defeat would be a trifle less bitter if we could deceive our conquerors. By the time the lofty and arrogant tax collectors arrived in their royally feathered capes, a great many baskets of dried maize and beans had been concealed. Thanks to his new facility with Nahuatl, my father was able to convince the suspicious Aztecs that the smallness of our year's surplus resulted only from the fact that their warriors had pillaged so voraciously. Warning us that they would expect much more next time the tax collectors departed, their *tamanes* lightly laden. Everyone looked mournful until they had gone.

Over the next few years this hidden surplus grew large and our communal spirit slowly strengthened. It became clear that Moctezuma had no interest in forcing on us his gods or his laws. All he wanted was tribute, not even the living tribute of men for his armies, already vast beyond all need. As for slaves to sacrifice to his war god, that deity was finicky, we learned, and preferred the hearts of brave warriors captured in battle. And if we remembered happier days when the long shadow of an Aztec ruler had not yet touched us, we still enjoyed all our traditional ceremonies and festivities, if on a less lavish scale.

The *emku* was a solemn rite. All the girls and boys who had reached adolescence in the past year were welcomed into adult life, the mother of each girl presenting to the high priest the symbol of purity worn since birth. In a space roped off with garlands below the gods' pyramid, the high priest sprinkled holy water on the initiates and declared them sinless and ready to assume adult responsibilities. After that they were honored with an outdoor banquet to which the parents brought delicious dishes, and all around the plaza other families ate. Some of the very old people drank too much pulque, but in them such rare drunkenness was not frowned upon. Everyone teased the girls and asked them whom they hoped to marry, and they always made the proper answer: "The man my wise father chooses for me."

At nine I was several years from my *emku* or the choice of my husband, a thin child carrying in my head a great weight of knowledge. Among much other lore, I had learned from my grandmother and from the young priest-tutor the story of the great flood that once washed over the whole world, destroying everyone and everything except for Tezpi, who had loaded plants and animals into his huge boat. And I learned that the Age of Water had been followed by the present Age of Fire when volcanoes erupted and earthquakes leveled towns and cities. I knew how to read the sacred calendar, to draw accurately the glyphs of the eighteen months of the year and those representing all the various units of time, from Kin, one day, to Alautun, more than 63 million years in duration. I knew the names of the gods and the feast days of each, and the phases of the moon and when each crop is best planted and harvested, or ears pierced, or honey gathered. I learned to identify a hundred herbs and plants and the uses of each, and which few are deadly poisons, which produce sleep, which give visions. I learned about the many animals of the forest and seashore, and that the barb of the stingray is used by priests to lacerate their own flesh, and that long ago mothers with much milk used to nurse the gentle little coati with its small black hands. I learned that the sacred quetzal bird, with its two long green tail feathers, lives only in the forests of the high mountains and would never be seen alive in our land. I was warned of a small serpent almost as rare, the Snake with Four Nostrils, whose venom is fatal within an hour.

I did not learn of any antidote. None was known. That serpent killed my father.

He had gone to visit the chief of the small satellite town to the west which had a plantation of the kind of maguey cactus on which the cochineal slugs feed. Their bodies produce a valued crimson dye and he had to barter for a quantity of it because mantles of this color had been requested by the Aztec tax collectors. Returning home, my father paused at the edge of the jungle that lay beyond our furthest maize fields to admire a strange bird on a branch before him. Large and sky-blue, it had a fan of yellow feathers atop its head. It was as my father gazed up at this bird that the Snake with Four Nostrils sank its fangs into his foot. Feeling the sharp pain, he looked down and recognized the creature and knew he was a dead man. Aware that activity speeds the venom faster through the body, he had the men who were with him improvise a litter from a blanket and on this he was carried to Paynala and into the palace.

They put the litter down just inside the doorway. Below the palace steps a crowd was gathering. Three of the men had gone running to get the clan heads and the high priest, while one who remained told me of the snake. I felt its fangs pierce my heart. I fell to my knees beside the litter; Ix Chan knelt at the other side. At his feet my mother sobbed, her face in her hands, her body rocking forward and back, but Ix Chan and I shed silent tears that ran down our faces. The five priests and four clan heads came in at a run, Ah Tok already brandishing his rattlesnake scepter. He dipped it in an urn of scented water and shook the water drops over my father's chest, and then, eyes closed, head back, he began to intone the customary plea to the gods that they listen to my father's last confession of his sins.

"Be silent," my father commanded in a voice like an echo of his own. The young priest swinging a censer in which tobacco unfurled its purifying smoke was so startled that his arm stopped moving. To die without confession?

"I choose my daughter as my successor," my father said. "Until Malinche's *emku* has been celebrated, signifying her adult status, my brother Dak Cho will sit at her left side on the council mat, and my mother Ix Chan on her right. After her *emku* Malinche herself will rule. I say this as I die."

The last words were whispers. In moments his breathing ceased. His half-closed eyes stared at eternity or at the time-faded mural on the wall, tall figures of warriors, priests, and nobles walking in procession around the room forever. Overwhelmed by my grief, I scarcely heard my mother's wild weeping or the wailing chants of the three old women who came to dress the body for burial. But I saw too clearly the four young warriors carrying in its rope sling the enormous clay urn in which my father's body would sit doubled knees to chest for all eternity, buried on the hillside where our dead formed one mute company, beneath each silent tongue a green jade bead. The interment took place that same day; we buried our dead quickly, I knew, because death was seen as a defilement of the living, corpses as unclean. But I knew too the human spirit outlived the body and that there were many heavens, each suitable to one's manner of life and death. There was a heaven for women who had died in childbirth, and one for dead babies where a beautiful milk tree grew, laden with breasts. There was even a special heaven for suicides presided over by the sad goddess Ix Tab, who had hanged herself. I told myself that my father would attain the bright heaven for brave warriors in the high realm of the Descending God, the sun.

BEFORE THE GODS ARRIVED

For three months my father's immediate family was avoided by everyone, being unclean until we had performed the rituals of placating the newly dead, who still envy the living, with gifts of food and flowers left at the burial place. We wore old ragged garments and people pretended not to see us when we crossed the plaza to leave offerings at the temple. During this time my uncle Dak Cho had to live with us. He agreed with me that the Realm of the Sun was the proper heaven for my father. This would have been of more comfort to me had Dak Cho been respected for his intelligence rather than liked for his amiability.

Five years younger than my father, he was his opposite in every way: short and solid with glossy skin darkened to copper by the sun, he had a round face and a rather trivial nature. Ix Chan once told me that as a boy he went through his training in martial arts without any belief that it mattered how far he could shoot an arrow or hurl a spear, and had also found every excuse to avoid lessons with the priest-tutor. Yet he was not lazy and worked hard on our family's section of the clan fields. His squashes were the largest, his maize the tallest, his bean and tomato vines the heaviest laden. He would have been happy with the life of any common man, raising his crops and paying his tithes and work hours to the ruler and the priests. He had not yet married, although many a girl had tried to lure him, but he was adept at slipping away. He had once lived in the palace with Ix Chan and my father, but soon after my mother arrived he went to stay with relatives, an old couple glad to have a strong young man under their roof. He worked their field and ours, too, and most cheerfully. But six months after my father's death I learned of the banked fire that had burned behind that amiable façade.

One night when we were all seated around the supper mat Chituche suddenly put down her bowl, looked defiantly at Ix Chan and said, "I am going to marry Dak Cho."

If the roof had fallen in I would have been less surprised. He leaned toward me and confided, "I have wanted your mother since before you were born."

I looked at my grandmother to see if she was as outraged as I. She was staring at Chituche as if she had never seen her before. Her dark deep eyes then moved to her son's face. He said respectfully, as if he had memorized the words: "I will be a good husband to Chituche and a good father to Malinche."

My anger overflowed and I jumped to my feet and cried out "I have a father!"

As I ran out of the room, I heard my grandmother say to Chituche, "You will wait a full year to show respect for my dead son."

"But I am alive," Chituche said. "And so is Dak Cho's child within me."

Stunned, I stood just outside the doorway and knew that my mother had soothed the pain of her loss by embracing kindred flesh. I could not understand such faithlessness.

Only a week later, Ix Chan and I watched the tying of the mantles which made my uncle my stepfather. Kneeling beside Dak Cho at the foot of the pyramid of the gods, Chituche's face was without expression, but he radiated such joy that many people smiled and wished him well despite the general knowledge that propriety had been flouted.

One year after my father's death, Chituche's second child was born, a son.

The season of rains set in soon after his birth and Chituche kept her baby wrapped in so many blankets that Dak Cho gave him the nickname Zub-Zub, saying he looked like an armadillo peeking out of its shell. Two years later the name still suited him, for the small, fretful baby became a timid child, often ill, forever hiding in his blanket or creeping into the shelter of his mother's arms. "Close the door curtain," she would command, "a breeze has risen." Or "Whisper. He is sleeping." Sometimes I wondered if she had ever shown such concern for me, and decided she had not.

But halfway into his third year, Zub-Zub suddenly bloomed. I thought my mother's preoccupation with him would pass, but she could not seem to bear to have him out of her sight. Carrying him on one hip, she boasted of how well he could walk. Nursing him still, she told how many teeth he had grown. Dak Cho began to resent this overabundance of maternal affection. "It's not natural," he said to me one day. "Why does she see this little boy of ours as a remarkable being? It's time for Chituche to face the truth: she had produced no prodigy in Zub-Zub."

I thought I understood her need to believe she had. Could her coupling with Dak Cho have been wrong if it had brought her not only the son she had yearned for but a marvel of nature as well?

Dak Cho summoned up the courage to confront her with the truth. "People are beginning to laugh at you. It is hard enough for me to get the respect of the clan heads and the warriors without that." He had hit on the one barb sure to strike home: Chituche's pride. After that she ceased to carry Zub-Zub with her everywhere and stopped praising him so often. But I soon found that her obsession with him had merely gone underground. Like the brown river that gushed from its hidden source near the Black Cave, it suddenly emerged, a torrent.

One day she and I chanced to meet in front of the palace and she astonished me with words of praise. "How tall you are growing, Malinche." She smiled at me. "I cannot believe that soon you will be a woman." She led me to the stone bench below the ceiba tree. I was flattered when she added: "And you will be beautiful, more so than I when your father chose me." Her next words were so astounding that I did not at once grasp their real meaning. "How fortunate you are that I have given you this little brother! Now you can have a happy life. You can marry the man you want. I have often felt sorry for you, knowing that as ruler you would have to tie mantles with someone the clan heads approved, whether you liked him or not." She leaned toward me with a rapt look and her voice was honey. "But now, if you wished, you could abdicate in favor of your stepbrother, for he, too, is of the royal line. Dak Cho could continue acting as ruler until the boy is of age."

I remembered the day when she tried to cut off my hair and saw the same madness in the black depth of her eyes now. I stood up, shaken by anger. "I will never do that. How can you think I would go against my father's last command?"

My vehemence startled her. "Don't get so angry. To rule a town is hard for a woman, unnatural. I wanted a happier life for you, that's all."

"You wanted your son to rule. My tying mantles with a man I wanted was just the rosebush hiding the snake!" I was the more bitter for having been lulled by her earlier pretense of affection.

Her face grew dark. "Brilliant as you think yourself, you do not know more than the woman who bore you. You have displeased me greatly. I do not want to see your face again today." She turned her head and stared out over the plaza as if I had vanished.

I walked toward the palace with my head high and my back straight. I did not see the little pile of pebbles Zub-Zub must have left on the step when he was playing there. I stepped on one of them. I was thrown off balance and stumbled and fell.

Chituche's harsh laughter appalled me. I got up and looked back at her. She was still sitting under the tree, her head turned my way, white teeth showing in a grin. In that instant I saw that she was not beautiful any more. The bones of her face were too strong and when she stopped smiling, her thick, chiseled lips looked cruel. "One who expects to rule a town should look where she walks," she called to me.

The words would one day seem like a mocking warning.

Even though I was eleven, I took my outrage to Ix Chan. "You must remember that your mother's people are less civilized than we," she said. "Chituche has the ignorant notion that women are not fit to rule a people. But here in Paynala our rulers have been directly descended for twenty generations from that brave young warrior who led us from a dying city, and to maintain this lineage it has been necessary that a woman rule from time to time. As I did. As you will."

Her voice was faint and I saw then that she was not well. The pain she confessed to was intense, as if her bowels had become two serpents, strangling one another. I ran to get the *ahmen*. This priestly healer left behind him a dense haze of tobacco smoke that did not relieve her suffering, nor did his medicine containing powdered moth wings and the ash of red parrot feathers. After he had gone she had me brew a tea of herbs that induce repose, and at last the pain subsided enough so she could sleep. I stayed all night on a mat near hers and lay awake a long time, hearing the sad two-note cries of a bird in the garden. It spoke to me of death. I decided that when my *emku* was celebrated it would be Ix Chan who reached up beneath my skirt to remove the Shell of Purity and she who presented it to the high priest, although this would be unprecedented for one whose mother was still alive. But in the morning when I told Ix Chan my decision, she refused.

"Your mother gave you light, and to her is due this honor. But what is more important, after your *emku* you will become Paynala's ruler. To begin by flouting custom out of mere whim would shock many, and would give enemies the chance to talk against you."

"I have no enemies."

"You have one. Ah Tok."

"Why is he my enemy?"

"For the same reason that he was mine: because you are your father's daughter. Taxumal believed, as my father did, that the power of the high priest must always be limited. Ah Tok was still young when I became ruler, and thought he saw the chance to regain some of the power the priests had lost since only a woman opposed him.

23

One day he had the temple drum sounded and called the people together and told them that unless a sacrifice of human blood were offered at once to the gods a great disaster would overtake Paynala. I refused to sanction such a sacrifice. The next day came one of those thunderstorms so frightful that the most stolid people begin to think the gods are angry.'' Ix Chan smiled at an old memory. ''Ah Tok was struck by lightning; it burned the soles of his feet and he hobbled about crippled for a long time. There is nothing less awe-inspiring than one who prophesies disaster and is himself struck down, and it was years before he got over his humiliation. It embittered him and has made him hunger all the more for the power he thinks should be his. Be aware: he will prove your enemy.''

Even she did not guess who else would be.

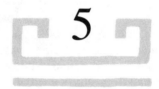

Three disasters led to my first clash with Ah Tok. A hurricane roared down from the north, trampling the young maize. It was replanted but had barely sprouted when a long heat spell dried the earth and then baked it, so that fields that normally would have offered stalks as high as a man's head produced stunted plants with dwarf cobs. And then the earthquake—which struck during the festival in honor of the corn god—leveled a dozen farmers' huts and alarmed everyone, dispirited as we were.

Early the next morning, two young boys came to the palace, troubled by what they had seen the night before. Daring one another on, they had stolen up the pyramid steps at an hour when they knew Ah Tok and the priests to be eating supper in their living quarters below and had entered the inner temple. There they had seen that the sacrificial altar of Chac Mool was stained with fresh blood. A heart was lying on a dish before the skull-faced image of Tlaloc, the rain god.

I went at once to the temple and sent Dak Cho to fetch the four clan heads. From the foot of the pyramid I called Ah Tok's name, and he appeared in the dark doorway above. His face had grown gaunter with the years and the cheekbones stood out like a skull's, but his deep-set black eyes burned with his strong life-fire. Today he wore his long white robe, dirty and stained. On one side was a dribble of blood.

"I am told you have committed a human sacrifice," I said.

"Who told you that lie?"

"Prove to me that it was a lie." I started up the steps. I do not think I would have dared to enter the temple atop, but I wanted to hold his attention until Dak Cho arrived with the clan heads.

He spread his arms out wide. "Women cannot enter the temple!"

"Nor can blood be spilled there." My earlier slight awe of him had vanished. I felt shrewd and capable of dealing with him.

"You have heard some rumor of the marketplace." His eyes left mine as he saw Dak Cho and the four clan heads hurrying across the plaza to where I stood.

"Then show them the inner temple," I commanded, triumphant. "Prove that it's clean of blood."

He made no objection, and I watched them ascend. In a few minutes they emerged, and as Dak Cho hurried down the steps to me he nodded and smiled. "It was only a deer," he said. "I saw the head and hooves. Ah Tok said a dream told him that Tlaloc and Chac Mool would be propitiated with merely an offering of deer blood and would send us better weather."

I said, "Blood is blood! Ah Tok is defying us."

Dak Cho frowned. "But a deer is only a deer. We must not make so much of this." The clan chiefs nodded in agreement.

As we walked away I felt Ah Tok's eyes between my shoulder blades and looked back. He stood at the top of the pyramid steps staring after me, the three red feathers in his hair stirring in a slight breeze, the rest of him statue-still. I think that may have been the first time he wished me dead: the clan heads and Dak Cho were malleable. I was not.

Far from procuring any good, it was as though the spilling of that deer's blood ushered in a year of sorrow that climaxed in two deaths. It was not Ix Chan's old malady that took her from me, although it recurred. Much weakened, she succumbed to a plague called *cil* that had already claimed several lives. Blood was vomited, the skin turned yellow, and chills alternated with a burning fever during which strong visions haunted the victim. I was kneeling by her pallet to sponge her hot forehead when she opened her eyes. "I had hoped to see your *emku* and your coronation, but it is not to be," she whispered.

A hard lump of sorrow filled my throat. I took her thin hand and held it and told her she would get well again, that the fever was gone now.

A film came over her eyes as eternity seeped into her. Then her eyes opened very wide. "I see! I see!" she spoke in her normal voice, not to me but to some vision within her mind. Her eyes turned to me in their deep sockets. "Changes. Many changes. You will survive them to rule in Paynala. Do not be afraid." Her eyes closed and I gathered her into my arms.

It was early morning. Gray clouds massing in the north promised rain by afternoon. By noon she had been carried in her funeral urn to the hill of the dead and interred in a narrow stone-lined crypt beside my father's. Standing there alone, unaware of the rain, I believed that no change she had envisioned could be as terrible as this one.

My *emku*, as yet uncelebrated, became a matter of general concern. The people wanted me declared their ruler, not only because they liked me but also because they needed the security of seeing tradition observed and my father's last command carried out, the more so now that Ix Chan was gone from us.

For as long as I could remember I had been friendly with the pretty woman who sold herbs on market days. A month after Ix Chan died, she offered me a bouquet of sweet-scented leaves and asked if there were any sign yet of the arrival of my womanhood. When I said no, she shook her head. "You have passed your twelfth year, yet childhood lingers on in you. But do not be unhappy, for there is an old saying that women whose blood is late are fruitful longer." She smiled and nodded. "It is also said that they are wiser than most."

Ato's early maturing seemed like proof of this, for to her slowness of mind was added a hopeless infatuation with Na Chel Cuy, who brought me occasional gifts of flowers or fruit. He was seventeen now, more arrogant than ever, and certainly not likely to have any interest in a slave girl. But it was Ato's foolish belief that one day he would come to realize that she was pretty, and want her. When she fell ill with the same disease that killed my grandmother, I sat with Ato listening to a rambling confession of her desire, and though my heart was heavy, to make her happy I told her that when I was caciqua

I would see that she was allowed to take part in the next *emku*. ''And when Na Chel Cuy sees you in new clothes, admired by everyone, perhaps he will take an interest.'' I thought it unlikely, but what mattered now was to try to lift her spirits above the clutch of her physical misery.

Chituche came in then and seemed very angry to find me there. ''This sickness can go from person to person. You escaped last year when Ix Chan died. Do not tempt misfortune twice, Malinche.''

Next day the *ahmen* was sent for, but after he left I disobeyed my mother's warning and looked into Ato's room to see if she were any better. Through the blue haze of lingering smoke her face was wan above her striped blanket and she did not know me. The next day she was worse and Ah Tok came. We met face to face as he entered and he drew back from me in alarm. ''Unlucky girl! I see death all around you!'' I did not consider that very astute of him, since he must have been told how ill Ato was.

''You will die before I do, Ah Tok.'' I spoke with arrogance to hide the chill I felt creeping through me.

With a last terrible glance he went to Chituche, who was beckoning him from the rear doorway that led to the garden and the hut where the two slaves slept. Alone in the main hall of the palace, I found myself sad and frightened. The fading murals of priests and warriors on the walls around me offered no comfort. Nor did Dak Cho when he hurried in looking for Chituche. He asked me to tell her that he was going to visit a village that had not yet sent us any tribute for Moctezuma. ''It will be two days before I return.''

I told him to be careful, for he would be taking the same jungle trail where my father met the snake that killed him.

''You're the one who must be careful, Malinche. Don't keep going to Ato's room as your mother says you have been doing.'' He hurried out of the palace then and down the steps, the sunlight warming his shoulders and the swinging rear panel of his loincloth, a simple man, unaware of the evil hatching in the room he had warned me from.

That night after we ate our supper, my mother told me that Ato was dead. I had expected this, but I could not keep from weeping. She came to my side and put her arm around me and spoke comforting words. For the first time since his birth, it was not Zub-Zub who claimed her attention, and when he whined she scolded him. He sat stunned, his beady little eyes on me, then crawled over and grabbed a piece of meat left in my stew bowl. Chituche slapped his hand hard and sent him away bawling, then brewed herb tea for me on the brazier. I remarked that the tea had an unusual flavor and she said, "I put in a strong herb that brings sleep, for that is grief's best enemy." Very soon I went to the alcove where my pallet was. I was almost asleep when I felt a presence beside it, opened drowsy eyes, saw her kneeling silhouette against the lighted doorway. "Some things cannot be helped," she said in a dull, brooding voice. I thought she meant Ato's death.

Then, as though from very far off, her name was called. She stood up and went toward the main room, and I heard Xochitl say that the *pochtecas* had arrived. The straw pallet beneath me turned to air and I floated into deep, dark sleep.

I woke on a narrow swaying litter and saw above me thick green leafage, bits of blue sky. Ahead was the broad red-brown back of the *tamane* who bore the litter's front poles. I was tied down by hempen ropes around my waist, wrists, ankles. When I tried to cry out only a croaking sound came from my dry throat. I shut my eyes and told myself I was still dreaming, but the flat pat-pat of feet on the jungle trail I knew to be real. "Water!" I croaked. I looked up into the inverted face of the *tamane* who held the rear poles of the litter as he bent forward to peer down at me. It was the face of a red-brown clay statue except that the eyes were human. He said something to the other *tamane,* who turned his head to peer at me over one shoulder. They did not understand me because I had spoken the Mayan word for water. I remembered how to say it in Nahuatl.

"She wants water," the *tamane* behind me said.

"I want water," the one ahead said. "We can't stop."

Now the dryness of my mouth and throat began to terrify me. Was I going to die of thirst between two walking clay statues? The clay feet pattered along the trail, which curved alongside a stream. The sound of water chuckling over stones maddened me, and again I screamed for water.

Then, from up ahead a voice called the procession to a halt. Because of the curve of the trail, I could see the six *tamanes* who preceded mine kneel and straighten, easing their burdens off their backs onto the ground with grunts of relief. I was set down with a slight thud. Turning my head, I avidly watched my two porters go to the stream's edge, each with half a dried gourd. They squatted and drank, and then one filled his and brought it to me. Cool water, filling my mouth and slipping down my parched throat, became the only reality in the universe. Sated, I let my head drop back, content for a moment to breathe without thirst.

But then the truth struck like a spear through the heart. My mother had drugged me. She had sold me to the *pochtecas*. They were not evil people and could not have been accomplices. She must have lied. She told them I was a slave that she was forced to sell because times were bad in Paynala. That was it. But how could she have been so foolish, even with Dak Cho gone and poor cowed Xochitl the only witness to the lie? Foolish? Mad!

"Is she awake yet?" The voice was a commanding one and I looked up at a thin *pochteca* with gray hair who seemed very tall in his high black hat and long red cape. Around his neck hung several necklaces of gold and silver and even one of jade.

I told him, "I am Malinche of Paynala, daughter of Taxumal. You must take me home at once."

To my surprise, he nodded. "She said you would say that." He frowned. "You must never say that again. No one likes crazy people. No one wants them."

Terror struck me. "It is Chituche who is crazy!"

"And is your mother Xochitl crazy too, Atotlotl?"

"Chituche is my mother! Atotlotl is dead!" My heart was beating wildly now.

He nodded grimly. "Chituche told me you'd say that. But I know everything. I know how you and Malinche were raised together like sisters, and how you refused to believe she had died."

"I'm alive!"

"You are, and you are Atotlotl. You are a crazed slave girl who put on Malinche's clothes and paraded about in them claiming the dead girl's identity. You reached such a state of frenzy that the priest gave Chituche a potion that put you to sleep."

"I knew Ah Tok was part of it! He doesn't want me to rule in Paynala."

"Stop!" He bent over me and now his eyes looked cruel. "If you

29

go on telling this lie you will end on some priest's altar. Do you want your heart cut out? Do you?''

Terror became a stone inside my chest and my brain fluttered wild wings in my head.

"Do you?'' The *pochteca*'s forefinger prodded my shoulder.

I shook my head.

"Then remember that you are Atotlotl, a slave and daughter of a slave. Hold firmly to that truth. It will procure you a better fate.''

"What fate?'' I whispered.

He looked pleased at my docility. "I plan to sell you to the most important cacique in all Tabasco. As a palace slave you will have a pleasant life. His city is much larger and richer than Paynala.'' He smiled down at me. "Now tell me your name.''

"Ato.''

"Ato?''

"That is what Malinche always called me,'' I said and laughed crazily. It didn't matter what I said because at the first chance I would escape and make my way back to Paynala.

But after I had swallowed a cold lump of maize paste and a tomato, he put a leather collar around my neck. It had a long rope attached and as I plodded along after him, my heart became more like a stone at every step. When the sun went down I knew that Ato's body had been interred as mine. I shivered and felt the cold jade bead under Ato's tongue. The cries of the birds turned to the laments of my people when they learned I was dead.

Chituche and Ah Tok had planned very well. With such a tragedy occupying everyone in Paynala, who would note that the slave girl Ato was missing? Later, when Chituche said she had sold her, who would care? Would Xochitl dare to tell the truth, overawed by Chituche and Ah Tok? When Dak Cho returned, would he believe what Chituche told him? I decided he would prefer to be deceived, whatever deep doubt he might feel, having left me quite healthy two days before I died.

By habit, my hand stole up to my golden pendant of Kukulcan. It hung next to my skin, hidden under the high square neck of my overblouse. When my fingers touched it through the cloth, a belated shock went through me. Chituche had forgotten to remove it and put it on Ato's corpse! Or else superstition had stayed her hand, since it was a god's likeness. Or perhaps sentiment had moved her. Who can say with a madwoman? Whatever the reason, its presence seemed a good omen and made me able to believe at least for a little while that Chituche and Ah Tok would not succeed with their scheme after all.

Any thought of escaping, of making my way home, left me the next afternoon when we stopped at a town near the bank of the Tonola River. In my ignorance I thought we had reached Tabasco, and then found we were not yet halfway there. But it was not only the distance from my home that disheartened me, nor the snarling of jaguars when we passed through the jungle, nor the night bats that suck blood. The farther we got from Paynala, the more all-enveloping became my dreamy, helpless mood. For I was of Paynala, and of my clan there, the way an arm is part of a body, or an ear is, or a tongue. Far from the sight and sound of my native soil and its people, my sense of identity grew frail. Sometimes it was only by clutching my pendant of Kukulcan that I could get back the feeling of being Malinche, whatever name the *pochtecas* chose to call me by.

I tried to imagine myself watched over by that god. I would stare up at the evening star, which is his star as is the star of morning, and I would whisper to him of the wrong done and try to invoke his help, but no feeling of comfort came. Gods might respond to priests' prayers after suitable elaborate rituals but a person of twelve far from home with a rope around her neck was as remote from their divine concern as if she were a monkey or parrot or lizard. The gods were supernatural participants in the communal life of an entire people. I was a leaf blown from that tree.

We reached the Tabasco River two days later, having stopped at several towns to barter. Men in dugout canoes took us downriver to Xicalanco, the capital city of Tabasco, for although the sun was setting, the *pochtecas* decided not to wait for morning. I shared their canoe and sat in the middle facing the shorter, younger *pochteca*. Suddenly he pointed to my gold pendant. "Where did you get that, Ato?"

For the first time I noticed the faint crescent scar on his left cheek. He had seemed vaguely familiar to me and now I recognized him. Hope stirred. I kept my voice calm so as not to seem crazy. "My father Taxumal bought it from you for me when I was three."

I thought I saw a flicker of recollection in his eyes, then his hand reached out for it. "Malinche told you that, Ato. It's too good for a slave. I'll take it."

"No!" I clutched it and leaned back to evade the reaching hand. "My father gave it to me. You know it. You know I am Malinche!"

My anger only amused him. "You are nothing. I want the pendant."

"No you don't." The other trader spoke. In the light of the setting sun his shrewd old face looked hard as gold. "It's worth more to us around her neck. It sets off her pretty face and gives her status so that we can ask a much bigger price for her." The reaching hand drew back. The old one added. "And there's something else to be considered." Their two heads in the tall black hats drew close together as the old one whispered at some length. I could catch only a few fragments, but these and my knowledge of the *pochtecas'* code of supposed integrity let me guess his message. Just in case I was who I claimed to be, and just in case the plot against me was discovered and I was somehow reinstated in Paynala, it would be best to be innocent of theft of the pendant. At the end he raised his voice and said, nodding wisely, "I have lived a long time. Stranger things have happened than justice prevailing at last."

The trader with the scar nodded and turned to me. "You can keep your pendant, Ato."

My frail hope vanished like smoke blown away, leaving me listless and at last I fell asleep curled against a straw basket. When I woke it was night, and I sat up to watch the dazzling broken reflections of the moon on the dark water into which the rowers' paddles plunged with rhythmic soft splashings. A deep resignation flowed through my veins.

Xicalanco was a great trade center on Pom Lagoon from which a wide brown river flowed east to the sea. There were big thatched stone warehouses for the salt, emeralds, cotton mantles, conch shells, turtle eggs, jade, topaz, alum, bitumen, gold dust, and countless other products and a barracks for slaves, in which the trade was brisk. The town itself was walled, and immediately around it the swampland had been filled in to grow palms and cacao trees. On entering, we crossed a wide plaza where several large ceiba trees cast pools of moonshadow. The palace we approached was enormous, of white stones. Four palaces the size of Paynala's would have fit inside it. We were admitted by a fat, sleepy servant who went to bring the cacique's wife, to whom the older *pochteca* had asked to speak.

The servant came back carrying a candlewood torch; its flame illuminated the ample, elegant figure of her mistress. Her pale underskirt swayed grandly below her square-necked chemise of deep Maya blue. She had weary eyes with highly arched brows, a narrow nose with a curved bridge, and wore a topaz on her pierced left nostril. "The hour is late for bartering," she told the *pochtecas* reprovingly.

"I remembered, respected Kukul, that you said you did not sleep well. I thought it might be a welcome diversion to glance at our merchandise." He pointed to me. "Many have wanted to buy her as we journeyed from her distant town, but I saved her for you, Kukul. She is a rare jewel and worthy of good surroundings." He spoke of my skillful weaving, sublime featherwork.

"Then how did her former owner bring herself to part with this flower of purest jade?" Kukul eyed me with slight interest.

"Poverty, and also a younger husband with a roving eye," he lied smoothly. "Anyone can see that the girl is going to be a beauty."

The cacique's wife spoke to me. "What is your name?"

"Ato," said the older *pochteca* quickly. "A common Aztec name."

"Oh, this girl is Aztec? We don't have any of those. What do you want for her?"

"We can decide that in the morning when I will show you many other rare items best appreciated by the light of day."

By now I was beyond shame or wonder. To be sold like a mantle or clay bowl had numbed me, and when the cacique's wife spoke to me I was not even aware of it and just stood staring ahead.

"Is she a mute?" Kukul asked.

"Say something, Ato," the older *pochteca* commanded.

"I am weary," I said, and it was true.

"Now say it in the Aztec language," the cacique's wife commanded, and I did. A kindly look came over her face. "Poor young thing. Of course she's tired after such a long journey." She told the short, fat servant to show me where I would sleep and I followed her out a curtained doorway, along a passage and across a moonlit courtyard to a low outbuilding with many doors in a row. "The slaves and the concubines live out here," she said.

"Am I to be a concubine?" My voice trembled.

"The old cacique does not take children to bed." She paused at one of the doors and held aside the cotton hanging. "This room was left vacant by a concubine who died, but the priest fumigated it." I saw that she was very cross-eyed, considered a mark of beauty among the Olmecan people. The mothers hang a bead in front of a baby's eyes to make them so. "Sleep well," she said indifferently, and left me.

On the floor was a thick straw sleeping mat with a serape folded

33

at the foot. The sight of it made me realize how weary I was. I took off my skirt, folded it and pulled the cover up over me. Moonlight paled the small square window beside the doorway. In the garden a night bird gave a harsh cry. I remembered my grandmother's last words to me. I would not be afraid. Kukul had seemed kind. Tomorrow after the *pochtecas* had gone I would tell her the truth and ask her to help me. The bird screamed again. It sounded closer.

I dreamed of a large sky-blue bird with a fan of yellow feathers on its head. With a flapping of great wings it settled in the window of my room. The moonlight was so bright that I could see its colors clearly and I knew it was the same bird that charmed my father on the last day of his life. First I felt afraid, but then a great rage filled me. It was clear to me that my father, who had always revered the Feathered Serpent, should not have died because of a snake and this evil bird. Then the bird opened its wings and swooped down to the floor. It turned its head to one side so it could watch me with one blazing yellow eye as it stalked slowly toward me. I knew that it meant to stab its long beak into my heart. I feigned sleep until it reached my pallet and then I seized its neck with both hands and summoned up all my strength to choke its life out. It opened its beak, making a terrible croaking, and flapped its great wings. I held on. Blood came suddenly welling out of its mouth and gushed over me in a stream, but I knew I must not let go until its wings stopped moving. . . .

I opened my eyes on the gray light of early morning, put aside my blanket and got up. It stunned me to look down at a red stain where I had lain. It was not the dream-bird's blood. It was mine. A vision came of that *emku* I would not take part in, of young girls in new clothes, smiling and proud in the sunlight of the plaza in Paynala, and tears filled my eyes. Anger seared them dry. One day, some way, I would return to Paynala and avenge myself. Chituche would grovel at my feet, begging for mercy. Ah Tok would crawl to me in the dust. And I would command that they die!

Kneeling on the mat with its red stain, I tore a long strip from one side of my skirt, and doubled it over and attached it to the belt from which my golden seashell hung. When I put on the skirt I twisted it around so the torn part was at one side. Heavy discomfort in my belly made me kneel again, which seemed to ease the pain. Then, hearing voices and footsteps outside the doorway, I got to my feet so that the next Tabascan to see me would find me standing, unafraid.

The short, fat slave woman with crossed eyes peered in. My torn skirt at once caught her attention and she pointed to it, giggling. Several other women appeared in the doorway behind her. A tall one with a kind face and a baby on one hip said her name was Ixlan and asked mine.

"Malinche," I said without thinking.

"Her name is Ato," said the cross-eyed one. "The mistress told me so."

"I must talk to her at once."

"She'll talk to you when she's ready. Who do you think you are?" said Cross-Eyes.

"She's only a child, Chu-Chu," the tall one with the baby said. "She's strange here and afraid. And she's probably hungry." She smiled at me. "Aren't you hungry?"

"Yes," I lied.

"Come on, we'll go to the slaves' kitchen and find you something to eat." Chu-Chu, jealous of her authority, came with us. The baby on Ixlan's hip woke and wailed, and she cradled it in her arms and nursed it as we crossed the garden, beginning to fill with children of all sizes who emerged rubbing their eyes from the many doorways of the barracks. "You'll find it isn't bad here," she said. "The cacique's old and doesn't bother us much any more."

"Doesn't his wife mind his having concubines?" I asked.

"She prefers it this way. She's had six children by him—ten counting the ones who died. The only time she ever gets angry is when the children make too much noise. She can't stand children yelling."

We had reached the kitchen, an open, thatched outbuilding where several slaves knelt chatting and slapping out the morning's maize cakes. A small, rough-coated pig lay under a table watching them. Several white ducks and a tame *guajolote* awaited crumbs. I found myself watching as hungrily as they.

"Now my mistress wants to see you," said Chu-Chu, after I had devoured three maize cakes. "She said to feed you first. She doesn't like liars. You'd better remember your right name."

When we found Kukul in the palace she arched her eyebrows even higher at the sight of my torn skirt and told me I must have a new one. Dismissing Chu-Chu, she took me to a large storeroom where many mantles, skirts, and chemises were stacked and she seemed to take an interest in selecting the proper costume for me. I told her what else I needed and she gave me some squares of soft, unbleached cotton and showed me how to fold one. "I welcome you to the world of womanhood," she said, and gave an enormous, groaning yawn. "I sleep very poorly. It is sometimes dawn before I close my eyes. I do not know why this is. I'm going to my hammock now. You can come with me and swing it."

The hammock, of coarse net striped with many colors, hung between two gnarled pepper trees in an enclosure beside the palace. She collapsed into it with a sigh and I set it swaying. Soon she was asleep and snoring, leaving me alone with my bitter thoughts. When she woke, the sun was halfway up the sky. She rubbed her eyes, smiled, and surveyed me with interest. "You look better by daylight, Ato. The old *pochteca* said you can do featherwork. Is that true?"

"The truth is that I am not named Ato. I am Malinche, the rightful ruler of Paynala. I was drugged and sold as a slave." I stood tall, my head high.

She blinked at me. "Paynala? Where is that?"

"Five days' journey to the north."

"I think I may have heard of it. It's a small place, isn't it?"

"We are over five thousand."

She smiled at me. "Do you know how many Tabascan warriors my husband can summon? Forty thousand."

"The size of my town is not important. A terrible injustice has been done to me and to my people."

"The world is full of injustice."

Her great calm in the face of my momentous revelation filled me with despair. "I would need only a small escort for the journey," I persisted.

"It is never wise for the ruler of one country to interfere in the internal affairs of another. Furthermore, I have just remembered something. Paynala is actually ruled by the Aztecs, isn't that so? Didn't they take over that town and several others up there many years ago?"

"They only want tribute. We still rule ourselves," I said. Bitter disappointment filled me now.

As though she hadn't heard me, she struggled to a sitting position and swung her legs over the hammock's side. Like a big bird on the edge of its nest, she regarded me kindly. "You must learn to resign yourself to circumstances. All women must learn this. Men are made to change circumstances, women to accept. You are much more fortunate than you realize. Xicalanco is no small backwater like your Paynala." She smiled at me. "I am not a native. I was captured after a battle with a town far to the west. At first I was only a concubine, but when the cacique's wife died in childbirth, I became First Wife in her place. Who knows what good fortune may await you here?" She leaned forward, an adult cajoling a child. "Forget the past. Bow to circumstance."

"I will not forget. I will not bow. I will return to Paynala."

She stared, surprised at my vehemence. Her tone was amused when she said "Before you leave us, I would like to see a sample of this featherwork you are said to do so well. Slaves are expected to earn their keep." She surged to her feet and moved grandly away, motioning me to follow, and then paused to deliver a final blow. "As for this unlikely tale you have told me, I shall call you Ato."

She gave me a loom and a spindle and cotton and a basket of feathers of many colors and ordered me to make a wall hanging showing the moon goddess. In my little room, with the voices of the children in the garden for company, my fingers soon remembered the skill they first learned from the mother I hated. For many weeks I lived as a recluse, numbing my feelings with the repetitive task that had been set me. But such a life was not in accordance with my nature and as Ixlan, the tall young woman with the baby, persisted in friendly visits, and some of the others too, I gradually emerged from my self-imposed loneliness and took part in the trivial and unimportant life in that small world of slave women and concubines who were endlessly spinning or weaving, pounding maize, shaping clay pots and straw baskets, and sharing the gossip of the palace and marketplace. Only a few were jealous when the cacique's wife praised my featherwork and rewarded me with a bracelet.

Had I been cruelly treated, I would have found a way to attempt the long journey to Paynala alone, probably ending as a huddle of bones in the jungle or else as a captive in one of the small towns we had passed, and much worse off than in Tabasco. But the kindness I met with as favorite slave of the cacique's wife allowed me to be cautious and patient. As months became years, my present existence often seemed like a dream; at other times it was my past life that seemed unreal. To relieve the tedium of endless featherwork, I began to tell stories to the children of the slave compound who came to watch me, and that led to my becoming their teacher. This pleased Kukul, because it kept them quiet and I think it saved me from despair because I found a satisfaction when their minds blossomed, and some I came to love.

Kukul came to my aid when I grew old enough to attract old Nan Chan's attention, though by that time he was nearly blind. She did not understand my disinclination to become a concubine, but humored me, and was able to convince her husband that I was a cold, plain girl best employed in weaving him a ceremonial cape and teaching children how to count. The other women did not enlighten him as to the fact that I was not as she described me, but her lie was useless to avert the sudden infatuation of one of her sons, who could see very well.

Akukum was a young warrior who had been living according to custom in a barracks with the others in training, but he came to the palace to stay when I was seventeen and one morning encountered me as I was swinging his mother in her hammock while she dozed off in her usual morning nap. The next day he came to the slaves' compound to visit me and brought a gift of turtle eggs, just as if he were visiting a person of some importance in her parents' home, and whenever I spoke he hummed politely to show he was interested. He returned the next day, and the next. I was less indifferent when he went to his mother and told her he wished to take me as his First Wife. Had Kukul not liked me, this desire to marry a slave would have caused great trouble and confusion, but as it was, she agreed to ask her husband to free me. Perversely, the old man refused. I think his son's desire for me had made him suspect that he had been duped.

To the other slave women and the concubines, Akukum's wish to marry me was a miracle, and several took to bringing offerings of flowers to the temple where Kukulcan's altar stood, attributing my good fortune to divine intervention of the deity whose likeness I wore and hoping he would provide them also with freedom and a handsome mate. But to me Akukum's infatuation meant much more than freedom and status: my dream of returning to Paynala to avenge myself and claim my proper destiny had not died with time. Now it sprang up fiercely. I saw Akukum as the ally who would make that dream a reality.

Summoning all my art as a storyteller, I told him of my betrayal. Because he desired me, he not only believed me but was incensed. He promised that when I was freed he would gather a group of warrior friends and take me to my birthplace so that justice could be done at last. But until his father granted me my freedom he could do nothing, for that would be to steal his father's property. The old man might even decide to exact the full penalty for theft, which was severe. All he could do was hope that Kukul would find the right moment to wheedle her husband into a generous mood.

This hope suffered a setback after Akukum told her one day of my desire to return to Paynala and the reason for it. I had always thought that she had never believed the story of my true identity. But now I learned from her that the *pochteca* with the scar had whispered before he left that he suspected I might be of high lineage. Kukul's eyes flashed with scorn when she summoned me into the palace for a private conversation after her son had left. "I thought you had finally come to understand that to rule in Paynala would have been a petty destiny compared with dwelling in a great town like this! Akukum might even succeed his father and rule Xicalanco! I will waste no more breath trying to get you freed. I should urge my son to forget all about you. Beauty and intelligence are nothing when they are coupled with a heart clenched on an old grief."

The shock of learning that she had always suspected my true status was worse than her angry words. What would it have cost her to have aided me long ago to return to Paynala? Was her self-centeredness so great that no other hand than mine could have rocked her hammock and woven her feathers? "You knew?" I whispered.

I found then that she regarded herself as my benefactress, believed she had done me a favor keeping me in Xicalanco, for she envisioned Paynala as a rude little town like the one where she had been born. And so I learned the bitter truth, that even affection can be blind to the deep needs of another.

After her tirade, she forgave me. "You are a rare one, Ato or Malinche, or whoever you are. I knew that from the first. I will not urge my son to forget you. I will somehow get my husband to free you. You will marry Akukum. And, who knows, one day you may be First Wife of the ruler of Xicalanco. And then you will thank me and know that you never had a better friend."

But old Nan Chan continued to balk at losing his valued slave. Ironically, the feather cape I had made was now used against me, and he irascibly demanded of Kukul that she show him one other slave

39

who could do work as magnificent. Soon a more important matter claimed his attention.

Word reached him that a small group of pale-skinned bearded mariners had landed on the seashore near the mouth of the Tabasco River. In some anxiety Nan Chan had bravely gone there to see for himself, bringing some gifts to placate the visitors. He returned to say that they were in no way awe-inspiring. ''These strangers, though peculiarly clad and possessing an unusual vessel to travel in, are mortal, mere men, unfortunate in being disgustingly hairy. They have now departed for their own land, wherever that may be, so let us give them no more thought and cease concerning ourselves with the possibility of a god's return.''

But less than a year after this the strangers reappeared. This time they came in many ships, eleven by the account brought to Xicalanco by some frightened fishermen. From these great vessels they had lowered boats something like canoes, and in them they had begun to row upriver. It seemed to everyone as if the strangers' earlier scouting party had fooled the old cacique as to their peaceful intentions. Five hundred warriors were sent to the river bank and a thousand more lined the shore of Pom Lagoon. But these attempts to discourage the strangers from entering Xicalanco were futile, for they camped that night on an island in the river, evidently planning to land on our shore the next day. Before dawn the city was evacuated, the women, children, and elderly plodding north on the causeway to a hilly jungle area where we could camp. The warriors stayed behind, concealing themselves behind a ridge of land to the west. By this time warriors from other Tabascan towns had converged on Xicalanco to swell our forces, spurred by fear of the strangers.

All of us who were encamped like savages to the north of the city believed our stay there would be brief. We were filled with fear and confusion when a runner came with the news that in a great battle our warriors had been routed. The strangers commanded supernatural weapons that thundered and hurled round stones that killed many people simultaneously. Worse, they had with them huge four-legged monsters, half beast, half human and utterly fearless. Akukum was among the many slain.

His mother wept bitterly, already dazed by this menace to the town she had believed to be as secure as the earth under her feet. I comforted her, but found that even while I grieved for her son's death I was grieving as well for the loss of my only chance to avenge myself on Chituche and Ah Tok and to astound my people of Paynala by appearing among them, risen from the dead.

When old Nan Chan, stunned and humbled, gathered together a retinue that would accompany him when he went to surrender to the gods who had conquered his city and his land, I was among the twenty slave women and concubines chosen to walk behind his litter. Curiosity was stronger than fear; the thought that I was going to see the returned Quetzalcoatl–Kukulcan in all his stern power filled my whole being with amazement.

A first intimation of the utter strangeness of the conquerors struck me when I saw one bizarre figure among those many armed creatures who stood watching us pass. He was beardless, with shining hair, dark gold. His eyes were like emeralds. He fixed them on me. The stare of those jewel eyes sent a thrill of fear all through me. I knew he was not of my world or any world I had even imagined, unless it might be Aztlán.

The old cacique descended from his litter and approached the large canopy in whose shade stood the warrior-god, bearded, stern-faced, and covered head to foot in smooth metal with the gleam of silver, but darker. We women were ordered to go forward to where he stood. As we obeyed, I heard my old master say: "In token of our humble surrender we offer these twenty slave women as hostages."

The shock was so great that I only remember looking down at my sandaled feet moving me forward, first one, then the other. The ground seemed to shudder under me as if an earthquake had struck. My head felt very light, filled only with air. Not even on that day when I awoke on a litter far from my home had such terror filled me. That journey had ended among people who spoke my tongue and worshiped my gods. But now, what would be my destiny?

I moved from the known to the unknown. The shade below the canopy both cooled and threatened me, for I stood near the great god's attendants. Some were bearded and helmeted like him; a few wore long brown robes. One of these, I saw, was acting as the god's interpreter. Nan Chan was offering gifts on a tray. The god's hand went out and picked up a small golden animal, holding it high and turning it in the sunlight. He offered a return gift, something he held up and shook so that it rang with a clear tinkling sound. Nan Chan took it and rang it again, looking pleased with the gift as he knew he should. The other women were huddled close together, mute with fear, but I moved forward so I could better watch the god and Nan Chan, my fascination stronger than my terror.

The god spoke in a strange tongue which the brown-robed interpreter translated into a Mayan dialect for Nan Chan. It seemed peculiar that a god should need an interpreter; I had imagined that gods are able to speak all human tongues at will. "Last year you gave some countrymen of mine some gifts of gold and now you offer me these golden animals. Do you have more gold?" I wondered why a deity should be interested in mere Sweat of the Sun when he could have asked for jade or emeralds.

Nan Chan showed his cleverness then. "If it is gold you want, what little we have is as nothing compared to what you will find if you go to Mexico or Culhua." I had to praise him in my heart, for he had mentioned the core of the Aztecs' wide domain.

"And where is this Mexico?" the deity asked. Strange, I thought, that a god does not know where Mexico is, or Culhua either.

"Far to the northwest, high in some mountains that I myself have never seen," Nan Chan told him.

"How far?" the deity asked.

"Very far. But in your great vessels you could easily cover much of the distance." I knew how eager Nan Chan was for the gods to depart and leave him free to deal with the problems their arrival had brought down on his poor head, chiefly to try to save his face and lofty rank after having been so wrong in his estimate of the strangers who had arrived last year.

"How many days or weeks would I have to travel to get to this Mexico, this Culhua?" the god asked.

"I do not know," Nan Chan confessed.

Nor did the god! I tried to find some explanation for his ignorance. Only one possibility occurred to me: he might be testing Nan Chan to see if he answered truthfully, in which case I had been wrong in my belief that deities can easily read mere human minds.

Suddenly I felt a presence behind me, and a mailed arm snaked around my waist. I smelled a peculiar stench, the smell of metal armor warmed by outer heat and the body beneath it. A low laugh blew hot breath into my ear. My head and eyes turned in that direction; my body was so tense with fear it could not move. A pair of narrow gray eyes stared into mine. Between beard and mustache teeth showed in an alarming smile. The lips whispered something, and I smelled the creature's breath, like rotten fruit. Then I felt a strong hand caress my hip, lingering on its curve. Outrage overcame my panic. As I struggled to free myself I heard an angry-sounding voice say "Captain!" One of the several brown-robed deities had approached and now spoke sternly to my molester, who at once released me, turning away with a shrug. Shaken, I stepped back among the other women.

I remembered Nan Chan's words when he returned from his encounter with the strangers who came to our shore last year: "They are no gods. Do gods stink? Do they hunger? Sweat? Belch?" Do they lust? I wondered now. Do they subject women to public indignity? Was I a hostage to gods or mere men? Very lustful men, with no normal respect for another's person! But then I recalled their remarkable instruments of warfare which thundered, and their supernatural beasts. I had not yet seen one of these, but had heard a vivid description: they were gigantic creatures like great stags but with human heads and arms covered by metal armor.

As if summoned by my thoughts, one appeared. I heard a thunderous drumming on the earth outside the canopy and saw one of those monsters prancing before it in the sunlight. Poor Nan Chan backed away in horror as the thing suddenly raised high its two front legs, its upper and somewhat human portion leaning forward against a lower, staglike head in which a wild brown eye gleamed and rolled. A terrible sound came out of its mouth. Behind me the women moaned in terror.

The principal deity who had talked with Nan Chan called something to the beast and in a moment it lowered its legs, whirled about, and thundered away and I felt the drumming on the earth with the soles of my feet while hearing it with my ears.

As Nan Chan tried to regain his composure, the great deity again asked through his interpreter, "Tell me, Nan Chan, do you have any more gold to offer me?" It was clear to me that he had summoned the supernatural beast to impress Nan Chan.

My mind was in chaos. Were these strangers gods or men? The one called Captain seemed no deity to me. But as if to reprove me for my doubt, one of the supernatural beasts had appeared in all its fury and splendor. I was hot and prickling still with the fear it had inspired.

A cool breeze touched me. I turned my head. The rear curtains of the canopy were partly open. Through the aperture I could see the grove of tall palms to the east of the town and beyond them the thick green mangrove jungle in which from time to time an adventurous child got lost.

BEFORE THE GODS ARRIVED

In that instant I knew that whether the strangers were men or gods or somewhere between the two I was going to try to escape them.

I edged over to my friend Ixlan and asked her to shield my departure by standing in front of me while I backed out. She whispered, "The gods will surely find you and be angry." I shook my head in denial of her warning and again asked her aid. She nodded.

By now the other women were engrossed in discussing the supernatural beast, and all the strangers were intent on the dialogue between Nan Chan and their leader. I reached the rear curtain without being seen, found the opening, and slipped through.

Outside, my fear was to encounter the supernatural beast, but it was gone. No one was in sight in the palm grove, and I hurried toward the mangroves, then began to run. The gray boles of the palms I passed seemed like old friends; far above my head their fans rustled in the breeze that had reminded me that freedom was possible. Soon my life would go on much as it had before the gods arrived, for surely Kukul would welcome me back and hide me until they departed. With a slight pang I remembered then that her son was dead, so that I could never be his First Wife or have any chance of returning to Paynala with his help. But even so the ragged remains of my former life seemed preferable to the fearsome future that awaited me if I had stayed with the gods.

The mangroves were only a short distance ahead when I heard a thudding like distant thunder, glanced back, saw with a thrill of horror that one of the supernatural beasts was pursuing me. It had a human voice; it shouted something in its strange language. But before it reached me I had flung myself in among the twisted slender gray trunks of the mangrove trees, not caring that their branches slashed at me as I plunged deeper in. Soon they were too thick for me to stand upright. I dropped to my knees and crawled, twisting my way deeper and deeper on sandy soil that grew moist under my palms as I neared the little stream that joined the great river to the south. In a deep green twilight I found that I could go no farther; the trees were too close together to pass between.

But of one thing I was certain. The great beast that had followed me could never get in here. Then my heart leaped into my throat. From the direction in which I had come I heard a faint rustling sound. Something was stalking me, coming ever closer. If it found me, what would it do to me? My heart was thudding so hard I was afraid it would hear it. Could the beast have told one of the strangers where I had gone? Perhaps the one called Captain who had molested me? I

44

tried to will my heart to beat more softly, and I listened so intently my ears seemed to move against my head. After a long moment I realized that the rustling was growing fainter. The maze of tangled trees had confused whatever was hunting me. It was moving away from where I trembled.

In the instant of false security this gave me I knew how horrible it would have been if it had pounced on me in anger or in lust. Then I knew this still might happen.

I had a choice. I could wait here like a frightened hare or creep out the way I had come, go back to the canopy, face with what courage I could summon up an unguessable future with those strange gods. I vacillated only a moment and then began to crawl with a growing panic out of the trap in which I had placed myself.

The dimness slowly brightened as the mangroves thinned. I stood and walked out into the sunlit palm grove. I stopped and stared, stunned by the sight that met my eyes: the lower half of the supernatural beast. It stood quietly beside a palm tree to which it was tied. Its large, long head was bent low on the strong arch of its neck. It was nibbling a clump of grass.

In a sudden new light I saw it as nothing supernatural at all, only a large animal of a kind unknown to me. It sometimes carried a god on its back. That was strange, but not alarming.

A sound behind me made me turn. From the mangroves emerged a god; the god who had ridden it. He wore a dark metal breastplate and a helmet that gleamed like gold. As he came closer I saw that it was the beardless one with emerald eyes. He spoke gently in a strange tongue, and then pulled out from under his armor a small silver cross suspended on a chain and held it out for me to see. As the cross swung before my eyes I looked up and saw the design on the side of his helmet. It was a true supernatural beast, clearly half-man, half-stag. It held a drawn bow. Apparently such creatures did exist in the land of the gods.

I knew what to do: I bent humbly, touched earth, and brought that hand to my forehead in surrender.

The god extended his hand toward me. I stepped back. He nodded and smiled and reached for my hand. I saw that I was supposed to touch his. When I did, some of my fear subsided, for I felt only warm human skin, paler than mine but not otherwise unusual. He went to the tree where the animal he had ridden on was tied and released it. Still holding my hand, he walked beside me toward the gods' canopy, the large gray beast ambling after.

45

PART II

TO THE UNKNOWN LAND
January 15, 1519–August 12, 1519

8

On a balmy Havana day, with just a little breeze to stir ragged palms bent by stronger winds, I stood on the cliff where our family land touched the Caribbean and stared west over blue, sun-sparkled water. A distant, unknown land waited beyond the horizon in all its mystery and promise, and waited for *me*. Then with equal yearning I looked to the east toward the emerald curve of the harbor, hoping to sight the fleet of Hernán Cortés sailing west from Trinidad. I was nearly eighteen, eager to risk death and lesser hazards to get a fortune in gold. I exulted in my great luck to be standing at this precise spot at this very moment.

I gave my father Francisco Mondragon too little credit for my whereabouts. When I was seven he had dared the unknown, lured from Spain to the West Indies by rumors of gold and plenty of subdued natives to mine it for him. But when he reached Hispaniola in 1509 he found a devastated island, the good lands gone—and the gold, too, such as there had been. So in 1511, instead of returning home empty-handed, he joined the expedition sent to Cuba by Diego Columbus, son of the Admiral, and led by a tough veteran named Diego Velásquez. Its purpose: to colonize this larger island to the west, overrun by savage Caribs from the north coast of South America. They were fierce cannibals and ate a good number of Spaniards before they were finally defeated. The other natives, Tainos and Ciboneys, were peaceful farmers who raised cassava, maize, and cotton; these were ruled by elected chiefs they called caciques. After we subdued an uprising and burned alive their rebellious cacique named Hautey, the island and its people belonged to Spain.

Velásquez established a settlement called San Cristóbal de la Havana, the original Havana, on the south coast. My father obtained a large grant of land near the harbor, where a fortress town began to grow. First my father had mined a stream bank on his land but got so little gold that he had his Ciboneys plant cotton for him; rare in Europe, it brought good money there. Using native labor he also built a house with an arcaded patio like that of his childhood home in Spain, then sent for my mother and me.

We left the safety of her parents' home at Medellín in southwestern Spain and from Cádiz bravely crossed the Atlantic in a tossing caravel, bringing with us a number of things of little practical use in Spain's newest colony. Among these were ten books, six of them weighty volumes given to my mother's family by a scholarly Jewish neighbor who had to flee to France in 1492 to escape the Inquisition. But my two favorites were *Amadís of Gaul,* a prose romance telling of fantastic adventures in strange lands, and *The Celestina,* whose young hero Calixto fell in love on sight with Melibea. Chaste and beautiful, she did not at first succumb to his ardor and died soon after the long-delayed consummation of their passion. Calixto joined her in the tomb, sprinkled by my young tears. The books were for me, my mother said, with the Azores just behind us. "For who knows if there's even so much as a Bible in this place called Cuba?"

My pretty mother, Elvira Flores de Mondragon, had hair of Spanish gold, sad brown eyes, and knew that she had married somewhat beneath her parents' expectations. My father was merely the second son of a Castilian who came south to Estremadura with a flock of sheep and enough money to buy a vineyard which the older brother would inherit. Whereas my mother's father had been a magistrate in Medellín since the days of King Fernando and Queen Isabel, was descended on his mother's side from the famed poet Manrique and was looked up to as a man of gentility and learning. It was my mother's hope that I might one day study at the University of Salamanca and follow in his footsteps.

When we reached Cuba and she saw my father's little house backed by a wide field of cotton and the round straw-thatched *bohias* of his Ciboney Indians, tears of nostalgia filled her eyes and she said in a tremulous voice, "An arcade! At the end of the world!" But I think she sensed even then that our landhold, for all its size, would provide a living for us, no more. Soon after we came, my father sank a second mine shaft in the hills to the south of our plantation. "Let us pray that your father finds a rich vein of ore so that you can go to Salamanca some day, Arturo," she would say, hugging me to her as

"To serenade her," I improvised. "Just a serenade, that's all."

As Aguilar spoke to Malinche, Father Diaz reached us and struck away my hand that held hers. "Lustful boy!" He placed himself between the two of us. His fanatical eyes blazed up at me, two black embers. "The holy drops that mark her transformation from savage to Christian are not yet dry before you seek carnal congress!" He hurried her away from me, grasping her upper arm as though she were a felon.

"She said she will await your visit tonight," Aguilar told me in a low voice. I knew he did not like Father Diaz; few did. Ugly and sallow and with a vulture's breath, Diaz had an Inquisitor's soul, alert for the devil in the flesh of men better favored. Aguilar added, "Remember, Arturo, I expect of you a serenade, no more."

I went happily away, my plans now concrete. I would find the dwarf and borrow his guitar again, and then I would wait until the Indian women had supped and retired to their huts, near those of the priests. As I hurried to Cortés' big canopy to find the dwarf, my eyes searched the sky in hope of a lovers' moon and found it floating large and low above the embers of the brief tropical sunset. With anticipation tickling me, I envisioned the charming scene that would soon take place. After I had serenaded her in true Spanish style, she would come out of her hut and we would stroll in the moonlight beside the sound of the eternal waves. And then—who knew?

To my dismay, the dwarf was not to be found. Under the canopy were only Pepe, the other page, and Cortés' valet and his lean secretary, playing cards by the flame of a candle. They said Orteguilla had gone out to the flagship with Cortés a short time earlier. Then I saw the guitar leaning against a tent pole and told them I had come to borrow it. The secretary and the valet didn't care whether I took it or not, but Pepe was dubious. I persuaded him, promising to return it that same night, and stood there strumming and humming until the secretary invited me to practice elsewhere.

By now darkness had fallen, the round lovers' moon was beaming down among the dunes and cooking fires were alight, wafting toward me smells of supper, but it was not food I was hungry for. I decided to sing her a *mañanita,* even though it wasn't morning. She wouldn't know the difference, and I sang it particularly well. My jupon and breastplate seemed unsuitable to the night's dalliance, and I went to my hut and from my sea chest got out my russet hose and doublet and one of the white shirts my mother had made for me. Then I slung the guitar across my back by its strap and trotted eagerly to the row of huts where the Indian women lived, reflecting that one good thing that could be said for Torquemada was that Spanish priests, who had been most licentious before the reign of our Catholic Monarchs, openly keeping concubines and mistresses and reveling in the sins of the flesh, were now very averse to carnal pleasures. So they could be trusted to live in close proximity to the Indian women and to act as watchdogs. When I reached the women's huts, I stood in the moonlight midway down the row, the perfect troubadour, and began my serenade.

But she did not appear, and it had dawned on me that the huts were empty when from the doorway directly ahead of me peeped a short fat Indian woman with crossed eyes. She beamed at me.

"Malinche?" I asked.

Her smile faded and she pointed a stubby finger seaward. I turned and looked that way but could see only the dark shapes of our ships, far out on the moonlit water.

Filled with foreboding, I hurried off to find Aguilar, telling myself that Malinche might have left a message for me. I found him with the other priests sitting in a circle around a small fire. He was eating a broiled fish. "Where is Malinche?" I demanded.

He looked up at the guitar, my ruff, my anxious eyes. His were gentle. "Have you had any food? An Indian kindly brought us these fine fish to grill. They are very delicious, despite their odd appearance." The fish he was eating had large spines along the backbone, very white flesh. "Have one, and then we can talk."

"No fish! Where is Malinche?"

My harsh demand had drawn the attention of the other churchmen, who looked at me reprovingly except for Juan Diaz, who wore a mean, small grin. Aguilar sighed, stood up, brushed a few bits of fish from his cassock and led me away from the other diners. "Try not to be too disappointed, Arturo." His voice was kindly, as if he spoke to a child who had demanded a missing toy.

"Where is she?"

"You must try to remember that man proposes, but God disposes."

"Where is she?"

"On the flagship."

"Why?"

He sighed. "Cortés is giving the Indian women to his various captains. Except for the fat one with the crossed eyes who is to be our servant."

In the rush of agony that filled me I found his calmness infuriating. "God disposes? Cortés disposes! You men of God baptized these women! But now you let him turn them into prostitutes."

My anger did not dismay him or bring me the reprimand I deserved. "No, they are to be *barraganas.*"

"Concubines!"

"A harsh word. Their status is somewhere between mistress and morganatic wife. This is preferable, I feel, to the licentious promiscuity of mere camp-followers."

"And Cortés, of course, got Malinche!"

Aguilar patted my shoulder soothingly. "If you loved her as much as you think, then you would find it in your heart to rejoice if she should find herself under the protection of our general."

"Aguilar, you know precisely nothing of love!" My voice broke on the last word and I turned and ran away across the sands, my borrowed guitar thumping against my back with a hollow sound, the voice of my loss.

I found myself at the foot of the high dune on which our white cross gleamed in the moonlight. I fell to my knees. I prayed that divine intervention would keep Cortés from keeping the woman I loved. "For now she's a baptized Christian, Lord. Cortés has a wife in Cuba. Malinche will only be his mistress. But if you let me have her, I will marry her! I swear it! Indian though she is, I will make her an honest woman!" Far above, the white cross shone serene, and above it the evening star hung brilliant in the sky. As I crossed myself came the fleeting thought of my mother's shocked face if I were to bring home an Indian bride, however beautiful, but I got up from my knees feeling a little better.

A hoarse voice spoke behind me. "He wants his guitar back."

I whirled. The young page Pepe stood there panting. Had he heard my prayer? Apparently not, for he pouted, "I knew I shouldn't have let you take it, and now a mariner just rowed in from the flagship to get it, because Cortés is holding a fiesta there for his captains and the Indian women. He wants Orteguilla to sing and play for them."

Inspiration struck me. "I'll return it myself and I'll take any blame for borrowing it without permission."

"That's only fair," he agreed with some relief.

As I walked to the shore where the mariner waited in a ship's boat, I turned to glance back at the cross. It seemed to me that this chance to go to where Malinche was, coming just after my prayer, was most uncanny. But what, precisely, could I do or say that would change the general's mind?

The mariner at the oars was a cheerful young fellow with a tasseled knit cap. He said, "Well, I guess the captains are all happy tonight, the lucky goats."

"And Cortés, too, having kept for himself the prettiest Indian of all."

"Doña Marina? The general hasn't taken any woman for himself. He gave Doña Marina to Puertocarrero."

Puertocarrero! Of course! The gold buttons from his cloak to buy a horse, and now another mount, my Malinche! In agony I imagined Puertocarrero embracing her. I clutched at the hope of error. "Are you sure?"

"I was right there on deck when Puertocarrero asked for her."

"But didn't she have anything to say about it?" I cried.

"She wasn't there. It was right after that I rowed ashore to bring the priests Cortés' written order for the Indian women. I waited while the priests rounded them up, two boats full, and none for me." Oarlocks creaked while I imagined Malinche's similar journey to the flagship. "How about a tune on that guitar to make the rowing lighter?" he asked.

And so it was to a mariner bending his back at the oars that I sang my serenade intended for Malinche, not without that twinge at life's bitter irony common to even lesser poets. While I sang, my mind was feverishly busy. What could I say to Cortés that might change Malinche's destiny? As I built up in my head a fervent denunciation of him for having baptized the Indian women only to make them concubines against their inclination, I wondered if I could summon up the courage to deliver it. Although Cortés made a point of treating his foot soldiers in a man-to-man fashion, he did not welcome criticism of his decisions. He had put in irons one Velásquez man too loud of mouth. And supposing I did let my anger out, even made Cortés aware that his disposal of the Indian women had been high-handed, was it likely that he would snatch Malinche away from Puertocarrero? And even if he did, would he then give her to a mere foot soldier with his blessing? I sat gritting my teeth so hard my jaws ached. I had set myself an impossible task. But I had to try.

When we reached the flagship I climbed the rope ladder, guitar strapped to my back. Two very different scenes drew my eyes. At the taffrail, several mariners were leaning out to scan the black water by the light of the ship's lantern one held at arm's end, giving the impression that someone had fallen overboard. In contrast, from the gathering on the foredeck came the robust voices of the captains singing with wine-induced sentimentality about the river Duero. Most were seated or recumbent, heads to the low rails, feet pointing inward, their Indian women beside them. I mounted a hatch for a better view, saw neither Malinche nor Puertocarrero. A lantern shed its dim yellow light on the wine cask at which Captain Olid was filling his cup, a grin on his black-bearded face. He swaggered back to his Indian *barragana* to lie beside her and smother her face with his beard, clutching her breast. I turned my eyes away as he roughly pulled up her skirt and I saw her pale brown naked leg helpless under the hand that convulsively kneaded the captive thigh.

Now, in the center of the cosy group, Orteguilla was standing on his head, kicking his legs in the air and singing a bawdy song about the joys of fornication—written, I happened to know, half a century earlier by a padre who kept several concubines, one a nun of the same order. Someone belched loudly. Someone laughed. Where was Malinche?

Cortés burst out of his cabin below the foredeck; his frowning face offered a sudden contrast to the carnal scene just above. He could not have failed to see me standing there on the hatch with my guitar, but for all the attention he gave me I might have been one of the white gulls wheeling overhead. "Any luck, Pedro?" he called, striding toward midship.

To Pedro Alvarado I was also invisible. He passed me with a lantern, shaking his blond head. "I searched the hold, the entire vessel, every nook, every coil of rope. She's not aboard, and that's for certain." His high-pitched voice exaggerated his alarm.

Mine was greater. She? Who? Malinche?

I ran to Cortés, stood face-to-face with him. "Who is he talking about?"

A glance at the guitar evidently reminded him why I was there. "Doña Marina has disappeared. It begins to look as if she may have jumped overboard." His voice rose; he turned to wave a fist in the direction of his own cabin. "And may God rot the balls of that hot-prick blunderer!"

Two of the mariners I had seen scanning the water approached. "No sign of her," one said. "Not a splash. Not a bubble."

Cortés wheeled abruptly and headed toward his cabin. I followed,

93

such a welter of emotions churning in me that my head seemed to be revolving on my shoulders. Cortés ducked his head to enter; I stood in the doorway. The small, low-ceilinged room was dimly lighted, but I saw Puertocarrero getting up from the floor. He groaned, holding his head, and sat down heavily on the edge of the bunk, elbows on knees, head between his hands. Blood still trickled out of his tousled hair in a narrow rill down his forehead and one cheek. From his open pantaloons dangled the organ Cortés had cursed, limp as a sea slug. Becoming aware of what he was exhibiting, he tucked it away and closed the gap, moaning to distract our attention. Looking up, he saw Cortés, fists on hips, regarding him with plain disgust. "That vixen!" Puertocarrero pointed to the floor.

There, serene face upward, lay a pretty painted statue of the Holy Virgin. Of wood, and about three handbreadths high, it had stood atop the small altar in the corner. "The Virgin?" Cortés demanded.

"That's what your Doña Marina tried to brain me with! She backed into the corner, seized that holy statue, and tried her best to kill me!"

"And what did you do to her?" Cortés demanded.

Puertocarrero looked up, saw the glare on Cortés' face, and lowered his head to his hands again, wiping a drop of blood from the end of his nose with the back of one of them. "Nothing! I did nothing that a Spanish countess would take exception to! Doña Marina is crazy, that's all. Don't blame me for that."

"I know what you did! You dragged her in here while I was aft with the pilot. You attacked her like a satyr!"

"*I* attacked *her?* You see me here bleeding to death and say *I* attacked *her?* You have it backward. *She* attacked *me!*"

"Good!" I shouted, coming at him. "You *pendejo,* backing her into a corner with your penis waving, what would any decent woman do?" I whirled on Cortés. "He treated her like a whore, but she was no whore, and now you know it! Do you think God wanted a baptized Christian Indian woman pronged like a strumpet? Do you condone that orgy on the foredeck?"

His face clenched, eyes blazing at me. I saw my doom: weeks in irons and maybe a flogging. But sudden caution shadowed his anger. I knew he had remembered the Royal Council of the Indies and its solemn mandate that Indian women were not to be raped by Spanish soldiers. He knew how swiftly I could spread word of Doña Marina's ill treatment; the Velásquez adherents would make the most of it.

In a strained voice he said, "I understand your outrage. I feel it myself."

"Cortés!" Alvarado's cry made us both turn toward the open door. "Come here, for God's sake."

On deck we found him pointing out over the moon-dappled water. "Look!"

My heart dropped into an abyss as dark as that sea. The triangular fin of a shark passed very near the side of the flagship, moving silent, swift, and deadly across the very patch of ocean into which Malinche might have plunged. "Over and done," Alvarado said. "The woman jumped, the woman drowned, or if she didn't that big *tiburón* or friends of his most likely got her."

Cortés' fist pounded the rail. "No!" He turned to Alvarado, his eyes wild and willful. "Search the ship again! She's clever. She could have outwitted you."

I saw that a very young mariner, most likely a cabin boy, had approached. "*Con permiso,* Cortés, sir?"

Cortés turned and glared down at him; the boy stared up. He swallowed. He tried to speak but his frail voice broke.

"Say it!" Cortés commanded.

"She's not on the ship, Cortés, sir. Doña Marina came out of your cabin, Cortés, sir, with her skirt tore and flying out either side and her bodice all tore open too so you could see her *pechos* all bare and she ran to the rail and went over and I heard the splash."

I heard it too, inside my head. Louder than Cortés' voice saying with terrible control "Why, then, did you not tell me this at the time? Right away?"

Voiceless, the boy stared up. Cortés' arm moved woodenly. His big hand came to rest on the boy's shoulder. He squeezed it as if to press the words out of him. "Why didn't you tell me this when she jumped?"

The boy swallowed. In a voice no more than a whisper he said, "It was *your* cabin she came out of, Cortés, sir."

Cortés released him and the boy backed away, then turned and ran. Cortés looked at me with stricken eyes. "How could he understand that I want no woman while my foot soldiers and mariners have none? That I choose to share their privation?"

"Privation?" asked a merry voice. Captain Francisco Olid had descended from the foredeck, winecup in one hand, an arm around his Indian concubine. Even in my trance of shock and misery I became aware that the incipient orgy on the foredeck had been broken up by the shouting and running about. Most of them were on their feet, the captains looking down at Cortés.

95

"I want these Indian women treated with decency!" he called up to them, and I saw Olid's arm leave his concubine's waist. "Or you can expect my very great displeasure."

Oh, very late for the warning, I thought bitterly. Too late! "You've locked the door after the loss," I muttered.

Orteguilla had joined us. "Loss?" he asked pertly. "All seems gains here tonight, if not for a somewhat short fellow like myself."

"Doña Marina jumped overboard," I blurted.

Cortés' look silenced further comment. He said, "Captain Puertocarrero was not sufficiently aware of her great modesty. And so I am without an interpreter." He reached out for the guitar; I unstrapped it; he handed it to Orteguilla. Catching his master's mood, Orteguilla at once strummed several brooding chords and began to sing a pavane. Tears filled my eyes as Cortés turned to me and said in a low voice, "Good night, Arturo. I trust your loyalty and discretion." He speared me with a searching glance. I turned abruptly toward the rail to hide my tears.

The mariner who had brought me pulled away from the flagship and began at once asking questions, but I could not have answered even had I wished for the lump of sorrow in my throat. When I turned and looked back at the ship I saw the chastened revelers clustered middeck like mourners at a grave below the dark crucifixes of the masts, their sails furled. Cortés stood alone by the rail staring toward the distant shore. A seagull swept low above him with a harsh cry.

12

As I crossed the wide sweep of water toward the beach where a scatter of campfires glowed no bigger than fireflies, a cruel grief tortured me. I might have passed Malinche after she leaped from the flagship as I was rowed toward it in this same boat. And she, in that black water and in need of rescue, would not have seen it as a source of help, containing as it did two Spaniards. Then I remembered that shark and agony tore at my guts, for I knew she might not have lived long enough ever to have seen the ship's boat in which I had sat trying to think how to get her away from Puertocarrero.

The shark did not get her, I told myself. That was only Alvarado's idea, but sharks do not attack swimmers as a rule, not unless they are bleeding. I smiled grimly to myself: it was not she who had bled, but Puertocarrero.

While these thoughts tormented or comforted me, I kept scanning the water hopefully, yet also I remembered the drowned woman washed in from a shipwreck off Cuba when I was a child. She had floated face-down, her long hair moving gently in the clear green water. With a thrill of horror I thought I saw a woman floating like that, but it was only a log with a branch like a human arm and seaweed clinging to it and floating like that woman's hair.

"The current's strong tonight," the mariner said, and I saw that the campfires were no longer directly ahead but to the left of the boat's prow. "It's a little arm of the big ocean current that sweeps in south of Cuba from the Atlantic, then around its western tip and out eastward again to the north of the West Indies. There's a couple of oars stashed beside you and I'll thank you to give me a hand, or we'll reach the beach so far north of the camp you'll spend half the night walking back to it."

Aware that he had just given me another reason to believe that I had lost Malinche forever, I did as he asked. We were able to correct our course somewhat after we reached shallower water where the current had little pull, but when I heard the crash of breakers and saw their white manes, the huts and campfires were no longer visible because of the distance and the intervening dunes. "You'll stretch your legs a bit," the mariner said, as a wave lifted the boat and sped it toward the beach.

Wet to the knees on that dark, deserted shore I watched him row away and then started toward camp, walking on the hard-packed wet sand for better speed. Looking landward, I saw above the mangroves that edged the beach the tops of palms and the moonlit *teocalli* atop an Indian temple, and I knew it marked the town of the natives who had come to the beach to bring us food, help us build our huts, and sell us their handiwork. I stopped in my tracks. If Malinche had managed to swim ashore, would this town not seem to her a place of refuge? Would it not be natural for her to throw herself on the mercy of people of her own race rather than again trust Spaniards? I stood pondering this notion to the forlorn and hollow crash of a breaker, the long sigh of spilled waters withdrawing into the sea. The sound reminded me that it had taken two pairs of arms to land the rowboat even at this distance from camp. A swimmer would be taken by the current even farther to the north.

I turned and headed northward, proving that hope can put out a frail blossom even on sand. To keep it from withering I called her name from time to time: her own name, not the one Cortés had given her. Only the waves answered me.

But after I had gone more than half a league, my heart gave a great bound and hope put out a hundred blossoms more. Far ahead on the shining sand at the water's edge a human figure stood. A woman, scantily clad in a few tatters of clothing that did not hide the curve of a thigh, bare arms, a naked breast. She had not yet seen me and bent above the mound of seaweed beside her to disentangle a long strand. My urge was to run toward her, shouting her name, but I forced myself to come nearer so that she could see who I was. As I closed the distance between us, she draped the strand of kelp, thick with flat gleaming leaves, around her neck, arranging it to hide her breasts. I knew then that the rags she wore were rags of seaweed to replace the clothing torn by Puertocarrero as he tried to rape her, and now abandoned in the sea as she swam toward this shore.

"Malinche!" I cried, and ran toward her, my arms stretching wide of their own accord to enfold her. Now I was close enough to see the gleam of the little snake-man pendant and to see the waterdrops still shining on her bare skin. "It's me! Arturo!"

No answering smile came to her lips. A long strand of her wet black hair hung down over the left side of her face. One dark cold eye looked at me. I saw then that she was spent. Her whole body was clenched on itself, knees clamped and shoulders hunched. As I neared, she crossed her fists over her breast and took a step back. She was not looking at me, but at something beyond me. I turned my head and saw the palms of the Indian village, the tip of its upper temple.

I spoke gently. "I only want to help you, Malinche." As her eyes met mine again she raised her arm to brush aside the strand of hair that hid the other, and the curves of that arm and the grace of the gesture belonged to a statue I once saw, except that this arm was not cold marble but warm flesh. With a sudden alertness a lustful imp between my legs announced that it, too, wished to help her in the only way it knew. The urge to embrace her came over me so strongly that I could almost feel her against me, cold seaweed, warm smooth skin, breasts pressed against my russet doublet under which my heart galloped toward hers. "I know what happened on the ship. I assure you that you won't have to go back to Puertocarrero, ever." As I spoke, doubt struck me, but then I told myself Cortés would surely not give her to him again.

Her eyes had left me to gaze again at the Indian temple. I turned my head. The uppermost tip of the white-painted *teocalli* pointed heavenward, quite as though blood had never spilled below it. "Aztecs," she said, looking at me once more.

I dared a step closer. "You don't belong with them. You're a Christian now. You belong with us."

Her voice was low but harsh. "Puertocarrero Christian."

"Cortés is very angry with him." I made a motion of cutting my throat with my forefinger. "Cortés did not know he would do what he did to you. Cortés was very sad when he thought you were drowned. And I—oh, Malinche, my whole world came to an end!"

She appeared to consider what I had said, head tilted to one side. Between the amber leaves tempting glimpses of firm flesh allured me. Battling down the urge to touch her, clasp her, roll with her on soft white sand, both of us joyous and aflame with the desire only I felt, I suddenly thought of the more than five hundred Spanish soldiers encamped to the south. My God, I thought, if any of them were here and saw her like this, they'd probably kill me to get at her! Thus I transferred my own desire to other, evil fellows lacking my own restraint and decency.

The first thing to do was to get some clothes on her. Yes, that is first and foremost, I told myself. She can't run around half-clad in some seaweed. I remembered the striped shawl I had bought for my mother from the Indians here. "I have a rebozo," I said. "At my hut. You can have it." I pantomimed wrapping myself in a large shawl.

She nodded, looking down at her improvised clothing. She raised her head and looked once more at the Indian temple. She looked into my eyes. "I go with you."

My hut had been built at the north side of camp, very near the mangroves. We made our way to it through them to avoid being seen, and I remembered how I had pursued her the day we met, which now seemed very long ago. When I went in to get the shawl, she remained outside; I found it and brought it out to her, bowing toward the open doorway to indicate that she might dress herself within. I stood with my back to the hut and imagined seaweed draperies falling to the sandy floor, leaving her naked as Aphrodite, that goddess who had also risen from the waves. To blot out this image and to subdue desire I congratulated myself on having the strength of will to dominate my carnal nature. Feeling somewhat noble and very pure, I saw a pure and luminous symbol against the dark starred sky: our great white cross on its high dune, bright in the moonlight. It reminded me of the gratitude I should feel to the good Lord who had brought her safely to shore. I crossed myself and sank to my knees.

With this act, a clear light seemed to shine in my brain as if reflected from that white cross. I saw the way out of her plight, a way that would not leave her dependent on the mood of Cortés when he learned she was alive!

A sound behind me made me turn. She stood just outside the hut, the striped mantle tied at one shoulder and wrapped around her body, held in place by a seaweed belt. She looked less like a Christian newly baptized than like a heathen goddess. I took off my rosary, stood up, and offered it to her. "It was blessed by the archbishop," I said. "Put it on." Obediently she hung it around her neck. The silver cross gleamed below her gold snake-man. I took her hand and led her to the dune where our cross stood. I pointed upward. "Wait up there for me." She nodded, and I ran to the huts where the priests slept and called, "Father Olmedo!"

In a moment his long pale face peered out of a doorway. "Yes, my son?" He offered no censure for waking him, just blinked at me with kindly bemused patience.

"Is the dune where the cross stands holy ground?" I asked.

"Holy? Why, yes, certainly."

"Like a church or cathedral?"

"Since we have no other, yes. But why did you wake me at such a late hour to ask me this question?"

"Because a Christian is waiting there to claim the right of sanctuary!"

As we hurried to Malinche I told him everything. She had trusted me; she knelt at the foot of the cross, shoulders wearily slumped, head drooping. When I called to her she stood up, staring down at us. Father Olmedo held out his hand to her, beckoned her toward him, his tonsure like a small moon. She looked at me; I nodded. She descended the dune and trustingly put her hand in the padre's. "Father Aguilar can now explain to her that she is safe, and that the Church will protect the virtue she had suffered so much to preserve."

As they went toward Aguilar's hut she turned her head and looked back at me. *"Gracias."* Her look was soft, and she even managed a little smile.

I went to my hut radiant with triumph and with joy. Triumph over my lower being, the part Satan rules, and triumph over Cortés as well, for now he could not decide the fate of my beloved. Joy came from that one word of thanks, that sweet smile she had sent me over her shoulder. I fell asleep to dream of her.

Alas, I did not wake until the sun was high. No morning trumpet aroused me, nor did El Galán. I dressed myself and hurried to the priests' huts. Too late. Malinche was gone.

Father Olmedo looked pleased as he told me that he had gone out to the flagship at dawn in the canoe of an obliging Indian fisherman, had told Cortés that Malinche was under the protection of the Church; he had censured him on two scores: for having been so hasty in baptizing the Indian women and for not having warned Puertocarrero in advance that his lechery must be controlled in his dealings with Malinche. "Only minutes after the Indian women joined us at Tabasco, Captain Puertocarrero was making lewd advances, to which I put a stop. But Cortés, as I can well understand, is in a difficult position. Puertocarrero must not lose face with the men he must continue to captain. We have reached an agreement, which Doña Marina has accepted: although it will be generally believed that she is under Puertocarrero's protection, she will actually be under the personal protection of Cortés." He nodded at me, pleased.

"Of Cortés!"

He hastily added, "Oh, no carnal knowledge is to be involved in this arrangement. No, no. She is to him his valued interpreter, nothing more."

"And where is she now?"

"On the flagship. She left only minutes before you arrived. Cortés sent for her. He wishes to offer her his personal apology for what she suffered. Captain Puertocarrero will also offer his. Father Jeronimo Aguilar is with her, I should add."

My fury with myself for oversleeping was so intense that I groaned aloud.

"Are you ill, my son?" the good padre asked.

"What makes you think he'll keep his hands off her?" I demanded.

"Cortés?" He looked shocked.

"Puertocarrero! He's a satyr! A lecherous goat!"

"He's also a caballero with noble antecedents. He will keep his word. I must add, my son, that such violent language concerning one of this expedition's captains does not become the young man whose Christian concern for this poor young Indian woman has borne such good fruit."

I took the censure and the praise and went in search of food to break my fast. I had lost the chance to ask her to accept me as her protector due to a delicious dream in which her brief visit to my hut the night before had been of longer duration and had ended less virtuously. But I soon enough came to realize that Cortés would never have agreed to let me have her, even if she herself wished it. With hundreds of womanless foot soldiers, could he endow one of them with a *barragana?*

But that might change in time. There might, before too long, be enough Christianized female Indians here so that every single soldier and mariner could have one. And in the meantime her well-established chastity would keep her safe for me. I still had hopes of getting her, and at barely eighteen hope is nearly as good as gold itself, or the real embraces of a woman clasped only in dreams.

One thing troubled me. Might she be too chaste? She had violently rejected a caballero with a horse and noble lineage, and I had neither. But there is a caballero more powerful than any other, and his name is Don Oro. The gold I had come here to get became commingled in my mind with the woman I wanted as much. Gold would make of me a future hero called Don Arturo by everyone in Havana. And it would make me equally worthwhile in Malinche's eyes. For, as my father once said, success is a seducer few women argue with, just as failure is a lapse they find hard to forgive. And gold is a proof of success as universal as it is rare.

So far I had only a thin gold medallion of modest value and had lost a helmet worth much more. I went bareheaded under the blazing sun that darkened my skin and paled my hair but could not wither the dreams of gold, glory, and Malinche rooted inside my skull. I would follow our banner; I had faith; I would conquer. Don Oro would one day be my humble servant and Malinche would share my blissful bed.

PART III

FIRE ON WATER

May 7, 1519–August 12, 1519

13

I got back my helmet after all. It was presented to Cortés, filled with gold dust. That, of course, I did not get.

Only a week after he had left us, Governor Birdcall returned with another of Moctezuma's governors from a nearby province. This Cualpopoca looked amazingly like Cortés, although darker and lacking a beard. Among the retinue of lesser Indians were several priests with long, tangled hair and black robes who chanted and swung incense burners to waft smoke over Cortés where he sat in his armchair below his canopy. After the Indians had knelt before him to touch their hands to the ground and bring them to their foreheads, a file of porters with baskets and bundles on their backs came forward to lay their burdens at his feet. It took six men to carry one flat package tied to a litter.

The extraordinary richness of Moctezuma's gifts astounded us all. Spread out on straw mats in the sunlight, a feast for avarice, those treasures drew our awed gasps, our cries of admiration. There was a golden disk as big as a cartwheel, engraved with intricate symbols in a circular pattern. A silver disk, somewhat smaller, lay by it like the moon beside the sun. There were many golden animals, dozens of necklaces and pendants, a large gold bow with a sheaf of golden arrows, crowns of gold and silver with plumes of green feathers and some golden fans. As though for variety there were at least a hundred mantles gorgeously woven of more colors than any rainbow and two curious feather capes that gleamed as richly as gems. But this was a farewell present. Moctezuma would not grant us an audience.

Cortés forced a smile to hide disappointment. "Then perhaps we will visit Moctezuma without an invitation."

Malinche frowned and made a vehement comment. Aguilar turned to Cortés: "She refuses to translate this boast. She says your small army could never enter his city by force. To pretend so is foolish."

Cortés barely concealed his displeasure. "My interpreter has never heard of Caesar: divide and conquer. We may manage to find some Indian allies." He added hastily, "Don't have her translate that, of course. Have her thank Moctezuma for his gifts and say that I return the same warm and friendly feelings that prompted him to send them." This done, he added, "And I now repeat my request for an invitation to visit Moctezuma."

With great reluctance, Governor Birdcall agreed to convey this message to his ruler.

Until an answer came, there was nothing for us to do but wait there on the beach, attacked by mosquitoes, dazed by ferocious heat, none of us knowing if Governor Birdcall would actually keep his grudging promise or how Moctezuma would react to Cortés' persistence if he did. The Indians of the area came to the beach in fewer and fewer numbers and ceased to bring us food, so we were reduced to grubbing for mussels and crabs to augment slim rations of salt pork. Our cassava bread, though it lasts for months, was now full of weevils. Two dozen men fell sick of a fever that turned them yellow, and six died. A wind rose and blew down three of the wooden crosses that marked their graves. And mutiny was beginning to stir with the blowing sand that stung our faces. The Velásquez men wanted to leave at once for Cuba. The rest of us wanted to wait and see what Moctezuma's answer would be.

Cortés tried to placate the grumblers by sending a ship north under command of a friend of Velásquez named Captain Montejo, with orders to explore the coast to the north for a pleasanter site; he returned in less than a week to report that there was a good harbor fifteen leagues away, near a large Indian town. The day we learned this, Governor Birdcall returned with Moctezuma's final refusal to see us.

The diplomatic wording did not conceal a threat: "Moctezuma regrets that he cannot enjoy a personal interview. The distance to my capital is great and beset with many dangers. You must return now to your own land with the gifts that prove my friendly disposition toward you, thus far."

The next day not a single Indian came to our camp.

When Cortés assembled the army below the dune where the cannons were and told us he wanted to go north to the harbor Montejo found, his words fell flat. After a brief silence, a voice shouted "Back to Cuba!'' In a moment it was a thunderous chant as a hundred voices joined the first. ''Back to Cuba! Back to Cuba!''

Young Captain Sandoval started a counter cry: ''On to Mexico! To Mexico!''

Others cried: ''North to Montejo's bay!''

Cortés signaled the priests to ring the bell for vesper service, and its persistent sound finally silenced the cacophony. We knelt below the cross but this respite meant nothing. On expeditions such as ours, cohesion was vital. Grijalva's men had forced him to take them home. Columbus had to lie to prevent a mutiny. Cortés, with his divided army, was in trouble.

Nor were the Velásquez men the only ones who took seriously Moctezuma's request that we leave: soldiers loyal to Cortés were beginning to agree with them. We now had more gold than all previous expeditions together. Why not thank God and go, while we were still alive to do so? ''There's no point to squatting here with empty bellies and sand in our crotches,'' Juan Morla said one night as Alvarado's company sat around a campfire waiting for a cauldron of mussels to boil. ''Cortés ought to divide the gold up fair and square and sail for home. God knows my woman will be glad to see my face, and for once I'll be glad to see hers.'' There was laughter and grumbling assent.

I said, misquoting the Bible: ''Cowards flee where no man pursueth.''

''*You* make brave bones here, Pollito. I'll be a rich coward in Cuba.''

During the next two days the heat got even worse and five more men died, yet Cortés clung to his desire to maintain a beachhead on this new continent. His captains went among us trying to convince the dubious that our best and only move was northward to Montejo's bay. Above the noise of arguments the stinging wind rose again, the sand blew into our eyes, and it seemed that the very air and beach were hostile to our presence.

Nor was I comforted by even a glimpse of Malinche. Cortés had given her a bed on the flagship, fearing that she might succumb to the fever that raged on shore and leave him without any means of communicating with the Indians of the town near Montejo's bay, assuming he could ever manage to get his army to go there. An angry group of Velásquez's men became so loud in their demands to be sent home that Cortés put them in irons until they cooled down. I said to

El Galán: "Why not let them go back to Cuba, and any others afraid to stay? That would leave Cortés with a loyal army, even if a smaller one."

El Galán shook his head. "It would leave him without stature as a commander. He cannot permit dissenters to have their way. He has to hold his army together, although I confess I don't see just how. At the moment, some diversion is needed badly."

A diversion was provided that same day when Cortés had his loyal captains talk with their men, reminding us that we had agreed in the contract with Velásquez to found a colony. If we returned to Cuba without doing this, we could expect the governor's severe censure, no matter how much gold we brought. Pedro Alvarado talked to us in a friendly, persuasive way, the flames of a campfire lighting his frank, open face and his short red-gold hair and beard. "The clever thing to do is to found a colony—on paper. Elect a regular town council and let them choose the town's captain and chief justice. That way a colony will legally exist, even if we don't actually get around to building a city hall." He winked and grinned and we all laughed, for the idea of getting around the letter of the law like this would please any Spaniard.

"Villa Rica de la Vera Cruz!" With a triumphant smile, Cortés announced next day the name he had chosen for our paper colony. All of us liked the sound of it, and soon shortened it to Vera Cruz. Until El Galán pointed it out to me, I did not realize that this Rich Town of the True Cross was a child born of our expedition, autonomous. Founded in the name of Carlos of Spain, it could serve to free Cortés from Velásquez's authority, for Cortés, of course, was chosen by the council as captain and chief justice, whereas the name of Velásquez figured precisely nowhere. Cortés appointed two mayors: Puertocarrero and Montejo—whose loyalty Cortés won when he trusted him with that ship in which he could easily have sailed to Cuba instead of discovering the bay to which Cortés hoped to lead us.

But not all the Velásquez men were as pliable as Montejo. Another diversion was needed, so Cortés named fifty of those dissenters as a special task force and sent them off on a reconnaissance mission along with Alvarado's company. We were to explore to the north five leagues to see if we met resistance or friendly tribes. Although it made me nervous to probe unknown terrain with so many discontented soldiers marching with me, I was glad to leave the sand behind for a while. A march of a few leagues took us onto a pleasant savannah planted with fields of maize and of maguey cactus, hostile-looking plants, each one a silent green explosion of thick, spearlike leaves. We soon came to a deserted village with a large warehouse full of clay pots of honey. After poking his finger in one to see what it contained, Alvarado licked it and reminded us that Cortés had forbidden any looting, but he left that pot open and a good many fingers were licked before we marched to the village temple. Alvarado decided to climb the pyramid for the view it would offer, and I was among the first of the soldiers to reach the *teocalli* atop where the idols were.

In its doorway I stopped, staring. On a blood-stained stone block was a human torso slashed open in a gaping hole below the rib cage, from which had flowed so much blood that it filled the hollow of the altar and ran down its side. The arms and legs were cut off. The heart, torn from the body, lay on a stone dish at the feet of an idol with a grinning skull face of dull gold. Lying all about were large pieces of paper steeped in dried blood, for what purpose I could not guess. The stone walls were layered with blood, old and black, dried and brown, fresh and red. The stagnant air smelled of butchery; nausea crept up my throat. I turned and pushed my way past the soldiers behind me as vomit filled my mouth.

Nausea had spared me another shocking sight. Alvarado told Cortés about it after we marched back to the beach. His face was red with righteous wrath. "Hiding in that temple I found a young boy dressed in women's clothing, and small clay statues showing the priests in the act of sodomy, and the boy made it plain that he had been so used and others like him. Oh, they are truly servants of Satan, those priests!" I did not know what sodomy was, but he showed one of the small clay statues he had brought back with him and it very much astonished me and made the word's meaning clear, although at the time I believed in my innocence that it was an act practiced only by Indian priests.

The news of that bloodied temple spread through the camp in an hour and fanned the fires of dissension to a new heat. The Velásquez minority were against staying even another day, and on learning of the sodomy our little padre Juan Diaz turned livid and went at once to Cortés. "If the rural Indians of that little village are so cruel and depraved, what must the Aztecs be like, whom they serve and fear? The men who wish to leave this place of evil should be permitted to go, in the name of God and all the saints!" And so the diversion of the march Cortés had ordered to keep the grumblers occupied had only intensified his problem. He looked sad that day. His page, Pepe, had been the twelfth man to die of the fever, and was buried with the rest.

This news alarmed me for Malinche, because Pepe had died on the flagship. I went up to Cortés after Juan Diaz had spoken up for the dissenters and asked if she was all right. "Yes," he said. "So far." He sighed. "That was all I needed. Severed limbs, excised hearts, and sodomy. And a Catholic priest who refuses to see that such depravity and cruelty should all the more move us as Christians to rescue these poor Indians from their hideous religion and bring them to God."

I said, "If you had seen that temple, I think you would be less concerned about the salvation of their souls than about saving our lives."

"In Cuba I saw humans barbecued on spits by the Caribs, but Cuba is now a Spanish colony and so, with God's help, will this continent be!"

Cortés' luck changed abruptly the next day. Our camp was visited by five strange Indians, very different in appearance from the half-naked natives ruled by Governor Birdcall. These wore full pantaloons like the Turks' and over them loose cotton robes. In their swaying earlobes were inserted huge plugs of gold, smaller ones in slits in their upper lips. Cortés came running to seat himself in his armchair under his canopy and learn why they were here and who they were. Aguilar and Malinche translated. She was dressed in the same kind of loose tunic and underskirt as when I first saw her, but these were emerald-green.

These Indians were of the great Totonac nation, they said, and came from a city to the north called Zempoalla. Itinerant traders had told their ruler of our great victory at Tabasco and they had been sent to see if we were as powerful and remarkable as rumor suggested. At this point Cortés paused to order several captains to offer a display of horsemanship, which awed the visitors. They revealed that their great cacique had long resented the heavy yoke of Moctezuma's rule, remembering when the Totonacs had lived in freedom and happiness. "He desires very much to meet with you and will welcome you to his capital city. We will escort you there."

Cortés lost no time in addressing the soldiers who had gathered to watch. "Perhaps those cowards among you who were so anxious to scuttle home to Cuba will now be willing to go with me and meet these rich potential allies." Every eye was riveted on the great gold earrings of the five Zempoallans who stood beside him.

Further questioning of the visitors had revealed that the town near Montejo's harbor was inhabited by Totonacs and was ruled by the same cacique who wanted to meet us. Cortés decided that our fleet would sail there with the treasures Moctezuma had sent, the Indian women, and the soldiers too ill to go on foot. The rest of us would march to Zempoalla.

Two days later, without a backwards glance, we left behind the little huts that had sheltered us. Of all the Indians who had once treated us so kindly, none appeared to watch us march away.

One thing bothered me. I had assumed that the village with the bloodied temple and its catamites belonged to Governor Birdcall's Indians. But we learned, to my uneasiness, that it was in fact a Totonac town, at the southern border of their territory.

But Zempoalla was a joy to see, a city of greenery and flower gardens whose civil robed Indians stood aside respectfully to let us pass. A palace was offered to Cortés and his captains, and we soldiers were lodged in its enormous courtyard, which had many apartments opening off it. Its walls were painted with white lime polished so it shone like silver. The plaza in which this palace stood was entirely walled off from the rest of the city and contained half a dozen temples, one with a colonnade of a hundred pillars. All were overwhelmed by a huge terraced pyramid beyond which we could see distant blue mountains, one peak capped with snow. The size and grandeur of Zempoalla was somewhat awesome and I realized that beyond those mountains were other cities perhaps even grander, ruled by Moctezuma. But then food was brought to us by files of servants: maize cakes, beans stewed with meat, fruits, and I forgot everything else, for the march had been made on slim rations. As soon as we had eaten, a group of high officials arrived carrying bouquets of roses and garlands of flowers, and they hung one around Cortés' neck and offered him a big bunch of red roses, smiling cheerfully below their lip plugs, and escorted him to another palace to meet their cacique. The captains and soldiers from each company followed.

The cacique of Zempoalla came down the steps of his palace supported by a noble at either side, for he was very fat. His great pantaloons would have clothed three men and his belly bulged through the front opening of his robe, his navel hidden by a fold of flesh like a thick, winking eyelid. His earlobes with their great golden ornaments hung to his shoulders and his crown with its feather panache was slightly crooked on his head, giving him a rakish air. After a greeting as flowery as the bouquets and garlands Cortés and his captains had been given, he offered him a golden brooch and yet another bunch of roses and called him "Lord of Lords." Then, his bulk heaving with indignation, he told how Zempoallan warriors had been taken to the Aztec's capital to be sacrificed to their war god, and how Zempoalla's gentle daughters had been insulted and even raped by Aztec tax collectors whose arrogance knew no bounds. "But which one of all the people the Aztecs have conquered dares to complain to Moctezuma of such actions?"

Cortés, in his turn, dwelt glowingly on the great power of our King Carlos across the sea and on the gentleness of our Deity, and on his own desire to put an end to such unkind behavior. "You say none of the conquered nations dares complain or rise up against Moctezuma's rule. An alliance seems strongly indicated. My king has no fear of the Aztecs, nor do I." But at mention of an alliance, the fat ruler backed away with a doubtful look. That was a grave matter, something he would have to ask his gods about and discuss with other Totonac leaders. "In the meantime, you might wish to visit your great houses that ride on the waves. A runner has just told me that they are waiting in the bay near my other city, Quiahuiztlán. There you will receive a friendly welcome."

After a good night's sleep, we marched to the sea and with no opposition entered that town. It stood atop a fortresslike eminence overlooking the harbor. It too had a large square with many temples, one almost as big as the great pyramid at Zempoalla. Two dozen Totonac nobles bearing bunches of roses came to meet us in a cloud of incense. One of them stepped forward and spoke to Cortés' black stallion in a timid tone and hung a garland around its neck, leaping back in fear when the horse tossed its head but then looking about proudly.

We were surprised when the fat cacique of Zempoalla appeared on a litter, having followed us. He wanted Cortés to tell him more about our king's great power. But before Cortés had more than begun, a messenger rushed up to the cacique to whisper something that alarmed him. With the look of a frightened child he ordered the litter-bearers to carry him away. It was too late, for five Indians in rich cloaks and embroidered loincloths approached us. Their manner was haughty and they ostentatiously smelled bouquets they carried, as though our smell offended them. They spoke harshly to the cacique of Zempoalla, who cringed. Obsequiously, several of the officials who had greeted us led them away to their quarters and Malinche asked the frightened fat cacique who they were. "Aztec tax collectors!" In a quivering voice he moaned that now they knew he was on friendly terms with us and soon Moctezuma would know this, too, and might draw dangerous conclusions.

Cortés strode forward. "Were you lying about your anger at their behavior?"

"No!"

"Were you lying about your desire for freedom?"

"No!"

"Then there is only one thing to do. Take a firm stand. Stop paying tribute to Moctezuma. Arrest these tax collectors, now!"

The fat cacique wavered only briefly. The commanding presence of Cortés, Malinche's ability to translate into ringing terms the great power of our king, and his knowledge that his fat would be in the fire if he let the tax collectors leave and tell Moctezuma of his friendliness to the aliens: all these factors tipped the balance.

Within an hour I saw those arrogant Aztecs tied to a long pole fitted with five leather collars, being led to the main pyramid. The cacique's plan was to offer them to his gods, thus achieving at one stroke their eternal silence and propitiation of the deities whose help he sorely needed. But Cortés sternly forbade this sacrifice, saying it would greatly offend him, our God, and our king. The cacique promised to forego it but insisted that the five stunned tax collectors had to remain in the custody of the Totonac priests.

Then came Cortés' next move. I was one of those he chose to carry out his plan.

I was summoned that evening to headquarters by Orteguilla the dwarf and was astonished when Cortés told me: "I want the Aztec tax collectors secretly freed. I think that if a pretty youth with golden hair were to visit the priests who are guarding them, he might fix their attention long enough so that another man could slip through the window of the prisoners' cell and cut them loose of those collars so they could escape."

I was stunned. It was Cortés who had insisted on their imprisonment. "May I ask why you want them freed?"

He smiled. "I'll leave that for you to puzzle out."

I said, "It seems to me that since I'm taking the risk, I should know the reason."

"Your risk is small. Doña Marina will be with you to interpret and she is too valuable to place in hazard.'' He turned and snatched a bouquet of red roses from an urn. ''Take this. These Totonacs love flowers as much as blood, it seems.''

''Who's going to get the prisoners out of the cell? How?''

''Yago the acrobat. Through the window. With a grapple. Don't worry about that part of it. Just concentrate on holding the priests' attention.''

''But what will I say to them?''

''Tell them a Bible story. Pretend that you have come there in all your young innocence to convert them.''

I said that if I were more innocent I would be less fearful and he laughed, giving me the rough map he had drawn which showed the rear of the main pyramid, the small room with one little window where the prisoners were, and the room where the two priests guarding them stayed. ''Don't fail me, Arturo. A great deal depends on your success tonight.''

I left with the roses and the map, puzzling over his wish to free the tax collectors, then gave it up and instead anticipated my reunion with Malinche.

14

It was a beautiful night with a silver slice of moon from a Moorish fairy tale. Near its tip was one bright star. Malinche's presence at my side was a great joy. I hoped that she might have learned a little more Castilian by now so we could converse. ''Are you happy being the general's interpreter?'' I asked as we crossed the plaza toward the great pyramid.

''I am happy. I am good. I believe in God, Father Almighty and in Jesuschristo, only son, our Lord.'' She spoke these memorized words of the Catechism in a gentle singsong. ''And I believe in Sainted Virgin, that Mother good and kind, and to her I pray most often.''

''And Cortés, is he behaving well to you?'' I wanted to ask if she shared his bed, but feared it might be true.

"He taught me to ride the horse of Puertocarrero." She smiled. "I remember when I was very afraid from horses."

The pyramid now loomed above us. I shivered as I imagined myself snatched into a bloodied temple like the one I had seen near San Juan Ulua and told Malinche, "If anything goes wrong and I have to fight the priests, you must run away."

She smiled at me. "Don't have fear, Hair of Gold. I no fear."

I could see that this was true. We might have been approaching that dread pyramid to visit dear friends waiting with cakes and wine. The dark bulk towering above us now hid the moon and star. As we turned the rear left corner, I became aware of the vast silence of the night and I was abruptly overwhelmed by the thought of all the cruelty and evil that had been done atop this manmade mountain and within its secret rooms. A dark figure loomed suddenly in front of me and I gasped.

"Shh! It's me, Yago." In that silence his whisper seemed very loud. "The grapple is padded, but it will still make a little noise when I toss it up through the window. I'll wait until you start to talk. Talk loud!"

Some forty feet ahead faint light spilled out from the only doorway of the stone prison cells built in a row against the rear of the pyramid. As we neared, I saw that the doorway was curtained with a leather hanging; when Malinche called out something in Nahuatl, it was drawn aside. A black-robed figure with long, matted hair made a wild silhouette against the light of a pine torch stuck into a stone bracket on one inner wall. The priest smelled like a corpse. Malinche spoke again, and like a marionette I held out my bunch of roses. He snatched them, grunted something, stepped back and held aside the curtain for us to enter. It was a small room with two straw sleeping mats on the floor. A black doorway to my right led to the row of prison cells. On one of the mats another priest lay asleep, his back to us.

Malinche's voice made me jump. She turned to me when she had finished her speech. "I said you came here to tell them about a God bigger than any, and that I will put your words in his language." It struck me then that she no longer needed Aguilar, but could translate directly from Spanish to Nahuatl. With the qualm of a schoolboy who has not prepared his lesson, I realized that I had no idea of what Bible story to tell.

The priest was staring at my blond hair. Clearly fascinated, he came closer and put out a hand to touch it. I could see the dried blood around the long nails, and under them. The smell of corruption grew stronger. My throat closed and I wanted to hold my nose. I stepped back. The horrible hand drew away.

I raised my voice to a shout. "Many centuries ago, into a town called Bethlehem, came a pregnant virgin named Mary to find a place to sleep and to bear her child." I paused and Malinche translated. My choice of this story seemed to me a good one, for all men, however evil, know they were born of a woman. I realized that I had left out Joseph, which might leave a wrong impression. "Her husband was with her, but there was no room for them at the inn, so the only place she could find to sleep was in a stable. And after her Babe was born, the only place she could lay Him was in a manger on straw. But Mary did not know that a shining star had led to Bethlehem three kings from afar." The priest now wore a dull, stupefied look.

Malinche nodded. "I know this story." She turned to the priest. With many graceful gestures she rattled out a long speech in Nahuatl. When she stopped talking, the priest seemed confused yet fascinated and had stopped staring at my hair. But a troubling thought had occurred to me. Cortés had forgotten to plan any signal by which we could know that Yago's job was done.

A grunt startled me. The sleeping priest had awakened. He sat on his mat, staring. Then he got to his feet and came toward me. He was taller than the other, more matted, and had an expression of habitual ferocity. He pointed to Malinche and spoke harshly to the other priest. Malinche stepped back to the doorway, drew aside the leather curtain and slipped out into the night. My blood stopped flowing as the taller priest approached me and peered into my eyes and said something which seemed to make the other one angry, for he stepped between us, talking rapidly, and grabbed my wrist. I thought, They are going to sodomize me and the only question is who does it first!

"No!" I shouted, wrenching my arm from that cadaver clutch to leap toward the leather curtain. A clatter of hooves and an enormous cascade of whinnying from just outside the doorway made one of the priests scream in terror. I swept the hanging aside and plunged out, colliding with the forequarters of a horse. "Run!" Captain Sandoval called and backed his mount so I could pass. He did not have to tell me twice. I ran to the corner of the pyramid and around it and clear to the center of the square before I slowed at all. In a moment Sandoval, with Malinche riding behind him, came clattering up to pace beside me as I panted along. "Well done!" Sandoval said cheerfully. "Yago got two of them free."

"Only two?"

"Two will do." He spurred the horse and, mystified, I watched them gallop away.

Having already thanked God for my deliverance, I realized that I could also thank Cortés, who had planned this interruption from the start.

I went directly to his headquarters, determined to learn how the two released prisoners could serve his ends. There I found those formerly arrogant tax collectors kneeling humbly on the floor, their sleek hair ruffled now, without their roses. Cortés smiled at me. "What Bible story did you tell?" he asked.

"The birth of Jesus."

"A good choice. Who could not be touched by that tale?"

"Two sodomist priests of Quiahuiztlán," I said grimly.

The dwarf Orteguilla came in then with a bowl of fruit, which he set before our two prisoners. Cortés looked at them with satisfaction. "I have told them that I was horrified by their imprisonment and I have promised to procure the release of their friends. I will see that these two get safely out of the city this very night so they can return at once to Moctezuma and tell him what has happened here." He looked at me blandly.

I was at first stupefied. Then a great light dawned: I thought I saw his plan. With this one stroke he would absolutely commit the Totonacs to the break with Moctezuma and also convince Moctezuma of his friendliness. He would get his allies and the Aztec ruler's gratitude as well.

When I told him this, he nodded with grim pleasure. "Duplicity is diplomacy's backside, on which even a king must sit."

The next morning the fat cacique, in an ecstasy of anxiety, came to Cortés to tell him about the escape. Cortés feigned anger and demanded that the remaining three tax gatherers be taken to his flagship in the harbor and there safely imprisoned. The cacique of Zempoalla took an oath of allegiance to Carlos of Spain and became our king's legal vassal.

The three Aztec tax collectors on the flagship were secretly released by Cortés the next day and sent on their way to Moctezuma with assurances of our general's friendship, even after our having been ungenerously left to starve on a barren shore.

Oh, the cleverness of Cortés! I myself was not clever enough yet to see precisely why he had schemed to force on Moctezuma this proof of friendship. Cortés' desire to march to that distant city of Tenochtitlán was as strong as ever: he hoped for a welcome there.

His next step was to make Villa Rica de la Vera Cruz more than a paper colony. He chose as the site a pleasant plain on the harbor Montejo had found. To erect a fortified town with a granary, church, city hall, armory, and barracks is a hard feat, especially when using the muscles and technical knowledge of an army divided against itself. After hundreds of friendly Totonacs had brought us load upon load of sun-dried bricks, stones, lumber, and mortar, it was not only the Velásquez followers who stood amid the heaps of building materials in sluggish and disgruntled clumps. Along with a dozen other soldiers from Alvarado's company, I stood staring sullenly at a great stack of adobe bricks. By Cortés' foresight, we had in the ranks an architect, a blacksmith, a stonemason, and a carpenter; the foundation of the city hall was already laid. Out of these bricks its walls would rise. Would they?

It was Cortés who turned the tide when he appeared, trowel in hand. With cheerful vigor he slapped down mortar, lifted one of the big bricks into place, and continued the row, whistling. El Galán and I were among the first to fall to work beside him. "Good, good," he said loudly. "A gentleman who thinks he is too good for this hard labor is no gentleman. This is noble work. I would be filled with shame if some of my own sweat did not wet these bricks. The first colony in New Spain! That is what we build here. More than a town: a gateway for the riches that will flow eastward to make Spain the greatest nation on earth!"

I wet many a brick with my sweat, and so did all of us. My hands grew calluses, and with pain I discovered muscles that marching had not used. We worked through all the daylight hours, well nourished by the good food our friendly Totonacs supplied and aided by many hundreds of Indians who labored cheerfully, as though they were to get the advantages Cortés had envisioned. In a little over three weeks we had built Villa Rica de la Vera Cruz.

We were still working like gentlemen or mules when an embassy bringing more gifts of gold arrived from Moctezuma. It included a number of richly dressed nobles and two of Moctezuma's own nephews. All were very solemn and reverential. The tax collectors Cortés had liberated had arrived to tell Moctezuma how they would surely have been sacrificed but for Cortés' great kindness. "Out of deference to you and your dislike of bloodshed, my uncle will postpone any vengeance against the rebellious Totonacs until after you have returned to your own land. He does not now doubt that you are those strangers whose arrival was announced to him by omens and oracles."

What strangers, I wondered. What omens? What oracles?

Cortés was amiable with these ambassadors, but they left with long faces after he told them that we were not going to return to our own land and still intended to pay personal respects to Moctezuma.

Although Cortés used a low tone, a number of watching soldiers heard this promise and I saw them stir uneasily and glance at one another. The scowling little priest Juan Diaz stepped forward, their self-constituted spokesman. "Are we to understand that you still contemplate this rash journey into Mexico?" He knew he was not loved like Father Olmedo, nor invaluable like Aguilar, but saw himself as the advocate who stood up for the rights of the dissatisfied.

"You are to understand what I want Moctezuma to understand, that he cannot command me or this Christian army according to his whim." Cortés had sidestepped the question neatly.

News of the gifts brought us by Moctezuma's nephews soon reached the ears of the fat cacique of Zempoalla, whose awe of Cortés was increased by this mark of respect. And so he asked Cortés to lend his aid in settling a dispute with a nearby ruler, believing that the mere presence of Spanish horsemen and soldiers would bring matters to a swift conclusion. Cortés agreed, and off we marched just after sunrise, Cortés himself leading us through a lovely countryside of wide rolling plains, groves of cacao trees, and tall palms whose fronds flashed silvery edges in the sunlight. I was feeling joyous, an all-conquering Spaniard in a land that was beginning to treat us with the respect we deserved.

Juan Morla must have felt this, too. When we passed a farm where there were some *guajolotes* in a pen, he ran and managed to grab one of the big birds, whacking off its wattled head with his sword, intending that he and his friends eat well that night. We were all laughing at his speed in getting the bird and catching up with us when a halt was ordered. Hoofbeats thundered toward us from the van and poor Juan Morla, with a big dead bird dangling from one hand, looked up to see Cortés glaring down at him from his black stallion. "You know my rule about looting. I must and will keep the trust of these new allies." Cortés turned and called to Captain Alvarado. "Hang him." Then he wheeled and rode back to the vanguard.

Juan Morla dropped the bird with a thud, not believing his ears. Neither did I. Hang a loyal soldier for one miserable *guajolote* bird? Alvarado ordered a rope brought and in a matter of minutes poor Juan was standing pale as whey under the branch of a large tree, a noose around his neck. I saw it catch on the rim of his steel gorget as he was slowly hauled, kicking, into midair. Even though Juan Morla had made fun of me often, I was very glad when Alvarado, on his sorrel horse, suddenly slashed out with his sword and cut him down, neck unbroken, to sprawl fainting in the dust of the roadside.

Remembering the command of Christ to treat kindly those who spitefully use us, I knelt beside him and gave him water from my flask. He was very shaken, and I put an arm around him and helped him walk until his own legs would hold him, then we double-marched and finally caught up with our own company. There are those who secretly hate one who aids them in a time of humiliation, but Juan was not of that sort. From then on he called me Arturo instead of Pollito. And the moment would come when his affection for me would turn the tide of my fortunes.

The fortunes of the expedition, however, were placed in sudden jeopardy that afternoon, by Cortés.

15

After our presence had aided the cacique of Zempoalla to cow the neighboring chieftain, we returned just before sundown to his city to be met in the plaza by smiling nobles with bouquets. A larger reward was soon offered, living tokens of the fat ruler's friendship and gratitude: eight Indian women, all of high status. One was his own daughter, who was thin and very plain. The other women were for the captains, he said. But his child was to be the wife of Cortés.

Cortés thanked him and said he already had one wife and that his religion did not permit him to have two.

This offended the cacique. Many wives, he said, are the well-known prerogative of power, and he particularly wanted his daughter to be the wife of Cortés.

Cortés ignored this and had his interpreters inform the donor that the women must all be baptized and become Christians before they could be given to his captains.

This greatly disturbed the cacique. "I do not want this done. It would offend my gods."

Duplicity was called for, but Cortés chose this moment to evangelize. "One reason why we came here is to wean you and your subjects away from false gods and from the abominations you perform to please them. You yourself must be baptized in our faith." He was still astride his black stallion, which stood with lowered head to nibble at some flowers that had been reverently placed before it. "Now! This very day."

"That cannot be," the fat cacique said. The man who had trembled before five Aztec tax collectors now gazed up with no sign of fear. "I promised loyalty to your king. I did not promise to worship your gods or abandon mine."

Cortés raised his voice; obduracy in the mound of flesh he had seen trembling with fear of Moctezuma clearly angered him. "Those idols must be removed from your temples! We must replace them with the Holy Cross of Jesus!"

In the brief pause while this was translated, Juan Diaz stepped resolutely forward, holding his silver crucifix high in one hand so that it caught the light of the setting sun and seemed to flame. Father Olmedo joined him, and so did the other churchmen, their faces shining with resolution.

The cacique looked very sad and stubborn. "My gods are good enough for me. For have they not brought me your aid? I will resist any violence to the deities of my people!"

The Totonacs filling the square gave a multiple growl of approval. A wild-haired priest screamed something and I saw other priests moving among the gathering crowd, exhorting them to defend their idols.

"Filthy sodomist priest!" yelled a soldier named Gonzalo, who had seen the same temple as I had. "We'll finish off your idols and you, too!"

Cortés turned his black stallion to face his own soldiers. "We are Christians and Spaniards, and I know that heaven will never smile on our hopes if we do not take a stand against the idolatry practiced here, and the atrocities. To close our eyes and let this people keep to their gods and so face an eternity in burning hell would be a sin, and unworthy of Christians! For my part, I am resolved that the idols shall be destroyed, this very day, this very hour, even if it costs me my life!''

Shouts of assent arose from many Spanish throats, but I stood dumbfounded. Cortés had got what he wanted—strong, compliant allies—and now abruptly he chose to turn friends to enemies. Why? What was the gain? I gawked up at his stern, armed figure and glimpsed another level of his nature: for his successes so far he owed Almighty God His due, and would pay it.

''Arrest the cacique!'' Cortés shouted, pointing to him with his unsheathed sword. ''Encircle him and the nobles with him!'' In only moments, we who were nearest had surrounded the group, our swords pointing outward in a hedgehog. At this moment an Indian priest burst from the watching crowd and came gibbering up to me and I slashed out with my sword blade and lopped off a lock of his long, matted hair, which fell to the ground and seemed to squirm there as though the poor victims' blood clotted on it had given it the power of motion.

Malinche's voice called out Cortés' threat to the fat cacique. ''If one arrow is shot at a Spanish soldier, or one spear raised, it will cost you your life!''

The Totonac ruler covered his face with both hands, then lowered them and called out to his people. ''Our gods are strong and will avenge any wrong these strangers do them. Offer no resistance.''

''Then let us see what vengeance these idols have in store for us!'' Cortés shouted. He ordered Puertocarrero's company to march across the plaza to the temple. The watching Indians, obeying their ruler, fell aside like the Red Sea parting for Moses. Our soldiers flowed up the pyramid's steep steps and sent the first of the idols crashing down into the square. With a vast moaning sound, the Totonacs drew back to the margins of the plaza, watching in helpless awe. A second idol tumbled down, and another, and more. The hollow sounds some of them made showed they were of wood; later we burned them in a great bonfire in the middle of the square, adding ones of clay and stone and smaller ones from the lesser temples. Night had fallen when the last of the wooden idols, the height of a tall man, stood upright in the flames the others had fed, and it suddenly seemed to me that I was watching an auto-da-fé and that the ugly thing carved of wood was really a living heretic burning in this life for having refused the Savior who could have offered salvation from an eternity in Hell.

A terrible scream gave an eerie reality to this illusion and the hairs on my neck stirred, but it was only one of the Indian priests standing with fists raised above his head and screaming up at an unconcerned evening star. He had gone mad and fell to the ground, where he rolled about with flecks of spittle coming from his mouth. Finally he rolled right into the fire and his hair went up in flames, but another priest rescued him, pulling him out by the legs and smothering his blazing head with his robe, and I saw that his body was crisscrossed with many gashes and scars. These priests lacerated their own flesh to feed still more blood to their gods, now mere smoldering ash and the one charred stalk still bearing its odd resemblance to a burned man.

But next day, what a reward after these unpleasant events! The Totonacs had lost faith in their idols, who had not avenged themselves. Following the orders of our priests, they cleansed the great *teocalli* of blood, and it was freshly stuccoed by Indian masons and painted white with lime. We saw atop that great pyramid a Christian altar raised, with our high white cross atop; the altar was hung with beautiful garlands of red roses. We all knelt at its foot. Led by an acolyte with a high, clear voice, we chanted a hymn to our sweet Jesus.

Rising from my knees, I felt ashamed that I had thought so much about getting gold. But then the soldier next to me nudged me and secretively showed me a flat heavy golden heart, almost as big as his palm; most of the idols, he whispered, had worn jewelry, and he had snatched this. Sudden covetousness claimed me, dimming my spiritual elevation of an instant before.

Raising my eyes from the heart, I saw Malinche, a Madonna-blue shawl covering her head. She was still kneeling at the foot of the pyramid, head bowed over clasped hands. I hurried to her side and stood quietly until she had crossed herself and risen from her knees. She turned and saw me. The shawl framed the dark purity of her face with the same soft folds as the pale-blue shawl framing the white face of the Virgin far above. The temple graced with Christian symbols had been the pyramid of Quetzalcoatl, and the idols we had burned had been gods she had once revered. What had been her feelings when she watched them thrown down and saw them go up in flames? And then I saw that she wore only the rosary I had given her. The little golden image of Quetzalcoatl was gone.

Its removal must have been a moment of greatest significance in her life. When Cortés had so valiantly insisted on that dramatic enactment of the power of Our Lord he had intended to convert our allies, the Totonacs. That it had so deeply moved Malinche was a benefit unforeseen. I smiled. "I see your pagan snake god is gone."

Her voice was soft and deep. "Now I believe. In the deep of the heart." My mind flashed to the golden heart the soldier had just shown me. How trivial such a heart was compared to the one beating in the breast of this woman now looking up at me with such childlike trust! "I was very afraid when the idols burned. I believed in God and Jesus and Virgin Mary. But I believed in Quetzalcoatl and some other gods too. So I thought a bad thing will come down on the Spaniards. But no. I know those Totonac gods are not real. The gods I had are not real. Cortés serves the true God. I, too."

I had been reminded that Puertocarrero had led that charge that toppled heathen idols from power. Could that have endowed him with a new stature in her eyes? I had to know. "Perhaps you feel less angry with Puertocarrero now?"

She cast me a glance around the austere fold of her shawl. "You may wish to know my feeling about him?"

"Yes."

She leaned toward me confidentially. "I do not like his smell."

I stepped back, felt the stench of my own sweat enveloping me like a thick haze, and I yearned for one of those bouquets the Zempoallans liked to carry about. "All soldiers smell a bit rank at times."

"Oh, yes. But he has a different smell. It offends me. He cannot help it. But so it is."

Hilarity seized me. Poor Puertocarrero! "And I, do I have a smell that offends you?"

"You smell young and good, like grass."

Like grass? "A million thanks!"

A hard, imperious voice spoke just behind me. "Mondragon!" It was Puertocarrero, who seemed to have grown slightly taller and whose narrow gray eyes were glinting like metal in his tense face. "This is my *barragana*. She is not to be accosted by you when my back is turned! Do you understand? It offends me very much."

The word *offend* reminded me how his smell offended the woman who was not really his *barragana* at all. "To *offend* you was not my intention." I slid a glance at Malinche, saw her barely contain a smile. How rare she was! Another woman would have laughed aloud to show her contempt.

But when Puertocarrero took her arm and tried to lead her away from me she refused to budge, only looked down at his hand. He removed it and walked off alone, his back very stiff. Then she said goodbye to me and went in the opposite direction. I watched her go, filled with pleasure at her true conversion.

We returned to Vera Cruz to find that a privateer from Santiago de Cuba had followed our trail and wanted to join us. He brought two horses, a dozen recruits, and some bad news. Governor Velásquez was publicly boasting that he had just received from Spain a warrant giving him and only him right to establish a royal colony on the new continent. Since we had just done this without his blessing, or that of our king either, I wondered where this left our little town. If not legitimately the first Spanish colony on these shores, then what was it? A mere headquarters, lacking any status with the crown?

This question was being asked and argued when Alvarado told us that Cortés had the answer: he was sending one of our vessels to Spain with a letter to the king himself telling of our gains to date and of the building of Vera Cruz, and pleading for royal approval of what we had so far accomplished, for permission to carry on our exploration of this rich new continent, and also for the reinforcements, arms, and ammunition that would guarantee our success. More impressive than the letter would be the Royal Fifth of our treasures. But fearing that it might not prove adequate to woo the king's favor, Cortés had added to it his share of the booty and had induced the captains to relinquish their shares, too. "Very noble—and smart, too," Juan Morla said. "Gold talks louder than words."

"I'm glad you know that," Alvarado said. His smile was, for him, rather cryptic.

Half an hour later Captain Francisco Montejo appeared with a document, a quill, and an inkhorn to ask the foot soldiers to give up our shares of the treasure, too. "For look," he said, "if what we send back to the king is inadequate to impress him, then all you will ever have is your little portion of what we have so far gained, and divided up into so many parts, your share is not going to look as large as you think. As for the future golden fruits of this rich land, forget them! Velásquez is out for those. It was only by good luck, the arrival of that privateer, that we even knew the governor intended to cut Cortés out. For if he had meant Cortés and the rest of us to benefit from the royal sanction he has been given, wouldn't he have sent us word of his good luck? We sweated to build Vera Cruz. Velásquez, safe and cozy in Cuba, boasts about his right to do what we have really done. Believe me, Cortés wants to get the king's approval of our efforts as much for your sakes as his own!'' Montejo's words had more weight in that he had once been Velásquez's friend. He held up the document. ''Those of you willing to relinquish your shares, as Cortés and I have done, sign this paper or make your mark.''

Stunned silence greeted his invitation.

Most of us in Alvarado's company were gathered around a large clay brazier where a few of us were roasting in the embers some nuts the Indians called *cacahuates,* which grow underground and have two kernels a little larger than peas. In the silence that followed Montejo's speech, the crackle of a nutshell which El Galán opened was very loud. We all laughed. Having got our attention, he said, ''We are on the eastern fringe of a vast new continent. All the riches we have seen are only a few crumbs dropped from Moctezuma's table. We need to buy our king's favor. Any price is cheap.'' He tossed the nutshells he held onto the coals of the brazier. ''I gladly offer my small share. Mere *cacahuate* shells.'' He took the document and the quill from Montejo and signed with a flourish.

I did the same, and so did all the rest. It took Juan Morla a long time to inscribe the nine letters of his name, printed very large. As he blew on the paper to dry the ink he held it in such a way that I would see he had not signed with an *X.*

Every single man in Alvarado's company signed away his share, and by the end of the day, every soldier and mariner had done so; the signing urge had spread like a fever and even the Velásquez followers were not immune. Cortés had used the same lure, in a sense, as that with which he hoped to win the support of the king, except that royalty was to be tempted with actual treasure and we soldiers with the promise of it. The hard labor we had expended to build Vera Cruz was also an issue; we wanted it acknowledged as the first legitimate Spanish colony on these shores. I do not know if Cortés had cleverly calculated on this when he came out that day with a fine speech and a trowel in his hand, or whether it was just luck.

When El Galán learned that everyone had signed, he indulged in prophecy. ''We are going to march to Tenochtitlán when Cortés is ready to go there, no matter what the cautious may say or do. For I have just found out that not only will we risk our lives for him, we will also unline our pockets of gold at his desire, which is more unusual.''

Juan Morla showed his buck teeth through his black beard in a wry smile. "The more I think of my woman's face when I tell her I did that, the more I like it here!"

But El Galán was only a fair prophet. He did not foresee that before we left for Moctezuma's city he and I would take part in an event so extraordinary that only two catastrophes the future held in store for us would impress me more mightily.

16

Before that climactic happening, I played an unwelcome role in a smaller unpleasantness that was to end with two hanged men swinging sadly from ropes. On the sunny morning after I signed away my share of the treasure the page Orteguilla pattered up to summon me into Cortes' headquarters in the city hall of Vera Cruz. Cortés was composing his letter to King Carlos, and since his frail secretary was sick with a flux, he had decided to use me for the moment, wishing to lose no time. He greeted me pleasantly and gave me a folio page to copy.

I dared to comment on one very courtierlike sentence. "Is it necessary to be humble, considering the gratitude our king will feel on seeing the wealth of gifts which will accompany this letter?"

He smiled at my innocence. "One does not expect gratitude from princes. They get their right to rule from God Almighty and do not feel that even He needs to be overwhelmed with thanks. Furthermore, young Carlos is the son of poor Juana the Mad and Felipe the Fair, son of Emperor Maximilian, and was raised at the Flemish court and does not like Spaniards much. I cannot know his mood when he reads my letter. He may have stabbed his finger on a rose thorn. A mistress may have disappointed him in bed, if so Christian a king allows himself such diversion. In other words, my words must bow to him, soothingly. And if I get his blessing and the arms and reinforcements I am asking, it will not be from gratitude, but because he smells more treasure in case I meet with success."

Ashamed of my naïveté, I bent my head to sharpen my quill, only to have it pulled suddenly from my fingers by the thin hand of the pale secretary, recovered from his flux, he claimed in a shaky voice.

As I rose to leave, Cortés said to me, "I have decided to employ you in a special capacity, Arturo." The secretary gave me a cold stare; his devotion to Cortés was absolute.

"In what capacity?" I asked.

"Not secretarial." The secretary relaxed and I heard his quill scratching away. Cortés smiled at me. "It is vital that I know the feelings of the foot soldiers, who do not always confide in their captains. From now on, it is your responsibility to report to me immediately any current of unrest, any remark that hints of insurrection."

"A spy." My dismay must have been evident.

"You will be helping the foot soldiers as well as me. I want to fulfill their needs when I can."

"Soldiers often grumble at this or that," I pointed out, "even the most loyal ones. I'd have no way of telling which grumble was caused by a bunion or gas in the belly and which had real importance."

"Let me be specific, then. I believe some sort of plot against me is brewing. See if you can ferret it out."

"Being no ferret, I do not know how."

"Then I will tell you. You will go about among the men saying you have heard there is a plot afoot. Rumors and guesses will fly. You collect them. I sift." His tone had crisped. This was an order. Then he stood up, dropped a hand to my shoulder, and walked with me to the door. "Do you know why I have chosen you? No? Because you I can absolutely trust. And you are also clever." He gave my back a pat and I grew suddenly tall. I shrank somewhat as I walked in the sunlight past other soldiers from whom I was now secretly alienated.

My first task as a spy was surprisingly easy. The gloomy, dark-skinned young Velásquez adherent named Gonzalo, much troubled by carbuncles and by memories of the bloodied temple we had seen, was one of a group of soldiers gossiping at day's end. I joined them and into their conversation I dropped the comment that I had heard the rumor of a plot against Cortés. Gonzalo stared at me in shock, then loudly denied the likelihood of such a thing. But later that night he sought me out and confessed it was true. The leader of the rebellion was the priest Juan Diaz. He and five Velásquez men had managed, with the connivance of a pilot, to get food and water aboard one of our ships, and they planned to sail it in to Cuba that very night. They believed that if they reported to Velásquez that Cortés apparently intended to march his army westward into great danger, steps would be taken by the governor that would save all our lives. Gonzalo bitterly regretted his earlier enthusiasm for this scheme, for fear of Cortés now outweighed fear of Moctezuma. "What shall I do?" he agonized, rolling his dark Moorish eyes toward heaven.

"You have no choice," I said. "You have to tell Cortés everything you know. If you don't, I will."

He writhed and begged me to go with him when he faced Cortés and put in a good word for his belated fidelity, which I did. Cortés listened to Gonzalo's halting story with an impassive face, but a swollen vein in his temple throbbed.

The other plotters were arrested and tried and treason was established beyond a doubt. The priest Juan Diaz claimed immunity as clergy, but the two other ringleaders were sentenced to death and the pilot who would have stolen the ship was condemned to lose his feet. The rest, including Gonzalo, were severely lashed. Orteguilla was present when the general signed the death warrants and told me that Cortés had cried out bitterly: "Before God, I wish I had never learned to write my name!"

After the executions, Cortés had me summoned and commended me for my part in so speedily uncovering the plot; this praise was so sweet that I did not stress how little I really had done.

We were alone in the room where the letter to the king had been written, standing by the window from which we could see a portion of the harbor and several of our vessels. Cortés was in heavy spirits. With dulled eyes he praised loyalty. "For what is any commander without men he can trust? Only a head full of plans that will never bear fruit. A cipher." He pointed suddenly to one of the ships. "That is the one that sails tomorrow for Spain. The treasure is loaded aboard. I have ordered them to avoid Cuba. Puertocarrero I know I can trust. Montejo, too. Yes, of them I am sure." Brooding there, he seemed to forget me and so after a time I left him. Dusk had fallen, the room was very dim, and he didn't hear me wish him good night.

So Puertocarrero was dispatched to Spain. As I watched the ship bearing him there sail away, all I could think of was what I had just learned from Orteguilla: Cortés had taken back the gray mare he bought for Puertocarrero with the gold buttons from his own cloak and had presented it to Malinche for her use. The dwarf had grinned as he added: "Cortés told Puertocarrero 'You tried to mount Doña Marina against her will. So she will now mount the mare I gave you. I consider this punishment lenient. And a mount for a mount would please even Solomon, I think. Or Moses.' "

"She will master horsemanship as rapidly as she did Castilian," I said.

"As for Castilian, I was of much help to her," Orteguilla said cockily. "She likes me well and we spend much time together. How many times I have corrected her amusing pronunciation! And I have told her the Spanish names of at least a thousand different things." The grin left his face as he said sincerely, "With Doña Marina, I never feel short. She sees that my mind and soul are large."

But the news of the gift of the mare was subtly disturbing. An idea flashed through my mind: from one favorite to another? With so few horses, it had been a lavish gift indeed.

That night I borrowed Orteguilla's guitar again. I was determined to draw her attention with the serenade that had been interrupted on the night Cortés gave her to Puertocarrero. This time, instead of standing outside a rude hut in the sand, I stood below the rear window of the building in Vera Cruz where Cortés and the other officials of the town had their sleeping quarters. From Orteguilla I had found out that Malinche had her own room there, and where it was.

In the moonlight, the window under which I stood with my borrowed guitar could have been somewhere in Spain, or at least Cuba. There was even a grille, though of wood. Once more, my voice rose in serenade. This time no cross-eyed Indian blighted my tender feelings. Looking up, I saw with a thrill of joy Malinche's face at the window, softly lighted by a candle flame. She listened, smiling, while I sang the little morning song of King David.

"Why are you singing a morning song at night?" she asked when the last note died away.

It struck me again how very much Spanish she had learned in less than five months. I tuned a flat string and sang the song I had written for her. "And now, if you were a Spanish lady, you would throw me a rose if you liked my serenade."

She disappeared and a moment later returned and tossed down a ripe mango. "I have no roses. And I am not a Spanish lady. Sing more."

Halfway through the next song I found we had an audience. From the darkness some soldiers and a captain or two had appeared to stand silently watching this ritual of Spanish wooing never before seen or heard on this alien shore. "Very well thung, Pollito," Sandoval called. Juan Morla said: "*Arturo* sings like the birds."

"But the birds are all asleep now," a commanding voice announced from a front window of the house. I looked up and saw Cortés staring sternly down at me. "Go to bed."

Picking up my mango, I waved to Malinche and traveled on air to the open thatched barracks where my company slept, sure that my serenade had touched her heart. I held the plump fruit in my hand for a while, smiling down at it idiotically, and then peeled and ate it with greedy pleasure, sucking from the big seed every drop of golden juice.

A blissful dream was shattered at dawn when Alvarado roused us and told us we were to march at once to Zempoalla in full armor and with all gear. When we demanded why, he said "Because Cortés has ordered it!" At first the rumor ran that this was the start of the march to Moctezuma's city, but that notion faded when Alvarado let us know that Cortés was remaining behind in Vera Cruz, along with several captains, himself one. He placed El Galán in charge of our company. Something unusual was afoot. I knew, but I did not much care when I saw that Malinche had come with us, riding on Puertocarrero's gray mare. Orteguilla the dwarf was perched behind her.

When we got to Zempoalla in the early afternoon, camping in the same enormous white courtyard as before, I rushed over to her and she seemed glad to see me, although more concerned about the horse, stroking its soft muzzle and feeding it maize from her hand until the soldier acting as groom came and led it off to be watered and fed with the rest.

Meanwhile Orteguilla had spread out a large striped serape against the shaded wall of the courtyard where already the men had settled down to dicing, cards, or conversation, waiting for food. He urged Malinche to sit down and rest, absurdly solicitous. She gave him a fond glance and told me he had ridden with her to protect her, and I thought that would have been fine if she had been menaced by a dwarf like himself.

They seated themselves and I sat down, too, and asked if they had any idea why we were here. They both shook their heads. I concentrated on flattering Orteguilla. "I thought that you, being in the confidence of the general, would surely have some notion."

He looked about for eavesdroppers, lowering his voice. "I can tell you one thing. The general was up very late last night discussing a matter of greatest importance with his most trusted captains.''

"I don't suppose you would tell me what it was?''

He smiled patronizingly. "A page may have large eyes and big ears, but unless he has a closed mouth, he will not be a page very long.''

Though the dwarf stuck close as glue, I gave myself over to enjoyment of the moment, seated close to Malinche on that serape, our little island around which the soldiers moved and talked and laughed, mere shadows in the sun. At last Orteguilla took a siesta, snoring gently on his small bent arm. Warmed by her presence and hoping for praise, I told her that the last song I had sung the night before had been written by me for her.

"Why?'' she asked, and I realized she was unaware of this European nicety or its significance.

"Because you are very dear to me.''

"Sing it again.''

I could not sing well without a guitar, so I recited the poem.

"What is a nightingale?'' she asked.

I told her.

"And what is damask?''

"A fine smooth white cloth.''

Her hand went to her cheek. "Skin is not like white cloth,'' she said.

"I was comparing the smoothness.''

The page had rolled over with his back to us and began to snore louder. I jumped to my feet and held out my hand to her. "His snoring annoys me. Let's go somewhere else.'' My audacity pleased and excited me.

"The cacique's garden is pretty.'' This was a retreat between his stone palace and a pyramid temple. It was his private park, unused by the townsfolk, but as one of the conquerors I had no hesitance about walking there.

It was shaded by a great jacaranda tree that seemed to shut out the rest of the world. Amid its lacy leaves hung clusters of sky-blue flowers like little bells. I sat leaning against the bole of the tree. She knelt on the soft grass. A bell flower fell and lay on her black, black hair. "I love you, Malinche,'' I said. I used the verb *amar*, which conveys a spiritual love. Honesty and my throbbing body prompted me to add *Te quiero,* the verb of desire.

"And I love you," she said, using *amar*. But did she understand the distinction?

"And from the moment I saw you I have wanted to kiss you." My voice had a tremor in it.

I saw on her face an oblique tenderness. She leaned a little closer to me, just a fraction. The motion made her loose chemise pull tighter against her full breasts. "Would God like that?" she asked with an innocence real or feigned. "Would Cortés?"

My male member rose in defiance of God, Cortés—and Aguilar, too. "Would you?" I whispered, and knelt facing her. The urgent desire to press my mouth against her full lips seemed to be passing almost visibly from my being to hers, a warm current of heat. That scent which was not Spanish answered it and enveloped me. But just as my lips touched hers, footsteps approached; I wavered, recognized El Galán's clean boots, and hated them.

He was smiling down as though he were not as unwelcome as a toad in the water jug. "Poor little Orteguilla is in a frenzy, trying to find where you are, Doña Marina. The soldiers are baiting him by pretending they don't know. He's afraid Cortés will ask for you any minute."

"Cortés is in Vera Cruz!" I cried.

"He *was* in Vera Cruz."

I turned to Malinche, but she was gone. I looked wildly around the garden, saw only the trembling tendril of a vine she had brushed in passing.

"You could hardly have picked a worse moment to come looking for me," I said as I stood up. We left the garden side by side.

"I think I picked a good one. Your ardor was visible from twenty paces. Last night you serenaded her and gathered an audience and a reprimand from the general. Yet today you march her off in full view of nearly the entire army. I have rarely seen a suitor more inept. I am only a simple soldier, God knows, but I did not get the name El Galán for nothing. I can tell you here and now that you must learn to plan things better. First, you arrange to get the young lady to suggest a more private meeting place. If she wants you she will prove adept at this. Only then do you let the little man downstairs rear up his head." We soon reached the steps of the palace that had been given to Cortés as his headquarters in Zempoalla. El Galán turned me around and led me up the steps with him.

"What are we doing here?" I asked.

"Cortés recruited me for a secret mission. He wants you too."

"What mission?"

"I'll let him tell you."

When we reached the palace throne room, Cortés and his captains were talking in low but excited voices, their heads together. When El Galán announced our arrival and Cortés looked over at us, it was with an appraising eye. He beckoned us forward in an informal fashion, dropped his hand to my shoulder. "Here is a soldier fit for our task," he said to the rest. "Like my friend El Galán here, he is totally worthy of our trust."

"Both Alvarado men," Captain Olid said jealously. "I have loyal men in my company, too."

"I do not doubt it, being the captain that you are."

"Tell them. Thee what they thay," lisped Captain Sandoval. The pupils of his brown eyes were large with excitement. All the captains seemed nervous and eager.

Cortés faced El Galán and me, smiling. Again I noted the small white scar below his underlip. "You have no doubt wondered why I remained behind in Vera Cruz. I will tell you. I have just ordered four of our ships scuttled."

I felt my mouth drop open but could not close it. Staring into those brilliant eyes it occurred to me that our commander had gone mad. "Four ships?" I whispered.

"They were quite wormy, unseaworthy. Their pilots have so testified in writing."

"That leaves us only seven ships here." My voice was shaky.

"It is my plan to sink and burn all but one."

"Sink . . . burn . . . ?"

"Do you approve?" His smile would have warmed a serpent; his magnetic stare would have charmed a dragon.

"No," I croaked, and then shouted, "No! Leave us stranded here? No way to get home? It would be the act of a madman!"

Smiling, he turned from me to El Galán. "And do you agree with Arturo?"

He said with a calm I could only admire, "And so will every soldier in the army."

"I said all along we didn't need any foot soldiers, that we can use Totonacs," said Alvarado impatiently.

Cortés frowned. "I wish a few foot soldiers to take an active part. I don't want it later said that only my captains knew and approved of this." Cortés turned back to El Galán and me. "I have determined to march to Tenochtitlán at once. The reward in gold and gems is beyond estimate. We have to trust in God, who has been with us thus far, and go bravely onward." I was beginning to kindle at the old, dazzling promise of great wealth. "But I cannot accomplish this march while a third of my army yearns to crawl aboard the nearest leaky vessel and head home. No general could; not Hannibal or Caesar. I need a united body of men, and I will have it! I will have it, that is, if there are no ships remaining at anchor to tempt their minds and dim what courage they possess. For let me tell you this: someone is going to march into Mexico; someone is going to penetrate this rich continent! Do we want to leave that to others? The English? The French? Or are we going to be the first?" Head high, he raked our faces with flashing eyes.

As always, he had inflamed me with his own passion. "The first!"

He threw back his head and laughed like a boy, joyously.

El Galán said, "You have found the only spur for the balky mules among us: no alternative."

Cortés nodded. "The balky mules cannot be allowed to spoil our venture for gallant and mettlesome thoroughbreds like yourselves." As my chest swelled, his face grew stern. "I now order you both to return to Vera Cruz with me and my captains to aid in the destruction of the fleet." He added, in a matter-of-fact voice, "The sails, rigging and ironwork are to be saved, of course. Wooden hulls can be built again when the time comes for our triumphant return to Cuba."

It was true that the wood of certain of the remaining vessels was well-drilled with wormholes and that others had suffered dry rot and could be called unseaworthy, but the caravel I helped to sink after it had been stripped was sound. To smash with an axe through the under-planking of the hull and see the water gurgle in caused me pain, and I felt as if I were killing something that had never meant me any harm. A tingle of fear stirred; I was helping to destroy my only link with home and its safety. As I climbed up and out of the slowly filling hold, I tried to think of the great adventure that lay ahead. The cowards could not be allowed to rob the brave of treasures beyond imagining, of fame that would ring down generations to come! Cortés was right. He had to be, or we were all lost.

The sun was low by the time Cortés decided to have two shallow-draft vessels that were anchored near shore dragged with ropes into the shallows, there to be stripped of sails, rigging, and ironwork. This took some time, even under the supervision of that excellent shipwright Martín Llopez. Even some nails were saved. Meanwhile, hundreds of astonished Totonacs had assembled on the beach to watch denuded hulls offshore go down into the sea.

By this time my initial high spirits had sunk with the sun, and this was true of all of us, I think, except Cortés. He had the buoyant air of a man who was building ships instead of destroying them. But he must have felt the general mood sag, for he had two hogsheads of good wine brought down to the beach from his private supply in the town. As I filled my clay mug with rich, cool wine, Cortés cried "A taste of Spain, from the vineyards of Jerez, to cheer us!" After we drank a toast to our king, the sherry flowed, and soon we were all laughing and a little drunk. Suddenly Cortés was at my side with a torch, a flaming shaft of pitch pine that the Indians light their houses with. He thrust it into my hand and pointed out to one of the caravels in the shallows near shore, and I waded out into the water to my waist and fired a sun-parched rail, which shot a flame out at me as if in protest. I waded in up to my neck, torch high, and set the other end alight, too, and by the time I got back to the sand, the vessel was blazing up, as hot as Hell itself.

Some Totonac musicians had appeared with a drum, a flute, and gourds filled with dry seeds to offer their savage music at this strange fiesta. A mariner who had gotten ecstatically drunk began to prance wildly, snapping his fingers like castanets, and soon all the Spaniards were capering in a mad fandango, our grinning sweaty faces reflecting the flames of the burning ships. Our frenzy consumed our regrets.

The fires sank down at last, leaving only poor black skeletons of what had been vessels. Out on the moonlit water of the harbor the prow of a ship that had refused to sink pointed at us accusingly as it floated, hull up. So Cortés had a cannon wheeled to the beach and ordered it fired at the stubborn ship again and again, and at last enough cannonballs had splintered the hull so that it settled slowly into the harbor whose dark waters closed over it and finally were still. Now only one ship was left afloat: the flagship.

The strange celebration had ended, and Cortés ordered us back to town to sleep; we were to march west to Zempoalla early in the morning. After all the others had left the beach, I lingered behind on the deserted sands, haunted by the doleful smell of charred wood and saddened by the black bones of the burned ships. Hugging my knees,

I sat near the water's edge and stared in the direction of Cuba, now as unreachable as the moon. Bits of charred flotsam washed up at my feet, no darker than the dismal mood that had engulfed me. A deep and awful doubt of our commander's sanity had edged into my mind. Cortés' reasoning, which had seemed so brilliantly right to me, now seemed only murky rhetoric. He had stranded us all in this alien land where our Zempoallan allies, learning we were at their mercy with no escape at hand, might soon be tearing down our white cross from the temple from which we had hurled their idols. A rat from one of the ships scurried past me, a dark and frantic shape against the moonlit sand.

"Waiting for a mermaid?" It was El Galán, who had missed me and had returned.

"Wishing our ships were still afloat." My hollow voice was funereal.

He grinned down at me and spoke kindly. "You swallowed a great deal of sherry. Come and get some sleep. You'll feel better tomorrow." He held down a hand and pulled me to my feet.

From somewhere down the beach came the sudden mournful wailing of an Indian flute. I looked that way and saw one of the Totonacs kneeling in the sand and staring seaward as if he piped an elegy for all the dead ships. Tears filled my eyes as I walked in silence beside my friend into the silent town.

But wine and sorrow were transformed into desire. I fell asleep yearning to hold Malinche in my arms. The burned ships seemed a boon, for now she and I could not be parted.

17

The march west to Zempoalla next morning was grim. My head ached from the fumes of the wine and my heart ached, too, nor did the memory of the salvaged rigging, ironwork, and other fittings stored in the warehouse at Vera Cruz bring any comfort. That act of preservation now seemed only another evidence of our commander's

lack of good sense: did he really believe our fleet could be rebuilt for
him whenever he snapped his fingers and commanded it?

As soon as El Galán and I rejoined the rest of Alvarado's company
in Zempoalla, I sensed a mood I had never felt before. All over the
courtyard men were gathered in angry clots to argue and debate the
report of the destruction of the first four ships, spread by a mariner
whose emotions had led him to ignore Cortés' command for silence.
His ship had been perfectly sound, he insisted, needing only to have
the hull scraped; seeing it go needlessly down he had thought that with
it went his last chance of getting home alive. But worse than this,
someone else had just let out the whisper that the rest of the fleet had
also been sunk, or burned.

This news spread like a grassfire. "Cortés has betrayed us!" a
soldier cried suddenly. "He's beached us!" My own concern over the
lost ships dwindled in importance beside the sudden looming fear of
a massive mutiny that even Cortés would not be able to quell. Stripped
of power over his soldiers, how long would he command the respect
of the Totanac cacique? And if the Totonacs turned from allies to
foes . . . ?

It was at this moment that I was summoned into the presence of
Cortés by Orteguilla. He moved beside me very fast on his little legs
and grinned up at me. His jaws seemed to have more than the usual
number of teeth. "I've put in a good word for you with Cortés," he
said, "but I warn you, he's very much annoyed."

"Annoyed?" An angry soldier I was passing made a sudden
violent motion with his arm which I barely ducked. "With me?" I,
who had torched a ship for him? I, his trusted spy, his thoroughbred
foot soldier? "Annoyed?"

"Oh, the innocence of Señor Green Eyes!"

My confusion took the form of anger at the dwarf. "I am jealous
of no one, manikin!"

"I referred to their literal color. Manikin is a term I despise, and
for obvious reasons. I want you to know that it was not I who told
him."

"Told who? What?"

"Of your little ramble with Doña Marina I said precisely nothing,
even though you left me asleep on a mat on the paving where I was
accidentally stepped on and then got splashed with horse piss."

I stopped dead. "At a time like this he can't be concerned about
a thing like that!"

"Correct. What pisses on his page is of no concern to him just now."

"No, no, I mean that little stroll you mentioned."

"You did more than stroll, did you not?"

"We sat under a tree for a few minutes."

"Sat, you say? Just sat?"

"Sat. Just that." For the kiss had missed. "Who told him?"

"Two soldiers. And considering that the entire army saw you take her off to that secluded garden, I would say that you must be quite popular." He added, grinning, "If not with Cortés."

We had reached the door of the palace where Cortés had his headquarters. Suddenly one soldier of a group gathered there pointed to me and nudged another, who stepped forward and blocked my path. "Deny it, you son of the great whore! Deny that the whole fleet is sunk and that you helped him sink it! Toadeater!"

I could not deny the accusation, but drew my sword to deny the epithets. His friend quickly stepped between us and begged me to forgive the remarks because my accuser had drunk too much fermented cactus juice and was not responsible. "And besides, Cortés happens to be waiting," Orteguilla said impatiently. So I accepted an apology, though feeling rather sick and shaken.

Inside the palace room where Cortés sat alone at a trestle table eating a late four-o'clock dinner, the angry voices of the soldiers outside were reduced to a mere hum. He was at his ease in only hose, breeches, and a white shirt that made his shoulders look excessively broad. As he ate, he studied a crude map. At the window some twenty feet away, a group of captains stood looking down at the soldiers in the courtyard below. "Here's that naughty Mondragon," said Orteguilla.

Cortés looked up at me, eyes cold. "You're not going to put horns on Puertocarrero. Stay away from Dõna Marina."

I was stunned. Orteguilla's grin stiffened my spine. "How could I put horns on him?" I spoke in what I intended as a tone of respect, but firm. "Their relationship was in name only. It ended when he left for Spain."

"Even so, what makes you think I would tolerate her dalliance with a mere foot soldier?"

Stung, I said, still very respectfully, "I am a little more than that, am I not? Your assistant secretary?" I leaned toward him and spoke low. "Your spy?"

"In your opinion, how deep is the anger of the men concerning the ships?"

"I think they are at the point of mutiny."

He nodded. "To return to the subject of Doña Marina and yourself: she is under my protection, in the sense that a ward would be. In addition to her value to me as an interpreter, there is her stature in the eyes of the soldiery to consider: they have her on a pedestal of sorts because of her great physical beauty and her high intelligence. Many may dream of her, but not as a woman they actually hope to possess. This is good; it keeps them manly and the keener to accomplish our purpose here and return to their women at home. Her conduct must be above reproach. She will bestow no further favors on *you*."

I imagined or heard contempt in his voice, and drew myself up to my full height. "With all respect, let me remind you that I come of good family and am an educated man . . ."

"Boy," he smiled.

"I care deeply about Malinche, and . . ."

"Why do you call her that?"

"Because it's her true name. I care deeply for her. I wish to marry her."

He stared. "Marry her! And how would that sit with the rest of my soldiers? I'll be brief. She is my voice, my tongue. I cannot talk to the Indians without her. I will not have her kissing under trees with you. Forget her. Bow in passing. Goodbye."

Shaken as I was, I stood my ground instead of going. "And what does *she* feel?"

Before he could give any answer but a basilisk stare, Olid and Sandoval had rushed over from the window, and one cried sharply, "It is worse than we believed! Down in the courtyard they're about to burn you in effigy!"

His armchair scraped on stone as he got up to see this sight. I went toward the door, but his voice arrested me. Standing by the window but looking at me, as if the sight of a straw dummy with his name on it were something he saw every day, he said very pleasantly, "I have made El Galán second in command to Captain Alvarado. You I have appointed his aide, which makes you the youngest such in the army." He turned his attention then to the demonstration below.

My wounded spirits soared, though when I emerged into the roar and turmoil of the great courtyard, I wondered if Alvarado would by tomorrow have a company to captain. As I went to look for El Galán, a very cheering thought struck me. Would Cortés have taken the trouble to send for me at such a time and speak at such length unless he knew Malinche cared for me? God well knew the sincerity of my feeling for her, and it was God, not Cortés, who would decide who got her.

The sun had set and the courtyard was in twilight. The crude effigy of Cortés had not been set afire because a squabble had developed over its possession; the Velásquez men lost to the soldiers who did not want to see their general's image go up in flame. Meanwhile, held aloft on the shoulders of a friend, an angry mariner harangued his onlookers: "Cortés said he would be loyal to us and our cause! Is this his loyalty? Leaving us stranded?" My mother's face with its large, sad eyes suddenly filled my mind, and with it the fear that I would never see that face again, or my father's, or ever again close my eyes sheltered by the safe walls of home.

Yago the acrobat bellowed: "Any ass knows how a rumor can spread and grow to a monstrous lie! Maybe Cortés burned a couple of rotten ships! Who cares?"

"More than two! More than two!" someone shouted.

"Where's Cortés?" someone else demanded. "Why doesn't he face us and put this rumor to rest?"

I expected Cortés to appear on the steps of the palace or at the window above to attempt to calm the soldiers, but soon a trumpet sounded from out on the plaza and the braying voice of Cortés' crier called to us to converge at the foot of the great pyramid. I looked up and saw Cortés partway up the steps in full armor. He was flanked by his captains, our standard aloft behind him. Far above his head I could see our altar and the cross. A rumble of discontent from the massed soldiers broke in waves at his feet, but then died away as he waited for our silence.

"Soldiers of Spain," he said in a tone easily heard yet lacking the thrust of authority, "I must tell you that a survey of our ships showed many unfit for service. I ordered them destroyed." Hot murmurs rose; he calmly waited for silence. "This was my great loss, for most of them were my property, all I possessed in the world." A new kind of silence fell now, for no one had thought of that. "But you, my soldiers, will gain an advantage: the addition to this army of the hundred and ten able mariners that were required to man those vessels." The army muttered its dissatisfaction with this boon. Cortés raised his voice up to the level of that ringing sureness I remembered from the speech at Cabo San Antonio. "But even if the fleet were still afloat, what good are those ships to us now? If we succeed in marching to Moctezuma's capital, we will not need them there. Nor will the ships help us if we fail in that venture, because we will by then be too far into the interior of this land to need ships." Cortés took a step down toward us, arms outspread. "Now I am going to speak to you frankly: I am glad for the hulls that were rotten, and I am glad those ships are gone, and I will tell you why. To be looking back over your shoulder at a means of escape is a sure way to fail in any venture. It is unworthy of the bravery you have shown me. If you now go forward yet again, with confidence in yourselves and in me, our success is certain. Certain!" One arm gestured upward and we all saw the Cross, our cross, elevated in this once-heathen land. "As for me, I have chosen my destiny! I will march westward and meet face to face with Moctezuma as long as there is even one man to bear me company!" A faint cheer sounded and I knew I was not the only soldier who was determined to be that man. "As for those cravens who shrink from sharing the future joys and dangers of this glorious venture, then, in God's name, let them go home! There is one sound ship left. We will let them take it and return to Cuba. Let them tell there how they deserted their commander and their comrades! Let them wait there until we who stayed return in triumph, loaded with the gold of the Aztecs, the riches of Mexico!"

My heart had soared as he spoke. "To Mexico!" I shouted, and heard other voices take up the cry. "To Mexico! To Mexico!"

There was a total reversal of mood. Now enthusiasm flowed from man to man like a fresh, invisible wind. A splendid exhilaration filled me. I threw my arms across the shoulders of El Galán and Juan Morla and the three of us chanted the names of Santiago and San Pedro, again and again, and marched singing across the square. The trumpet sounded, a cannon was fired, and once-surly faces beamed with smiles and the glow of comradeship.

Young though I was, I was aware that Cortés had achieved a miracle of generalship, using the very act that had enraged his men to prod them suddenly forward into commitment to the journey westward. And I knew the scuttling and burning of those ships was a crucial moment in history as memorable as any other I could name. In choosing to commit the only act that could keep his army together so he could thrust us onward to the distant land of the Aztecs, Cortés unlocked the continent north of us to penetration. He knew he was doing that. True, this was inevitable: If he had not, another would have, in time. But the fact is, he did. He did, knowing that whatever else history remembered of him, it could never forget this.

And I am not without pride that I took that torch from his hand and used it, though less proud of the wine-sad youth who later sat on the shore mourning the deed to the wail of an Indian flute.

PART
IV

THE MARCH TO TENOCHTITLÁN
August 16, 1519–November 6, 1519

18

Three days later we set forth for Tenochtitlán: the cream of the force, four hundred soldiers, fifteen horses, seven cannons. Behind us marched thirteen hundred Zempoallan warriors and a thousand *tamanes* to carry the ammunition and baggage. The remainder of the soldiers and most of the mariners stayed to man Vera Cruz, under the command of Captain Juan Escalante, who looked a little like my father. It was the sixteenth of August, six months and six days since we sailed from Cuba. As though to mark my new status as aide, my mustache had turned a trifle darker than my hair, and I let it grow out, though I still shaved my chin. The trials I had passed through merited at least this badge of manhood, I felt.

Orteguilla the dwarf had accompanied us, riding on a litter or on one of the caissons when his legs gave out. I was more surprised to find Gonzalo the traitor among our select number. His carbuncles had disappeared magically after his lashing, and a fervent devotion to Cortés now consumed him. "Our great leader" he called him, rolling Moorish eyes heavenward. "The equal of Alexander, by God!"

Six days of hard marching took us upward from the torrid clime at sea level through a green and temperate zone to frigid mountains thousands of feet high. There an icy rain and hail chilled our bones; a few of the poor *tamanes* were so numbed by cold that they stumbled and fell to their deaths as we made our way along perilous precipices with steep drops into canyons where we could see far below us lush tropical foliage instead of the pines that grew where we were. The breath out of our nostrils often condensed in cloudy plumes, and at night we huddled around campfires that kept dying in the wind and the rain. But Cortés' spirit burned high as he moved among us when

147

we stopped to rest, assuring us that the worst would soon be over. Rain stood in droplets on his armor; he had lent his hooded black woolen cloak to Malinche. Marching beside El Galán in the vanguard of the foot soldiery, I saw ahead, as our trail curved around a mountain flank, the imposing figure of Cortés on his black mount, Malinche in his black cloak riding beside him on the gray mare, and I thought suddenly of the young French maid of Orléans, who had so bravely led an army against the English nearly a century before.

That same afternoon we came to Xocotlán, a fortresslike town whose thin dour cacique, instead of offering food and shelter to such cold and weary visitors, took us to view a local monument in which he took great pride. It was a huge boxlike structure shelved to display rows of white and grinning skulls: thousands stared out with their sad, hollow eye sockets, his precious harvest of the sacrificed, his crop reaped by Death. "But these trophies are few, compared to the skull rack of my great lord," he confessed. When Cortés then asked, through Aguilar and Malinche, if he were a vassal of Moctezuma, he stared in surprise. "Who is not?"

"I am not," Cortés told him. "I serve a king whose least vassals are as powerful as your Moctezuma."

The cacique of Xocotlán was not in the least impressed. "Indeed? Moctezuma can muster up thirty great vassals, each master of a hundred thousand men. His revenues are immense, and this wealth he expends on his city of Tenochtitlán, which is magnificent beyond any idea you may have of magnificence. His vast armies have garrisons in sixty cities. Every year, year in and year out, at least twenty thousand victims are sacrificed at the altars of his gods. Many years ago, at the coronation of his uncle Ahuitzotl, more than seventy thousand victims were sacrificed. For days on end they were marched across the city and up the steps of the pyramids in the great central plaza. Priests dropped exhausted from the killings, dripping with blood from head to feet. My grandfather saw this with his own eyes, having gone there as a newly conquered vassal to see his new lord crowned."

As I stood stunned, Cortés asked calmly, "Have you yourself seen the city?"

"I can tell you what it is like. It stands in the middle of a wide lake in the center of a broad and verdant valley ringed by mountains. The only approach to the city is over causeways. There are four, each several miles long. In places these have wooden bridges which can be removed, making it impossible to enter or leave. In the city live a hundred thousand families. Every man, woman, and child reveres Moctezuma as both their ruler and as a god.''

In the silence that fell, Malinche said to Cortés, ''I will tell him about your victories and of the gifts Moctezuma has sent.'' There on her gray horse, her hands waving gracefully against the black cloak, she spun a tale which seemed to alter the boastful cacique's disdain of us. He led us to some large stone buildings where he said we could rest, and then sent to us a file of women who made us hot maize cakes on braziers.

We stayed there four days, resting and regaining our strength. The cacique's first hostility seemed to abate, and he readily answered Cortés' questions about the route we should take. We could approach Moctezuma's city by either of two routes. One led to a large city called Cholula. The other passed through the republic of the Tlascalans. This was the route Cortés decided on after the cacique of Xocotlán revealed that the Cholulans were cowed by the might of Moctezuma. The Tlascalans, on the other hand, had rebelled against Aztec domination a century ago and had fiercely maintained their independence: they were civil to everyone but Aztecs. In Tlascala, we could expect a warm welcome.

Our march there took us through a green valley with a lovely little river and many woods in which birds sang sweetly. Along the river were many small Indian houses; their occupants sometimes came out to stare at us, astonished but not unfriendly. The four Zempoallan envoys Cortés sent ahead to take gifts for the Tlascalan ruler and to ask friendly passage through his land would certainly face no troubles en route.

Our journey ended abruptly. Ahead was a stone wall. Nine feet high and with a parapet atop, it looked as if it extended a length of at least a league, buttressed at either end by mountains. We had reached the border of Tlascala, but this barrier did not seem to me to fit the description of a friendly people. The wall had only one opening, at the end of the wide trail we had followed. It was a curious one, formed by two semicircular walls overlapping for a distance of some forty feet and providing a curved passageway ten paces wide, perfectly controlled from the top of the inner wall, empty against the sky. But even though this bastion seemed undefended, Cortés rose high in his stirrups to call back to us, ''Forward, soldiers! The Holy Cross is our banner!'' I knew then that this formidable wall, which proved ten paces thick, had impressed him, too. I lifted my eyes to our cross for courage, and as I did I saw the long black hair of Malinche blowing back in the wind that had risen. With sudden clarity I realized that our lives were in her hands. Our four Zempoallan envoys had not yet returned with permission to enter this land, so her tongue was our only means to convey our peaceful intentions to whatever horde of Tlascalans might await us beyond the wall. I entered that passageway with my sword half-drawn.

It debouched into a narrow gorge that sloped upward for a considerable distance. No warriors menaced us. We marched along in good spirits, though at first wary about possible Tlascalan arrows and spears from the cliffs at either side. At last our scouts came back with the word that some fifteen Indians were waiting for us ahead where the top of the gorge met a high level plain. Cortés led four of the cavalry forward to meet this welcoming party.

But when we foot soldiers caught up with those horsemen, we found that a furious fight had taken place. To my horror, I came upon the body of a horse lying stiff-legged with blood still gushing from the neck stump; the severed head lay a few feet away. I looked up and saw Malinche on her living mount staring down at it with a horror that seemed to equal mine, and then Cortés galloped up and furiously ordered her to ride back to the rear, out of danger.

In a moment I saw why. Across the open plain, a horde of Tlascalan warriors, three thousand at least, was bearing down on us. But on that open ground, our full cavalry was able to maneuver. Within minutes fifty of the enemy lay dead, our musketeers and crossbowmen accounted for a hundred more, and the rest of the Tlascalans ran away across that plain like scared children. Cortés at once ordered the carcasses of our two dead horses buried, hoping to preserve to our advantage the Indian belief that they were mythical monsters. The Tlascalans who had slaughtered them and those who saw it done were all killed now, and could not testify that centaurs can bleed and die.

In low spirits, we camped that night in a wide dry riverbed and supped on some small fat dogs we found in a pen; the Indians breed them for food. Needing oil with which to dress his wounds, one of the men in Alvarado's company, lacking certain sentiments I felt, cut fat from an Indian corpse and rendered it down into oil in a pan over the campfire. I was glad I didn't need to use any, my only injury being a swollen and purple eye for which El Galán advised a poultice of raw dog meat.

As I held it in place, my spirit seethed with rage at the cruel duplicity of the cacique of Xocotlán. I had been there when Cortés had asked him, through Aguilar and Malinche, about the best route to take. And that miserable Indian had said to avoid Cholula and go by way of Tlascala, where we would be welcomed. What a warm welcome we had had! Just below my anger lay uneasy doubt of Cortés for trusting the proud owner of so many dead men's heads. I said to El Galán, "Cortés should have been suspicious when our envoys failed to return. It's clear now that the cacique of Xocotlán deceived us when he said this route was safe."

"Maybe it wasn't he who deceived us," a voice behind me said. I looked around and saw Gonzalo, the former traitor, firelight glowing on his brooding face. He squatted between us and stared at me with eyes both malicious and somber. "Would Aguilar or Cortés have known the difference if that cacique had really said just the opposite? To *avoid* Tlascala?"

In the tense silence that followed, a pine cone in the fire went up in a spurt of flame. Malinche rode across my mind, black hair blowing back.

"A traitoress?" El Galán demanded. "That beautiful creature, so noble in appearance, so gentle-voiced and kind?"

"She's an Indian," Gonzalo muttered. "Just because she speaks some Spanish now and lights a candle to the Virgin doesn't change that. Blood to blood. She's not of our race. Look at how Melchorejo deserted us."

"Melchorejo was Melchorejo!" I shouted. "Malinche is Malinche. She would never betray us."

He gave me a smug and irritating smile. "I am not the only one who has realized that she could have told Aguilar anything she pleased, and like a parrot he turned it into Spanish for Cortés. He wouldn't suspect a thing!"

I suddenly hated this former traitor now relishing his suspicion of treachery in another. "Why are you vomiting this on *me?*"

He smirked. "You are Cortés' eyes and ears, no? You are his spy, no? I'm just giving you the chance to do your job again." A mean triumph gleamed in his eyes. It was clear to me that he had done some brooding and had concluded that it was not by pure chance that I had drawn from him the confession about the plot in which he had taken part. He must also be aware of my high regard for Malinche.

"For a former traitor you're very zealous, Gonzalo," I said with contempt.

His eyes took on a doglike look; squatting there he made me think of a hound, the fawning sort that pants and slavers at the master's feet. "Cortés punished me with a flogging when he could have had me hanged. And when I begged to march with him to Moctezuma's city so as to have a chance to redeem myself, he let me come. And I am going to merit his faith in me. He is going to know what I suspect about this Indian girl." Inflamed by his own loyalty, he jumped to his feet. "I gave you your chance to be loyal to Cortés, and don't be surprised if I tell him you refused it!" He turned and ran in the direction of Cortés' tent.

I stood up, intending to run after him and stop him if I had to knock him unconscious, but then I knew that unless I killed him he was going to bring Cortés his bone of suspicion.

I sank down and sat staring into the embers of the fire and moodily fed them a few twigs and leaves, the voices of El Galán and the several others mere wind to me. Imps and devils leered from the brief bursts of flame, mocking me for my impotence now, in contrast to my nights of secret passion. Ever since Cortés had forbidden me to speak to Malinche, I had lived a secret life with my Indian princess. In reveries and in sleep, she and I became companions of the night, sometimes as innocent as children picking flowers and singing songs together but sometimes locked in thrilling embraces that emptied me of lust. The priest at home had once warned me against those succubuses that fasten themselves onto a man in the night, the Devil's temptresses that make him fornicate against his will. But he had never warned me that one could assume the face and form of a woman who walked by day quite innocent of those dreams I had of her.

Innocent! She was innocent of any treachery! But would Cortés know that as I did? Or would he believe Gonzalo? I leaped to my feet, furious at myself for having brooded by the fire so long instead of starting at once on my mission: to defend Malinche. El Galán asked where I was off to; I told him; he tried to deter me, saying I had no proof of her innocence beyond my evident infatuation with her. Ignoring him, I raced toward Cortés' tent, wondering what I could say in her defense and whether I could even get past Cortés' sentry.

The tent was large, four-walled, peak-roofed. Lighted from within, it glowed softly. Outside the closed flap of the doorway, Orteguilla was standing beside a sleepy sentry. I had almost reached him when Gonzalo came out looking both pleased (a small smirk) and chastened (a somber backward look). Seeing me, he detoured abruptly.

As I panted up, Orteguilla said, "Do you know what that whoreson just told Cortés about Doña Marina?"

"He has babbled his suspicions. I'm here to defend her."

"Save your breath. When I spoke out in her behalf Cortés dismissed me. There's nothing you can do where I failed. He sent a sentry after her. He's in a cold fury. I think he believes Gonzalo, halfway anyhow. Here she is."

I turned. Malinche was coming toward the tent beside a tall sentry. Her face looked serene. She smiled at me and at Orteguilla as the sentry who had brought her opened the tent flap so she could enter and then hurried away. The other one roused himself for an instant, then fell into his doze again, resting on his pike as sentries do. Orteguilla and I, as one man, moved to the tent flap and laid our ears against it.

I was the luckier. My right eye was a handspan from the crack where the tent flap was not tightly closed. I edged that way and peered through. I could see only part of the interior: Cortés was seated in his carved armchair; much of his armor had been removed; the greave for the right leg lay on the floor where Orteguilla had evidently dropped it on being ordered out. The helmet, pauldrons, and gauntlet had also been shed. At either side of the breastplate Cortés' wide shoulders jutted; his face looked as hard as the metal below it. I knew how much his emotion had mastered him, to let a woman see him thus half-clad. And yet his somber air of authority was such that his appearance did not diminish him. To me the contrast between the vulnerable exposed arms and the armor he still wore expressed his state of mind: somewhat vulnerable to Gonzalo's suspicions, his heart armored against Malinche's defense of herself. He was saying, "A serious accusation has been made against you, Doña Marina. You are suspected of treachery, of sending us here to our possible deaths. The Tlascalans' hostility makes it impossible for me to dismiss this possibility." Parting the tent flap a trifle I was able to see Malinche, facing him.

Something hard prodded my shoulder. It was the butt of the sentry's pike. "Get out," he advised me succinctly. Orteguilla was gazing up at the moon as if he had never eavesdropped in his life. The sentry's crooked nose had been broken. He raised the pikestaff as if quite ready to break mine. "Get out," he said again in the same flat tone. I saw in his small cold eye that breaking noses might be his favorite pastime. I left.

But having disappeared into the nearby grove of plane trees, I quickly circled through them and came to the rear of the tent, unguarded as I had hoped. No doorway there offered me a slit to peer through, but I laid my ear against the tent's fabric. Cortés was saying "You deny any wish to ingratiate yourself with Moctezuma by defeating my effort to reach his city. You tell me the Aztecs are not dear to you. But the blunt fact is that they are Indians and you are an Indian, and most people feel loyalty to their own kind."

Her voice was low but did not sound frightened. "My own kind? At San Juan Ulua that night I swam ashore I did not return to my own kind. Did not choose slavery with them, or death. I stayed with Spaniards.If Tlascalans defeat you, I am defeated. Why would I lie, betray you? If you die, I die."

"By my conscience! You are very cool-headed for a woman!" Did I imagine it, or was there a note of admiration in his voice?

"You are not a fool," she said. "There is another explanation for the hostility of these Tlascalans besides my treachery."

"What?"

"The Zempoallan envoys you sent ahead may have boasted of the gifts Moctezuma sent you. So these Tlascalans see you as friends of the Aztecs."

"I never thought of that, I must admit!"

"I want to leave now. I am very tired."

"You will leave when I give you permission to leave. Do not get above yourself, Doña Marina." Cortés' voice was no longer harsh. "I want you to stay here awhile. There are matters I wish to discuss with you." His light tone changed to a shout. "Orteguilla! Where are you? I want the rest of this armor off!"

Was he going to undress in front of her? Or did the tent have some sort of screen or curtain? What did he want to "discuss" with her?

"You again?" The sentry's pike had preceded him around the corner of the tent as he made his rounds; he thrust it toward me. I leaped away and raced for the grove, my feelings in turmoil. Instead of going toward the pine grove where Alvarado's company was camped, I doubled around and hid in some bushes through which I could peer and see the door to Cortés' tent. The sentry was back at his post, dozing upright. In the stillness of the night I could hear faint voices within the tent. Orteguilla wished Malinche good night. He emerged, closed the tent flap with care, and trotted away.

Kneeling there in those bushes, I waited for Malinche to emerge. At any moment she would, I told myself. The moments passed. I heard Cortés' laugh, the sound of his voice but not the words. More moments passed, a veritable army of moments, as many as the multitude of cold stars looking down at me, but she did not come out of the tent. Exhaustion after the day's long march and battle proved stronger than my urgent need to clarify my doubts. I woke with a start and looked wildly about, not sure at first where I was. I saw then that the tent was dark. Had she left while I slept? An urge to creep to the tent flap and peer in was stilled as the sentry coughed.

I plodded to the pine grove, spread out my blanket beside El Galán, who lay on his back, snoring gently. The sound was comforting as I lay wide-eyed beside him, for all around us was the dark expanse of this land where they hated us. I suddenly remembered what El Galán had once told me: great danger can be a stimulus to sexual desire.

"What happened?" he asked me sleepily. "Where have you been?"

"I didn't feel like sleeping."

"Did you have any luck defending Doña Marina?"

"There was no need to. She defended herself very well."

"I don't imagine Cortés was too hard to convince." Now he was up on one elbow, facing me. "I've lived some and I have eyes in my head. Lately he's regarded her at times with that look a man sends toward a woman he intends to enjoy."

The wind of truth howled in my hollow, aching heart. I knew the look he meant, had seen it, but had chosen to confuse myself with thoughts of Juana of Orléans, noted for her purity as much as for her valor and her voices.

"And there's something else to consider." El Galán sounded ready to chat all night. "Cortés is a general, and knows he needs her voice. Gonzalo's accusation of treachery has sharpened Cortés' awareness of her importance to this venture. To bind her to him with the tie of physical passion would not be a stupid move. A well-bounced woman tends to feel a definite loyalty to the source of her pleasure. I think that before long Cortés will have her on his wrist like a hooded falcon."

"Do you intend to pitch a tent and dwell on this one subject forever?" I cried.

"Poor Arturo. And you found her first." His voice was amused but kind.

Tears stung my eyeballs. I turned my head away; the moonlight might make them glimmer. As I feigned sleep a voice in my head insisted that El Galán was wrong, all wrong. But the hollow inside my chest through which a night wind blew told me he was right.

155

19

I woke foggy-headed after troubling dreams; soon enough I was as alert as the rest of the army, keenly aware of our peril, ready for another Tlascalan attack. But late in the morning two of our missing Zempoallan envoys were returned to us, brought by polite Tlascalan messengers who said, we soon learned, that we had been attacked by mistake by a border patrol that had been alarmed by our appearance. A cacique named Xicotencatl the Younger sent his regrets for this mistake.

"But nonetheless we'll sleep in our armor tonight," Alvarado said when he told us this, "because Indians are very tricky."

He was soon proved right. Later that same day the other two Zempoallan envoys came back to us, weary and frightened. Because of the fluke of an unlatched door they had managed to escape from a cageful of sacrificial victims where they had been imprisoned after being severely questioned about us. Cortés had the captains tell us what he had learned from them: that our invasion of Tlascala had caused great turmoil and a sharp division of opinion among the caciques and nobles of the various towns when they met in council in the capital. Some were in favor of letting us pass westward unmolested, but the most revered leader in the republic, a blind old man named Xicotencatl the Elder, was convinced that the weight of evidence favored our being friends of the Aztecs and therefore enemies of Tlascalans. The gifts Moctezuma had lavished on us and the fact that a great number of his conquered Zempoallans accompanied us were two indications of this, he said. To tamely let us pass through Tlascala would seem to Moctezuma a sign of weakness of which he would surely take advantage later by mounting an all-out attack on the republic neither he nor his ancestors had been able to conquer. Our two envoys, who had observed a part of this debate before being imprisoned, had no doubt that this blind old man would persuade his namesake and other dissenters to believe as he did.

Nonetheless Cortés and the captains determined that we had to march forward toward Moctezuma's city. Retreat would be a sign to these indomitable Tlascalans of timidity that would release a savage scorn and provoke attacks as savage. Warily we set forth the morning after the return of the envoys. From the high flank of the mountain we rounded we could see what lay ahead to the west: other mountains, among them volcanos like the one looming above us. Behind we could see the white cone called Orizaba; ahead were two stupendous peaks, only their snowy summits jutting above the lower sierra that formed our horizon. The Zempoallans knew their names: Popocatepetl and Ixtaccihuatl. The last meant ''Sleeping Princess'' because, from the high valley of Anahuac where Moctezuma's city stood that mountain had the form of a shapely woman reclining on her back. A lesser peak far to the south interested me much more when they said it was called Malinche.

I marched forward wondering why a female child had been given the name of a mountain. Later I learned from her that it was only a soubriquet her father had chosen when she was an infant, since among her people it was considered bad luck for a child's birth-name to be bandied about outside the immediate family. But all such idle thoughts were cut off abruptly when we heard drums and shrill flutes and saw on a plateau ahead thousands of Tlascalan warriors running toward us, shooting arrows and hurling spears. The sight of our horses caused a sudden wavering, but the enemy summoned the courage to attack with massed fury. It was lucky for us that they chose this wide level place for their show of bravery, for Cortés could use the Spanish phalanx in which we had been well-drilled, the cavalry driving a deadly opening wedge into the enemy ranks, leaving a great number of them dead. The living retreated, but almost at once thousands more burst out of some woods nearby, all in red and white, armed with pikes, slings, lances, obsidian swords, thick cotton breastplates, and huge shields of wood and leather with bright feather designs. They did not carry their banner to the front as we did, but to the rear—a white crane with wings spread. They yelled like devils. We fought them until sundown and killed eight of their chief warriors, but they managed to kill another of our horses and they dragged the body off the field when they retreated. Soon they would know that it was no supernatural creature, just meat and bone and sinew.

My knowledge of what happened on the large scale in this battle and all the rest was pieced together from what others said after the fighting was over. I entered each encounter with a prayer to God and I assumed that he wanted me, a Christian and a Spaniard, to have a longer life than whatever heathen opposed me, and by this faith and a certain cold exertion of my own will I turned myself into a kind of machine for killing, to make sure that no one killed me. I discovered that I disliked killing even heathens, and I wondered if it had been the same with my father when he was helping to rid Cuba of Caribs.

That night we found a large empty temple which we could use as our fortress and for several days Cortés made brief forays, leaving the main body of his troops to defend this bastion. We left it on the fourth day, thinking the Tlascalans subdued, only to hear their drums and flutes and conch horns and to confront an army of them so vast it made the earlier battles seem like children's play with toy soldiers: later Cortés estimated this Tlascalan army at one hundred forty thousand. But again we fought them on level ground, and again our cannons, musketeers, arquebusiers, and cavalry cut great lanes of dead men in their ranks. After several hours of this there was a division of the enemy, some leaving the field, others staying. But these soon saw the severe losses they had suffered, and disappeared pell-mell, a rout marked by scattered shrieks of fading defiance and the slow drumbeats of defeat. None of our horses was killed, and we lost only one man. About sixty of us were wounded, but I was not among these. We all knelt in prayer on the battlefield and thanked God for this victory.

It had seemingly impressed the Tlascalans, for the next morning when I got up I was startled to see an Indian coming toward me in a cloak tied on one shoulder in the Tlascalan manner. He was holding out a big basket of cherries and urged me with a nod to help myself. I saw many other Tlascalans passing among us with baskets of fruit and tortillas, and I decided they were peace offerings.

I had just popped the first cherry into my mouth, savoring its sweet juice, when I saw Malinche talking to one of these friendly Tlascalans and saw that he looked uneasy. She turned and hurried toward Cortés' tent. I ran after her and fell in step beside her, offering my handful of cherries. She shook her head. "Enjoy them. They may be the last you will ever eat. I think the Tlascalans who brought them are spies, pretending that the younger Xicotencatl now wants to make peace."

In a few minutes I saw Spanish soldiers rounding up the Tlascalans with the cherries. Later I learned that under questioning the smiling visitors first protested their innocence but at last admitted that they had been ordered to our camp to spy out what they could about us. Under further "questioning" at the hands of a fellow we called The Executioner, who had flogged Gonzalo and hanged his cohorts, they confessed that Xicotencatl the Younger planned a night attack on us because their priests had said that Spaniards turned coward after the sun sank. Cortés sent the spies back to Xicotencatl with their hands cut off, punishment for having brought gifts that were false evidence of friendship. I was at first very sickened, for it seemed to me unnecessarily cruel to have treated them so, but then I realized that Cortés was dealing with a savage people who did not understand subtleties and that he was desperate for us, vastly outnumbered as we were, and with retreat down that gorge impossible. I had learned, too, what Malinche had meant when she said those cherries might be the last I would ever eat. She had instantly suspected the worst, as if she had heard the old adage "Beware of Greeks bringing gifts."

Thanks to her suspicion, we were prepared for their night attack as we otherwise would not have been, believing that Indians will never fight after dark. With that day's dusk, some ten thousand Tlascalans moved silently down on us from the neighboring hills, but since they were unfamiliar with night fighting, we routed them by moonlight.

After three days of sporadic battles, Cortés attempted to parley with Xicotencatl through our interpreters. A Tlascalan we had captured pointed the young chieftain out to us, and Cortés had Malinche call out to him that we had come here with only peaceful intentions, had fought because we had been forced to defend ourselves, and now asked only permission to pass through their country. One of the warrior chieftains surrounding Xicotencatl then stepped forward and shouted something at Cortés. Malinche translated his words into Spanish with no evidence of fear, though I saw some soldiers around me turn pale. "Feel free, strangers, to make your way to our capital city. There we will sacrifice you all to our gods, and strip the flesh from your bones and cook it with chili sauce and vend it in the streets!"

This threat might have seemed merely the ferocious boasting of an angry child had we not learned that these Tlascalans were cannibals. In a town where we had camped for a night on finding all the warriors gone and only women and children there, we had found big wooden cages full of men and women being fattened for sacrifice, after which their bodies would be eaten by the populace, they told us. We had set the poor creatures free; having nowhere else to go, they stayed with us. Such victims had either been captured in battle or had been sold to the Tlascalans by slave traders who procured them in various ways, sometimes from parents facing starvation.

The Tlascalans made a last bold effort to overwhelm us, were decimated by our guns and crossbowmen, and retreated tossing back defiant cries that included the word *chili* a number of times.

The next day, to our surprise, Xicotencatl the Younger arrived in person, along with fifty warrior chiefs, to offer peace. He was a tall Indian with a long, pockmarked face, a high feather headdress, and a toga with a horizontal frieze reaching just below the knees and tied at one broad copper-colored shoulder. He carried himself with royal dignity, acknowledged our victory, and begged us to enter Tlascala's main city. "Either you must kill me now as I stand here or accept my lifelong friendship," he declaimed. Cortés embraced him, said he accepted his friendship and offered his in return. I witnessed this meeting at quite close quarters and I did not have the slightest doubt that Xicotencatl was sincere.

On September 23, having entered Tlascala on the first day of the month, we marched six leagues to the capital, where we were met by a procession of nobles and priests and learned that the city's usual thirty thousand inhabitants were swelled by thousands more, come from near and distant towns to see the white gods enter. We made a fine procession ourselves, three hundred ninety-nine Spaniards and nearly twenty-five hundred Zempoallans, counting the *tamanes*. We foot soldiers behaved like the victors we were, heads high and marching brisk.

And we were treated like victors, given six stone buildings around the main plaza with braziers of charcoal in all the rooms. But the food we were offered tasted flat and strange and we learned that for nearly a century the Tlascalans had done without salt, for that commodity was controlled by the Aztecs. Cotton, too, was scarce; most Tlascalans wore a coarse cloth called *nequen* woven of cactus fibers.

But Cholula, the city lying between us and Tenochtitlán, suffered no such lacks, Xicotencatl the Younger told us bitterly. The Cholulans were abject and servile toward the Aztecs and could be expected to do Moctezuma's bidding. Our Tlascalan ally had now learned that we were proceeding westward against Moctezuma's command, and he said, "Do not go to Cholula! The rooftops will be piled with stones to pitch on your head as you pass. Stay here with us as long as you wish. But do not go to Cholula."

Cortés smiled and said that since he had been told to expect a friendly reception at Tlascala, he would not avoid Cholula on the basis of mere rumor, and asked for further information about Moctezuma, who interested him more than Cholula did.

The Tlascalan said, "He has ruled for nearly seventeen years. In his youth he was a warrior, I have heard. He now lives in idle luxury. But I have been told that from the day of his coronation he has been plagued by many evil omens, and by prophecies of disaster to the Aztecs." He grinned. "Your defiance of his command to leave must disturb him deeply."

That we would ever see the famous Moctezuma was thrown suddenly into doubt, for two weeks after our welcome to Tlascala I found out that a good many soldiers wanted to abandon the march to his city. They had rallied around the Three Moors, brothers we had nicknamed that because of their dark coloring. Rosario, the tallest, fiercest, and darkest, spoke out to at least thirty Spanish soldiers in his deep, hoarse voice. "These Tlascalans treat us good, feed us nice, but how long can we trust cannibals? What we ought to do is thank them for the warning about those Cholulans with the rocks on the roofs and turn around and march back to Vera Cruz and wait there until King Carlos sends us reinforcements. There's too few Spaniards here."

Nods and murmurs of approval greeted this. I said, seeing all hope of my meeting Don Oro go glimmering: "But we have our Zempoallans. And what about the Tlascalan soldiers Cortés hopes to get from Xicotencatl?"

"There's too few Spaniards," Rosario boomed.

"Three hundred and ninety-nine. Only three hundred Greeks held the pass at Thermopylae against the whole Persian army," I said.

Rosario shrugged. "I don't know about any Thermop-whatever, but defending a pass is one thing and marching into enemy territory is another, and I want more Spaniards by me. And I'll wait for reinforcements in Vera Cruz if I have to march back there by myself."

"Be careful, Rosario," Gonzalo called, looking at me. "When Cortés learns you talked like this you can look for a flogging!"

"Yours was well-deserved," I said, reminded of my duty as a spy. I faced Rosario, a good bit taller than I was and twice as wide. "When I tell Cortés that some men want to go back to Vera Cruz I do not intend to mention your name or any other."

I found Cortés in the palace of Xicotencatl the Elder, Malinche at his side. The younger Xicotencatl was there too, and many Tlascalan nobles, gathered in a large stone hall with impressive bas-reliefs of warriors and gods. The blind ancient ruler stood at the center of the group, eyes staring fixedly below the band that crossed his forehead, binding his gray hair which hung nearly to his shoulders. His legs were not withered but still muscular, and his square-jawed face had also retained its strength. Even facing Cortés, he was so impressive that I felt hesitant about interrupting with even so important a message.

But Cortés, knowing I would not intrude except for a good reason, beckoned me forward. I saw that he was elated. "The elder Xicotencatl has just promised me ten thousand Tlascalan warriors to march with us to Moctezuma's city!"

"Five hundred Spaniards would do you more good," I said.

He sobered. "Meaning?"

When I told him his face darkened. "In other words, a mutiny is brewing?"

"It might come to that." My eyes wandered to Malinche. Was her face softer, or did I imagine it? Did she look somehow different? Cortés' voice drew my gaze back to him. "You were wise to bring me this news promptly. By God, I'd make a good muleteer! *¡El Arriero!* I have to keep driving balky cowards toward the destiny they want to flee!" He turned to Malinche, told her to make his apologies to the elder Xicotencatl, and strode from the council hall.

A few minutes later I heard his crier call the soldiers to form ranks below the palace steps where he stood. He told us of the huge Tlascalan contingent that would join us, and once again he was able to shame the cowards, inspire every man to march with him to the land of the Aztecs. Smiling, confident, without a fear or a doubt, he aroused in each of us the courage that would not have been there without him. Like a magical mirror he reflected back into us everything we wanted to be as men.

When he stopped speaking all faces were animated, eyes flashing, smiles parting dark beards. And then I saw Malinche. She stood at the foot of the steps, Orteguilla beside her. She was looking up at Cortés as though she saw God himself standing there.

I had lost her. And I could not blame her for this adoration, or him for having succumbed and made her his mistress, for he was flesh and blood after all. But it was bitter to realize that those two would never have known each other except that I had looked up one sunny day in Tabasco and seen walking toward me a vision who embodied all beauty and all desire.

Cortés chose to take only six thousand Tlascalan warriors with us; he did not want to be too vastly outnumbered by our new allies, allies as yet unbaptized, although an oath of loyalty to King Carlos had been sworn. The day before we left, Cortés made Xicotencatl the Younger promise that he would see to it that the Tlascalans did not eat any more people, but this was a promise easily made since we would not be there to see that it was carried out.

On the morning we marched from Tlascala, one sorrowful face stood out to me. It was that of Xicotencatl the Elder, who appeared at the top of the steps to his palace with some old nobles who surveyed the ranks of soldiers massing in the square below. His blind eyes stared at nothingness from deep sockets. At last he shook his head slowly and departed, followed into the palace by the others. His evident sorrow suggested to me that through some rare gift of inner sight he had envisioned many perils that lay ahead of us. Xicotencatl the Younger would remain in Tlascala, but two other sons of the old man were marching with us that morning toward whatever dangers he saw or imagined.

20

The road to Cholula was a dogleg of a little more than twelve leagues, though the two republics were closer than that as the crow flies. We were a dragon with a small body of Spaniards and a monstrously long tail: nine thousand Tlascalan and Zempoallan warriors and above a thousand *tamanes*. In a land without any pack animals or wheeled vehicles it was natural that a low class of human beings should be used as burros or mules are in Spain, but I felt rather sorry for them. I wondered what our toilsome adventure looked like from their eyes. Perhaps it was all as puzzling and incomprehensible as God's ways often are to us.

It was sunset when we neared the city of Cholula. Cortés decided that we would camp for the night on the border of a stream and enter in the morning, rested. We had just settled ourselves there when several Cholulan caciques and their attendants came along the road to the city. They were dressed in a manner quite different from any Indians we had seen, in flowing burnooses of fine cotton.

THE MARCH TO TENOCHTITLÁN

They offered us a fulsome welcome to their city but balked at admitting our Tlascalans, ancient enemies. Cortés courteously agreed that these allies would camp outside the wall to rejoin us when we left to march on to Tenochtitlán, so next morning we entered Cholula followed only by half of our Zempoallans. Hordes of citizens lined the street to see us pass: tiny children, tottering old men, and every age between. Flowers were strewn at our feet and music from flutes and horns made it all seem like a great public fiesta in our honor.

The main part of the city was in a bowl in the hills overlooked by a vast pyramid of Quetzalcoatl, the base covering forty acres, and there were three hundred smaller temples. The whiteness of the great pyramid in that cool bright sunlight hurt my eyes; it had just been given a new layer of stucco. This was done every fifty-two years, the most significant time span among the Aztecs and the people they dominated, for they believed that at the end of such a cycle the sun may cease to appear in the sky and all things perish. In Aztec cities there was a very solemn celebration of the safe passage through that dread hour: a new fire was kindled in the breast cavity of a sacrificial victim and priests lighted torches from it and brought this sacred flame to all the other temples. But even after we learned this, we did not realize that our approach to Tenochtitlán at just this time added to our dread significance.

We were offered quarters in several large palaces, and in the great courtyard of one a feast was spread by slaves who brought many dishes we had never tasted, among these a chilled and frothy sweet drink made from *chocolatl,* the favorite beverage of the great Moctezuma himself, we were told. Noble Cholulans in burnooses came to our courtyard with their wives to welcome us and again music played delightfully and an air of gaiety prevailed.

We sat on straw mats alongside lengths of fine cotton cloth on which, among the various bowls and platters of food, were scattered flowers. There is an old Spanish saying that too many flowers may hide the stench of a murder, but I truly believed that envy as well as an ancient hostility had made our allies speak so harshly of Cholulans. By opting to stay on peaceful terms with the Aztecs, they certainly had a better life than the Tlascalans—they even had beggars in the streets, a sure sign of affluence. Thousands of visitors came to worship at the famous pyramid and to buy the many wares in the markets scattered through the town, particularly gauzy cottons and delicate pottery.

Watching Malinche sip from a goblet shaped like an open lily, I noticed that the wife of one of the Cholulan caciques knelt close beside her and seemed very enamored of her, if that is the right word for the admiration of one woman for another. This Cholulan woman was much older than Malinche, stocky, with flashing black eyes, heavy gold earrings, and a brooch of carved jade. Before long she and Malinche had their heads together and were conversing intimately and with great animation. Cortés was paying no attention to his "tongue," for his real one was wagging in merry conversation with the captains seated near him. As I watched Malinche and her new friend, it occurred to me that the older woman might have been instructed to strike up this acquaintance for the purpose of learning what she could about us. Would Malinche be wary? I even thought of going to where she knelt to remark, in Spanish, that there was something about this overly friendly woman I did not like. But then Orteguilla, drunk on the pulque served, was urged into reciting some ribald rhymes that took my attention from Malinche, though when we departed from the feast I noted the older woman still beside her.

During the next several days all went pleasantly. I wandered along clean streets, stared at by Cholulans upon whom my blond hair made the usual impression. Along with other visitors, El Galán and I went up the hundred twenty steep steps of the main pyramid to its vast top level, an acre across, where an enormous statue of the god wore a headdress of flames, seen at night for many leagues. With greater awe I looked out at those two great volcanos we had first glimpsed in Tlascala. Popocatepetl was sending up a great volume of smoke or steam that rose in spite of a strong wind straight as a pikestaff far into the sky. As I stared, a priest sounded the hour on a long trumpet; it was a haunting, mournful wail, like the yearning complaint of that fuming mountain which could not ever hope to awaken the serene Sleeping Princess at its side.

On our return to our quarters, El Galán and I learned that in our absence some messengers from Moctezuma had arrived. Juan Morla said they had been very sharp with Cortés; their master was angry at our stubborn approach to his capital and they urged us to retrace our steps to Tlascala immediately. "Oh, but they were arrogant dogs," Juan Morla said, "and they passed by us common soldiers as if we were turds on the pavement, and that's why I made it my business to overhear when Doña Marina translated their words to Cortés. And I hope Xicotencatl was wrong when he said these Cholulans are kissers of the Aztec ass.'' He gestured at the hills surrounding the city. ''Because we're in their pocket, no?''

The change in our hosts' attitude was abrupt. No nobles or caciques visited us that night, and the next evening—when Cortés made a point of sending several captains to invite them to dine—they all pled sudden illness. The slaves brought us only scanty food and left without serving it to us.

That night Cortés sent out some Zempoallans disguised in burnooses to mingle with the populace, and they returned to say that stones and spears were stockpiled on the flat roofs of the buildings overlooking the road out of town, just as we had been warned. Big holes with upright spikes fixed within had been dug at intervals as though in hope of trapping and killing our horses and, even more chilling, they heard that a number of slave children had been offered up as a special sacrifice to the gods, in the hope that these deities would smile on some venture the Cholulans contemplated. That it concerned us we could not doubt. But what was their concrete plan against us?

When I left Cortés' headquarters after learning this bad news, I saw two familiar female figures crossing the plaza together, lost in deep conversation: Malinche and the Cholulan cacique's wife, with whom she had been on such good terms at that first happy banquet. When they saw me, the Cholulan woman abruptly hurried away. Malinche went toward the stone building where she and Cortés slept. I ran forward and stopped her as she began to go up the steep stone steps. ''Malinche!''

She turned. New clothing had been provided her in this city of beautiful cloth, and she wore a burnoose of a pale green cotton so fine it floated as she moved. Heavy gold pendants hung from her ears. A hood gave her a mysterious look. Beside her, forming a balustrade, was a great stone serpent head, grinning to show wide-spaced teeth. ''No one ever calls me Malinche any more,'' she said. ''Except Indians.''

''I will call you Doña Marina if that is the name you prefer,'' I said stiffly. ''I did not mean to offend you.''

''You didn't offend me.'' She smiled down at me, waiting.

I looked up and realized once more that she was perhaps the single most important member of our expedition except for Cortés himself. How could I have dreamed this outcome when I first saw her in Tabasco, stricken with terror at her capture by a god? ''Your friendship with that Cholulan lady might be dangerous,'' I told her.

"Why?"

"She's older than you and has a wily look. She could pry secrets out of you."

"Or the reverse."

"What?"

"Perhaps I can pry some secrets from her."

"She sought you out. I think she had a reason."

"She did. She wants me to marry her son."

"What!"

"I have told her that I am a princess being held hostage and that I am very unhappy. She says that her son saw me at the banquet and liked me very much. She has invited me to come and live at her house. Her husband is an important noble. I will be safe there, she told me. Why, she asked me tonight, should I share the fate of my captors?"

"What fate?"

"That is what I hope to find out when I visit her tomorrow."

My skin prickled with alarm. "It could be a trick! They know how important you are to Cortés. You could be held there as hostage!"

"Then you can come with me as my bodyguard." Her serenity was maddening. "Yes, I must have a bodyguard. For if I were really a prisoner as I told her, I would never be allowed to go freely about the city, true?"

"Does Cortés know about this plan of yours?"

"No. I don't want him to. He would refuse to let me go." She came down two steps so our eyes were level. "No one knows but you. If he learns, it will be you who told him." She paused, eyeing me sternly. "I am sure that Cholulan woman knows the plan they are going to use against us. I think I can squeeze it out of her. At least I must try. Will you help me, Arturo?"

The Devil himself would have agreed, persuaded by those dark, yearning eyes, that sweet voice, and I was no devil, only a very young man trying to forget that I was in love with her. "If you will come to visit me when I am put in irons."

"If that happens, I'll demand that I be put in irons too." We both knew that this disgrace was not the risk we faced. If the Cholulan woman had set a trap for Malinche as I feared, we would both be the hostages of a people who killed little children atop the pyramid of the gentle god who had preached to them of mercy.

We said good night and as I watched her climb the steps, the hem of her full skirt swaying from side to side, I realized that now she spoke Castilian with no more accent than if she had been born a Portuguese. I remembered El Galán telling me that were it not for that miserable law that forbade our sleeping with Indian women, we would all by now be able to speak the Nahuatl tongue with some fluency, as there is no better place to learn a strange language than in bed. I turned abruptly away, but then was cheered at the thought that even if she slept tonight at Cortés' side, a secret would lie there between them, a secret she had just shared with me.

My anxiety about tomorrow's venture took form in a troubling dream of the Cholulan woman, who had hidden Malinche in a big chest and sat on top of it, grinning at me evilly, holding in one hand a knife of black obsidian with which she made curious gestures in the air which I knew were very obscene.

The next day, wearing full armor, I went with Malinche to the house of the Cholulan lady. They sat together on a stone bench in a pretty garden and I stood frowning a few feet away, watching Malinche for the signal she would give me; when she brushed her forehead with her hand I would interrupt them and say that it was time for Malinche to leave. After they had talked quite a while, Malinche made the motion I had been watching for. I stepped forward and pointed toward the street. "Did you learn anything?" I asked in Spanish.

"It is worse than I thought." She turned to the Cholulan woman and said something to her, then stood up. "I told her that I have to return with you now, and that I will gather together my clothing and jewels and escape tonight."

Her hostess stood up, too, and spoke to Malinche in an imperious tone.

Malinche turned an uneasy face to me. "She is coming with us."

They preceded me out of the garden and along the street to the courtyard of Cortés' palace. As we went up the stairs to Malinche's sleeping room she turned to me and said, "I asked her to come into my room with me to help me pack. I'll leave quickly. You keep her there."

I waited outside the room, sword drawn. Malinche ran out, but when the Cholulan woman tried to follow I barred the way with my sword and she stepped back, her face sharp with suspicion as she stared after Malinche's receding figure. I took hold of the woman's shoulder and turned her around and pointed into the room with the sword. She stood there staring about her, trapped. In minutes Cortés,

Malinche, and several captains hastened along the corridor and into the room and I watched from the doorway while Cortés questioned her through Malinche.

The terrified woman admitted that Moctezuma had sent bribes to the most powerful of the Cholulan nobles, among them this woman's husband, and had asked their aid in his plan to dispose of us before we came any nearer his city. When we started to march out of Cholula, impeded by the holes in the road, the missiles on the roof, and the barricades, thousands of Aztec warriors now bivouacked a few leagues from the city would march in, dispose of our Tlascalans, and then join the Cholulans in defeating us. Of those who lived, twenty would be sacrificed in Cholula, but the rest would be marched in fetters to Tenochtitlán, there at last to meet Moctezuma and his hungry gods.

"Why is Moctezuma so afraid of our reaching his city?" Cortés asked.

Malinche conferred with the Cholulan woman and then told us: "This is the year Two Cane, the year, according to many omens and prophecies, when a great disaster is to overtake Tenochtitlán and all the Valley of Anahuac."

And then the Cholulan took a step toward Malinche and spoke to her with a look of puzzlement and reproach.

"What is she saying?" Cortés demanded.

"She asked me why I have treated her like this. I told her that I am a Christian now."

Oh, the Madonna sweetness of her face as she stood there in her barbaric finery proclaiming this! I was struck by a kind of awe, for I thought I saw the hand of God and a reward for all those heathens we had baptized and all the idols we had thrown down and destroyed.

Cortés acted swiftly. First he bribed two Cholulan priests with Moctezuma's gold while threatening them with instant death and they confirmed the truth of what the noble's wife had said. Cortés next had Malinche instruct a Cholulan messenger to ask the nobles of the city to come to him to discuss our immediate departure. Since this was what they wanted, they arrived swiftly. Feigning sorrow, Cortés told them that since it appeared to him we were no longer welcome guests, we would march in the morning to Tenochtitlán. He asked only the aid of some two thousand men to help us transport our artillery and baggage out of the city; to this the Cholulans agreed readily. He then called all his captains and laid the plot for the morning of our exodus.

THE MARCH TO TENOCHTITLÁN

Before dawn, Cortés on horseback arranged the trap in the big central plaza where the Cholulans would send the two thousand men he had demanded. Buildings surrounded this square on three sides, a high wall on the fourth. There were only three entrances, at three corners, and these our cannon commanded. Our muskets and arquebuses were ranged along the walls, our crossbows atop the one. When the Cholulans had all marched in, most of them mere *tamanes,* Cortés took aside the nobles who had brought them and sternly revealed his knowledge of the wicked plot. They were thunderstruck. Then, at a signal from Cortés, every musket and crossbow was leveled at the leaders and the poor creatures in the center of the square, killing at least half of them, and then Cortés signaled the foot soldiers to rush in with lances and swords. Hearing the sounds of this massacre, hordes of other Cholulans outside the square poured in to aid their countrymen, but were instantly cut down by artillery or steel.

Of all this horror I was not wholly aware at the time. A terrible thing had happened to me. For the first time a lust for killing took over my being. I suppose it was caused in part by fear we all felt because of the trap we found ourselves in and in part because I had to steel myself very hard to murder those poor *tamanes* for whom I had only gentle contempt. The thunder of our guns reverberating against the buildings that enclosed the abatoir added to a madness in me as I saw my blade pierce and slash at flesh I tried to imagine as a sort of vegetation around me, a vegetation that bled.

Meanwhile our Tlascalans had poured into the city from their camp outside its walls. The Cholulans fled up into the shelter of their buildings, which we set afire, and then were hounded up their pyramids, from the tops of which they poured down javelins and burning arrows, but in our steel armor we got up the steps and set afire the wooden temples at the top so that enemies in them threw themselves headlong to earth or died in the flames. Then, through the streets, our cavalry pursued others and our Tlascalans killed and looted most savagely; this massacre went on for hours. The clean and beautiful city we had entered was finally a scene of horror, the streets lined with dead Cholulans, white walls blackened by flames. Among their six thousand dead were many nobles, including the unfortunate husband of the woman who had whispered his secrets to Malinche.

By the end of it I was not only physically spent but was also filled with an intense sorrow that alienated me from rejoicing Spaniards and loot-laden Tlascalans. Long after my sword blade was clean I sat on a step, wiping blood from it with a length of blue cotton a passing Tlascalan had let fall. Tears ran down my face, and for the first time I found it strange that such butchery should be required of a Christian soldier. The great white limestone cross that was erected atop the pyramid where the flame-crowned Quetzalcoatl had reigned did not raise my spirits.

I was present when a group of envoys arrived from Moctezuma, bringing Cortés many more gifts of gold. They said that Moctezuma sent his deep regret at the catastrophe at Cholula and disavowed any part in any plot against us. By now, the stupidest soldier among us knew that the great ruler must be trembling or raging at his failure to stop us in our march to his city in the lake.

The day before we left Cholula, our Zempoallan allies left us. Because of their recent rebellion, they feared to enter Moctezuma's city. Cortés sent word by them to Vera Cruz telling of our successful progress and urging Juan Escalante to send us immediate word of the arrival of any reinforcements from the King of Spain or any message from him telling when to expect them. I copied this letter for Cortés, the massacre having almost fatally undone the delicate bowels of his secretary. We left Cholula in the hope that at this very moment a Spanish fleet was already on its way to Vera Cruz and proud that we had come this far without the king's sanction or that of the governor of Cuba, only on the strength of Cortés' imperious will.

It was to take us farther still, up a steep sierra into cold piercing air and through the pass that lay between the great volcanos. Popocatepetl still sent up its column of smoke into the blue sky and now was rumbling like contained thunder. We had learned that this mountain was thought to be the abode of the spirits of the wicked departed rulers of the Valley of Anahuac, and there had been many. When we camped below that tremendous dark bulk at dusk, its snowy peak lost to sight above us, the intermittent rumblings we felt through the soles of our feet sent a thrill along my spine as though at any moment the mountain might send its boiling lava streaming down on me in punishment for the Indians I had killed. I was evidently different from the other soldiers, gathered cheerfully enough around their campfires, cooking an evening meal from the abundant provisions we had brought with us out of Cholula. I could not eat and all night kept waking from horrible, bloody dreams.

In the morning one of the captains, Diego Ordaz, proposed to

THE MARCH TO TENOCHTITLÁN

Cortés that he wanted to climb the volcano and asked for volunteers.
I leaped to my feet. Eight others joined, and a few Tlascalans. Cortés
smiled on the enterprise and congratulated us in front of all the other
men for our daring. To get to the top had a point; from there we
thought to look down on Moctezuma's valley.

First we passed through dense forests of fir trees that finally thinned
out and disappeared. In the thin air as we ascended, we grew light-
headed and hilarious, even though the going was hard, but at last we
were panting and pausing for breath after a dozen steps. Under our
feet the rumblings grew louder and more frequent. The Tlascalans
turned back when we reached a slope of dark gray pedregal, twisted
as it had congealed from its molten state into tumbled and fantastic
shapes. Over this I scrambled upward into the perpetual snow of the
volcano's utmost peak. All around us yawned frozen chasms. The icy
glaze underfoot was so treacherous that at one misstep we could vanish
down into one of these forever. To breathe was pure pain, like icicles
piercing into the chest, and my legs ached so that I could hardly move
them. But we pressed on upward toward the rim of the crater until,
all at once, it belched out smoke, sparks, and bits of burning cinder.
Our eyes stung and our hair and clothing were charred where the
cinders struck. Half-blinded, coughing, and believing ourselves in
peril of an even worse explosion at any moment, we had to turn back
without peering over the edge of its mouth into the bowels of this
monster mountain and without a glimpse of the fabled valley.

I broke off an enormous icicle, one of many hanging in a row off
the edge of a rock. To bring it safely down without its breaking became
a challenge and I swaggered into camp with the icicle cocked like a
musket over one shoulder. Seeing Malinche standing beside Cortés
where he had watched us making our way down the final slope of the
volcano, I went to her and, with a bow, presented her proof that I had
reached the icy summit. "A small trophy for the lady who saved our
lives at Cholula," I said, and she thanked me very sweetly.

I saw El Galán laughing at me, and I will not repeat what he said
to me privately about the icicle's shape in relation to its recipient; a
stubborn imp had not abandoned all hope.

The next morning early we pressed onward and reached the crest
of a sierra called Ahualco that rises between the two volcanos, though
lower. The night had been bitterly cold; we had weathered it by using
some great stone houses built by Moctezuma to shelter his couriers
and travelers to his capital. But the morning air was diamond-bright

and the sunlight had slowly warmed our bones as we ascended the sierra. Our spirits rose, for we knew that when we descended its other side we would tread on Moctezuma's own land and at last see the city we had suffered so much to reach.

I was in the van of the foot soldiery as usual; ahead were the captains on their horses following Cortés, with Malinche riding beside him. The trail we followed made a sudden turn around a flank of the mountain, and as the last of the horses vanished around it I heard the rider cry out "God save me!"

I rushed ahead to offer aid, but stopped, petrified like the stone from which I had broken the icicle. Below us lay the Valley of Anahuac. Never had I seen such a vista, and never will again. Awe filled me, and that uplifting of the heart that great beauty provokes.

Immediately below us were forests of oak and dark cedars, and beyond these were miles of wide fields of maize and maguey, orchards of fruit trees and gardens of flowers. These all flourished around the rim of a vast basin perhaps seventy leagues long and thirty wide, surrounded entirely by high mountains. In the center of the valley a wide blue lake was shining in the sun, and all around the irregular shoreline stood towns and hamlets, walls gleaming in the bright air, distinct at that high altitude where you could see very far, all details clear and colors vivid, the way things must look in the height of heaven. In the center of the lake stood Tenochtitlán, a jewel on blue water. Its white walls and pyramids caught the sunlight and dazzled it back into my eyes. A horse whinnied and I found that I was crossing myself.

"There!" I heard Cortés cry, exultant. "The promised land, gentlemen! The silver city!"

Behind me other soldiers were pressing forward and we began the descent. We had been nine months reaching this place and hour, and now faced the travail of the birth of that twin expectation fathered by Cortés: wealth beyond any dreams, glory for all time to come.

"I have never seen anything to equal it," El Galán said. "I feel as if I were in a dream, or a tale from *Amadís.*" The strange, rapt look of his face and the awe in his voice sharpened the edge of an emotion that was beginning to cut into my marveling wonder. It was terror.

We inched down the steep narrow trail. Behind me murmurs grew. Ahead floated our battered banner. The velvet nap was rubbed off in places and the golden fringe was dulled, which called to my mind the dented armor of the soldiers and our many wounds, some scarred over and others not yet healed. No doubt we were valiant, but valor can have an end, like youth or beauty or life itself. We were fewer than four hundred Spaniards against that formidable city; I felt that I was a fly about to entangle my feet in the outermost strand of an enormous spider web. How many more suns would rise before I looked up at the last thing I would ever see on this earth—an obsidian knife flashing downward toward my supine and helpless body?

Yet I was so young that wonder prevailed, and joy. I had reached the Silver City at last! Now for the dishes of gold, the emeralds, the pearls as big as my staring eyeballs!

Far ahead I could see Malinche, for the trail had curved outward around another shoulder of the sierra. Cloaked against the cold, a silhouette against blue sky, she stared toward Tenochtitlán, turning in her saddle to keep her eyes fixed on it. Very soon, unless we were destined to be killed first, she would encounter the ruler who had conquered her people. What was she feeling now? To hide my awe I began to whistle, a small sound in that bright air above that immense, peopled valley. A moment later a great eagle flew above us, so near I could hear the flapping of its pinions. It headed straight toward Tenochtitlán, as if to bring a warning of our alien presence.

PART V

IN THE SILVER CITY
November 5, 1519–May 15, 1520

21

When I looked down at Moctezuma's capital from a mountain pass between two volcanos and realized that I was now riding the gray mare that once had frightened me, I felt for a moment as though I, the real self I had been for nineteen years, was concealed inside the body of a strange woman in Cortés' black cape. How could that earlier Malinche be breathing this chill bright air? How could her eyes be staring down at the vast and beautiful Valley of Anahuac, at Moctezuma's city, that once-distant and legendary place?

It was a long journey that I made after I came out of the mangrove swamp in Tabasco to discover that the beast which had pursued me was no supernatural creature but only an animal called, I soon learned, a horse. The first step was taken when I dared to face that monster and those gods in armor. The next seven months took me not only from a town by the sea to the mountains surrounding Anahuac, but from pagan ignorance to knowledge of God, and from virginity to passion.

An eagle's shadow drew me into present reality, and I watched the great bird sail off over the valley in a long descending flight, its spread wings as wide as a man is tall. I looked at Cortés riding his black stallion beside me, enthralled by those far gleaming towers rising from the wide lake. He turned to me, eyes dazzled, and I saw the same smile of surprise that I had seen in his tent in Tlascala when he first saw me naked.

As we descended the wide trail, well-marked by the feet of Moctezuma's many couriers and visitors, recollections of that long journey from Tabasco passed through my mind. I could feel again the silent terror I had felt down in the ship's dark hold when a storm had the vessel groaning and tossing; I could hear once more the moans and wails of the other women huddled around me. I knew that no supernatural beings would keep the ship afloat, for Aguilar had assured us that the Spaniards were not gods: a dying horse confirmed the mortality of our captors. But what a strange race of men they were, and how incomprehensible to me a God who died in agony nailed to a cross! I did not believe Aguilar when he came down to the hold to comfort us with the promise that his God would not let us perish but would bring the ships to safe harbor.

The sunny day when we reached San Juan Ulua seemed to me a confirmation of his faith. How proud I was to find myself Cortés' interpreter, and to learn that "Doña Marina" was a name that showed his respect for me. But at that same place, what anguish I was soon to know!

A secret expectation had filled me when I was rowed with the other women hostages out to Cortés' flagship after our hasty baptism. When Aguilar said we were to be *barraganas,* I believed Cortés wanted me for himself. Because of my feeling for him, the excitement of his presence, my intense awareness of his virility, I believed he must feel corresponding emotions toward me. The shock of being given to Puertocarrero stunned and crushed me so that I let myself be led into Cortés' cabin, never expecting any lewd attack in that place. The first thing my eye fell on was the Blessed Virgin, serene on her stand in the corner. What a contrast to the scene that occurred only moments later! My horror only inflamed the half-intoxicated captain; grinning, he opened his lower garment and I saw the protruding thing reaching out toward me like a blind enraged sea-creature. When he pulled me toward the bed I broke free and tried to reach the door, but he was there before me to seize my tunic and rip it open. Backing away from him into the corner I reached blindly behind me for the statue of the Virgin; as he bent to seize the hem of my skirt I brought my weapon down on his skull. He fell heavily to the floor, a trickle of blood running down the side of his face. I could not think, could only run out of there to the ship's rail and drop like a stone into the black water of the bay. As I fell I heard the loud cheerful singing of the captains on the foredeck.

The cool depths restored some of my sanity. The shore looked a long way off, but I believed that by swimming and floating alternately I could reach it. I shed my torn clothes, which would only hamper me, and began the long swim. The pull of the current did not dismay me; it flowed to the north and away from the Spanish camp to which I had no idea of returning. When I saw a boat coming toward the anchored ships and heard one of its occupants speak in Spanish I submerged: Spaniards I would never trust again.

At last I reached the beach, deserted of even so much as a gull. I flung myself down beside a tangled clump of kelp, flotsam like myself, and lay there a while, panting and exhausted. I opened my eyes and saw the wide night sky, the evening star brighter than the rest, and I knew it was no god, as I had once believed. The stars were many and far, and the gods too, if there were gods. Neither could help me.

I sat up then and began to consider my alternatives. I could throw myself on the mercy of the Indians of the town near the beach, even though they were Aztec-ruled, or go south to the Spanish camp, tell Father Aguilar why I had attacked, perhaps killed, Captain Puerto-carrero. Having lived among the civilized people of southern Yucatán, Aguilar would understand the significance of the golden Shell of Purity, which still clung to me, and might explain to Cortés my terror of the attempted rape. Remembering it I felt shame, then outrage, then anger at Cortés, who had not wanted me.

Two choices I had, and only two. In the town of the natives here I would be a vagrant without status and would find myself a slave again, or a concubine. And if I proved unruly I might end on a stone altar. If I went back to the Spaniards, one thing could save me from whatever punishment might be in store for me: I was of use to Cortés. Without me he was mute. I began to see I had been hasty in my wish to avoid the Spanish camp. But it was a bitter choice: slavery or even death against a life spent with the Spaniards as interpreter for a man who needed only my voice and had no use for the rest of me.

A breeze from the sea touched my body and I knew that whatever I decided I had to cover my nakedness. All I had was the tangle of seaweed beside me. I stood up, loosened several long strands, washed off the sand in the sea, and fashioned a skirt by looping the kelp's stem through the belt from which my seashell was suspended.

To my astonishment, I heard my name called. Along the beach a man was coming toward me. A Spaniard. Arturo Mondragon. In the distance behind him I saw the upper temple of the Indian town. My alternatives faced me. But even before he reached me and offered me a shawl he had in his hut I had already decided to stay with the Spaniards, although I did not then let myself know why: Cortés.

In addition to the shawl, Arturo gave me his rosary. I thought it clever of him to provide me with Christian sanctuary after Aguilar explained to me what it meant. In the morning, dressed in the clean skirt and tunic I had in my hut I went with Father Aguilar to the flagship when I learned that Cortés wished to offer me his apology. I was cold and formal with him even after he made Puertocarrero, head bandaged, humbly ask my pardon. With lowered eyes I hid my pleasure when Cortés told me that from then on I was to be under his personal protection, no carnal knowledge being involved in this arrangement. I agreed to pretend that I was Puertocarrero's *barragana* in order to save his face. From that day on he treated me with the wary respect a man might give a wild animal that had once turned on him in fury.

My feelings toward Cortés went through many changes. During the time when so many soldiers were sick with the *cil*, twelve dying of it, he gave me his own cabin on the flagship, sleeping outside with the mariners. I would lie there on the high bunk hoping the door would open and he would come toward me, but he never did, and I knew that he had protected the life of an interpreter whose services he needed and who happened to be me. It did not occur to me that he had put himself to some discomfort in giving me his bed. It was only after he gave me Puertocarrero's gray mare, sending him to Spain without it, that I knew I meant much more to him than a voice that spoke Nahuatl. I was secretly amused as he explained at length how convenient it would be to have me ride beside him, ready to parley instantly with whatever natives we met. I knew how few horses he had.

His later anger with me after I went walking in a garden at Zempoalla with Arturo absolutely confirmed my secret conviction that Cortés desired me. I told myself, again, that I was wicked to use that boy's affection in order to enrage Cortés, that such behavior was alien to my real nature. I would always be ashamed of it because from the very first Arturo was good and kind with me. . . .

I was startled out of my reverie by Cortés' voice. "In what dream do you wander, Marina?" I turned toward him. Those dark and often somber eyes of his seemed to glow. Without waiting for an answer he leaned closer, smiling. "See? I did it!" His mailed arm swept out to claim as proof of valor the valley below.

Some of his exultance leaped from his body to mine. It remembered being held in those strong arms. "No other man could have brought us here," I said, and then added piously, "with God's help, to be sure."

He threw back his head and laughed. "You always prick my arrogance when it needs it!" He reached across to press my thigh, then spurred his horse and galloped ahead; a hill now shut off his view of what lay just below. My mind looked back over time past, for that caress evoked his tent in Tlascala and the night that began with an accusation of my treachery but ended so differently.

I defended myself as best I could with what Spanish I spoke then, less aware of Cortés' stern face than of his bare arms, for he was sitting in his carved armchair half undressed. The broad shoulders and biceps were the color of ivory; on the forearms a little dark hair grew. The hands were darker from having been exposed to the sun; a diamond on the forefinger of the right hand sparkled when he gestured. "If you die, I die," I told him in denying the false charge of having betrayed him. But I felt my face flush because I knew I had told a deeper truth. He was as necessary to me now as sunlight, as water, as food.

I knew that he believed me and not my accuser when he ordered me to remain with him and called Orteguilla to remove the rest of his armor. They retreated behind a drawn curtain that parted the tent to make an alcove where there was a cot and a stand holding the Virgin Mary. I stood waiting, my heartbeats marking time, my mind blank. I told myself that Cortés wanted to question me further, and at the same time I knew this was not true.

Orteguilla emerged first. His glance as he wished me good night was roguish and wise. Then Cortés strode around the edge of the curtain, and it was like seeing another man. He wore a long Indian robe of deep red, one of the many sent to him by Moctezuma. By now some of the captains occasionally wore these for comfort and to spare their Spanish clothing, but I had never seen him dressed so. He looked very tall, and less unfamiliar than in armor. He smiled. "Will you take a cup of wine with me?"

I nodded, my mouth dry as sand. He went to the trestle table where a wine keg stood, around it some pewter mugs and also the silver goblet I had seen him drink from more than once. When he turned he was holding it out to me. "Sit down, Doña Marina. And don't be nervous. I have no doubt whatever of your loyalty. Gonzalo once played the traitor, and traitors see treachery everywhere." He turned back to the wine keg and held under its spigot a plain pewter mug for himself.

My knees went weak. I sank onto a camp stool facing his armchair, into which he sank with a sigh of ease. As I tasted the wine I was only aware that his mouth had touched the cool smooth rim now pressed by mine. When he lowered his pewter cup after a long swallow he smiled again at me, lips moist with wine. I wanted to reach and touch the small white scar between his underlip and beard. I could not take my eyes from it, that small evidence of his vulnerability. To disguise my fascination I pointed to it and asked, "In what battle?"

"In no battle. I got this scar when I was seventeen, climbing a high stone wall to get into a lady's bedroom window. The wall was old, the mortar rotten, and it crumbled under my weight. Down I went, and my face met the upturned blade of a garden hoe." He smiled, one eyebrow raised. "I wish I had a more glorious adventure to tell you, Doña Marina."

"The window of your present wife?" I asked, taking the wall-climbing to be some curious Spanish courtship ritual.

"Marriage was not what I had in mind." He tipped his cup and drank again, eyes watching me with crinkles of laughter in the outer corners. "The lady was already married."

I knew what he meant: mere coupling. I also knew that this was what he wanted now, with me. My blood tingled, but I said, "In Paynala what you did is thought shameful."

His laugh was forced; I knew he did not like this reproof. "At seventeen I was an actor playing a role. A very devil with the women, less out of lust than pride. My father sent me to a famous school. But he found he could not afford to keep me there. I had to come home. I did not want people to know my family was that poor. I made up a lie to explain my return. I said I was thrown out of that school because of my many seductions of women. To sustain this lie, I climbed to that window. With very shaky knees, and a wealth of inexperience." He gave another laugh; his eyes were looking at me in surprise. "By my conscience, I've never told anyone this before. I don't know why I am telling you. Did you understand anything of what I just said?"

"I understand pride."

He leaned closer, "Do you know why I asked you to stay here with me?"

"Yes."

"You are under no suasion. I will not command this favor of you. Do you wish to stay?"

Those dark and somber eyes engulfed mine. I saw yearning in them. "Yes."

His hand reached out to touch my cheek. His eyes were half closed; his lips opened a little and I heard his breath sigh in through them. His touch was gentle. I thought how often that hand had held a sword. He opened his eyes, took my hand, raised me to my feet, rising with me. His arms went around me and drew me to him and he kissed my mouth. Paynalans do not kiss, and his lips on mine seemed as alien as his beard. His tongue opened my mouth; his hand caressed me. A haze of pleasure stole over my senses. I did not know time or place, only the sensations his touch gave me. Then I heard the distant mutter of Tlascalan drums. I became aware of the danger all around us, of the night full of enemies eager for our deaths. I clung to him tighter. The kiss ended. He led me to his narrow bed.

It seemed to give him pleasure to remove my tunic, untie my skirt and let it fall. When he saw me naked by the small flame of a candle that burned at the feet of the Virgin his smile of delight was as pleasing as his touch. But suddenly he saw something that puzzled him. My golden seashell of purity. He asked me why I wore it and I told him. Then I took it off.

At dawn when we awoke clasped in each others arms, I gave it to him. Propped on one elbow, he looked down at the small gold shell on his palm, then closed his hand around it. He seemed moved. "With this gift I will never part," he whispered. He smoothed my hair in a long caress. "Nor with you." His face was tender and unguarded and I knew how he had looked when he was young.

The thudding of hooves coming up the trail startled me from my reverie. Cortés galloped back from his brief sortie well pleased: in the nearest town below there was no sign of any warriors to impede us. But then Captain Sandoval rode down to him to say that some of his men, overwhelmed by Moctezuma's city, were too frightened to continue toward it. "It's the same in Alvarado's company, and Olid's, and I guess the rest as well, so you had better talk to them." He pointed up to where a huddle of soldiers had sat down on the trail, blocking passage for the others behind them.

Cortés looked from them to the Tlascalan warriors massed at the topmost point between the two volcanos, spears aloft as if in defiance of their ancient enemies. He spurred his stallion and galloped uptrail, followed by Sandoval. He roused the valor of the frightened Spaniards, gold and the Tlascalans' courage his main themes.

We continued down to where the woods thinned out and came to the first patches of cultivated land surrounding a village where the inhabitants came out to welcome us. To my surprise, we learned that this close to the capital there was bitterness against Moctezuma. The rustics of the valley shared none of the affluence of the dwellers in the city in the lake or the others built at intervals around its irregular shores. A villager who was the son of the cacique summed up the plight of his people. He was slender and sad-eyed, his skin a dark copper from working in the sun. "I am not an Aztec. We are of Toltec ancestry," he told us. "Moctezuma takes our young maidens to be his concubines and our young men for his armies, and this is not just." When I translated this for Cortés his face lighted up and he glanced back at the looming bulk of Popocatepetl. "I see that Moctezuma lives in the shadow of more than one volcano." He had me tell the young Toltec that we had come here to redress such wrongs.

"Long, long before the Aztecs came to this valley, the Toltecs dominated it," the young farmer said, "and before us there was a people even more ancient. The Toltecs built great cities, like Tula and Texcoco, and the great pyramids to the sun and moon at Teotihuacan. It was the Toltec ruler of Texcoco who permitted the Aztecs, then only a small band of wanderers, to inhabit an island in the lake." He shook his head in regret. "Who could guess that they would grow in number like weeds? They came here three and a half centuries ago; Toltecs had built cities here for nearly fifteen hundred years by then. But the Aztecs, being ferocious, became allies of Texcoco after only a hundred and fifty years in this valley. A young prince of Texcoco went to them and asked them to help him put down a rebel upstart who had caused a civil war and had killed his father. They did, and the alliance continued to exist until this very day."

This was, he said, of great advantage to the Aztecs, who borrowed Toltec manners, knowledge, laws, and gods. "Quetzalcoatl first appeared among the Toltecs at Tula, not among the Aztecs, as they now claim." Standing beside a field where autumn maize stood taller than he, the young farmer shook his head at life's injustice: ferocity, avarice, and unceasing industry had enabled the Aztecs finally to outdo and dominate their betters. "But for many years now there have been prophecies that foretell a great disaster to the Valley of Anahuac, and in this very year." He nodded with pleasure, as though his village would be spared this general woe.

As we advanced by easy stages toward Tenochtitlán, often along a road lined by curious natives, Cortés asked me several questions about the Aztecs: How had they grown like weeds on only a small island? Would the Toltecs be possible allies? I could only tell him what I had learned about the Aztecs' beginnings from Ato and her mother when I was a child.

In their long southward wanderings in search of a place to settle they had been sustained by their war god, Huitzilopotchli, which one of their priests found in a dark cave. The deity told them that as long as they fed him the hearts of defeated enemies he would always bring them victories. And he told them, through a priest, that one day they would come to a spot where they would see an eagle on a nopal cactus devouring a serpent held in its talons. That was the place where they would settle and prosper. After they came to Anahuac and were encamped in the thick reeds on the lakeshore and eating salamanders and algae, their chieftain went out in his canoe on the lake and came to a deserted island where he saw that eagle and serpent. So he went to the ruler of Texcoco and asked permission to live there. His name was Tenoch, and so the town his people built on the island was called Tenochtitlán, which means "city of Tenoch." They were then called Tenochans.

Hearing this, Cortés smiled. "That has the ring of myth, like the story of Romulus and Remus to explain the founding of Rome. It certainly does not explain how that small island grew into a city now said to hold a hundred thousand families."

An embassy from that city made me postpone the explanation. Several Aztec lords, to judge from their jewelry and richly embroidered *atl* panels, were followed by a dozen *tamanes* bringing Cortés gifts from the emperor: more gold, more feathered capes. They also offered a bribe: if Cortés would turn back now, return to Vera Cruz and embark for his own land, Moctezuma would give him and each of his captains four large loads of gold and would also pay a yearly tribute to his sovereign.

Cortés had me say, with great courtesy, "I could not answer to that sovereign if I were to turn back without meeting Moctezuma in his capital. There it will be much easier to arrange such matters as tribute in a personal interview. We come here in the spirit of peace. We will leave if Moctezuma should find our presence burdensome."

As soon as the nobles left to deliver this message, Cortés showed his elation. "It begins to appear to me that this Moctezuma is a woman, not a man! His superstitious nature makes him fear us very much!"

His people shared his awe of us, as we learned in an Aztec city built on the edge of the lake near one of the causeways. Many houses were on piles extending out into the water, and canals penetrated into the city. We later found that this was in imitation of Tenochtitlán. We were well received and were housed for the night in stone buildings of austere elegance, and there we rested two days.

And there we received a visit from Cacama, the ruler of Texcoco, who rode into the city on a palanquin that was decorated with gold and precious stones. Many nobles accompanied him, and two had brooms and swept the ground before him as he walked toward us. Cacama was a man of about twenty-five, handsome and stately. He acknowledged Cortés as being of high rank when he bent to touch earth and bring that hand to his forehead. Cortés embraced him; this is what European kings do when they meet. "I have been sent by my cousin Moctezuma to welcome you to his capital," Cacama said.

When I told Cortés this his eyes gleamed with pleasure; the gleam was brighter when Cacama then presented him a golden bowl holding three large pearls. In return Cortés hung around Cacama's neck a string of twinkling glass beads called margaritas. When the Texcocan prince left, Cortés said he was very impressed by his noble bearing. "To say nothing of his three pearls!" He told me that any one of them would grace a king's crown in Europe. "As big as pullet eggs!" A pullet, he explained, was a small chicken, but as I did not know what a chicken was except that it must be a bird since it laid eggs, I was little wiser.

The army resumed its march around the borders of the lake, past fruit-laden orchards and fields of waving maize, all irrigated by canals from the lake, although there were many patches of uncultivated woodland. At last we came to the longest and most impressive of the four causeways that connected Tenochtitlán with the lakeshore. It proved to be wide enough for eight horsemen to ride abreast.

And for the first time since reaching Anahuac I felt fear as the hooves of the horses thudded on the planking of a wooden drawbridge some ten paces long; removed, it would leave a gap of water too wide to leap. Ahead I saw another such bridge. I assumed they existed on the other causeways, except for the aqueduct. If ever a perfect trap had been constructed by the mind of man it was this city built on water, its only roads to the rest of the world interrupted by these removable bridges that could prevent invasion from without or the escape of enemies from within. And I suddenly wondered if Moctezuma had really been so innocent as to believe that his lavish gifts would drive Cortés away. Had he rather intended to lure us toward him? The ambush at Cholula having failed, was he now permitting us to enter his city to slaughter us at his leisure, provide hearts for his war god?

"I don't like these bridges," Cortés said thoughtfully. "Still, we must cross to the city. If Moctezuma intends to kill us, he can do it as easily if we retreat as if we advance. Advance has another advantage: If I make as good an impression on Moctezuma as I did on Cacama, then we will meet like two kings, and what king wants it known that he invited another to his city and then slaughtered him?"

I said that Moctezuma might not be as concerned about others' opinions as Cortés hoped. "His authority is absolute, remember. And he is considered a deity himself, or nearly so."

"But don't forget that Toltec farmer! Unless Moctezuma has very lazy spies, he knows that outside his city are many potential rebels. He must keep up a noble front." Suddenly he pointed. "What is that thing out there on the lake?"

I saw my first *chinampa,* a little garden floating along amid the many canoes laden with Aztecs making their way to the causeway and staring up at us in wonder. In the middle of the garden was a small shade tree, under which the farmer dozed. It seemed to me a lovely life, to move over the blue water while one's garden grew. Yet I knew that this *chinampa* was a living relic of the early grim days of the Aztecs. I told Cortés, "What you see is the answer to the question you asked me three days ago: how did the little island the Aztecs settled on grow into a great city?"

And I told him what I had first learned from Ato and her mother, long ago: On that small island, needing to raise more food for a growing population, the Aztecs found a solution. Seeing chunks of earth that had detached themselves from the lakeshore in the rainy season floating along held together by the roots of their verdure, a clever farmer got the idea that large baskets of tightly woven reeds could be filled with mud dredged up from the shallow lake bottom, planted with seeds fertilized with human excrement. Eventually *chinampas* moored to the shore of the island sent roots down through the shallow water to the rich lake silt. The farmers paddled along canals left between them to splash them with lakewater. And so, over more than two centuries, the island of Tenochtitlán spread out wider and wider, a city of canals.

"Such ingenuity merits admiration," Cortés conceded. "I never thought to find a Venice high in these mountains." He lost himself in thought, perhaps wondering how canals might be used to his advantage in case Moctezuma's reception of us did not look promising.

The Ixtapalápa causeway on which we advanced went first due west and then, about a league and a half out in the lake, turned north straight as an arrow to the city. The three other causeways each led out to a different compass point and were of different lengths due to the irregular curving of the lakeshore. There were actually, we learned, several lakes, two being formed by three causeways. Lake Texcoco was the largest. The shortest causeway led to a town called Tacuba.

The nearer we came to the city of Tenochtitlán, the more it overwhelmed me. Now I could see that many of the largest buildings were white, but others were of a rust-red stone, and some were gray. Cortés and I and four mounted captains led toward it the Spanish army, fewer than four hundred soldiers, their battered armor polished to give a brave appearance, Cortés' worn banner floating overhead. Behind them came our Tlascalans, dressed as for battle, their white crane banners held high. Last of all plodded the *tamanes* with their loads on their back, and back there on a litter rode little Orteguilla. I thought how the sights we were seeing must awe that tiny man.

The horses' hooves thudded on yet another wooden bridge. From either side of the causeway wondering Aztec faces smiled up at us from canoes laden with flowers that were tossed to the causeway to make a carpet for our feet. Walking on bright petals I found my earlier fear melting into the pleasant feeling that this was a holiday in our honor. And then I recalled that I had felt the same on entering Cholula.

Ahead a great double gate between two stone towers was opened wide and through it came at least a thousand citizens to greet us, among them war chiefs in the strange costumes of the various military orders, with helmets like jaguars or eagles or serpents. Seeing them I remembered the defeat of my little town of Paynala by warriors like these. A dreamlike mood descended on me for a moment. Was this really happening? Was I really here? I looked at Cortés and knew all this was true. Not only was I here, but I had to translate the formal speeches of welcome delivered by a large number of nobles, one of whom explained that Moctezuma was ill and so had not come in person to greet us. This did not please Cortés, and he accepted the nobles' deep bows of humility rather coldly. At last we proceeded through the great gate to continue into the city itself on a wide avenue that was half stone-paved street and half canal, solid with dugout canoes that had followed us in. I glanced back at the great gateway. When finally it clanged shut after the last of Cortés' army, either a trap would have closed on us all forever or we would be feted as honored guests, all the marvels of the silver city at our disposal. Which would it be?

I looked at Cortés, my mouth dry. He was staring straight ahead. A large palanquin was approaching from the center of the city. It seemed to float on the shoulders of the cluster of richly dressed attendants surrounding it; ornately decorated pillars supported its green canopy, thick with *chalchihuites* and other gems, quetzal plumes nodding at its four corners. Seated on a gold chair in its center was a man as motionless as an idol. From his golden crown a towering fan of green quetzal feathers spread out. His ceremonial cape, open to frame his body, revealed a massive pectoral necklace of gold and jewels. The wide front panel of his *atl* was encrusted with pearls and emeralds. Wide bracelets on both arms almost hid the flesh.

Yet in spite of the color and gleam and glitter of all this magnificence, as the palanquin came closer it was his face that stood out most clearly to me: a delicate face, very pale, with sad eyes and a slight narrow beard cut off square just below the chin. He looked as if he had recently been very ill, yet at the same time seemed above the usual human complaints. All about us humble onlookers had prostrated themselves, faces to the ground. Moctezuma!

His head turned slightly. His eyes looked straight at me. Suddenly I quivered; my throat grew tight, and I was cold with fear. Moctezuma!

The palanquin was slowly lowered to the ground. He rose from his chair and stepped from the litter to approach us with slow dignity, a noble supporting him at either side. I tried to swallow so as to moisten my parched throat. In moments I would have to speak to him for Cortés.

Moctezuma!

22

Cortés dismounted; I followed suit, looking desperately about me in hope of seeing Aguilar, who had learned some Nahuatl. But at Cholula I had found that I could translate directly from that language into Castilian, and so he had ceased to aid me. I walked beside Cortés toward the advancing Moctezuma knowing how much depended on this first meeting with the ruler into whose absolute power we had so bravely marched. My parched mouth demanded water, and I remembered my thirst on the litter going toward Tabasco. Now that helpless slave child was about to speak to this ruler of rulers! I saw that a length of green cloth was being unrolled before his feet by two richly clad attendants who bent to this task as dextrously as if all their lives their main occupation had been to keep the ruler's golden sandals from ever treading where other feet had walked. The awe I felt was as intense as when I first saw Cortés and thought him a god. This memory was my salvation: Cortés was no god; neither was Moctezuma.

Now he stood directly before us. He was shorter than Cortés, but the green panache, symbol of his power, made him seem to tower over him. Smiling, Cortés stepped forward and spread his arms to embrace him. Seeing his intention, Moctezuma took one step back; two nobles ran forward to push Cortés away, their faces shocked. One was Cacama, who said, "No one must touch the First Speaker unless by his command!"

Undaunted, Cortés held out a necklace of glass margaritas that was longer than the one he had given Cacama, who took the sparkling strand and clasped it around Moctezuma's neck, being careful not to brush his flesh. I knew these beads had little value in Europe, and so to me they looked strange sparkling against the massive golden necklace of the Aztec ruler.

He raised his arm and a tall, fierce-looking noble, his brother Cuitlahuac, brought to him a golden necklace with pendants made in the shapes of various shellfish. I knew these were symbols associated with the god Quetzalcoatl, who came from across the eastern sea, and I explained this to Cortés. Moctezuma himself hung the necklace on Cortés, who bowed to him to show that he knew he had been greatly honored. Then Moctezuma stepped back. A noble attendant announced: "The great Moctezuma speaks!" His words soon confirmed the significance of the shellfish necklace.

"Our lord, you are weary, for you have come a great distance to your city here in Mexico where you will sit on the golden throne which has so long awaited you. Kings who have gone before me have guarded it against your coming. Oh, if they could see what I see now! It is not a dream! I am now walking in my sleep! I have seen you at last. For many days and nights I have been in agony of spirit, my mind lost in the Region of Mystery as I sought to know the truth of your coming. But now I know you have indeed returned, as was long foretold. Rest now, and take possession of your royal palace. Welcome to your land, my lords.'' His melancholy eyes left Cortés' face to look up at the mounted captains behind him.

When I heard the sad and hollow voice speaking the flowery words, I knew that he had indeed been in an agony of indecision, and that the legend of the return of Quetzalcoatl or his descendants to judge and punish must have been confirmed as present fact by whatever new omens and oracles he had discovered in his Region of Mystery since Cortés' triumph over the Cholulans. Moctezuma was now resigned to the probability that Cortés and the captains on horseback were no mere mortals.

I thought of the file of Spanish soldiers now halted on the causeway behind us by this ceremony, battered weary men, some scarred in Tlascala, some wounded in Cholula, and very far from being gods or even a god's attendants. And I knew that some of them were afraid. But I also knew that many would march into this city looking all about with eager eyes, convinced as Spaniards and Christians that any land on which they trod was merely a potential colony of Spain.

Cortés thanked Moctezuma for his gracious welcome and the Aztec ruler turned and walked back to his palanquin, the ceremonial cape sweeping the green carpet behind him and forming an iridescent background for the two tapered lengths of quetzal plumes extending downward from his headdress nearly to the ground.

As Cortés and I remounted to follow him into his city a breeze from the lake caught the Spanish banner held aloft behind us, and the blue-and-white flames around the central red cross seemed for an instant to flicker as real flames do.

I glanced at the gold necklace that gleamed against Cortés' steel breastplate: a crab, a nautilus, a scallop caught the sun. Honored as Quetzalcoatl, he would bring to Moctezuma his first knowledge of the one true God, and that seemed to me most fitting, and almost as though the legendary return of that merciful deity was in a sense taking place. But then I knew I was slipping back toward my old idolatry and crossed myself.

As we rode at a slow pace toward the heart of the city following Moctezuma's palanquin along that wide avenue, the houses we passed became larger and grander. At the city's fringes by the lake were only reed-sided homes of the poorer folk built out over the water on piles. Then came one- and two-story dwellings of *tetzontli,* a porous rust-red stone; on the flat rooftops bloomed gardens from which Aztec faces stared down at us. Nearer the city's center temples and public buildings were covered over with a gleaming white stucco against which the colorful clothes of the Aztecs lining the street to watch us pass stood out boldly.

Among the multitude I saw young women with long black hair and full skirts below triangular *huipiles* woven in varying designs, vivid colors. Many wore their hair braided with bright ribbons for some festival. Sunlight gleamed on their bracelets of silver, gold, and copper and lighted their cheekbones, prominent below their jet-black eyes of almond shape. They were squat in build, like the men, whose hair was cut off just above the eyes and below the jaws; many wore narrow headbands. Over their loincloths, the front panels woven in varying motifs, some wore cotton cloaks tied on one shoulder like the Tlascalans', only these were not of coarse *nequen*. Both men and women looked very clean and gave off no smell of sweat because of their custom, I learned, of bathing daily in steam baths attached to their homes or in public ones. But as we penetrated deeper into the city I became aware that it had an odor, which came in part from the canals that crisscrossed it, from the food the people cooked, from incense burning in the many temples, and from the stench of the offerings made on their altars. It was not entirely unpleasant, only strange.

"This city is cleaner than any I have ever seen," Cortés remarked. "Cities in Europe . . ." His voice broke off in midsentence, because at that moment we entered the vast central plaza, thronged with Aztecs who had left a wide lane down which Moctezuma's palanquin and attendants had preceded us. My mare stopped in her tracks as if as stunned as I. Cortés reined in his stallion. Side by side we stared about us.

To the north was a high white pyramid of five levels with stone steps going up its steep face—the temple of Huitzilopotchli, the war god. To the east stood an enormous palace, a high wall enclosing its many buildings of that rust-red stone. It was both imposing and desolate; no curious figures stood on its ramparts or roof garden to stare down at us. We learned that it was the palace of Moctezuma's dead father. His own was even larger and grander, separated from it by a spacious walled garden: above its treetops soared a giant aviary; wickerwork domes emitted a constant bird music. In the square itself, facing the garden, was the temple of Tezcatlipoca, creator of the universe, in whose polished shield he could see all that happened everywhere. The temple of Quetzalcoatl's entrance was an enormous open serpent's mouth, so hideous that the soldiers named it the Inferno. These and the other religious buildings were white and gleaming and the pale stone paving was as clean as though a thousand slaves had scrubbed the immense expanse in the night (which proved true). The southern half of the square was an enormous open market, its stalls loaded with every kind of ware and produce, buyers numerous as bees swarming over a hive. But the huge splendor of the temples and palaces dwarfed them and ourselves, backed by the circular range of distant mountains, snowy tops glistening against the hard blue sky against which a plume of smoke rose from the crater of Popocatepetl.

Cortés was barely able to hide his wonderment from Cacama, who came to tell him that Moctezuma offered us the entire palace of his dead father Axayacatl, unused by anyone for seventeen years out of respect to his memory.

In the first courtyard we entered Moctezuma himself had waited to welcome us, then left us there to marvel at our quarters. The many rooms we saw that day had ceilings of sweet-smelling carved cedar and stuccoed walls adorned with hangings in bold Aztec designs and colors. One hall alone was large enough to sleep a hundred fifty soldiers; this and two others nearly as vast were furnished with thick straw pallets, one for each foot soldier, showing the accuracy of Moctezuma's information as to their number. Evidently his enemies the Tlascalans were to content themselves with the various courtyards. Since it was winter, charcoal braziers on stone tripods gave off a pleasant warmth. Stone wall brackets held unlit pine torches for the night to come.

The sleeping room into which Cacama ushered Cortés was large and low-ceilinged with a narrow window overlooking the main square through which we had just passed. There were many rich hangings, several braziers and wall torches, chests for clothing, tables, chairs, and a raised platform with a large thick sleeping pallet with a jeweled canopy above it. Along the wall by the doorway a row of ten servants waited to see to Cortés' needs. My room, Cacama said, was adjacent. "If there is anything you require, Lord, send word to Moctezuma by one of these servants. For the First Speaker wishes you to be comfortable, with all to your liking."

"Is this First Speaker Moctezuma?" Cortés asked.

Cacama concealed all but a hint of surprise at such ignorance. "Yes. Moctezuma speaks first and last at all meetings of the thirty clan chiefs he graces with his presence. What he says is then law, and cannot be changed except by himself. Even the Council of Four cannot act contrary to the word of Moctezuma, although they may make recommendations to him."

Cortés thanked him and said he was pleased with his room and Cacama departed. We were, for the moment, alone; ten slaves who did not understand Castilian might as well have been furniture and stood as motionless as though they were. Cortés went to the narrow window and stood looking down at his Spanish soldiers now crossing the wide Zocalo between staring Aztecs. Behind them came the first of the Tlascalans; I saw that they stared straight ahead on entering the heart of the city of their ancient enemies.

Cortés removed his casque and rubbed his forehead where it had pressed. "It strikes me as somewhat forbidding that Moctezuma has housed us in a mausoleum." He smiled grimly. "I am pleased that it is walled like a fortress, however." He put the casque on again and started for the doorway. "I must see to the soldiers' sleeping arrangements and to the stabling of our horses. I must also decide on the best placement of our cannons and artillery."

His intended exit was halted by the arrival of the tall, fierce noble who had walked at Moctezuma's left when he met Cortés. He offered only a token inclination of his body and did not touch the floor with his hand. I translated his curt words; they confirmed my immediate feeling that he did not like or revere Spaniards. "I am Cuitlahuac, a brother of Moctezuma. The First Speaker desires an audience with you. He will visit you here, at your convenience." His rigid body and obsidian eyes deplored his ruler's courtesy.

"As soon as I take care of certain important matters I will send for him," Cortés had me say. As I finished speaking, faint cries and jeers floated in through the window, and I knew that the Aztecs were responding to the arrival of Tlascalans.

"Why have you brought our enemies here?" Cuitlahuac asked coldly.

"The Tlascalans are my friends. They have accepted my sovereign and my God," Cortés said. "In this the Aztecs will be wise to emulate them."

"Aztecs do not emulate," Cuitlahuac said flatly, and left us without other farewell.

Before sending Moctezuma word that he could visit him, Cortés assigned his troops to their several quarters, had cannons placed on the palace's front rampart to command the main gate, positioned other ordnance to command approach over the other walls, and stationed many sentinels. It was as if he expected a siege instead of a visit from a generous host.

Moctezuma arrived bearing in his own hands a vase of flowers.

He was followed by a cluster of nobles and by servants bringing other gifts. In a large lower hall, evidently an audience room with many benches, Cortés' captains and Moctezuma's nobles all seated themselves, Moctezuma and Cortés apart on a low dais, each in a carved gilded chair or throne. I stood between them, aware that my earlier thirst had returned, although not so intensely. The questions Moctezuma asked Cortés surprised me, and I decided that the reverential speech he made at the causeway had been a mere formality, perhaps intended to impress the many nobles and citizens who heard it. Now the Aztec monarch asked about the government of the country Cortés came from, its distance, size, and the number of vassals its king commanded. Here was no oratory, but an intelligent mind seeking knowledge. "Tell me why you came here," Moctezuma demanded.

"I wanted to meet so distinguished a monarch. I particularly came to declare to you the True Faith as practiced only by Christians."

Moctezuma was not interested. What he wanted to know was whether earlier pale bearded strangers seen by a cacique of Yucatán many years ago, at the start of his reign, had been Cortés' countrymen.

"He must mean Columbus!" Cortés said to the captains after a moment's reflection. "On his third voyage he came to Yucatán." I, for my part, remembered a child in Paynala, charmed by a little gold snake-man. Cortés' voice brought me back to the present. "Tell him I am surprised that he knows of this."

Moctezuma said, "I also have been aware of all your movements since you first came to Tabasco." He explained that rulers before him had perfected a widespread courier system with runners so swift that in relays they brought to his breakfast table certain fish caught the morning before in waters near Verz Cruz. "It is a fish I am very fond of," he said, "although it is spiny and ugly in appearance. But you and I know that appearances can be deceptive." His eyes roved then to the shellfish necklace Cortés had been given, which I had supposed was offered to Quetzalcoatl returned.

"I intend to be open and honest with you," Cortés said, with dignity. "On my part there will be no deception."

Moctezuma withdrew to his palanquin outside the main gate after ordering his servants pass out gifts of fine cotton robes to each soldier and golden chains to the captains. Cortés stood looking after Moctezuma, his face dark. "Yes, appearances can be deceptive. Lavish hospitality is no exception." He turned to me. "Would you say Moctezuma thinks me a god returned now?" I had to admit that his attitude seemed suddenly to have changed.

IN THE SILVER CITY

That night Cortés celebrated our arrival by ordering a discharge of all artillery, including the cannons; the thunderous noise reverberated against the walls of the palace and the air was filled for a while with the stink of sulfur and niter. "Supernatural beings have commanded thunder and lightning ever since Jove's thunderbolts," he told me later. "Let these Aztecs fear me, the sooner to bow to my God and my king!"

Moctezuma's response was to send nobles early the next morning to invite Cortés and his captains to his palace. "Malinche is of course included in this great honor," one of them said, so evidently Moctezuma not only knew my Indian name but preferred it to my Spanish one, although he pronounced it *Malintzín*.

The nobles had been told to show us some of the palace of Moctezuma, and we passed through courtyards and corridors and huge halls filled with strolling Aztec nobles and visitors of high rank, the sweet smell of incense, and the music of flutes. The walls were gorgeous with featherwork tapestries depicting animals, flowers, birds, and butterflies, all glowing with colors both brilliant and subtle. There were three large marble steam baths with pools of crystal water, several vaults for wine and one for chocolate pressed into cakes. In a large annex giving onto the gardens hundreds of pretty concubines passed the day in idle chatter and embroidering. In contrast, the arsenal was a grim, immense room stocked to the high ceiling with racks of javelins, obsidian swords, bows and arrows.

The owner of all this magnificence was seated on his carved golden throne, which occupied a dais at the far end of a spacious audience room, a similar golden chair empty beside him for Cortés. He was surrounded by many nobles, among them Cacama and Cuitlahuac and a straight-backed eagle warrior named Cuauhtemoc, who eyed us boldly. Moctezuma's humility made clear to me that the cannonade of the night before had deeply impressed him. "Thank you for accepting my invitation so promptly," he said to Cortés while indicating that he was offering a seat beside his own.

Cortés at once seized the opportunity to speak to Moctezuma of the Christian Church; the Trinity; the Crucifixion; the Resurrection; the origin of the world; the temptation of Adam and Eve by the Serpent in the garden. "That was Satan who caused the fall of man. All your idols are other forms which Satan has taken. They must be removed from your temples. I have come here to save your soul and the souls of your people from the eternal flames of Hell. I plead with you to accept the Cross of Jesus!"

Moctezuma raised both palms outward in shocked negation. "I cannot be false to the gods who have raised my land to prosperity and me to great honor! Their shrines have been entrusted to my keeping. I do not deny that your God is good, but so are my gods to me. Your story of the creation of the world is not what I have been taught to believe. I am sure you are good, and came here with kind intentions. Once I felt otherwise, hearing about your sending thunderballs to kill people, throwing down their idols, crushing them under the feet of your great beasts. But now I think all this was lies or exaggeration." He leaned toward Cortés. "I think you are mortals of another race than mine, wiser and more valiant, and for this I honor you."

Cortés, still wearing the necklace of golden shellfish, stiffened in his chair. "Whether mortals or not, we are valiant in one cause: to save your soul from Hell!"

"You too have heard lies of me," Moctezuma said. "You have been told, perhaps, that I am a god and live in a palace of gold and silver. But you can see that my palace, although large, is of stone and wood like any other." He held out his arm, touched the bare skin of the biceps with the other hand. "And my body is of flesh and bone like yours. It is true that I have a great domain inherited from my ancestors, and own lands and palaces and gold and gems and receive huge yearly tribute from near and distant places." He stood up; staring fixedly down at Cortés he seemed to be addressing all his watching nobles as well. "But still I accept your great sovereign as my rightful lord. You are his revered ambassador. All that I have you will share. So rest now from your long journey. You are here in your own land, and I will see that your wishes are obeyed as my own."

He spoke calmly. This did not minimize the importance of his concession: Cortés, though probably mortal like himself, was the emissary of a sovereign superior to Moctezuma. This could only be Quetzalcoatl. The legend was still working in Cortés' behalf.

Moctezuma's next words confirmed this. "My ancestors were not the original proprietors of the Valley of Anahuac. We have occupied it for only a few ages. We were led here by a great Being who gave us laws and other knowledge and ruled over us for a time, but then withdrew to the land where the sun rises. He said before his departure that he or his descendants would again visit us and resume his empire here. Your wonderful deeds, and the direction from which you come, all show me that you are this Being's emissaries, sent from him to us."

To my surprise, I saw tears in Moctezuma's jet-black eyes. I knew

197

why. I had seen such tears gather in my father's eyes as he told of his surrender to the Aztecs. I could not help but feel a certain compassion for Moctezuma, and not just because of some tears. It seemed to me that the Toltec farmer had been right; the Aztecs had borrowed the god Quetzalcoatl and made him their own, yet without ceasing to revere their bloodthirsty war god. And so Moctezuma's nature had been imbued from birth with a greater split between good and evil than are most men's; it was as if he revered both God and Satan.

Cortés was quick to seize on Moctezuma's belief that Quetzalcoatl's descendants had entered his city. "Yes, it is true that my sovereign is that great Being you revere. But I promise you he will not interfere with your authority here if you swear to be his faithful vassal. What he greatly desires is your conversion to Christianity, of which I have told you something, and of which I will tell you more."

Seeing the confusion on Moctezuma's face as Christianity was again mentioned, and as he recalled Cortés' earlier and hurried indoctrination into matters very strange and unreal to an Aztec's mind, I recalled how many things had puzzled me when I first learned of them, how I had told Aguilar that Jesus was stupid to have let himself be crucified instead of choosing to live and teach men good things as Quetzalcoatl did in his human form. Nor had I first believed in the Resurrection. I thought it only meant that Jesus had deceived everyone by only pretending to die on the Cross. So I quickly turned to Cortés and whispered that he should avoid any more talk of Christian doctrine at present. "Let Moctezuma ponder what you have already said. And then let our priests do the work they came here to do. They are more skilled than you at getting converts."

He gave me a cold glance, proud of his power of persuasion, but then with a nod admitted I was right. Moctezuma concluded the interview with another display of generosity: a gold necklace for every Spanish soldier, two for each captain. As we left for our palace, they all bowed deeply to Moctezuma, helmets in hand, and on the way back they commented on his gentle breeding and great courtesy. I do not think it was only the golden gifts which had impressed them, because I myself had undergone a great change of opinion concerning him.

I had expected arrogance and had found humility. I had imagined a cruel, proud face and had found a gentle, sad one. None of my one-time hatred of an oppressor had flared up in me; instead I felt some sympathy. His need had been to prove to himself that Cortés and his men were not gods or a god's descendants, just mere men. Everything Cortés had accomplished since Tabasco had proved just the opposite. And so Moctezuma found himself the victim of a legend, faced with a situation nothing had prepared him to cope with. How could he have dreamed when he was crowned at twenty-three that during his reign the long-promised Return would occur? That after seventeen years of absolute authority in accordance with precedents known and changeless he would find himself attempting to comprehend beings so bewilderingly different from any he had known or imagined that they might as well have dropped to earth from another planet?

That night Cortés asked me to share his bed. Head propped on his hand, he lay facing me. "I think I could have done well as an evangelist to Moctezuma if he had only understood Spanish. As it was, my words had to be filtered through you, a neophyte in Christian doctrine."

"You are a commander of men. Do you need to excel as a priest as well?"

He forced a grin at the pricking of arrogance. "What do you think of Moctezuma? Is he a man to fear or a man to love?"

"I think he is sincere, and that we will continue to be well treated by him."

"Have you so soon forgotten Cholula? Do you think he did not order that ambush of us?" He sat up, staring coldly down at me. "Fair words mean nothing to me! Nothing! Has it occurred to you that he could only be pretending to believe we were sent here by that deity of his in order to lull us into a sense of false security? I must proceed as though that were his plan, to disarm us, to make us careless." A sudden crooked grin made his face look sly and somewhat cruel. "When you find yourself in a web, do not look for gnats. Look for spiders!"

When he extinguished the torch and drew me to him I found him in a state of unusual excitement: insatiable, devouring. At last he fell into a deep and sudden sleep, lying prone beside me, sprawled as if though flung there by the great hand of the passion that had possessed him. I lay for a long time staring up into the alien darkness. Here, as in Tlascala, Cortés felt danger all around us. I knew that deep within and probably unacknowledged by himself was fear of Moctezuma for his great power which at any moment, and because of some omen or oracle beyond Christian understanding, might be turned against us in all its mighty fury.

And there was reason for fear. The awed Moctezuma was not used to feeling awe for any human alive. After the impact of the Spaniards' strangeness had been lessened by propinquity doubts might arise as to their descent from a deity.

And I was the only link between Cortés and Moctezuma. Through my voice they would come to a better and peaceable understanding— or fail to do so. I dreamed that night that I was a child back in Paynala, my father alive and Ix Chan too. All was golden sunlight there, and no unbelievable future threatened me.

Shortly before dawn the light of a pine torch in a wall bracket awakened me. Cortés, in his red robe, sat at a table near the bed, quill in hand. I was sure he was writing another letter to Carlos of Spain, telling of our arrival in this city, of the warm welcome by a potentate soon to be Spain's vassal, and asking again for reinforcements. I knew by now the long distance this letter would have to travel to reach the king: up the mountains walling this valley, then down the long eastern slope to Vera Cruz, then across to Cuba in the one remaining vessel Cortés had. From Cuba, on another ship, the letter would then have to cross a wide ocean to another continent, then go by land to a place called Madrid where the King Carlos might or might not be in residence at the time it arrived.

Cortés plunged the point of the quill into the inkhorn, then drove it scratching across the page once more. And it seemed to me he was holding the only weapon he could at this moment use against the inner fear that threatened him. Looking at his face in profile, eaglelike with fierce concentration, I knew again that I loved the bravest of men.

23

The next few days passed pleasantly. Cortés and the captains were elaborately banqueted, reverently attended by a swarm of servants. Moctezuma first allotted three slaves to each Spanish soldier, but when Cortés laughingly protested such extravagance he reduced the number to one. The horses were fed maize and bedded down on pallets of flower petals, yet Cortés did not know from day to day when he would ride his black stallion to the lakeshore to find a causeway's first bridge removed and a gap of twenty spans of water separating him from the rest of the world. He was uneasy with the perfect courtesy of Moctezuma, his apparent willingness to have us with him forever, his refusal to embrace the Christian faith. He foresaw clashes between the Tlascalans and the Aztec citizenry, was worried lest a life of sudden luxury would soften his Spanish soldiers, yet could not forbid them to visit the vast marketplace at the southern end of the central plaza.

When he and I went there, I could not believe such plenty, such variety. Each type of merchandise had its regular place: building materials such as stone, lime, and lumber; pottery in all sizes and glazes; cotton cloth of every hue, and cloaks, tablecloths, bedcovers, handkerchiefs, serapes; a feather stall with rare birds in cages and artisans who turned a handful of feathers into a butterfly, a bird, a flower so perfect as to seem real. In the silver market there was a silver parrot that could move its head, feet, wings, and tongue. Cortés bought it for me. He said no Spanish silversmith could better such workmanship. At meat stalls you could buy almost anything that moves: fat little dogs, moles, maguey slugs, mice, deer, hares, muskrats, fish, flow. There were stalls for fruit, for vegetables, and eating counters where the soldiers bought cooked meats and omelettes and fried beans. A shop sold herbs to cure any ailment, another any color dye. There were barbers, doctors. One shop sold only cooking oil, another pine and candlewood for torches. The paper shop sold *amatyl* in many colors, and every tint of paint and ink. The sweets stall offered honey of many sorts, aloe sugar, candy made from cactus and sweet potatoes. This and the pulque shop were favored by the soldiers: the pulque was flavored like strawberries, cherries, melon, mango. There was a nursery with every kind of plant for sale, even small-sized trees. The air was noisy with bartering, with the piping of flutes and the shuffling rattle of dried gourds; in time to the music a man danced on stilts. Cortés was surprised that cocoa beans, small tabs of tin, and bird quills filled with gold dust were the only money used, the latter carelessly valued by size rather than weight. When he saw a child dragging a toy dog with four small wheels he said he could not understand that a people so clever had never thought of a better use of the wheel; they did not even have potters' wheels, he pointed out, but built up bowls and urns from long ropes of clay.

The busy marketplace offered a sharp contrast to the great five-story temple of the war god. In its forecourt stood a skull rack: tier upon tier of gleaming white skulls formed a wall between two towers built entirely of skulls mortared together and topped by forty poles bristling with pegs, each impaling five skulls. "Is there any spot on earth so soaked with blood, so laden with death as this one?" Cortés asked, and told me that one hundred thirty-six thousand skulls had been counted by one stunned soldier. "And almost in the shadow of this horror these Aztecs buy food, eat it, bargain and chat!" The skulls did not represent human death and suffering to them, he said, but only proof of Aztec power. The hearts of the victims fed the gods; priests and nobles dined on the arms and legs, and the rest was taken home by humbler folk to be cooked into a man-and-maize stew. This cannibalism particularly horrified him, even after I pointed out that it was a religious rite, not mere appetite.

A deep-voiced drum boomed from the top of the temple; Aztecs began to hurry toward it. We returned to our palace, not wishing to view the rite that drum announced.

I was surprised the next day when Moctezuma and a group of nobles arrived to invite Cortés and his captains to inspect the holy of holies, Huitzilopotchli's inner sanctum atop his pyramid. For the first time in my life I, a woman, was to ascend such a temple; as Cortés' interpreter I was indispensable, regarded less as a separate person than as an extra member of Cortés' corporeal being. Sometimes, to his annoyance, Malinche was the name used by Aztecs to address him as well as me.

In the three-story *teocalli*, topped by two elaborately carved wooden towers, were two blood-spattered holy chambers through which flitted dozens of black-clad priests, stinking of the dried blood on their robes. In the larger room the war god stood, fashioned, we were told by a noble, of every seed that grew, ground fine and mixed to a paste with the blood of virgin girls and boys. He was colossal, his face hideously distorted by scowling brows and two fangs. In one hand he held a sheaf of arrows, in the other a bow. A tiny hummingbird was attached to one ankle; a thick snake of precious gems coiled around his waist, and chains of gold hearts hung around his neck. Three fresh human hearts lay in a bowl at his feet. One of his names was The Hummingbird Wizard, but why I do not know.

In the adjacent chamber stood Tezcatlipoca in the form of a young man of black stone decorated with ornaments of gold and gems and holding a burnished silver shield in which he could see all that happened in the universe, so his soubriquet was Smoking Mirror. Five human hearts had been offered before him.

These two were the principal deities of the Aztecs, but hundreds of different idols were worshiped at various seasons for various reasons: in homage to the goddess of young corn a virgin boy and girl would be set afloat in a canoe and stoned to death from pursuing boats; to honor Xipe, The Flayed One, a priest would put on the skin stripped from a sacrificed victim and dance wildly to the frenzy of flutes and the throb of the huge snakeskin drum atop the war god's pyramid. In the course of one Aztec year, Moctezuma calmly told us, there were twenty ceremonies to honor various gods. All required sacrificial victims. "One of these is deeply moving," he said, "and I believe would impress you."

After we left the temple, Cortés remarked grimly that blood seemed to be the glue that held the Aztec people together as a political unit. "Remove it and you would have fragments that could be welded together with a purer substance, such as faith in God."

A few mornings later, just after dawn, Moctezuma sent a messenger to invite us to see that beautiful rite he had spoken of to Cortés. We were conducted to the royal box in the *tlachtli* court that adjoined the forecourt of the temple and whose highest tiers offered a good view of the platform atop where the stone altar stood.

Shortly after the sun had risen, a splendidly dressed young man was led by two Aztec priests to the foot of the stone steps of the white pyramid, which he ascended alone. He seemed to walk toward the altar at their top in a trance. He was laid on the altar. The huge snakeskin drum boomed in slow cadence. With a swift downward thrust of a sacrificial knife the high priest slashed open the boy's body just below the ribs, reached in, wrenched out the gushing heart, and held it high in both hands to the morning sun.

I shut my eyes, felt faint, heard the silence as the drum abruptly ceased to beat just as that poor young man's heart now had. Moctezuma's calm voice explained the beauty of this rite. "For one year he has lived as an emperor, known every luxury, slept each night with a different beautiful woman. He had been feted and adored, a national hero." He paused for me to translate this for Cortés, which I did in a somewhat weak voice. "He enjoyed all this in the knowledge that the most splendid of all honors would be the moment when he walked up to the temple altar, the finest gift we could offer our gods." He waited for Cortés to comment.

When Cortés merely shook his head, unable to find words to express his horror, Moctezuma said, "I thought you might see the similarity between our boy hero and your Jesus Christ, who also died for the people of his land, you told me."

"*¡Jesucristo!*" Cortés whispered, instead of his usual oath.

As soon as we left he found Father Olmedo and conferred with him about the necessity of immediately suggesting to Moctezuma that the Cross of Jesus be erected atop the temple where this boy had died. Olmedo counseled patience, but Cortés went without him to Moctezuma's palace. "Our Cross must at once replace that sacrificial stone! And ultimately all your temples will have to be swept clean of your cruel pagan gods! This terrible rite that you insisted I see has convinced me of this as nothing else could!"

Moctezuma's sad face changed as if a mask had been snatched off; the lips thinned, the nostrils flared, the eyes turned to black slits. "What you ask is not possible! Our gods have made us a great people in this land. My five thousand priests would never permit such a desecration. You are foolish to believe that any wise ruler would turn his back on the gods of his nation or let harm come to their places of worship!" He turned his back on Cortés and walked away. Cortés stood looking after him. His face was white, as though sudden recollection of the Spaniards' precarious position here had drawn all his blood down into his still-beating heart.

It was with a show of humility that he went to Moctezuma the next day to ask his permission to build within our own palace a Christian chapel. Moctezuma not only agreed to this but also said he would send to us any wood or stone or masons or carpenters Cortés might need. After a large room in the rearmost palace building was chosen for our church, it was decided among the priests that no heathen hands should build its pews and altar. There were several carpenters among the Spanish soldiers; one named Nuñez was very skilled. He said that with half a dozen volunteers to help he could have our place of worship ready in a week. The priests had agreed to accept the sweet-smelling cedar planks Moctezuma had offered to send us; these would not profane God's house in that trees are not heathen, having no souls.

I was with the other Indian women who had been given several rooms near mine while all this was being decided. I was fondest of Ixlan, who had been given to Captain Sandoval and liked him very much, but I had become very friendly with the earnest, slender daughter of Xicotencatl the Elder, who had been baptized Doña Luisa.

She had no protector; her great desire for Father Aguilar had been transformed by him into a very devout acceptance of Jesus. "Jesus be praised!" she said when Cortés came in to tell me that the wood for the chapel had already arrived.

"I agree," he smiled. "That Moctezuma has allowed me to turn one room of his father's palace into a Christian place of worship may well be a first sign that his stubborn resistance to God is beginning to weaken."

At that moment El Galán and Arturo Mondragon arrived in haste. Arturo had grown a beard, darker gold than his hair; it still made him seem like a stranger to me. Out of boredom both men had volunteered to help Nuñez build chapel pews. Arturo said, "When El Galán and I pulled down one of those barbaric hangings which didn't belong in any church, I happened to notice something odd about the wall where it had hung. The shape of a bricked-up doorway showed through the thin stucco that covered it. Nobody closes up a room that way for nothing, and I was all for getting a battering ram, but Bernal thought we ought to tell you about it first."

"It wouldn't do to antagonize Moctezuma by smashing into his father's crypt," El Galán said. "If that's what it is."

"If it is, we will reverently close it again," Cortés said.

He had little trouble opening it, because the two large stone blocks at floor level were not mortared and could be pushed into the hidden chamber, leaving enough space to squirm through. Not wishing to crawl on his belly, Cortés had Arturo and El Galán batter out the two above them, and then entered crouching and holding a wall torch. I followed, Arturo and El Galán just behind me.

The gleam and glitter of the treasures crammed into that small windowless stone vault astonished us all: the most precious objects amassed during a twelve-year reign had been hidden away from all eyes by a miser of misers. There were statues of gold and jade, piles of gold bracelets and necklaces; a chest full of precious stones carved in the shapes of animals; huge disks of gold and silver showing the Aztec calendar; a slit-eyed turquoise mask with human teeth; a gold alligator ten hands long; a large crystal skull on a green onyx pedestal. Dozens of chests and baskets rose to the low ceiling except on the far wall, where a great feather ceremonial cape was hung outspread and seemed like a giant bird guarding this hidden hoard, wings wide.

The crystal skull fascinated Cortés. It was the size of a real one, and he picked it up and held it in both hands, turning it this way and that. "It seems to be carved from one giant crystal," he said. I shivered as the hollow eye sockets caught the light from a certain angle and seemed suddenly to blaze at me, fiery. Cortés returned it to the pedestal and grinned at it. "We thank you, Axayacatl, for guarding all these riches for us!"

Serious once again, he proposed to Arturo and Bernal Diaz that it would be wisest to replace the stones that closed the doorway and have it plastered over as before. "There's no need for Moctezuma to know that we have found this room. Let it be our secret, except for the mason we will need." He smiled. "And Nuñez, the carpenter. He can make a large pedestal for our biggest statue of the Virgin, and she can guard this crypt for us."

He was elated, and I knew why. The hoarded wealth of a dead idol-worshiper might prove the lever that would finally impress King Carlos. A sudden thought made me cross myself: had Cortés not wanted to build a chapel, it might never have been discovered.

Of all the marvels there, the crystal skull stayed most vividly in my mind; in a dream that night I was tormented by those blazing hollow eyes, that grin.

The next morning a frightful piece of news shattered Cortés' joy at the marvelous find. As I heard the two Tlascalan runners gasp, I could only think of the crystal skull's dreadful smile, as if it had known that good luck would be followed by bad.

There was grave trouble at Vera Cruz.

Juan Escalante, the captain in command there, had recently sent two emissaries to Cualpopoca, the Indian governor who resembled Cortés. They politely requested that he swear allegiance to the Spanish emperor. Cualpopoca refused and had the two Spaniards killed. Learning of this, Escalante at once led a punitive expedition of fifty armed Spanish soldiers and thousands of loyal Zempoallans. The ensuing battle had been fierce; it ended with seven Spaniards killed, including Escalante. His horse, a light chestnut with white stockings, was also dead. And then the Tlascalan messengers delivered a final blow: the severed head of a Spanish soldier had been sent by Cualpopoca to Moctezuma to be offered to the gods as hideous proof of the defeat of the Spaniards, the governor's fealty to his deities and his ruler.

From sorrow over his friend Escalante's death, Cortés went to a state of controlled fury on hearing of this decapitation. The twisted vein on the left side of his forehead swelled and throbbed; the edges of his compressed lips were white. "There's very little doubt that Moctezuma ordered this slaughter of Spaniards, that sly son of Satan!" He called for Orteguilla and sent him to fetch his five most trusted captains: Alvarado, Sandoval, Lugo, Leon, and Avila. "Cualpopoca would never have dared such a thing without his ruler's approval!"

We had been breakfasting in his room when this news came; with a sweep of his arm he sent a bowl of fruit off the table; mangoes, melons, cactus fruit, and cherries went rolling over the floor, the stunned servants staring in astonishment. I too was astonished, for I had never seen him so out of control. "It is not surely known yet that Moctezuma knew anything about what his governor did," I said.

His eyes scorned such innocence: "It will be known. It will be made clear beyond any doubt. I have reached the limit of my endurance. Blood and violence are all these Aztecs understand. Violence he will get!"

I knew I was not welcome or needed at conferences with his captains, yet I lingered out of anxiety. He told them what had occurred at Vera Cruz and said that Moctezuma had to be confronted with this breach of trust. "For days now Moctezuma must have known what Cualpopoca did. His couriers make the run from that coast in a day's time. Yet he has said nothing. He did not come out like an honest man and tell me that to his chagrin a rash governor of his exceeded his authority and slaughtered nine of our countrymen. No! It seems plain to me that he ordered those two Spanish emissaries to be slaughtered, and then the rest followed. For what motive? To test me! To see how we will take it. And I tell you, if we are passive now out of fear of him, we are finished!" He had mastered his anger and spoke with his usual ringing authority.

"But what can we do?" Sandoval asked.

Lugo said, "If we try and question him, he can just lie and say he knew nothing about it."

Alvarado shouted, "I'd like to lop *his* head off, like that Spanish soldier's!"

Avila looked pale and sad. "I hope it wasn't Juan Escalante's."

"Feeding a Spanish head to his filthy gods!" Alvarado shouted, red in the face. He whirled to me, pointing to the servants, who by now had picked up the scattered fruit and waited in a row, looking somewhat uneasy. "Ask them if that's what happened! They'll know!"

I obliged him, and questioned one whose brother not only worked in Moctezuma's palace but served a noble who enjoyed the ruler's confidence. He had overheard a discussion concerning the fate of the Spanish head. It had been brought in a basket by a runner, but it had been so hairy and ugly that Moctezuma had ordered it taken away and buried rather than offend the flayed goddess Xipe by offering her its skin.

When I turned back to Cortés and the captains, they were gathered close and had reached a decision I did not learn of until later that day. They were all grim and tense, and I decided not to tell them about the rejection of the Spaniard's head.

"All right," Cortés said, summing up. "It's agreed. We request an interview with Moctezuma. We confront him with the facts we know. But first I want all soldiers armed. I want thirty or forty to filter into Moctezuma's palace. I want a large detachment stationed in front of it."

When the captains left to carry out these orders he returned to the breakfast table and sat down to eat cold fish. I asked him what had been decided, my anxiety like a cold knot inside me. "To tie up a spider with its own web," he said and would tell me no more.

In his throne room Moctezuma was seated on the dais, surrounded by his nobles, and seemed in a good mood. He offered Cortés a wife from among his concubines, and when Cortés refused he joked about whether one wife was enough. But then Cortés grew serious, and the captains too. "I am astounded that you, Moctezuma, a valiant prince who had declared himself our friend, would order your governor Cualpopoca to take up arms against Spaniards."

Impassive, Moctezuma said, "I gave no such order. I only recently learned of this."

I felt relief at these words, but when I turned to Cortés his face told me that he did not believe them. "Your governor's soldiers have slain a countryman who was like a brother to me. I wanted to believe that you did not order our ambush at Cholula. Now I cannot. Nor can I believe you innocent of this."

"Cualpopoca acted without any order from me. Just as your dead captain acted without orders from you when he sent two Spaniards to tell my governor that he must transfer his allegiance from me to your Spanish king."

Cortés shook his head sadly. "I would like to believe you. How can I?"

"I will summon Cualpopoca here and we can investigate the truth of the matter." Moctezuma slid from his wrist a gold bracelet from which dangled a small jade image of the Aztec war god. "I will send to the east coast several of my nobles with this, which gives them the power to enforce my commands."

Cortés was not mollified. He pointed to the bracelet. "How do I know that little green fellow has not just returned from a trip to Cualpopoca when you commanded him to kill the two emissaries of Juan Escalante?" These words, translated into Nahuatl, had a great many sibilants; Moctezuma drew slightly back from me, as from a menacing serpent.

"I am innocent of any such command."

Cortés strode forward one step. "Then prove it!"

"How can I prove it, my lord?"

"Come with me to my palace and remain there as my guest until Cualpopoca arrives to clarify his slaughter of innocent Spaniards."

I stared at him, not believing the words I had just heard. An impatient nod urged me to repeat them in Moctezuma's language. When I did his face turned white, then turned red with anger. He straightened his back, staring down at Cortés. "Who ever heard that a great king like myself ever left his own palace to become the prisoner of strangers?"

Now murmurs arose from his nobles; they turned to look into one another's shocked faces. Of this Cortés seemed unaware. He took another step forward, his voice as hard as steel. "Not prisoner: hostage. I cannot any longer trust you. You must be my hostage until the truth comes out."

Moctezuma now looked dazed. "That, of course, is impossible. But if it is hostages you require, I offer you three of my children."

"I want you and only you! Your willingness to comply will tell me much about your innocence as to Cholula or this new aggression against me. Hostage is perhaps too harsh a term. You will be my guest. My men will obey your every command. You will live in whatever rooms of your father's palace you choose. But I insist that you now show me your good faith. If you did not order Cualpopoca to kill my men, then you will feel no hesitance about leaving this room with me, and now."

The murmurs from the nobles were louder now. They buzzed inside my head like angry bees as I respoke these words. Cortés' courage had turned to folly! Here in the heart of this city of several hundred thousand Aztecs all fanatically devoted to Moctezuma he dared to make this demand!

"What is the use of all these words?" Alvarado shouted. "Why

209

waste our lives bickering with this barbarian? Either he comes with us or we kill him, here and now!'' And he half-drew his sword. As I stared at that gleaming steel, Captain Juan Velásquez shouted ''Yes, here and now!'' The other five captains, faces resolute, closed their fists on sword handles.

I said to Cortés, in a low, warning tone, ''Surely I am not to say *this* to Moctezuma!''

He did not look at me but kept his eyes on Moctezuma's. ''Tell him to dismiss his nobles.''

I did so. After a moment's confused hesitation, he obeyed. He did not seem to be able to remove his eyes from those of Cortés. With a whispering of sandals, all the Aztecs who had surrounded their ruler crossed the room and left. Then Cortés said, ''Now tell Moctezuma what Alvarado said about killing him.''

Looking up at the Aztec ruler I made my voice pleading. ''Please, my lord Moctezuma, do as Cortés asks. If you go with him to his palace, he will treat you with all respect and reverence. If you refuse, you will expose yourself to violence, even to death.''

Cortés raised his arm. Steel rasped on scabbards as six captains drew out shining blades and held them out at arm's length, all pointing toward Moctezuma's heart.

The sight of those swords had a stunning impact on a man never touched except at his own command. Staring down at them his cheeks seemed to grow hollow; his lids veiled his eyes to shut out what he saw. The threat of murder had unnerved him as though from the clear blue sky lightning had pierced through a palace window to sear him with its white heat. On that golden throne he seemed to shrink. Cortés grew taller.

In that moment which seemed like an hour I waited in terror for the cry of outrage from Moctezuma that would summon his nobles, then his warriors. But he rose slowly from his throne, stepped down from the dais on which it stood. His eyes did not seem to see Cortés, or me, or anything, but stared inward at some dreadful vision there, some imperative that drove him to obey Cortés. ''To prove my friendship, I will do as Lord Cortés wishes.'' His voice was low and dazed.

I breathed again. My translation was scarcely necessary: his whole being spoke of his submission. Cortés gave no sign of the enormous relief he must have felt. He bowed to the Aztec ruler, then turned to leave. He and Moctezuma crossed the throne room side by side like dear friends. The captains sheathed their swords and followed. A throng of nobles filled the corridor; I held my breath for fear Moctezuma, seeing them, might be reminded of his great power, tell them he was to be made a captive by Cortés. But he merely nodded at them and asked that his royal litter be brought to take him through the plaza to the gate of Cortés' palace. "There I wish to visit for a time," he said.

There was only one answer: he thought he walked with a god's descendant whom he must at any cost appease. It seemed most fitting to me that a Christian soldier should have been confused with a gentle pagan god who had asked that only fruit and flowers be offered at his altars, and never blood. Then the reality of what had just occurred gripped me, and I looked up at Cortés with something of the awe I had felt for him long ago in Tabasco. Kidnapped! He had kidnapped Moctezuma from his own palace in the heart of his own city in the center of a world that had been his to command. Who else would have planned and dared it? I knew then what his earlier cryptic words had meant: he had entangled Moctezuma in a strand of his own web, superstitious fear of the Aztecs' borrowed god.

Tension riddled the next few weeks, though on the surface everything was pleasant. Moctezuma was amenable, the perfect guest. He did not object to the large guard of Spanish soldiers who went with him on his daily visits to the main temple to worship his gods. He seemed pleased when Cortés willingly gave him his own bedroom, for which Moctezuma asked because it had been his father's. When his nobles came to visit him, I had to be present to learn of any orders he might give them to our detriment; he accepted this graciously. He even mustered up a mood of gaiety, as though he were there by choice. One day he ordered three of his canopied pirogues to take Cortés, his captains, and me with him across the lake to Chapultepec, a wooded shore where his other palace stood and where an outdoor meal had been arranged for us by its staff. He took a great liking to little Orteguilla, whose quick mind had enabled him to learn to speak Nahuatl quite well, and Cortés gave him Orteguilla to serve as his page. The two would sometimes stroll together through the palace garden, followed by the usual bodyguard of Spanish soldiers; it was strange to see so great a ruler with a dwarf as his chosen companion.

The underlying tension came from the fact that Moctezuma did not send for Cualpopoca. One day, assuming that this had been done, Cortés saw the bracelet with the jade token of authority still on Moctezuma's wrist, found that he had not yet used it to command his governor's presence in the capital. Charged by Cortés with failing to keep his word, Moctezuma evaded the issue: "I find it pleasant here with you. There is no hurry therefore." He continued to vacillate about the questioning of Cualpopoca, one day promising to bring him before Cortés, the next day refusing to hurry the matter.

"He shows an indecision of mind unbefitting a ruler, or else guilt," Cortés fumed.

Another sore point was Moctezuma's continued resistance to the Christian faith. "I have given my word before my own nobles to accept your sovereign as my own. Do not make further demands on me at present," he said with a cold and haughty show of authority. Nonetheless, our priests and I spent many hours with him, using every power of persuasion to break down Moctezuma's loyalty to heathen gods, to no avail. He was perfectly polite, perfectly unmoved. His occasional remarks reminded me of my own thoughts before the patience of Aguilar and Father Olmedo and the flaming destruction of the idols at Zempoalla made a wholehearted Christian of me. Moctezuma, for example, found the notion of the virgin birth of Christ absurd, since Mary had already married Joseph and therefore was not a virgin at all. Nor did he think it likely that Eve had been made of a rib of Adam, since in that case all men now living would lack one rib, but this was not true. He conceded that the Spaniards clearly worshiped a powerful deity; he denied that it was the only one. "My people, like the Toltecs, have long understood that there may be a One and Unknown God much greater than any represented by our idols. This Force never took the form of a man or died on any cross. This Force is above and beyond mere human understanding. This Force is not your God or your Jesus."

Moctezuma surprised me one day by asking me to walk with him in the gardens of his own palace: perhaps the absence from his wives and concubines had left a yearning for female companionship, although Orteguilla had told me that he had remarked favorably on my appearance and intelligence. "All I ask is that you do not speak of religion," he said in a weary voice as we set forth, followed by the clanking Spanish guard.

"What would it please you to talk about, Lord Moctezuma?"

He paused before his menagerie of wild animals near the great aviary, stared at a caged jaguar, then moved on to the reptile house to watch a rattlesnake coil itself in its feather-lined trough. "You may choose the subject," he said.

I seized the chance to ask about the disquieting omens spoken of by the Toltec farmer. His face grew even more somber. The rattlesnake raised its tail and issued its sinister warning.

"Omens, disturbing oracles, strange happenings have marked my reign from any other," he said. The arrival of the pale bearded strangers at Yucatán had been only the beginning. Ten years before the arrival of Cortés, the waters of Lake Texcoco had become violently agitated during an earthquake, had poured into Tenochtitlán, sweeping away many smaller houses. Then the coldest winter in history iced the whole valley so that thousands froze to death. Not long after this Popocatepetl erupted, its lava burying an outlying temple to the Aztec war god. Then a strange bird with a mirror in its head was found and brought to Moctezuma, perhaps sent by Tezcatlipoca. The bird died. Only a few years before the Spaniards' arrival, a weird crackling blaze of light, broad at the base and tapering to a point and sparkling with tiny stars had appeared in the eastern sky; from it came a wailing as of many voices. At this time one of the wooden turrets atop the war god's temple caught fire from no known cause and continued to burn, inextinguishable, for a long time. All these events, unprecedented as they were, had seemed to the priests of Tenochtitlán and of Texcoco to be warnings of a disaster that would befall the Valley of Anahuac at the end of the Aztec calendar's Fire-Sun era of fifty-two years. "The last day of each such cycle of time is one of great danger," he said. "For the ancients knew that the sun may fail to rise in the sky, and all things cease. But these extraordinary phenomena, clustered in so brief a time and in this valley, indicated a more particular danger than the sun's death which would affect all the earth. My old friend Nezahualpilli of Texcoco was warned many years ago that if this disaster was to be averted an extraordinary propitiation of the gods was required. His priests told him that unless his favorite son was offered up as a sacrifice, doom was certain. But he refused to let this son be killed, saying that he disdained to placate gods so cruel. The fact is that he privately believed only in the One and Unknown God, though he of course rendered the customary public homage to a large pantheon of other deities in which his people believed." Moctezuma smiled sadly. "He was a poet. In his old age he made many songs about the shortness of life and the need to enjoy its roses. One day he and I bet on different players in a *tlachtili* game; the wager was that if I won, the danger that threatened our kingdoms would be averted. But I lost. He died soon after that." He gave me a sad, grim smile. "His city had already declined; chaos followed his death; I chose the next ruler of Texcoco."

"As to the One and Unknown God he believed in: did you never come to believe in Him too?"

"I told you, my friend was a poet, not a realist. He would have been wiser to have sacrificed his son, for he had a great many." His eyes met mine in a chill and remote look. "I told you that I do not wish to discuss the gods."

The tranquility of that lovely garden was suddenly shattered by the roar of a jaguar. A flash of fear prickled through me. In great part the strange events Moctezuma had just described had contributed to his present belief that a god had sent Cortés to judge him. But if newer omens caused that belief to waver, Cortés would find that it would have been less dangerous to have brought into his bedroom all the wild animals and venomous reptiles in the garden's zoo.

Moctezuma's next words were like a confirmation of this thought of mine. "The strange events I have just told you of show one thing very clearly. The gods I worship and shall continue to revere gave me many warnings. They will continue to reward my devotion. As of now, they indicate that I am to wait with patience."

We passed then to the House of Freaks, where I saw a girl with white hair and skin and lavender eyes, a boy with skin like a snake's, a creature whose hands grew from its shoulders, a woman so fat she could not walk, a man with a pointed head no bigger than two fists clenched together, a man with a huge round skull, and a number of dwarfs all smaller than Orteguilla. "In these creatures, appearance and reality truly meet," Moctezuma said. "Nothing can disguise their true nature, which is their deformity." His eyes searched my face. "You appear to be of my race, yet you live with people of another and speak their language. What is your true nature, Malinche?"

Taken off guard I said, "I am a Christian and the tongue of Cortés and beyond that of no great importance."

He smiled. "Beauty is never unimportant. At an earlier time I might have made you my concubine."

"At an earlier time, Lord Moctezuma, I was a slave in Tabasco, and before that daughter of the cacique of Paynala and named by him to rule after him."

His interest in me suddenly faded. "I am tired and will rest now, then bathe and change my clothing." Each day he dressed in new garments, all very splendid. As we turned toward the palace he had given Cortés, I knew that even if I had told him of my childhood betrayal, he would have been little interested. Tribute flowed to him from many conquered towns and nations; their internal problems were their own.

Walking through a rose garden he had the wan air of a man whom reality has abandoned. He paused to stare at a red rose; a fish in one of the marble pools then caught his attention. Perhaps these simple forms of life soothed his complicated mind, patiently waiting for his gods to let him know whether he should summon Cualpopoca or defy Cortés.

That night he maintained his royal dignity in spite of the shocking experience of dining in public and not behind a carved and gilded screen so that no mortal eye might see him chew and swallow: Cortés had arranged for a huge banquet in honor of his royal guest. As always, Moctezuma's wine was chilled with ice from the heights of Popocatepetl. His frothy chocolate drink, thickened with honey and spices, he ate with a tortoiseshell spoon from a golden cup. A curious mark of Aztec sophistication was that before the meal and after we had eaten servants brought us basins of warm water and cloths with which to wash our hands. But despite delicious foods—meats with rich sauces; fowl stuffed with fruit; luscious pastries of maize flour, eggs, and aloe sugar—I could not really enjoy the feast. Watching Moctezuma sip from his golden goblet, I was very much aware that for all the extreme luxury and indulgence that had so long surrounded him, the fierce blood of his indomitable ancestors flowed in his veins. Would Cortés be the serpent he at last held in his talons and devoured?

Cortés tried to use the feast as a means of persuasion. "If Cualpopoca were here tonight, and had convinced me that the slaughter of my Spaniards was in any way provoked or justified, then he would be sitting here as my honored guest, second only to yourself."

Moctezuma said almost petulantly, "I have made many sacrifices and have asked the gods to enlighten me on this matter but they have not."

Cortés could not hide his irritation. "There are times when we are expected to behave on our own accord and use the brains we have been given!"

"That may be true for you, Cortés, but it is not true for me." Moctezuma's personal steward knelt to offer him a long pipe of gilded wood and he inhaled the tobacco smoke with pleasure, emitting gray clouds that veiled from him Cortés' urgent face.

The next morning Cortés had another chance to reprove Moctezuma for Cualpopoca's absence. It was reported to him that one of the soldiers of Moctezuma's bodyguard had spoken rudely to him and had urinated in his presence. Cortés had the man arrested, brought before Moctezuma and himself, and flogged. "That is how I treat anyone under my command who does you an injury, Moctezuma. I expect like respect from you. Yet you continue to protect Cualpopoca by refusing me the chance to question him. How long must this continue? Why do you make it so hard for me to believe in the innocence you profess?"

Moctezuma urbanely deplored such a cruel punishment as flogging for so minor an offense, a sentiment flagrantly insincere coming from so clean and elegant a king, in a city whose people were so devoted to bathing, as if to wash away any guilt they felt over all the blood spilled on their many altars.

But rites of sacrifice at one of these altars must have provided Moctezuma with the omen or oracle he claimed to have been awaiting. Three weeks after he became a hostage he announced that Cualpopoca had been sent for and was arriving that very day.

He rode on a litter, accompanied by one of his sons and fifteen other attendants. Entering the audience room where Cortés and Moctezuma awaited him on the dais in two golden chairs, he paused at the door to put on over his fine attire a humble robe of *nequen,* then came forward to kneel at his ruler's feet. Moctezuma spoke coldly and firmly. "You must answer all Cortés' questions honestly." He stood up then and left.

"Are you a subject of Moctezuma?" Cortés asked the governor.

"And what other sovereign could I serve?" Cualpopoca had risen and faced Cortés boldly.

"Did you order two Spaniards killed when they visited you?"

"I do not deny this." Cualpopoca stripped off the *nequen* robe and let it drop to the floor.

"Did you order your warriors to fight against Spaniards, and were seven of them killed?"

"That, too, occurred."

"And was this done at the order of your ruler Moctezuma?"

After a moment, Cualpopoca said, "I have authority in the area I govern and do not always have to ask his permission."

"Then Moctezuma did *not* instruct you to take such extreme measures?"

Now the governor's voice was less assured. "I am trusted by him to a very great extent."

Cortés gave him a smoldering look. "I, too, am trusted by him! In fact, he has placed your fate in my hands! That fate may well be the immediate arrest of you, your son, and your attendants. There is nothing Moctezuma can or will do to prevent this. So cease all this evasion and give me simple honest answers!"

Cualpopoca paled; his throat moved as he swallowed. "No one had to tell me to remain loyal to my ruler and not swear to obey another king."

"But did he tell you to kill my Spaniards?"

"They tried to tell me to forsake my gods as well."

"I want straight answers! If I tell you this evasion will mean your death this very day, will that bring the simple truth out of you?"

Cualpopoca's bearing changed. His shoulders drooped. He looked at his frightened son. "What truth do you mean?"

"Did you decide on your own authority to kill Spaniards?"

There was a long pause. Cualpopoca stared straight ahead at the empty golden chair Moctezuma had left. "In such an important matter I would not act merely on my own authority."

Cortés' fist pounded down on the arm of his chair. "I knew it!" He turned to his watching captains. "Take this man and his retinue away. Put them all in irons."

I left the audience room filled with uneasiness. All along I had believed that Cualpopoca had acted alone. In sudden fear of his life, and deserted by his monarch, did he lie or tell the truth?

This uneasiness refused to leave me. If Cortés was convinced that Moctezuma had planned the attack on the soldiers at Vera Cruz while treating Cortés as his guest and friend, would Cortés retaliate? Would he forget that Moctezuma's fatalistic patience might snap at last?

Finally I sent a servant to find Cortés and tell him I wished very much to speak with him. Before she returned, one of Moctezuma's attendants came to say that Lord Moctezuma wished to talk with me, and at once.

He was alone in the sleeping chamber where Cortés and I had first stayed, and which had been turned over to him. He sat in a carved and gilded chair near the narrow window overlooking the great square. Beyond its far buildings the sun was setting, the sky a blaze of orange light. The glow was reflected on the gold wine cup in his hand. Instead of any panache of plumes he wore only a narrow jeweled headband. His black hair, slightly graying, hung straight nearly to his shoulders. I had never seen him so simply attired. "What did Cualpopoca tell Cortés?" he asked in a rather querulous voice.

"He admitted that you ordered the killing of the Spaniards." I watched his face closely, but saw no hint of guilt.

"That is not true."

"He was in great fear of Cortés."

"What will happen to him?"

"He and his son and attendants have been arrested."

He sighed heavily. "All over my domain people fear my name. Yet I have been powerless to prevent this. I do not think my father or my uncle would find themselves helpless as I am now. I cannot believe what has happened to me in these last weeks." He raised the cup, swallowed wine. "When I was young, I was a very brave warrior. I attained the highest of honors and was made a member of a select military order. I did all this as a means of becoming First Speaker. There were others as eligible: my brother Cuitlahuac, and my cousin Cuauhtemoc, for example. As you may know, succession among us is not from father to son, but from uncle to nephew or brother to brother. Before my uncle Ahuitzotl the Cruel chose another nephew to succeed him, he told me privately that I am unlike our ancestors, that I lack in my nature a certain fierceness which an Aztec ruler must possess. Deeply hurt, I reminded him that fierceness can take horrible forms, and mentioned a daughter of his who married Nezahualpilli, and demanded a separate palace, to which she brought her many lovers, all of whom she killed and had minions make statues around their bodies, keeping some in the bedroom where she reveled. Her husband found out and had her publicly strangled. It was stupid of me to remind my uncle of this crazed daughter. It lost me any faint chance I had of becoming his successor." He drank again, and suddenly he smiled. "But it is surely the gods who rule our destinies. The chosen nephew died suddenly, soon after Ahuitzotl did. That left it to the Council of Four and the thirty clan chiefs to decide on a new ruler. They selected me. It was I, not the fiercer cousin my uncle had chosen, who walked up the steps of the great pyramid to address the people with humility and have the green panache placed on my head." His eyes looked back in time at that great day.

I was in part amazed that he spoke to me so intimately, yet I also knew that he was speaking as much to himself, trying to grasp the threads of his life which had been ripped, unraveled, and tangled by the hand of Cortés.

"As a boy," Moctezuma said, "I thought that if I ever became First Speaker I would inaugurate an old Toltec custom. They used to have Battles of the Flowers, in which no blood was shed. Prisoners were taken as proof of victory after being touched by blunt spears, but then they were garlanded with flowers and released to fight again. And after my coronation I abandoned warfare and turned my mind to the great mysteries, to astronomy and astrology, to the interpretation of omens, to the secrets of the universe. Do you know that the earth, which seems flat, is a round planet like the moon, and also moves through the sky? Do you know that when the heart is taken from a sacrificed person he feels no pain? As his eyes see the knife raised above his body, the god to whom he is being offered sucks out of him all power to feel it so that no screams of pain or writhing of the body can occur to destroy the sacred moment." He nodded. "As a high priest who must order many sacrifices, it comforts me to know that."

"If you are also a high priest, how is it that you can have so many wives and concubines? Christian priests have none, nor did the high priest in my town of Paynala."

My question seemed to bewilder him. "But I am also First Speaker! One of the many prerogatives of such power is the acquisition of wives and concubines. This is expected of me, demanded by precedent. The common people must live monogamous lives. They enjoy the thought that their ruler is able to revel in pleasures denied them. It pleases them that I never wear the same clothing twice, but give away what is once worn. My palace also gives them pride. My palace is exquisite, is it not? I have gone further than any monarch who preceded me in matters of elegance and style. By comparison, my ancestors were as barbaric as the Chichimecas of the northern deserts." He found his wine cup empty, held it out. A steward I had not noticed came and took it from his hand. He straightened in his chair. "No one can say now that we are inferior to the Toltecs. We have outdone them!"

"Your city is very marvelous and beautiful." I felt almost as if I were praising a child for some feat.

The steward returned with the filled goblet. Moctezuma did not notice him, but leaned forward, his eyes filled with woe. "Yet here I am, a prisoner of Cortés!"

I spoke gently. "You are his hostage because you refuse to accept his God. God wants your soul, not your body."

"My soul?" He accepted the goblet of wine which the steward had continued to hold out until his ruler might deign to take it. "I am not dead."

"Those who believe in God will never die. They will live with Him in Heaven, forever."

I thought I saw a gleam of interest in his brooding eyes. "I have listened to a great many words concerning your religion. But for some reason I did not understand that your God offers immortality. Perhaps I turned off my ears. I did that often. Immortality? Or do you merely speak of the long journey of the disembodied spirit to the dark realm of the dead called Mictlán?"

"Heaven is bright and beautiful, filled with angels and with good Christians."

"By Christian standards, I am not good," he said. "Of this I am well aware."

"God forgives all our sins if we believe in Him and confess our wrongs."

"One of your God's commandments is not to kill. I have killed many men. Would this be forgiven me?" He was half smiling, as if he believed I would have to answer *no*.

"Yes," I said.

"I also remember that your Deity can heal afflictions."

"He can heal all ills of the mind and spirit, if we believe in Him."

"And can he make impotent men virile once again?" Our eyes met; I knew what he had admitted. "Since Cortés came here no woman can arouse me."

"I believe that when you kneel humbly and accept Him above any other gods he will remove this affliction." Moctezuma's great candor had amazed me, yet at the same time I felt strong within. Was I to be the one who reached his heart?

"Are you suggesting that I do as Cortés asked and remove my

people's gods from their temples?'' I could feel his resistance, see it in his frowning face.

" 'You shall shall have no other God.' That is His first command.''

"Again you confront me with this alarming renunciation of all that I have ever believed in!'' He stood up; the steward took the golden goblet from his hand. "My priests would never consent! My people would refuse to have their gods taken from them!''

"But you are First Speaker. Your word becomes law. You have the power to save yourself and all your people from burning forever in Hell.''

He winced; Christian priests are very effective in describing the eternal torments in store for sinners and heathens. With weak defiance Moctezuma demanded: "As for this Hell, where is it? And where is your Heaven, since earth is a planet?''

I pointed down at the stone floor. "In the realm of the spirit, Hell is the lowest place, Heaven the highest. It is like the bright Realm of the Sun where I once thought brave warriors go when they die, only Heaven is even more beautiful, and more filled with peace. It is like the loveliest moment of the happiest day you have ever known, stretched out to last forever.''

"Peace! I have known very little peace since I first put on the green panache of power. Pomp and luxury and worship, yes. But very little peace.'' He sank into his chair. "If I were to accept this God of yours, how can I be sure He would not condemn me for things I have done? Send me down to Hell?''

Now a sense of power touched me; it filled me as the wind fills a ship's sails. "God does not want you there! He wants your soul to be with him in Heaven!'' I took a step toward him and dared to say again what Cortés had told him. "Your war god is Satan. I beg of you, do not revere him a day longer! Kneel humbly, as I have done, to the only God, the God of Cortés! He will forgive your worship of false gods, for you knew no better. He will remember a little boy who wanted all battles to be Battles of the Flowers. For He is called the Prince of Peace.''

When I saw his eyes gleam with unshed tears I knew that God had inspired me to touch a deep chord in his nature. My whole being was tense with hope. I might succeed where wise priests had failed! I knew I must not say another word but let the gentleness at the core of Moctezuma's being flow up in his heart and wash away the now-crumbling wall of his resistance.

Night had now fallen. Through the window behind him I saw the evening star. Suddenly a bright glow was there outside as though the sunset had returned. I walked to the window and looked out. I heard a cry of horror. The voice was mine.

In the Zocalo below the window stood a long row of stakes each amid leaping flames where Cualpopoca and his retinue made living torches. The fires lighted the faces of stunned Aztecs watching their first auto-da-fé and were reflected on the breastplates of Cortés and his captains. The stench of burning flesh filled my nostrils. I heard myself cry "My God!"

"Your God of mercy," I heard a voice behind me say. I turned. Moctezuma's face was lighted by those fires below. "Your Prince of Peace!" A burst of flame leaped up to the height of the window and was reflected in those hard black eyes. "Go from me. Ask your God to explain such mercy as this!"

As I turned and walked numbly toward the doorway, a male servant entered with a blazing torch to light those in the brackets on the wall. The pleasant resinous odor of this smoke did not eradicate the stench of charred human bodies. I turned my head to look back in anguish at Moctezuma. His face was lighted by the torches within the room. Behind was the glare of those other flames. Back straight, he looked every inch a king. And I knew he was lost to God forever except by some miracle God might send.

25

Heavy footfalls thudded on the stone floor of the corridor. Cortés entered with a burly soldier who carried iron manacles: black chains and a heavy ball. At a lope, bent by the weight in his hands, he approached Moctezuma, knelt, and clamped the leg irons shut around his ankles. At a gesture from Cortés he pushed the carved gold chair to a place behind the chained ruler so he could seat himself. Moctezuma bent his head to look down at his fetters. From his throat came a deep groan. The flames of the wall torches and the glare of other flames below the window made him look to me like a man chained in Hell. The staring servant with the torch backed to the door and ran out.

Cortés beckoned me and said, "Moctezuma, your governor has admitted that you ordered the murder of Spaniards. Such a crime merits death for your subjects who were responsible. Even for a sovereign, this crime cannot be atoned for without some punishment."

He waited for me to speak. My tongue refused.

He turned to stare at me. "Speak up! Tell him what I said!"

Nausea from burning bodies clogged my throat; my hand covered my mouth; I held down rising vomit.

"By God, what is wrong with you?" Cortés' harsh voice would have alarmed me if I had had room for any more emotion than I now felt. "Speak!"

I swallowed and repeated in Nahuatl: "The crime of killing the Spaniards merits death for your subjects. For you, this punishment." Moctezuma stared down at the iron ball resting beside his gold sandal. He moaned.

Cortés spoke again. "I want you to reflect on how you deceived me and tricked me after saying you would hold me in honor."

This time he did not have to urge me to speak; like that silver parrot in the market that opened its beak when a wire was pulled, I told Moctezuma what Cortés wished.

"I have never deceived you," he whispered, and sank down slowly on his chair, staring at nothing with dazed eyes.

Behind me I heard the loud and growing noise of many sandals in the corridor and turned as the crowd of Moctezuma's nobles poured into the room, somewhat hesitant about entering without having been sent for. They spread out along the two walls at either side of the doorway. Cortés, the soldier, and I were between them. Others filled the exit. All stared at their chained ruler, awaiting his command.

Cortés turned and faced those in the doorway, waiting imperiously for them to let him pass. The human wall awaited orders from their ruler. It was Cuitlahuac who said, "Do you wish the strangers to leave, Lord Moctezuma?"

I felt my flesh shrink, watched Moctezuma's face for the first sign of his rising anger, reminded by the question of his status and his power. In his pale face pale lips opened. His eyes looked at nothing, or everything. "Let them leave me," he whispered.

Obediently, the human wall parted, flowed aside. Cortés, the soldier, and I passed into the corridor between angry and bewildered faces. The soldier grinned up at Cortés. "That was a narrow one!"

Smiling grimly, Cortés shook his head. "No. I knew the irons

would break his spirit if the sight of his governor in flames had not
already done so."

A moan like the one that had come from Moctezuma's throat now
came from mine. "Lost. We have lost him."

Cortés looked down at me. "What is wrong with you, Doña
Marina? You are not like your usual self today."

There was an interval of blankness between walking beside Cortés
along that corridor and the moment I found myself in the chapel on
my knees before the statue of the Blessed Virgin. Votive candles
burned at her feet; her serene white face looked down on me; one pale
hand was raised in benediction. High above the altar hung a large
crucifix; on Christ's gaunt cheek shone a glass tear. My body was
rocking backward and forward as it had the day my father died. Now,
too, my tears were silent ones. "Hail Mary, full of grace, be with us
now and in the hour of our death," I whispered. But when I tried to
raise my hand to cross myself it did not move.

I knew then why I had come here. My faith in the Christian God
was in peril. Mere statues of stone and wood had burned in Zempoalla,
but now this stench of human flesh was still lodged in my throat so
that even the sweet aroma that came from the new cedar pews could
not take it away. I willed myself to be aware of that smell of the wood
of trees first made by the hand of God and now serving His purpose
here, destined by Him when they were mere seedlings to grow large
and tall and be made into these seats in the first Christian church in
Tenochtitlán. This thought soothed me. I too was God's humble
creature. Humility, Aguilar had told me, is the first duty of a Christian,
who must accept that God's ways are mysterious, not always to be
understood by us. Faith comes from such humility.

A cry went up inside me: but how humble is Cortés? How humble
is a man who burns other men so cruelly? Chains a captive king?
Where is the humility of Hernán Cortés? What sort of Christian is he?
Is he one at all?

The Virgin to whom I raised my eyes had no answer. Her gentle
face and upraised hand seemed to counsel patience until God chose
to enlighten me.

But patience did not come; instead another emotion began to burn
in me: anger. Anger at Cortés. And, for the first time, contempt. He
believed himself so astute, yet had ordered set alight those flames in
which Moctezuma's tenuous rootlet of belief in God had been
consumed.

From the chapel doorway behind me came the animal noise of someone retching. I turned. One hand against the corridor wall opposite the wide aperture, a Spanish soldier was bent double, vomiting. His helmet tumbled from his head and clanged to the stone floor. A gilded helmet. Arturo Mondragon's.

The little figure of Orteguilla, who must have been following, ran forward; he picked up the helmet. "Well, at least you didn't do it in the chapel!"

Arturo straightened, wiping his mouth on the back of his hand. Through the open door he saw me. Orteguilla did too, and came running toward me. His cocky grin was gone. "Cortés has put Moctezuma in chains. I saw him. In leg irons. He was weeping. Some of his nobles, too. They could not comfort him."

"I know," I said.

Arturo joined us, casque under one arm. His voice was loud yet unsteady. "I rarely vomit. Only once when I was seasick. It was the auto-da-fé. I never saw one before. My father once told me about a Carib cacique in Cuba who was put to the torch for refusing the Christian faith. As the faggots were lighted at his feet he asked if being burned would send him to the Christian Heaven anyhow. No, they told him. He showed great relief and said that was good, as he would not care to go to a place occupied by such Christians as he had known." He looked down at me uncertainly. "I can't help but think that Moctezuma may feel much the same."

"One thing is sure," Orteguilla said. "He must be released from those leg irons. How much can he be expected to endure? Those nobles of his are going to work on his mind, believe me! Cuitlahuac and Cuauhtemoc in particular. I am trying to get up the courage to tell this to Cortés."

The deep feeling of the little man and his desire to reprove Cortés moved me. "He doesn't take rebuke kindly, but he is good at plucking the truth from mere opinion or rhetoric." Many nights beside Cortés seemed now like irrelevant dreams I once had. The daytime man who had laughed when I pricked his arrogance might listen to the dwarf.

"I have my methods," Orteguilla nodded with some of his usual assurance. "Oh, he listens to me, all right. That's what jesters are for, to offer truth with a grin."

"If you can joke about what happened today, you belong at the court in Madrid," Arturo said.

Orteguilla turned to me. "Will you come with me, Doña Marina? I've noticed that he sometimes listens to you, too."

"Well," Arturo said, "I came here to pray and had better do it."
He knelt near me before the Virgin, clasped his hands, bent his head.
"Holy Mary," I heard him whisper, "help me to understand this
thing and then to forget it. Amen."

As we left, several Spanish soldiers approached the chapel, casques
in hand, followed by half a dozen more.

We found Cortés in his room, sunk low in his armchair and
evidently in a dark mood. His captains were just leaving. They were
unusually quiet and said good night to their commander in subdued
voices. "Good night, gentlemen," Cortés said. "Perhaps my dwarf
can cheer me after this momentous day. Play me a song, Orteguilla.
Something on the merry side, if that will not annoy Doña Marina,
who appears to prefer a funeral dirge to go with her dismal mood."

Orteguilla sat cross-legged at Cortés' feet, looking up. "As I do
not have my guitar with me, I will tell you a fable. It concerns a brave
rat-knight who led his band of rats into a sleeping lion's lair. The
rat took some jewels, and the lion slept on. He drew his sword and
killed a few of the lion's cubs, and still the lion slept. But then, made
bold, the rat-knight tied the lion's paws and muzzle. The lion woke,
snapped the bonds and gave a roar that summoned a thousand lions,
who pounced on the rats and ate them all up."

"I could wish that you had not made me a rat," Cortés said with
a forced smile.

"Cat and mouse, lion and rat," Orteguilla said, paling slightly.
"The point is, sire, that until today Moctezuma was as docile as that
sleeping lion before he was fettered."

"I know the point! But there's much that you do not know! None
of you!" He glared at Arturo. "What are you here for?"

Arturo raised his head high and I noticed for the first time that his
beard was trimmed exactly like that of Cortés. "I came to say that the
auto-da-fé seemed to me excessive punishment, and that other soldiers
feel the same."

Cortés stood up, glaring down at Arturo. "Excessive! Rat-knights
and lions! Has it occurred to none of you that Moctezuma is playing
a feline's waiting game? The murder of those Spaniards was a test of
my power! I could not let it pass. If the auto-da-fé is what bothers
you, then let me point out that this is the means the Church has long
used to deal with heathens. I did not invent it. All Cualpopoca had to
do was kiss the Cross. Aguilar made that clear. He refused. If his soul
is frying in Hell, don't blame me!"

"And the chains on Moctezuma?" Orteguilla asked.

"I had to cope with his anger on seeing his governor burned! The best way was to humble him."

By now I had seen that Cortés' defensive anger showed that he was uneasy about the chains, if not the flames. I stepped toward him. "You may get more than his humility," I said.

He turned to me, frowning. "More? What more? I want no more."

"If you keep him chained, he may choose to die."

"Die? He has no weapon. Do you mean he could command an adulating noble to kill him? A *coup de grâce?* Is that what you mean?" His voice was urgent now.

"A man who chooses to die can will himself to die."

"Nonsense!" But now Cortés looked both thoughtful and alarmed.

"If Moctezuma chooses to die, because his terrible humiliation makes him believe his gods have abandoned him, another First Speaker will be chosen. Perhaps Cuitlahuac. Or Cuauhtemoc. They do not like Spaniards, and I do not think they are owerawed by you as Moctezuma is."

"They are not." Cortés looked grim.

"You need Moctezuma alive, don't you? None of his subjects will make one move against you unless he commands it. His successor's first command might be your death. The death of all of us."

He stood staring at me alertly. Then he went to his writing table and took something from a carved box: a key. The key to Moctezuma's chains! His face was resolute. "I have degraded Moctezuma. But I can also exalt him." I followed him down the stone corridor to Moctezuma's room.

Surrounded by Aztec nobles who looked confused, sad, anguished, or stoic, the ruler sat huddled in his golden chair, head bent low. Cortés crossed the room, knelt before him, and unlocked the leg irons. He unclasped and removed them. Still kneeling, he spread his arms in a gesture that implored forgiveness. "I regret the disagreeable necessity of subjecting you to this brief punishment, Moctezuma."

As I repeated those humble words, the discovery that his legs were again free brought Moctezuma back from his deep trance of sorrow. In a weak voice he said "I thank you for my freedom." He stood up, walked a step or two, shaken.

Cortés also rose. "I offer you a further freedom. I am convinced that you will be loyal to me, whatever your governor did. So I offer you permission to go back to your own palace to live."

IN THE SILVER CITY

Amazement unnerved me. I knew Cortés had gone too far in his effort to regain Moctezuma's friendship. Once removed from Cortés' personal magnetism, once in daily frequent contact with those nobles who wanted the Spaniards dead or banished, how long would Moctezuma continue to protect us?

As Moctezuma heard Cortés' offer of this freedom, his face had a wistful look; it was replaced by one of resolve. "Many of the nobles in my palace want me to take up arms against you. If I were living among them it would be hard for me to avoid that alternative. But it would pitch my city into a war of great bloodshed and violence. Your weapons would kill thousands of my people. I will not do that to my city."

I felt my tense body suddenly relax. I repeated these words for Cortés in Spanish. But Moctezuma added these: "Nor can I let anyone believe that I purchased my liberty at the price of my governor's terrible death. I must remain here with you, Cortés."

Smiling, Cortés rushed forward to embrace Moctezuma joyously. "I will love you from this day like a brother! Every Spaniard will have your interests first in their hearts!"

Moctezuma stared stoically out, suffering this embrace, he who was never touched. Murmurs of amazement rose from the nobles watching, and I saw Cuauhtemoc stare, mouth open, at Cortés embracing the First Speaker as if the sight would be engraved on his mind to the moment of his death.

As we left, Cortés smiled down at me. "You gave me good counsel, Marina." But I could not return his smile.

A little later, Cortés having gone to tell his captains of the new status of affairs, I removed my clothing and other possessions from the room we shared and took them to the one where Doña Luisa and Ixlan slept. A pallet was brought by servants for me, and it was soft enough for a queen or Moctezuma's favorite concubine, but it was a long time before my eyes would close. I was tense with anxiety, fearing that Cortés would demand my presence in the other bedroom. But it became clear that he was too proud or too angry to do more than ignore my absence. I said a prayer at last and composed myself to sleep among women for the first time in a very long while.

I knew that fear and not repentance had brought Cortés to his knees to remove those shackles. Once again he had created a crisis; once again he had met it with apparent success. His ambition had created all the crises he had overcome. In resolving them with violence or with craft, he had created a new Cortés who seemed more of a stranger to me than that god in armor I first saw in Tabasco.

For many nights my dreams were haunted by bodies aflame, Moctezuma in chains, and by the heavy hand of Cortés on my arm, shaking me awake to come to his bed, and from this dream I awoke with a scream. Yet by day our relationship of commander and interpreter continued as before, except that no intimate words were spoken between us. He was as courteous and as distant as if we had never touched and never referred to my change of sleeping place. After a time I was torn in half between the frightening executioner of my nightmares and the Cortés I saw by day, and within me these two were in conflict; my emotional reaction after the auto-da-fé was on one side of the battle, but on the other was the knowledge that Cortés was in an excruciating position. His letters to the King of Spain had gone unacknowledged. His bold unauthorized march to the Aztec capital would certainly anger Governor Velásquez when he learned of it, for it had placed in jeopardy the expedition in which he had invested much money and much hope. Cortés could not relax his strong grip on the emotions of the Aztec ruler. Was it just of me to blame him for maintaining it by means of a custom to which he had been used since birth, however appalling it might be to me? Even gentle Father Olmedo, even Aguilar, with his fondness for Indians, had told me that the auto-da-fé had been a grim political necessity that might eventually prove a boon to untold thousands of heathens who by that terrible example could more easily be converted to Christianity, fear being a good persuader. Moctezuma, alas, was not one of these.

26

Moctezuma spent long mornings atop the great temple in worship of his gods, lost in his Region of Mystery. Any enlightenment he received must have counseled continued patience. He continued to ignore those nobles who urged that the strangers be forced to leave the city. As though no subjects of his had ever burned, no leg irons ever chilled his ankles, he returned to his former false amiability: he taught Cortés to play *totoloque,* an Aztec game of chance, and ordered a game of *tlachtli* to be played in the ball court, that large sunken enclosure surrounded by high tiers of stone benches from which we had watched the boy hero die. The towers of skulls in the forecourt of Huitzilo-potchli's temple stared down from thousands of hollow eye sockets at the muscular, agile players who—though wearing heavy yokes of polished stone—sent a ball of *olli* rebounding from walls and finally up into a high stone hoop. Watching this game, I remembered the bet Moctezuma had lost to his old friend Nezahualpilli of Texcoco. It did not surprise me when he turned to Cortés and said, "We will each choose a player to score highest. If mine wins, it will mean that you will leave my city of your own volition."

Cortés agreed, and Moctezuma watched the game with intensity. When his player won he was overjoyed; I knew he took the triumph to be an omen. The next day he took Cortés hunting on the royal game preserve near the Chapultepec palace across the lake; he killed a deer but Cortés missed his. The dead stag was brought back in the pirogue to Tenochtitlán to be butchered and eaten. "Tonight you will eat the proof of my superior marksmanship," he told Cortés, smiling. He held in one hand the blood-stained arrow, glancing often at the obsidian point of his trophy in a way that made me uneasy. He had bested Cortés twice. Would a third time complete the charm?

But the mood of false tranquility and the days of playful competition came to an abrupt end; any comfort Moctezuma might have taken from small triumphs was shattered by the message sent to him from Cacama of Texcoco. It accused him of abject cowardice.

That same day several nobles who had been in Cacama's confidence came to Moctezuma to tell him that the Texcocan ruler was trying to spur a rebellion against him. He had been going to many neighboring caciques of the lakeside towns and farther ones to speak against the Aztec ruler, insisting that he should be replaced by a First Speaker who would either force the Spaniards to leave or kill them all. I was sure that this revolt had been ignited by the flames that killed Cualpopoca even before a sorrowful and deeply disturbed Moctezuma summoned Cortés to his room to tell him of it and to say: "Now you see, Cortés, that your cruel punishment of one of my governors was unwise; it will make all my vassals fear like treatment."

Pale and stunned, Cortés had no answer. He knew that all our lives hung on the outcome of the rebellion. He vigorously urged

Moctezuma to summon his army to put it down in its first stages; Moctezuma vacillated, not wanting to destroy the century-old alliance between Texcoco and Tenochtitlán. And such intervention proved needless: few caciques or governors were willing to rise against Moctezuma. Cacama was captured in his city of Texcoco by traitors he had trusted and was brought in fetters to the capital. With him were several Aztec nobles who had conspired against their ruler. One was Cuitlahuac.

Moctezuma chose not to have him or Cacama executed for treason, and they were imprisoned in a cell in our palace. Remembering how Cacama had come to welcome Cortés, I could imagine what he must be feeling now. Cuitlahuac had taken his imprisonment with a stony indifference, showing no gratitude that he had escaped execution by his brother Moctezuma's forbearance.

Knowing how deeply this unprecedented uprising had disturbed Moctezuma, Cortés decided the time was ripe for him to proclaim his allegiance to Carlos of Spain in a formal ceremony. Moctezuma did not object, and called together all his most important vassals, some of whom came long distances. When they were gathered with his nobles before the golden throne in the large audience hall he told them that Cortés represented their great deity Quetzalcoatl and that the time had at last come when he wished to resume his supreme authority.

"For my part, I am ready to acknowledge this authority. You have all been faithful vassals of mine for as long as I have sat on the throne of my fathers. I now expect you to show me this last act of obedience by acknowledging the great king beyond the eastern waters to be your supreme lord. I shall serve him as he commands me. It is your duty to behave likewise. In doing this you will give me much pleasure." The tears running silently down his cheeks belied the words.

Many of the gathered nobles wept with him, for with those words Moctezuma had relinquished the absolute power that had come down to him from a succession of eight rulers. Yet obedience to his authority was deeply ingrained in them; since he thought the sovereign of Cortés to be their ancient god, they believed this too. The oath of allegiance was solemnly administered. To my surprise, many of the Spanish captains and those foot soldiers who were present seemed deeply moved. I saw tears in Arturo's eyes, and in El Galán's and Sandoval's. Cortés looked grave; when he spoke his voice was husky, although his words were resolute. "First my emperor, next my God," he said to Sandoval. So ended a dynasty.

But Moctezuma steadfastly refused to do away with his pagan

gods and become a Christian. Nevertheless he complied with a request Cortés had made before the rebellion: to send an expedition to the province where there were many gold mines and bring back this raw gold for Cortés' use. Francisco Pizarro, a distant kinsman of Cortés, and several other Spaniards were placed in charge. When the gold arrived, Moctezuma generously added to it many golden objects from his treasury. To me it was painful to see artifacts of rare beauty smashed to bits and then melted down in the stone crucibles of Aztec goldsmiths, to be poured into clay molds that, broken off when cold, left only squat heavy ingots. It took only three days to eradicate the excellent work of many lifetimes.

But Cortés had decided on a division of the spoils, and this was the only way the value of the gold itself could be measured. After the Royal Fifth was set aside, and Cortés' share and that of Governor Velásquez, and double shares for priests, captains, musketeers, those with horses, the foot soldiers got only about a hundred gold pesos' value each for more than a year of faithful service amid great dangers. This caused great anger among them—a small rebellion, in fact, set off by Arturo Mondragon. I learned from Sandoval, who was present, that when the modest heap of nuggets and gold dust was doled out to him, he pushed it right back across the table to the officer who was doing the doling. "Give it to Cortés with my compliments! I would not want our commander to come out of this with empty pockets!"

"But as he turned angrily away, El Galán stopped him," Sandoval told me. "He said that except for pain and the pox, a little is better than none. So Arturo took his share. But a great many other soldiers imitated his gesture of spurning so poor a reward, and Cortés finally went among them and spoke kindly and gave every foot soldier a gift of gold which he said came from his own share." Sandoval sighed. "I wish this division of the loot meant that we could march out of here tomorrow. But I fear not. Cortés is determined to bend Moctezuma to his will in the matter of religion. Sometimes I wish his only interest were gold. Or even glory. He could go back to Cuba a rich man."

But he had undertaken to Christianize the people of a land larger than Spain itself. And he had discovered that Moctezuma could accept Cortés' emperor as his own ancient deity but not Cortés' Deity as the one true God. The visits of the Spanish priests were endured with adamant disinterest and blank eyes.

One day Cortés' patience snapped. Summoning me, he strode into Moctezuma's chamber and told him that the devilish rites of the Aztec priests must be stopped at once. The lengthy thudding of the great snakeskin drum suddenly ceased. "I command you to order the removal of your heathen gods from the temples!"

On the same chair where he had sat in chains not long before Moctezuma was as rigid as one of the idols he now defended. "Perhaps some of our rites seem wrong to you, but I warn you that the destruction of our idols is a sacrilege that neither I, nor the priests, nor the common people will ever permit."

"Permit?" Cortés looked outraged, as if he were the ruler and Moctezuma the intruder. "Permit it they shall!"

He ordered me to follow him, collected a dozen armed soldiers in the courtyard, and led us at a fast pace to the pyramid of the war god and up the steep steps to the *teocalli*, where he entered the chamber in which Huitzilopotchli stood. The hideous colossus glared down on us; today half a dozen human hearts filled the bowl at its feet.

Cortés clasped his hands and stared up toward heaven with anguished eyes. "Oh God, why do you permit such honor to the Devil in this land? But we are here, God, to serve You, and serve You we shall!"

A number of Aztec priests burst into the sanctum. In a loud voice Cortés commanded: "Bring water at once and wash the blood from these walls!" He pointed to a gory inner altar, the spattered wall and floor.

When I translated this the oldest priest rushed toward Cortés, pointing with a blood-red hand. "This is the house of Huitzilopotchli! To honor him the people of this city hold as nothing their lives, or their fathers' or mothers' or childrens'. They will rise up in arms against you! Take heed, stranger, for they will gladly die for their gods!"

Cortés turned and ordered a soldier quickly to bring more armed Spaniards to the temple. Then he faced the priests again. "And I will fight for my God and if need be die for Him!"

"Our god will eat your heart and we will eat your arms and legs!" the old priest screamed with a sneer.

Cortés turned, seized a long pike one of the soldiers carried and began to smash at the war god, striking high at its face. "Something we must do for the Lord!" he cried to his soldiers. At once they began to attack the idol too. A sword slashed off the little hummingbird on its ankle and it fell to the floor at my feet.

Even though I knew that only an ugly statue was being desecrated, reverence for such idols taught me in childhood surged up in the form of fear. I backed slowly toward the doorway, trembling as if some dreadful retaliation would be sent down by the now-battered war god. There was a more real danger: at first immobilized with astonishment, the Aztec priests came at Cortés and the soldiers with raking fingernails and stone sacrificial knives. More soon joined them. The soldiers had to leave off attacking the idol to protect themselves against the maddened priests. One saw me in my corner and ran toward me with a knife raised high. But at that instant the soldiers Cortés had sent for burst into the room; one felled the priest who menaced me. At that instant Cortés turned and saw that I had been in great danger. He strode over, took my arm, and pulled me with him to the doorway and out. We all but hurled ourselves down the pyramid's steep steps. When we reached its base I was panting, fear still beating in my throat.

"Forgive me," he said, "for placing a woman in such jeopardy. I had hopes of talking with the priests up there, of convincing them to at least make a small beginning toward the end I must attain. And as you know, to do this I needed the aid of your tongue." He amazed me with a smile. In a low, intimate tone he said, "And there are many times when I need more of you than that, Marina. When are you going to stop this game you have been playing? My bed is cold without you."

What kind of a man is this? I thought. How can he leap from righteous fury to carnal desire? But at the same time my body itself responded to his words, to the look in his eyes, that warm bright look that said he desired me. My knees seemed to melt; a languor softly filled the very hollows of my bones while excitement made my blood go hard and fast. My throat wanted to say, "Tonight! Now!" But my mind stayed cool and apart. "It is not a game to sleep among women and not with you," I said. "It is a necessity of my being. I do not want to be touched by you until you can make me understand why you burned seventeen people alive."

His smile turned to a scowl. "I will explain nothing to you! If you are too dull or too fond of Indians to grasp the necessities my duty forces on me, then to hell with you! You are standing there breathing God's air because I had those heathens burned. Anything less and I would have lost Moctezuma's respect, and with that, all! The news of that blaze you hate me for is going to spread like a wildfire. It may be the one thing that eventually gets us back to Vera Cruz alive, because you can be sure that it will make all Indians very afraid of killing Spaniards. So sleep where you will, Doña Marina! Dream sweet dreams about some other man than Cortés! Some gentle fellow who does not have to control an alien nation of many millions of bloodthirsty savages by means of fewer than four hundred Spaniards and a weak-kneed captive king!'' With a last cold stare he turned his back and strode away.

I took a step after him, belatedly realizing how he had left his soldiers fighting the priests in order to be sure of my safety. But had I been saved by the commander who needed his interpreter, or by the man who needed me? I felt tears sting my eyes. I wanted to be loved for myself alone by the man I had just sent striding away from me by charging him with inexplicable cruelty: if the thought had not made me weep a tear or two it might have made me laugh, if harshly, at the miserable knot of confusion that fettered me where I stood watching Cortés mount the pyramid again, sword already drawn. I walked back to the palace, passing below the rack of skulls that silently testified to more than two centuries of cruelty far more terrible than that of Cortés.

Within the hour I was performing my daytime function; for Moctezuma summoned him to an audience and asked as well for the soldiers who had been with him when the war god's temple was so brutally desecrated. Now the monarch who had wept in chains sat as unapproachable and impassive as when he first rode out on his palanquin to meet us. With a look that combined horror and sorrow he said even he could not save us now from the inevitable results of the damage to the idol and the wounding of Aztec priests. His people would surely rise up against us when they learned of the affront to their gods. "The priests have not made your terrible act public because they do not want it known that they were unable to defend the deities. They offer an ultimatum: you must all leave this city and this land, going back to whence you came."

I saw all self-assurance leave Cortés' face. Yet still he tried to play for time, perhaps in the hope that he would learn at any hour that reinforcements had at last arrived from Spain. With the might of Spain solid behind him, he could try to use Moctezuma's status as vassal of its king to force him to take a stand against the Aztec priests. He spoke quite humbly, for him: "You must tell the priests that we cannot leave this land until a fleet of ships can be built at Vera Cruz. The vessels we came in have been destroyed."

Moctezuma said he would have his subjects on the coast supply the wood needed to build us ships, and would so inform the priests and continue to placate them. "Do not blame me for the situation in which you find yourselves. I do not think it was Quetzalcoatl who inspired in you such foolish savagery." But for all his reproachfulness, I saw on his face a glimmer of triumph. By his own act Cortés had made our exodus inevitable.

I knew our situation was very ugly. Cortés could not know from moment to moment if the Aztec priests might suddenly decide to make public the sacrilege and demand the obvious penalty: our hearts to propitiate the war god whose idol Cortés had all but demolished. The soldiers all slept in their armor. Our palace was readied for a siege. Masses were heavily attended and a special one was held in memory of Spaniards who had died. But Cortés knew well that our only actual strength was his hostage Moctezuma's continued desire and ability to protect us with his hereditary authority.

That was how it was when disaster struck.

Cruelly, it wore the smiling mask of the good news Cortés and all of us had been awaiting.

27

I was picking roses in the palace garden when Orteguilla's excited voice spoke behind me. "Cortés wants you at once!"

I pricked my finger on a thorn. Blood rushed to my face. The words had meaning to that part of me that wanted Cortés.

"I was with Moctezuma when an Aztec courier came up from the coast," Orteguilla said as we walked toward the palace. "A large fleet of Spanish ships has arrived! Eighteen of them! Anchored offshore near Vera Cruz! The King has responded to Cortés' letters at last."

The surge of relief that rose in me was dimmed by a dreadful thought: Vindicated at last and provided with the ships he needed, would Cortés leave Tenochtitlán? Would he return to his wife in Cuba? Or would he be summoned to his emperor's side to be rewarded for gaining him a vast new colony? I found my steps slowing as my spirits sank.

"I can hardly wait to get out of this place," Orteguilla said. "I am reasonably brave, but lately I have had to keep telling myself that if I am to die here at least it won't be on one of their hellish altars, for which of their gods would be honored by the heart of a dwarf?"

"Then you think Cortés will leave now?"

"Why wouldn't he? Moctezuma has sworn allegiance to Carlos of Spain. The ceremony was recorded and notarized and went to Vera Cruz the next day to be delivered to his royal majesty. There's nothing to keep Cortés hammering away on that hard Aztec head, I assure you."

Moctezuma, dressed for some ceremony, wore a panache and looked almost cheerful. When I arrived, he beckoned forward the courier who had brought the news; he knelt at the ruler's feet to spread out before his eyes a brightly colored pictograph. Cortés stood at one side of Moctezuma's chair to look down at it, I at the other. On it were painted eighteen Spanish ships, many men in armor on each, and cannons and horses. "Now you will not have to build any ships," Moctezuma said, "and can leave at once."

Cortés bent forward to examine the detailed drawings, then straightened and had me ask the courier several questions. "Are these ships anchored at Vera Cruz?"

"No. They are a half day's walk south of it."

"Have the banners on the ships been correctly depicted?"

"Yes."

"Are all of them shown?"

"Yes."

Cortés nodded thoughtfully, thanked Moctezuma, and left. I followed him, aware that he seemed disturbed rather than excited by the news of a Spanish fleet at last. He walked frowning down at the floor, his feet moving with a slow, heavy tread as if he did not want to follow where his thoughts were leading him.

"You do not seem very happy," I said.

"I'm not." His glance showed slight surprise to find me at his side, but no warmth. At that moment there was the crack of a musket from the courtyard, followed by several more. We were passing a doorway that opened out onto a stone balcony; he went to it and we looked down on the jubilant crowd of soldiers below and at several captains galloping its length, wheeling to gallop back again. "*Viva Carlos el rey!*" one shouted, heartily cheered by the rest.

"One of the soldiers guarding Moctezuma must have rushed to

spread the news," Cortés mused, to himself rather than to me. "Too bad."

"Bad? It seemed good news to me."

"Indeed? Well, enjoy the illusion while you can." He turned his back on the cheerful scene below.

"Forgive me, but illusions do not interest me. What is the truth?"

"It's a matter I prefer to discuss with the captains."

"Forgive me," I said again. As I repeated the phrase, intending to make it cold and formal, my voice betrayed me. The words sounded gentle, almost a plea, and I knew then that I wanted his forgiveness for having deeply wounded his pride and his love for me. How right Aguilar had been when he told me that God judges us, and that to judge another harshly is not a mortal prerogative! What right had I to judge Cortés, and also to punish him for what I had thought wrong?

He must have heard more than the words themselves, for he looked at me squarely, studying my face. "I sent to Carlos a detailed map of the coastline from Tabasco, showing the exact location of Vera Cruz. I do not think he is in the habit of paying good money to inept pilots and mariners. Why is this fleet not anchored at Vera Cruz?" He watched my face as I nodded. "Second: these Indian artists are wonderfully precise in what they depict. Yet the flagship did not fly the royal banner of Aragón and Castile, the flag any fleet sent by the emperor would have flown. Why not?"

"This particular artist might have left it out, not knowing how significant the banner was."

"I'll allow that. But then there is the third point: If King Carlos was enough impressed by the treasure and the letters I sent him to decide to aid me with reinforcements, that good news would have arrived well ahead of the fleet. It takes time to assemble and launch such an expedition, but very little to send word it is on its way. If Carlos had such concern for me as to send it, he would also want me to know as soon as possible that he was going to do so."

"If the king sent no fleet, then are you saying there is none? That Moctezuma is lying? That it is a ruse to get you to leave Tenochtitlán and march down to the coast?"

"I wish that were true. But I think a fleet has arrived. I think it is an expedition sent here by Governor Velásquez of Cuba."

"Velásquez?"

He nodded. "And in that case I doubt very much that the soldiers down there have any reason for rejoicing. I think Velásquez has learned everything: the building of Vera Cruz as a royal colony, the treasure I sent to the king, and my determination to march here without telling him.''

"But how could he have learned these things? From the King, you mean?''

"Doubtful. He has been living out of Spain, at the Flemish court, and may not even have read a single letter from me as yet. I think Puertocarrero and Montejo may still be dangling in Madrid, waiting his return. No, there's a very simple way in which Velásquez could have been supplied with all the information I did not want him to have. When Puertocarrero and Montejo left for Spain, I specifically ordered them not to stop at Cuba. I did this knowing that Montejo owns some property on the north coast which he wanted to visit and would be passing, eastbound. I think this order was disobeyed. Probably what happened is that some mariner jumped ship, as they will do, and spread the news of treasure, my letters to Spain, and a projected march to the interior: everything! Such news would inevitably reach the ears of the governor.'' He gave a mirthless smile: "And I doubt that these ships he has sent are here to render me aid.''

"Then why are they here at all?''

"His way would be to first complain of my insubordination to the Royal Council of the Indies, claim I had defied his orders and cheated him as well. If he got no immediate favorable response, he would set about on his own raising the money and soldiers for a second expedition to Mexico. Probably he would put his friend Pánfilo de Narváez in command, the man he came close to choosing to lead this one. And I do not have the least doubt that Narváez has orders to take over this expedition of mine, just swallow it up, and arrest me on sight.''

He left me there stunned and went to confer with his captains. Within an hour the entire Spanish army was mustered in the largest courtyard. From the top of a flight of stone steps leading to the front rampart he bluntly told them the worst, much as he had told me, except for heavy emphasis on the greed of the governor who was striking out because of envy that no gold had been sent to him.

Stunned faces looked up; his voice rang out angry and assured. "You all know, and God knows, that the governor's share has been fairly apportioned and set aside for him. You all know, and God knows, the hardships we have endured and from which Velásquez, safe in Cuba, is going to reap great financial benefit. And what is our thanks for making him rich? He has sent out an armada against us!''

He waited, nodding in agreement as a low growl of anger arose from the men. Then he smiled down at them, that warm and brilliant smile, and cried, "But I say Velásquez has made a great mistake! He does not know the men we are, nor how all our sufferings have strengthened our valor. Did he really think we would let him arrest and punish us for all we have done to his benefit? We are seasoned! We know this country and its Indians, and we have allies among them. Narváez's men may outnumber us, but they are raw, untrained. I say that these ships have brought us arms and horses we badly need. Let us march down to Vera Cruz and take them!" As the first shouts of approval rang out, Cortés shouted over them: "We will swallow Narváez and his men just as they thought to swallow us!" The roar of agreement broke over him like a wave.

And I, I stood there on the balcony where he had told me the truth about the ships and felt the old admiration of him well up in me, as strong as it had ever been. Who but Cortés could have used such evil news to wring from those soldiers shouts of approval? Granted that the tense situation here made the prospect of a swift departure not unwelcome, still his army would march out not as undesired guests who have been asked to leave but as a band of heroes ready to stand up for their rights against a greedy tyrant. And safe in Tlascala, there would be time, I thought, for Cortés to evaluate the situation and make careful plans either to confront Narváez and his army, or avoid them.

That night a more personal problem faced me: how should I now behave toward Cortés if he asked me to return to his bed? For there would surely be an awkward time between us; an estrangement like ours does not mend itself in a matter of minutes, I believed. Would it be best not to refer to the recent past? Or should I try to explain the deep emotional impact of a spectacle I had never seen before, as well as my compassion for Moctezuma, whose nation's history held him in a strangling anaconda grip?

I might have spared myself these questions: Cortés did not send for me. Not that night, nor the next, nor the next. I faced the fact that I had wounded Cortés too deeply for him to forgive and forget with ease. Under other conditions, he might have found time to perhaps make some gesture toward our reconciliation: an hour's conversation, or a meal shared. But as it was, he had problems of much greater import confronting him.

For I had learned that Narváez commanded some twelve hundred

Spanish soldiers, nearly a hundred horsemen. And that Cortés had decided to take with him only two hundred men, including horsemen and some seventy well-seasoned fighters whom he considered the most devoted to him. This meant that he was leaving in Tenochtitlán about a hundred forty of his Spaniards, who would have ample ammunition, cannons, and fourteen musketeers and crossbowmen. He supervised the building of additional barricades and fortifications, then announced his plan to the soldiers. "Against Narváez I need to use a small, mobile force and the element of surprise. The duty of you who will remain here is the all-important one of keeping Moctezuma captive. I believe he is on the verge of becoming a Christian and is already a vassal of the Spanish crown. You who hold this city can do so knowing that both your God and your king will smile on your fortitude." A loud cheer went up when he announced that their commander, to be obeyed as they would obey him, would be Pedro de Alvarado.

An instant feeling of foreboding told me this was a mistake, that a cool man was needed here, not a hot one. Alvarado's tendency toward headlong action was known to Cortés, although his bravery and the love the men felt for him had to be weighed against this, as did his unique status with Moctezuma and his nobles, who called him Tonatiuh, "Child of the Sun," because of his red-gold hair, ruddy skin, and exuberant warmth of manner. I knew the disdain of Indians it hid, and had guessed that under this lay fear of a people whose ways he did not understand.

My doubts concerning him led to others. Suddenly, for all Cortés' assurance when he had spoken of his plans and decisions, the grim reality of his situation struck me with full force, and his decision to maintain his grip on Moctezuma seemed a great folly. Surely a hundred forty more soldiers would be of some help when he was so outnumbered? As for the gold with which, Sandoval told me, he hoped to bribe some of Narváez's soldiers into changing sides, would enough respond to this lure to even the odds, even after the enviable sight of Cortés' soldiers wearing the gold necklaces and bracelets they had taken to putting on out of ostentation?

As if the forthcoming situation at Vera Cruz were not bad enough, the plight of those soldiers ordered to remain behind certainly equaled it for sheer danger if Moctezuma's belief that Cortés was a god's emissary should finally waver. I did not know if I felt more concern for the soldiers who would leave with Cortés or those who were to remain in the city.

IN THE SILVER CITY

I had decided that I preferred to be going to Vera Cruz; at least half our Tlascalans would accompany Cortés, and I knew I would be needed to relay his orders to them as well as to the Zempoallans and Totonacs the fat cacique might provide. Orteguilla spoke Nahuatl quite well enough for Alvarado to communicate with Moctezuma. My spirits rose at the thought of riding once more beside Cortés, his indispensable voice. Under those conditions, surely our estrangement would fade away.

An interview with Cortés which Moctezuma requested made it plain that my concern for those to be left behind was even better founded than I had thought. I went to his audience room feeling happy that Cortés had requested my help when he might well have used Orteguilla's. Cortés was in good spirits too.

Moctezuma's words changed that, abruptly. "I have seen that your captains and soldiers seem agitated. You have not come to visit me to tell me why. I asked Orteguilla. He said you intend to go out against your brothers who came in those ships, leaving Tonatiuh here to guard me. But those in the ships are also vassals of your emperor. Yet it seems they have come here to capture you, even kill you. I do not understand this at all."

After a hard glance at the dwarf, who turned pale, not having guessed that Cortés had told Moctezuma nothing, Cortés assumed a casual air and told me to say: "If I did not come to tell you about this, it was because I love you and did not wish to grieve you, knowing how well-disposed you are toward me. As for the white men who came in those ships, it is true that they are also vassals of my monarch. He rules over many provinces, and their people are very different from one another, some more valiant than others. We here in your city are Castilians, the most brave of all. So do not concern yourself about my well-being, Lord Moctezuma, for I will soon return victorious."

The sad face did not brighten. "They are fourteen hundred in number and have eighty horsemen and twenty cannons as well as seventy of the weapons men hold in their hands to shoot out small thunder. A courier has also told me that they possess crosses and images of your God and his Mother and hold Masses. Yet they say you have fled from your rightful ruler, and were not sent to me by him."

Cortés raised his chin and seemed to grow taller. "They are bad people and have come here with a bad purpose. Our God and His blessed Mother will give more strength to us than to them. You will see that we will bring them here as prisoners. So you need have no anxiety about our departure. I beg of you only to stay quietly here with Tonatiuh and his soldiers. He will not allow any disturbance after we leave the city, nor must you."

The crucial instant had arrived. Did Moctezuma believe Cortés? Or did the size of the army sent to capture him seem more convincing? The delicate, mournful face gave no hint of what he was thinking as he stared into Cortés' eyes. The name Moctezuma meant "he of the sorrowful countenance"; for a long moment he epitomized his name. Then he said, "If you should need assistance, I will send you five thousand warriors."

"I am grateful for this offer," Cortés said. "I need only the help of God and my brave companions. I ask you merely to supply my people here with food, and that is all." He went to Moctezuma and embraced him. Moctezuma returned the embrace, his face still sorrowful.

With a daring induced by his earlier amazing candor after his governor was arrested I said, jokingly, "I think you are only pretending sorrow at our departure, Lord Moctezuma. For I know it will please your priests and nobles and reduce their complaints of us to you."

He gave a swift glance but ignored the remark. "If there is anything more I can do to aid you I will do it with all good will, Cortés. I do not want any calamity to befall you." He sounded sincere, and Cortés embraced him again and then we left.

"A pox take the dwarf for babbling," he said.

I defended Orteguilla. "I doubt that he told Moctezuma anything he did not already know or would have soon learned, his espionage system being as it is."

Cortés' annoyance with the dwarf had made him forget our changed relationship, as I realized when he answered me with a return to cool formality. "I am sure that is true. But his spies and couriers have served me too. I did not know that the odds against me were quite that severe."

In as cool a tone I said "Then why worsen them? I cannot understand why you need to leave anyone in this city at all."

He stopped walking, stared down at me as though at an idiot. "You can't, Doña Marina? Then I will tell you. I signed my name to a contract with Governor Velásquez. In it I promised to make Christians of heathens. The fact that he now intends to arrest or kill me does not change the fact that this is what I swore to do. The difference between a caballero and a commoner, as my father told me long ago, is that a gentleman keeps his word, not so much for others as for himself. I will keep mine. But there is an even larger reason why I must keep the foothold I have gained here and refuse to admit failure in making a Christian of Moctezuma. These cruel barbarians must be brought to God! And I seem the one God has chosen for the task.'' He paused portentously, then added, ''Your responsibility is a heavy one. I pray you will show your gratitude for your own salvation by giving of your best in helping our priests reach Moctezuma's heart at last.''

My own heart gave a throb of anguish, then sank, aching with every beat. Cortés was leaving me behind! I tried to conceal my feelings. ''I thought you would need me to interpret your commands to the Tlascalans and Totonacs.''

He sounded pleased when he said ''Fortunately, Sandoval has picked up enough Nahuatl to do that.''

Part of me wanted to cry out ''And can he hold you in his arms? Can you turn to him in the night and forget all dangers and find joy?'' But I said ''Yes, that is very fortunate.''

''Incidentally, I must part you from the mare I gave you. She is spirited, an excellent mount in battle. But do not fear, I will bring her back safely, and she will be yours again, like anything else it has been my pleasure to give you.''

Perhaps he did not know the wrench it gave me to part with that particular gift. Perhaps he did not know what it had meant to me to mount and ride the animal that once had filled me with superstitious terror. Perhaps the smile he gave me as he promised to return the horse was not a cruel one but it seemed to me that he knew these things, and also was aware that this particular gift had once conveyed to me that he loved me. Shaken, I said, ''Since you have taken back the gift that most mattered to me, I will not weep at losing a mere horse.'' And with that I turned and left him.

The gift I meant was his affection. I wanted with my whole being to weep for that loss, yet would not let myself. He had his pride; I had mine.

''Marina,'' he called after me.

I wanted to stop; I wanted to turn. My feet kept on walking away from him. I told myself that never again could I be open with him, vulnerable to such pain as I now felt. Yet all the muscles of my back were tense; my ears yearned for the sound of his footsteps behind me, my shoulders waited for his hand to fall on me and whirl me around. But he did not follow me.

May 15 was the day set for his departure. During all the preceding day I struggled with my yearning to go to him to wish him well and say goodbye; I knew that with the first light of dawn the departure from the city would begin. In the chapel I knelt and prayed to the Blessed Virgin to remove from me this sin of pride, this fear of again being hurt by his cold response. I rose from my knees, went straight to his headquarters, where I was sure he would be. And I was right. There he was, seated at a long trestle table, surrounded by his captains, all of them preoccupied with a large chart spread out before them and a discussion of Vera Cruz and its environs. I watched them from the doorway for a moment and then left, relieved and yet disappointed. This frustration of my good intention served to stifle it completely. Bitterly I told myself that to Cortés I had been just one more woman he had conquered, like the one to whose window he had climbed at seventeen.

Doña Luisa and my old friend Ixlan had long been aware of the changed situation between Cortés and me, of course. When Ixlan left us to wish Sandoval, her protector, farewell she turned in the doorway to say to me, "He may never return, but we will have had this hour." Her words pierced me; I started to my feet, for the first time facing the truth I had hidden from myself: Cortés might not return.

But Doña Luisa chose this instant to be her most sanctimonious. "God says to hate the sin but love the sinner. You are behaving without an ounce of Christian charity if you do not go to Cortés at once and wish him well, for the peril he faces is great."

I sat down again.

But not for long. The bell that hung outside the chapel to call the men to Mass and vespers and to mark the passing of the hours was tolling nine when a voice in the corridor asked permission to enter, using the Aztec tongue. I knew I would see one of Cortés' servants, and the curtain was pushed aside by the one who had told me what happened to the Spaniard's head. Cortés was in his room and wished to speak to me.

Doña Luisa was asleep on her pallet; Ixlan had not returned; I was still dressed, waiting with lessening hope for some word from him. Now it had come. I stood up and preceded her down the dark stone corridor where all but one torch at the far end had been extinguished. Cortés was in his bedroom alone. There too only one torch burned, so placed that it threw his huge shadow on the wall behind his chair. He looked weary, and had on a long robe of deep blue embroidered with disks of gold and silver. "I did not wish to leave without saying farewell to you.'' His voice was neutral, perhaps because he was so tired.

"Farewell. Go with God, Cortés.'' No emotion, I told myself as the poignance of parting stirred.

"I debated with myself for some time about taking you with me, Marina.'' His beard was sunk on his chest, his eyes looking up at me. "And that was a hard decision, because of the great help you have been to me in the past.''

The tongue, the voice, the silver parrot that opened its beak when a wire was pulled. "But now you have Sandoval.''

He ignored that. "I had to evaluate the relative danger between your staying here and riding to Vera Cruz with me. You will be safer here.''

"Then you see no possibility of losing Moctezuma even though you are gone?''

"None. Having treated us as his god's emissaries, he must continue to do so and put a good face on it. As for his priests and nobles, they are placated by the fact that so many of us are already leaving the city.'' He stood up. "So don't be nervous, Doña Marina.''

We stood staring at each other for a moment, and then he turned and went to the table where a wine cask stood surrounded by cups of fine Cholulan ware. He picked up the silver goblet he always used, filled it, and came toward me holding it out. He smiled. "And now, Doña Marina, will you take a cup of wine with me?''

My heart raced back to that August night in Tlascala, and my whole body took command of me and responded to him with all its ardor, heart pounding faster, breasts yearning for his touch. He looked at me for a long moment, then in two strides reached me and put his arm around my waist and drew me to him. His eyes were bright with desire; my finger went up and touched the small white scar below his lip. As our mouths met I thought of the danger he would march toward in the early morning, and I held him tighter.

"Stay with me,'' he whispered then.

To feel that strong body close to mine on that soft wide pallet below its jeweled canopy was such delight I could not believe I had lived apart from him so long. He kissed me gently, many times, and then more fiercely, and whispered the pretty words he used to say, that I was his beloved Amazon, more beautiful than any imagined in any chronicle or legend. I told him that I loved him, and we kissed again for a long, sweet time, my yearning for the consummation growing almost unbearable. But then his body went slack, and although the arms embracing me still clung, I knew he was asleep.

Lying beside him, knowing the stress he was under, I forgave his weariness while I yearned for my girlhood body, chaste and passionless, that did not betray me with this yearning. He suddenly stirred, flung a heavy arm across me. "Marina. My Doña Marina," he murmured, the words slurred. I held his weary body close and was content with that. I fell asleep at last, able to rejoice that our enmity was ended, even though with dawn he would be marching to face Narváez. But for this brief interval, he was almost mine.

When I woke he was gone. I heard the noise and clamor in the palace courtyard; soldiers' marching feet, a captain's loud command, the drummer beating the tempo. A trumpet sounded. I leaped from bed, dressed myself hastily and ran along the corridor to the door that led to the front parapet, filled with soldiers watching their comrades leave. They made way for me, and I looked down at Cortés and his captains starting to cross the main square toward the avenue leading to the causeway across which we had come half a year earlier. It surprised me to see that Moctezuma, on his palanquin, followed behind Cortés. Many silent Aztecs stood in the gray dawn watching. "Cortés!" I cried. I do not know if he heard; he did not pause or turn. "Go with God," I whispered, and tears filled my eyes. I knew I might be seeing him for the last time on this earth: a man in armor on a black stallion riding away to meet his destiny or his doom.

I could not leave, but stood there watching until he had vanished and only the foot soldiers were crossing the square, as if this silent vigil could somehow be known to him. I turned away then feeling hollow, spent of all emotion. For the first time since I had known him I faced the task of women: the waiting. It touched me that in silent sympathy the Indian women had joined me: Ixlan looked sleepy; Doña Luisa was holding her rosary, telling the beads, eyes shut and lips moving silently; Chu-Chu sniveled and wiped her nose with the back of her fat little hand.

"Doña Marina?" I turned. Arturo Mondragon stood a few paces away, in breastplate and helmet. Behind him the sky above the mountains was turning pale and rosy. He approached me, politely removing the casque. "It is a very great honor Cortés has paid me," he said solemnly.

"What honor is that?" My dull voice could pretend no interest.

"I was to have marched to Vera Cruz. But just before he left,

Cortés told me he wants me here. He has charged me with the protection of your person in the event of any danger that may arise.''

"You?'' It seemed a strange choice. Cortés was aware of Arturo's affection for me.

Arturo stiffened. "He trusts me above any other soldier for this responsibility.''

I knew then why Arturo had been chosen: his very affection would make him more zealous about my safety than another might be. And I had learned that Cortés' final concern before he left had been my protection. I told myself that this was a better farewell than any last embrace.

The bright arc of the sun slid up behind the mountains. Its light touched that dark gold hair that had once aroused my wonder. "But Cortés foresees no danger here,'' I said.

"Even Cortés cannot read the future, Doña Marina.''

I became aware that now he used my Spanish name. In the square below the Tlascalans were marching after the Spanish soldiers, white crane banners held high. And now the sun had fully risen on the first day of my long waiting.

The voice of the dwarf shattered my self-preoccupation. "We have been betrayed!'' I turned to look down at Orteguilla, and in the next few minutes I learned that the odds against Cortés had worsened, though he was as yet unaware of this. I did not guess that the treachery of Francisco Pizarro would precipitate the horror that left me facing Death and my own great fear of dying.

PART
VI

NIGHT OF DANCERS, NIGHT OF TEARS
May 15, 1520–July 1, 1520

28

I was glad when Alvarado told me I had been one of those chosen by Cortés to fight Narváez. I was proud, too, because I knew it meant that Cortés thought well of me as a fighting man. In the gray light before dawn I stood with El Galán, teasing him about his gloomy mood, yet knowing there was good reason for it. Now we faced battle with well-armed Spaniards who outnumbered us four to one, counting our soldiers who had remained in Vera Cruz, he reminded me—not with superstitious Indians who had never seen a horse or heard a cannon or musket. It was then that Cortés' groom came to tell me our commander wished to speak to me.

He had just mounted his black stallion. I stood at the stirrup, looking up. When he told me I was to stay behind as Doña Marina's personal bodyguard, I thought at first he must be joking, for it seemed like asking the fox to guard the hen coop. But his next words sobered me. "She is in particular danger from being closely identified with me. If another rebel like Cacama should arise, he might well get the idea of kidnaping her in imitation of my coup with Moctezuma. He might believe that he could use a threat against her life to persuade me to evacuate the city entirely, which would guarantee him the favor of the Aztec priests and nobles. And so I need someone who would guard her with his life. The concern for her you have shown in the past convinces me that you are that man." He leaned in the saddle to grasp my shoulder. "You I know I can absolutely trust."

Pride outweighed disappointment at suddenly finding myself left behind in the city. I nodded. "You can trust me."

"It will be best that she does not leave this palace at all."

"I understand. But do you really believe another revolt against Moctezuma is likely to happen?"

He smiled. "What has happened before can happen again, as I am

251

going to prove when I frustrate Velásquez in his desire to remove me as commander and put Narváez in my place.'' The trumpet sounded then; the drummer rattled off a first fast flourish and then settled into a marching beat. The great gate creaked open and the black stallion paced toward it, head high, as if it knew Cortés would lead the army from the city.

I ran back to El Galán to wish him well. He managed a grin after we embraced: ''If it so happens that we do not meet again on earth, no doubt we'll be good friends in Heaven or Hell, depending on how God may judge us.''

His uncharacteristic pessimism left me feeling uneasy as I climbed the stone steps to the top of the front wall of the palace, a long stone platform with a crenelated rampart, where I stood with other soldiers, their faces wan in the cold dawn, watching nearly two-thirds of our small force march away from us toward the causeway over which we had come. Gazing out over that vast square with its pale pyramids to heathen gods, I saw it with unaccustomed eyes. Once again its bizarre grandeur astounded me, all built and conceived without the help of God, without any ancient Greek or Roman or Moorish examples to copy. And we few Christians held its heart and its ruler. My eyes found El Galán then, and I cupped my hands to my mouth to shout that I would see him soon. ''You'll come back a hero!'' He turned in the saddle to shout back something I could not hear over the sound of our drums.

As I turned away I saw our Indian women clustered at the parapet's far end. Where they were, Malinche was apt to be. I went to find the woman for whom I had pledged to lay down my life, if need be.

As I told her I had been appointed by Cortés to guard her, I saw the sorrow in her eyes, and that her face was no longer that of a girl. She was no less beautiful, but it seemed clear that her life with Cortés had not been smooth. And then, with a thrill of recognition, I saw that she wore the humble little rosary I had given her, the jet beads, silver chain, and filagree cross barely visible against the barbaric embroidery of her triangular *huipile,* a gift undoubtedly from Moctezuma. The fact that she still wore this gift from me took on enormous significance and suggested to me that she wore it because of affection for the giver until her response to the news that I was to guard her stabbed my pride. ''You?'' she said, as if Cortés had selected a weakling or a dwarf like Orteguilla.

Oddly enough, he suddenly appeared shortly after I had responded to her in a stiff and prideful manner. There was a stirring among the

Indian women surrounding us, and the short fat one giggled as the dwarf pushed his way past her, his small arm holding aside the full skirt of the tall woman next to her like a curtain. Orteguilla's anxious face and staring eyes were a sharp contrast to the women's amusement. "We have been betrayed," he gasped. "By three of our own soldiers!" He paused for breath, one hand on his small, heaving chest.

"Betrayed? How? What soldiers?"

"Francisco Pizarro, for one." He eloquently cursed first Pizarro and his mother, father, and more remote ancestors, then broke off as Malinche, who had been gazing out over the square, its white temples now gilded by the newly risen sun, turned to look down at him. "Pardon me, Doña Marina," he said. "But Pizarro is all I just said, and worse. Here is the situation: Just now several of Moctezuma's nobles came to his apartment to visit him. An ungodly hour, but they knew he had decided to honor Cortés by riding with him to the gates of the city and wanted to be there when he returned. I happened to overhear what they were discussing while they waited. They were much intrigued by a certain message one of Moctezuma's couriers had recently brought him and of which I knew nothing. I tell you, the hair rose on the back of my neck when I realized what Pizarro and the two other traitors with him had done!"

"But Pizarro isn't here! He went down to the province where the gold mines are, sent back the gold, and remained behind to explore the area further," I reminded him.

"Oh, he explored! He went down to the coast and he learned that Narváez's fleet was anchored near Vera Cruz. And he and the two whoresons with him went aboard the flagship, got drunk on wine, and told Narváez he was lucky to have come so soon after Cortés had piled up another fortune in gold. And he also told him how near they were to Vera Cruz, and that there were fewer than two hundred Spaniards there, some of them invalids. And he told Narváez he could easily capture Zempoalla, overawe the fat cacique, and lose Cortés some valuable allies!"

All I could think of was El Galán's unusual gloom; it seemed to me prophetic. Cortés could reach the coast to find Vera Cruz in enemy hands and even Zempoalla an enemy camp.

"But that's not all," Orteguilla said. He lowered his voice to a hoarse whisper. "Moctezuma has known all this for many days!"

I felt the blood leave my face. "That means he thinks Cortés went marching down there to his own funeral!"

"Exactly," Orteguilla said.

NIGHT OF DANCERS, NIGHT OF TEARS

A mass funeral was what I saw for us left here, a multiple Aztec sacrifice that would end for me when a stone knife took my heart out and my skull joined the thousands below the war god's temple, just one more pitiful bone pate to grin and gleam in the sun. Malinche's voice made me turn toward her.

"Pizarro's treachery will change nothing as far as Moctezuma is concerned. To him the battle between Cortés and Narváez is still another game of *tlachtli* on a larger scale." When I said I did not understand, she told me of his bet with the king of Texcoco. "He still believes that Cortés was sent here by his sovereign, as Cortés told him. And that Narváez and his followers are bad people, as Cortés told him. He is awaiting the outcome of the battle between them. If Cortés wins, it will prove to Moctezuma that he is the god's emissary. If Narváez wins, it will prove Cortés a mere pretender."

I tried to think with a mind addled by shock. "So we're safe until news comes to Moctezuma of Cortés' victory—or defeat."

"And Moctezuma would prefer his victory. It will mean that Cortés is all Moctezuma believed, and that in revering him Moctezuma has done the right thing, perhaps the only thing that could avert the prophecies of doom. He is still as fettered by the power of Cortés as if he sat in leg irons."

"But Cortés isn't here," I cried. "And with every minute that passes his personal impact is fading away!"

"It is with his spirit that he has overpowered Moctezuma. Spirits are more powerful than bodies, and can remain where the body is not."

"Just the same, I wish Cortés were here in body now," Orteguilla said, glum.

Malinche looked down at him, her face kind. "All Moctezuma can do is wait. I think he must be the loneliest man in the universe."

"Thank God for that!" I said.

She turned to look out over the parapet, and pointed. "He's coming back."

For an instant I thought she meant Cortés, and rushed to look; Moctezuma's green and jeweled palanquin was now heading toward the palace past bowing or prostrate Aztecs. Malinche started toward the steps leading down from the rampart. "Where are you going?" I asked, remembering Cortés' suggestion that she should not leave our stronghold.

She turned. "To beg him to send a runner after Cortés with this news of Pizarro's treachery.'' With a whirl of her full skirt she was gone.

Orteguilla was staring after her in admiration. ''God sometimes bewilders me, to have placed a mind like that in the body of an Indian!'' He turned to me. ''I meant to ask her opinion, but I guess you'll have to do. Shall I tell Alvarado about Pizarro?''

''As commander here, I think he should know the worst.''

''Now answer this: if I tell him, how can I prevent him from doing something foolish? Such as putting Moctezuma in a jail cell or otherwise humiliating him for having said nothing to Cortés about Pizarro?''

''You've convinced me. Say nothing.''

''But if he later finds I knew and didn't tell him, he won't be very pleased with me, will he? My fondness for the idea of sitting in a cell on maize cakes and water is not excessive.'' Suddenly he clapped a hand to his forehead. ''Ha! As God is my witness, I forgot a thing of great importance. Pedro Alvarado hates Francisco Pizarro! As dogs hate cats, he hates Pizarro. Pizarro's treachery will merely confirm this odium. He will rage, but at Pizarro, and it will give him such satisfaction that he won't feel so harshly toward Moctezuma.''

''I didn't know Alvarado hated Pizarro. How do you know this?''

''I use my ears for more than holding wax in. It is Pizarro's cold cruelty that Alvarado hates, to be expected of a man who never killed anyone except with his blood at the boil.'' He gave me a nervous wink. ''Come with me, please, to spread over two heads the wrath that can descend on the bringer of bad news.''

Alvarado was seated at the long trestle table in Cortés' headquarters. He was eating a mango, of which he was very fond. The juice trickled down into his beard, almost the same color, and he wiped it off with the back of his hand, nodding as he listened to the dwarf's brief summation of Pizarro's betrayal.

''I have a good nose for filth,'' Alvarado said. ''I told Cortés when he decided to send Pizarro to the gold mines not to trust him just because he has some trickle of Monrroy blood in his veins. But Cortés chose to believe that blood would tell. Well, something has moved Pizarro to tell too much in the wrong place, and I suppose it was not his Monrroy blood but that of the great goat-bitch that spawned Pizarro on a heap of dung.'' He calmly selected another mango from the bowl on the table. ''How long did you say Moctezuma has known of this treachery?''

"Oh, a very short time. Doña Marina is asking him to send word of it to Cortés."

"Good." He peeled back the mango's thick skin with a thumbnail. "Continue by all means to spy for me, Orteguilla."

We left reassured by hot Alvarado's cool reception of our news. Evidently it seemed to him that a bad situation had not grown much worse.

I was wrong. Alvarado must have conceived it as proper to his position as commander to conceal his inner fears. Events proved that it had stunned him to learn that Moctezuma had not shared with Cortés this crucial information. He believed that Moctezuma yearned for Cortés' defeat; it did not occur to him that to Moctezuma a god's emissary would not be affected by the information Pizarro had given Narváez. That the Aztec ruler did as Malinche asked and sent a runner after Cortés with the crucial information did not reassure Alvarado because he believed that the courier would have been privately instructed not to deliver that news. That the Aztec ruler continued to be docile did not reassure him either. Although Alvarado appeared so bluff, frank, and outgoing, he secretly saw himself as a man of considerable cunning and subtlety. He confided in no one his conviction that Moctezuma was only waiting to learn the outcome of the unequal struggle between Cortés and Narváez. If it proved to him that we were mere pretenders he would then crush us with a clear conscience. And Moctezuma, because of his many spies and his swift couriers, would learn before we did whether Cortés had met with triumph or defeat. Politely, Alvarado visited Moctezuma daily, hiding his misgivings. He let the soldiers see only his cheerful face, reassuring us in his high-pitched voice that one Cortés was equal to a hundred men like Pánfilo Narváez.

And at last came the night of the dancers.

29

For a week and then another we soldiers, like Alvarado, hid our tension and our secret fear. No news was bad news. And such news as we got was mediocre. After one of Moctezuma's couriers told him that the Narváez fleet had sailed north to Vera Cruz we all became military strategists, devising ways in which Cortés could defend the little town against worse odds. When we learned that Narváez had set up a camp right in Zempoalla and had requisitioned, in the name of the Spanish monarch, the Indian women and other gifts the fat cacique was keeping against our return, we loudly affirmed that the Zempoallan ruler would remain loyal to Cortés. When we learned that he had, and had moreover told Narváez that he intended to complain of such behavior to Cortés, we cheered our faithful ally. We were delighted to learn that Narváez was very stingy, keeping the gifts he extracted for himself. We assured each other that Cortés' plan of bribing away his soldiers with gold was sure to succeed.

An elaborate political development briefed in a short message to Alvarado from Cortés gave us no comfort. The Royal Audience of Santo Domingo, knowing of the treasure Cortés had sent to Carlos, in turn sent an officer called an *oidor* to Vera Cruz to rebuke Narváez, who promptly made him a prisoner. Those who had come with him escaped arrest and joined Cortés, indignant but helpless. Cortés confessed that his letters to Moctezuma, in which he had tried to make him see that the important thing was to keep control of the Aztec capital and urged that they join forces to accomplish this, had not been honored with any answer. What Narváez clearly wanted was for Cortés, overwhelmed by the odds, to give up after a few brief skirmishes. In short, all this news was inconclusive, the first mutterings of thunder before the storm.

I saw almost nothing of Malinche. With Aguilar, Father Olmedo, and the other priests she spent many hours with Moctezuma in fruitless efforts to convert him. It had not been necessary to remind her not to leave the palace; she had become obsessively busy in weaving a large feather tapestry, the loom Moctezuma provided set up in the room she had shared with Cortés where she knelt for hours among baskets of feathers. I thought of Penelope awaiting the return of Ulysses.

Like all the other soldiers, I gambled. We used cards made out of the thin stiff hide sold in the market to make drumheads. Our original cards were long since worn out, and ones made of *amatyl* paper did not hold up at all. My luck was bad; I lost my gold dust and nuggets first, the gold necklace Moctezuma gave me, and even my first gold pendant bought from the boy at San Juan Ulua, although I managed to win back the gold chain Cortés had bestowed the day I rejected my soldier's pay. One gold necklace! That was all I had to show for nearly a year and four months of danger, toil, and frustration. These losses induced a forlornness that rarely left me. Fear lay just under it and would suddenly flare up whenever I heard the booming of the great snakeskin drum atop the looming pyramid of the war god. It was beaten in slow cadence, most often just after sunrise, and for a reason I wished I did not know.

I became very fond of the drink called pulque, and on many an afternoon I would wander through Moctezuma's beautiful garden with a clay jug of the stuff, reciting poetry to the freaks and animals and birds. My deep sense of impending doom intensified.

The single cheerful note was the young slave girl Moctezuma had given me. She was named Xochitl, but I called her Sochi. Short, plump, and rather pretty, her black braids twined with red ribbons, she always had a smile for me. Most of the other soldiers slept with theirs, but I did not. She had a little girl, which probably meant that she was married, and that would have been adultery even though she was only an Indian. One evening, though, after too much pulque, I found that I very much wanted to bed with her. She came to my straw pallet with the smallclothes she had washed for me, and knelt beside it smiling, waiting. I think all that stopped me was that her little girl was with her, a tiny thing with braids like her mother's. I put my arms around the child instead, and sang her songs from my own infancy. This served to remind me of home, safety, another life. Nostalgia was soon stronger than my dark sense of doom or the urge to escape in a slave girl's arms.

Abruptly, circumstances merited all my foreboding.

Through Malinche, Moctezuma courteously asked Alvarado's approval of the annual harvest dance honoring the fruitful labors of the Aztec farmer-warriors on whose shoulders rested the whole grand hierarchy. The dance was to be held in the *tlachtli* court just after sundown. Alvarado agreed that it should be performed.

Unfortunately, at sundown on the day of the dance Alvarado learned from Orteguilla of the boastful message Narváez had recently sent to Moctezuma, which the dwarf had translated from Spanish. Narváez had written that since Cortés had refused to surrender peaceably, and instead was suborning many of his men with gold and promises, Narváez was now forced to wipe out Cortés and his whole army in an immediate pitched battle of which the outcome was a foregone conclusion. This battle had probably by now been fought. We who would be so crucially affected had no way of knowing the outcome except from Moctezuma.

The harvest dance had already begun when a tense Alvarado called together those of his own company still left in the city and some thirty others, making fifty in all. Abruptly, he revealed to us all those doubts of Moctezuma that had been gnawing in him ever since the news of Pizarro's defection to the enemy. "If Moctezuma learns that Cortés has been defeated, then we are dead men, in my opinion! Even if Cortés manages to avoid an outright defeat by a strategic retreat, that will not satisfy the Aztec. As I see it, Cortés will have to capture or kill Narváez. This is unlikely." He pointed toward the ball court, from which a faint barbaric music could be heard. He reminded us that the dancers were warriors as well as farmers and might well be working up their savage spirits for an uprising against us if Cortés did not attain a conclusive victory. "A show of our strength and valor is needed now," he cried in his high, nervous voice. "A show of Spanish arms!" He proposed that we march to the ball court in full armor with muskets, pikes, and swords and surround the celebrants.

The ball court was lighted by dozens of pine torches in stone holders around its upper rim; all the tiers of stone benches were filled with Aztecs, both common folk and some nobles. There were a number of women, undoubtedly the wives and mothers of the male dancers. Alvarado led us into the court itself, where we spread out and stood against its walls. We saw what must have been a thousand male dancers whirling and posturing to the thumping of drums, the blaring of conch horns, the screaming of bone flutes. The dancers overflowed into the temple forecourt. Far above, the hollow eyes of the skulls distantly observed this exuberance of life and motion. The men's bodies, gleaming with the sweat of their exertion, were garbed in the clan jewels, gold necklaces and bracelets, pearls and precious stones, and the plumes that nodded on their heads made them look tall. The beat of the music was simple and repetitive, shrill flutes echoing deep drums: "Dum, dum, *dum/* dum, dum, *dum/* deedle, deedle, deedle, deedle/ dum, dum, *dum.*" Dancers who moved in a wide outer circle around the rest in the ball court carried rude musical instruments; I saw a notched human femur which a dancer in an ocelot skin scraped at with a stick to make a harsh, rasping noise. Many wore anklets of dry pods and small seashells that clashed together constantly with a soft sliding sound. In the very center, on a pedestal or large drum, stood a young man very splendidly costumed, plumed head back, eyes closed, arms raised to heaven as though he were in a rapt trance.

As the frenzy of the dance and the music intensified, so did the throttled fear I had been hiding ever since Cortés had marched away. And yet the spectacle drew me, numbed my mind, captured my eyes, left me like one enchanted, eyes dazzled by motion and ears by that barbaric music.

I wrenched my eyes away, blinked, and scanned the Aztec faces on the stone tiers above, all solemn and entranced. My heart gave a great lurch. Malinche was seated on the lowest tier to my left. With her were our Indian women. She was leaning slightly forward, her face rapt and childlike. She had disobeyed Cortés' warning that she should not leave the palace.

Then Alvarado's shrill voice rose above the sounds of music and of broad dancing feet. "I want the two entrances blocked at once!" He ordered me and five others to the west doorway near which we were already standing. Other soldiers positioned themselves at the eastern one. Why, I wondered, does he want to prevent the dancers from leaving? For it looked to me as if they might dance until dawn.

I looked up at Malinche; she had noticed the soldiers' movements and looked from one gate to the other, then at Alvarado.

His imperious voice startled me. "We must strike first! This is no harvest dance! This is a war dance! We get them or they get us!" Two muskets cracked. Alvarado was the first to fall on the bewildered dancers, running one through with his sword. The Three Moors accounted for three more. The muskets cracked again. I stood for an instant frozen with horror. It was as terrible as the ambush at Cholula; worse, because then we were fighting for our lives. In a few moments Spaniards were everywhere, lopping, hacking, stabbing. One slashed an arm off a drummer and then hacked off his head, which went rolling across the smooth stone paving, eyes glaring in surprise. This set the tone; two other heads joined it. Abdomens slashed open leaked entrails. A crossbow's arrow impaled the central entranced Aztec, who toppled forward from his pedestal like a statue, arms wide. Those butchered, jeweled, dead and dying Aztecs I was never to forget, helpless victims of a long-suppressed fear that had given rise to a fury that was scarcely human.

A woman screamed. I looked up. Malinche stood with both fists clenched against her face, mouth open between them in another scream. The women around her were bemused, and that seemed true of the watching Aztecs; they had not had time to believe what they were seeing. At her scream some stirred, rose. And she was up there among them, voice of the absent leader of the insensate Spanish killers in the ball court! All my training as a soldier deserted me. I abandoned my post, ran to a point just below Malinche, raised both arms to her and yelled "Jump! You must get out of here!"

She came to herself, lowered her fists from her face, and lowered herself to the ball court, hanging by her arms and landing heavily beside me. I took her hand and ran with her to the gate I had been guarding; the soldiers let us pass. As we ran toward our palace past Aztecs in the square who did not yet know what was going on, I found I was groaning like a wounded animal. I knew without any doubt that this was the final night of my life. No Spaniard in this city would live to see tomorrow. Even if Moctezuma should want to—and he would not—he could never protect us against his aroused subjects' wrath when they learned how those dancers had died.

I pounded on the great gate and we were admitted. Seeing Captain Lugo, I went to him and gasped, "For God's sake, take command here! Alvarado's gone mad. He's killing all the dancers. Within an hour or less you'll have armed Aztecs storming this place by the thousands!" I could see it as I spoke: wave after wave of Aztecs swarming up over our walls like ants, like monkeys. Lost! We were lost!

A choked cry turned my attention back to Malinche. She was holding out her full skirt, staring down at the splash of blood across it. I remembered the headless Aztec torso that had thudded down at her feet when we started our run for the gate. How unfair her plight: splashed with blood Spaniards had spilled, she would die with us! And how in God's name could I protect her? A thin hope lighted my racked mind. I took her cold hand in mine. "Come on!"

She obeyed me like a child. We ran to the rearmost palace building, to the chapel there, to the secret vault that held the treasures of a dead Aztec king.

30

The chapel was empty and dim, lighted only by one votive candle burning at Mary's feet. Directly behind Her was the section of wall I had helped burst through, now bricked up and plastered over. I moved out from the wall the wooden pedestal concealing the two large floor-level stones which were not mortared in place. Kneeling, I shoved against one with all my strength. With maddening slowness it moved inward. I was sweating with the exertion, but more from fear of being found before I had hidden Malinche. I lay on my back when the stone was clear of the wall and with a series of sharp kicks that jolted my back teeth I sent it far enough into the vault so a person, if not too large, could squeeze through. The opening was only about four handbreadths high and perhaps nine wide, and it occurred to me, irrelevantly, that to get inside I would have to remove my breastplate. The way cleared, I stood up and faced Malinche. "Get in, and quickly!" I thought then of something I had overlooked: food and drink to sustain her. And light, for in there it was dark as a tomb.

I ran to the chest where I knew the priests kept the necessities for Mass and took the clay olla of pulque, used for Christ's blood now that our wine had run out. Beside it were half a dozen maize cakes, very stale, which served as His body. But now they were just ordinary pulque and tortillas. I took them and then stole the votive candle burning in its glass cup at Mary's feet. Olla in one hand, flame in the other, and the maize cakes held by one bent arm against my chest, I turned to the opening in the wall. Malinche had not yet entered the vault. "What are you waiting for? Get in so I can close it!"

"And you?"

"I'm finished. It's only a question of whether the Aztecs kill me before Alvarado strings me up for deserting my post." I had meant to sound the hardened soldier but my voice betrayed me and seemed bitter.

"Would he?"

"What do you think?"

"Hide with me, then."

I realized I had wanted to, all along. "A soldier does not leave his comrades to die for him," I said. "And what's the point of my hiding anyway? I'm a Spaniard. If you can manage to live through the Aztecs' first fury at us, Moctezuma may well decide to pardon you. You're a woman, and of his own race and had nothing to do with the butchery tonight."

Her face, lighted by the candle I held, showed no sign of interest in this line of reasoning. "I will not go in there alone."

"You mean you're afraid?"

She nodded.

"But it's out here where the danger is! Get in, I beg you."

She shook her head stubbornly. I thought I saw a gleam of tears, and knew then how badly that sudden slaughter of the dancers had unnerved a woman who had always been brave. After all, I had been ordered by Cortés to protect her, and did that not include helping her conquer her terror at being sealed alone in this crypt? "All right," I said. "I'll stay with you, Malinche. You go first."

She obeyed, and when she had squirmed inside I passed in to her the candle, the olla, the maize cakes. Then I removed my breastplate and shoved it through the aperture, opened out. I moved the pedestal and the Virgin as close to the wall as I could and still leave space behind it to writhe into the vault. There I turned around and wormed back the way I had come until my arms were in the chapel, my hands on the base of the Virgin's pedestal. Bit by bit I edged it toward me, squirming my way backward, until I had it close to the wall again. Inside the treasure room once more I shoved the stone block into place. We were sealed into the crypt.

Malinche stood holding the votive candle high to light the crystal skull that had so fascinated Cortés. He had thanked it for guarding the treasure; now it would guard Malinche. And the foot soldier who still loved her. A bitter thought occurred then: Malinche and I were alone together at last, companions of the night, but not as I had ever dreamed it. "I dreamed of this skull after we first saw it," she said. "It had the power of motion and followed me. I knew if it touched me, I would die." She turned her back on it and looked about her at the other treasures. Even though those made of gold had been melted to ingots, the display was still dazzling. The great gleaming feather cape that hung outspread on the rear wall seemed like a winged symbol of the enormous brooding power of the Aztecs whom we had foolishly thought to overcome.

I saw a pile of folded mantles on a chest and went to them. "We may as well make ourselves comfortable," I said, and took some and made a cushion for her on the floor, another for myself. The floor space unoccupied by treasures, chests, and hampers was quite small; our seats were almost side by side. "And when we get tired we can add more and make pallets to sleep on," I added, and felt a tingle go through me.

She knelt on her mantles in that humble, compact pose Indians seem to find comfortable and set the votive candle on the floor between us. I sat cross-legged, facing her, but in that position the crystal skull behind her seemed to stare right down into my eyes, so I changed position. Her face, dimly lighted from below, had a sudden new aspect, ghostly and mysterious; I got lost for a moment in the midnight depths of her eyes. "You were clever to think of this hiding place," she said. Her voice was low; how had I failed to hear the velvet in it? "And so for the third time you have saved me."

"The third?" I rolled onto my side and propped my head on one hand; from this angle I could enjoy her face in profile.

"From life as a heathen when you followed me in Tabasco. And in San Juan Ulua you brought me to sanctuary."

I sat up; it occurred to me that she was right. "Moctezuma likes you; I'm sure of it. He'll prove reasonable."

She shook her head. "I am linked in his mind with Cortés, and with Spaniards." Above her the skull grinned. "I think this will be my last night on earth."

"Please don't say that!"

"There's only one chance. For me, and for the soldiers who had nothing to do with that butchery. If Moctezuma were to learn tonight that Cortés has decisively defeated Narváez, then I think he would defer retaliation and let Cortés punish the butchers."

The chance seemed to me so thin as to be almost invisible. "But can Cortés defeat Narváez?"

"He will fight to the death to do it." Her voice was passive, brooding. "I have seen the two I loved most die. My father and my grandmother. She had a gift for prophecy, and foresaw many changes in my life. I wonder if she saw me in this treasure room with a Spaniard with golden hair?" She smiled, her eyes sad. I knew that her faith in those prophecies of her grandmother had faded, replaced by a new Faith.

I spoke staunchly. "Still, we are breathing! And the Sainted Virgin herself is guarding the entrance to our . . ." I nearly said "tomb" but changed it to "sanctuary."

She crossed herself, bowed her head over clasped hands. I knelt facing her and together we said the Hail Mary I had known for as long as I could remember, she for one brief year. "Hail Mary, full of grace, be with us now and in the hour of our death. Amen."

Our candle, burned low when I seized it, flickered and went out. In the utter blackness I heard my heart beating and thought I could hear hers. I imagined, behind her, the icy grin of that skull. But I could not let myself give way to the awful notion that our lives would end in this darkness. "I have heard that flame eats air," I said. "And there is only so much in here for us to breathe."

Creating the illusion of life in that blackness we began to speak of the past, of our short lives, living them again in words to keep from thinking of our peril. Our voices might have been the only sounds in the universe; so thick were the walls around us, so far the chapel from the main buildings that no sound of any conflict reached us in there, not even the boom of cannons. Then it occurred to me that Indians do not fight at night, that dawn would bring these sounds of battle. The thought brought me to the present; I wondered if Captain Lugo had taken command of our palace-fortress or had believed Alvarado. "Captain Sandoval would have been a better choice than Alvarado," I said. "The men like him as well. But I guess Cortés needed him in Vera Cruz."

"Any captain would have been a better choice."

"Well, Cortés had to take the best ones with him. Without a triumph there, he won't be able to hold this city. With it, he can."

"Even if we're all dead by then, he could come back a victor and still have the respect of Moctezuma."

"Which wouldn't put the breath back into our nostrils or the hearts back into our bodies," I said bitterly.

Her tone was light: "You forget we won't have any bodies. The Aztecs will have eaten them."

A loud laugh burst from me, unlike my own. "And they'll hang our heads up there on the skull rack to dry!"

"We'll see all the *tlachtli* games."

"And bet on the winner."

"And watch the Aztecs bargain in the market."

"But we won't watch any sacrifices."

"No, we'll close our eyes to those!"

Our hilarity abruptly ebbed. We knew that the fantasy of those two skulls observing life in the great square might become, in part, reality. By our laughter we had denied that, tried to make the possibility seem impossible. Men about to be hanged, my father once said, can joke about nooses.

Time flowed with nothing to mark it. We grew thirsty and drank a little of the pulque, melon-flavored and quite good; we grew hungry and ate a maize cake each. At last our eyelids began to close; our voices slowed and there were long silences. We spread the mantles thinner and turned our cushions into pallets. I dozed, then woke to find myself shivering from the penetrating chill within the vault, the cold of stone, of night at a high altitude, of ancient guarded treasure. In that absolute darkness the crystal skull made itself felt to me. It was a presence that defied mere sight; I fancied that some of the chill in the room was exhuded from its smile. I could feel its hollow gaze.

My teeth began to chatter. I imagined the skull as cruelly awaiting my death, I, the last living Spaniard left in Tenochtitlán after the rest of our palace had become one vast charnel house. My mother's face loomed in memory, and I could not bear the sorrow of her eyes.

"Are you cold too?" Malinche asked.

"Yes." My father told me again to forget about poetry, to just concentrate on staying alive. The present was no longer real to me; the golden past claimed me. I swam again with Rubén, I knelt in the little Havana church between my parents, and the sound of the liturgy was sweetest music. In distant Medellín in the vineyard of my father's family I plucked warm purple grapes . . .

I heard footsteps. Malinche was up, moving about in the darkness.

The grapes were sweet. From the cork oak where I climbed to eat them I gazed down like a prince at the workers picking them for my grandfather's wine press. A warm summer breeze made the leaves about me rustle . . .

A whispery rustle filled the cold room where I relived a summer long ago and I heard the sound of something dragging across the floor.

"What's that?" I asked her.

"The feather cape. I got it down. For a blanket."

From cold and sorrow and remembered grapes, my mind raced toward warmth under feathers, and more than that, to the warmth of two bodies giving out to one another their gentle heat. The thought was delicious. I let my hand creep toward Malinche's pallet and felt the soft smoothness of close-woven feathers under my palm. I edged closer and my hand slipped under the cape's edge, into the warmth.

Blessed warmth. Life itself. With a slow sigh, I lay supine on my pallet, intensely aware of her breathing body so close to mine, which promptly responded with a carnal glee; I waited tensely for her command to remove my hand from her bed. Instead, the great cape rose into the air and settled down over my whole body as she shared it with me. I thanked her and lay smiling as I grew warm, willing the imp to subside.

"Are you afraid?" she asked after several moments of silence.

"No," I lied. "Whatever happens, it is God's will for us."

"I know," she said, "but I'm still afraid."

Her honesty shamed me. "I don't look forward to being dead

myself.'' I found that until this moment I had not really believed I would die. I remembered hearing that men walked up the steps of the gallows still thinking that some miracle would save them, and fear gripped me in a clutch as icy as the grin of that crystal skull. Anger came on its heels. ''And we have Cortés to thank! How little he really cared for us left here, to give so reckless a man as Alvarado full authority!'' I turned toward her, reached out, found her hand, gripped it. ''But if I burn in Hell for it, I will tell you this. I have loved you since I first saw you in Tabasco, and I have dreamed of you, and yearned for you! But instead I am to die without you.'' To the little demon between my legs, Death might have been the most seductive enchantress, for it arose in high anticipation, waiting alertly. ''Without you,'' I sighed.

''With me,'' she said. ''I do not hope for kindness from the Aztecs.''

With me? It could have two meanings, that we would die together here, or that I would die after possessing her.

''Do you think God will take us to be in Heaven with Him?'' she asked.

That query half-subdued the rampant demon. I knew to what horrible circle of the inferno fornicators went. ''We're Christians. We have committed no great sins.'' I lay for a time like a stone effigy, while every rivet of my jupon ground steel teeth into my flesh. Deciding that the pain of desire was enough to bear, I got up and removed it and put it on the floor with my breastplate, sword, and helmet.

''You said you were cold,'' Malinche said. ''Why are you taking your clothes off?''

''I will never sleep if I don't, and I must try to, because God knows what we will face tomorrow.'' In only my smallclothes and hose I crawled under the feather cape again. My heart was thudding first fast, then regular, then faster still, trying to beat its way through the wall of my chest and tumble into Malinche's arms. With wild insistence, my male member reared again to attention, throbbing like my heart. All at once, although she said nothing, I knew Malinche was aware of me, of my agony of desire. She found my hand, drew it toward her, and let it come to rest on her breast.

I rolled onto my side, toward her. My lips found hers as unerringly as if the bright sun shone on us. With a moan I kissed a mouth more sweet than even in my dreams of her. From the dark behind me I could feel the icy glare of the crystal skull, chilling my spine. Drawn by her and fleeing it, I escaped inward and upward and outward into the deep warmth of her body, into the ecstasy awaiting me there.

It was over too soon. Lying beside her, I felt suddenly shy. I wanted to say something memorable, words that would express my infinite gratitude. I summoned up one, but *gracias* seemed inadequate to the occasion. I turned my head toward her and listened to her breathing in the dark. What was she thinking?

"I wish I could see you." The words came out of me without forethought. I reached and found her warm hand. "I remember you on the beach at San Juan Ulua. You were like Aphrodite."

"Who is that?" Her voice was low, husky.

"The goddess of Love and Beauty."

She drew her hand from mine. She slipped out from under the feather cape. I heard soft, sliding sounds. She was taking off her clothes! I sat up, blood pounding in my ears. In a moment she lay down beside me. My hand went out and chastely touched her face, traced the line of her cheek, found her lips, moved down her throat. As it followed the smooth curve of her breast and found the nipple a shiver of desire convulsed me and then I felt her shiver too. Her response excited me because before she had lain passive, receiving my blind hungry thrust. I felt a terrible urge to place my lips there. It seemed to tighten and grow firm and her body turned toward me. I felt great wonder that I was doing this and then it seemed quite natural. My hands turned into eyes that had to see every inch of her, and all my manhood saluted her body and the beauty of it that my hands now knew forever. I left her long enough to make myself as naked as she, and this time was as unique to me as the first because my body and hers kissed down all their length just as our lips were doing. When I entered her I was no soldier storming a castle but a welcome guest who gently arrived and moved slowly in the home of her body until the dancing began to a wild beat, all the flamencos in Spain and Portugal . . .

We fell asleep at last clasped in each other's arms beneath the ceremonial cape of a dead Aztec king. For all his great riches he had been a poor man next to me, for I had attained my heart's desire.

I awoke suddenly. The air was stagnant, thick, and it was hard to breathe. My head ached dully and my dim brain knew that no matter what awaited us outside our crypt, I had to let air in. I found Malinche's mouth and kissed it. "Wake up, my dearest, or we'll die before our time." She stirred and murmured something as I got up and put on my jupon and carrying my breastplate made my way through the blackness to the chest by our low doorway and pushed it aside. I could not manage to pull the heavy stone inward by only my fingertips, so at last I lay on my back to edge it outward with my feet. Careful as I was, I heard the pedestal or the Virgin or both topple and crash to the floor of the chapel. Prickling with terror, I crossed myself, said, "Forgive me, Mary," and shoved the stone the rest of the way out. Along with fresher air a hint of daylight seeped in. Our long night was over. Only silence filled the chapel, and I began to breathe again.

And then a frightened voice demanded, "What thing is that in there?"

I knelt with my cheek to the floor and peered out. I found myself face to face with a young Spanish priest peering in, the same one who had cauterized my shoulder at Tabasco.

"Hasn't the battle begun yet?" I asked, astounded.

"What battle? What are you doing in there, Arturo Mondragon?"

Dumbfounded, I turned and called to Malinche that it was safe to emerge.

With his eyes roving to the fallen Virgin, the young priest told us that even when Moctezuma learned of the massacre of the dancers he had refused to command his warrior chiefs to attack us. Without his orders, they had not dared to proceed to revenge.

Malinche and I shared a lost look. In the shadow of what we had thought was sure death we had committed a great sin. And Death had passed us by. I felt very guilty, as though I had deliberately deceived her with a lie. By now the priest was much more concerned about the damage to Mary than about us, but still I explained to him that Cortés had ordered me to protect Doña Marina. I put on my breastplate and then I helped him right the pedestal and the statue. The end of Her nose was chipped off, and the priest wrung his hands as he wondered aloud if it could be properly mended.

In silence, Malinche and I walked into the palace I had imagined as a battleground. Sudden jubilant shouting reached us from the courtyard, and we hurried down a corridor that led to a balcony overlooking it. Below us men were hugging, shooting off muskets, dancing like fools to the fast thrum of Orteguilla's guitar.

He looked up and saw me and shouted the good news. "Cortés won! He defeated Narváez!"

NIGHT OF DANCERS, NIGHT OF TEARS

Elation flooded me; my spirits rose and rode that tide. Alvarado was astride his horse, sword aloft and gleaming, cleaned of last night's blood. He was beaming, roseate, a true child of the sun. Around him soldiers capered in a circle like the now-dead dancers. His horse reared; sword still pointing at the sky he cried shrilly: *"Viva Cortés!"*

"Viva Cortés!" the soldiers shouted with one voice.

"Arriba Cortés!"

"Arriba, arriba!"

I turned to Malinche. She was in profile to me, staring down. One hand was clenched on the rosary I had given her. She turned her head and looked at me. Her face was impassive. But as one sees pictures in clouds or flames, I saw in her eyes the truth of what I was, and knew with bitter pain that my joyous passage into manhood had made me a man I would never have chosen to become. It did not matter if the Devil had seized his chance while fear of an early death and a desire long felt had weakened me. I, Arturo Mondragon y Flores, had put horns on the great and victorious commander the men below now cheered. Worse, I had marred Malinche's chastity in the name of love. Mortal sin had claimed me. And yet there was a voice within me that defied these desperate facts as nonsense, denied my unworthiness. Shocked by the bloodbath in the ball court, believing death faced us, we had celebrated life. "I will love you, Malinche, until the day I die," I whispered.

Her hand left my rosary, let it fall. "Dying is not the danger we face now," she said. "Only living." She turned and walked away from me and I knew enough not to follow her.

A shouted word drew my eyes to the courtyard below. Alvarado was pointing his sword at me on the balcony. "Coward!" he shouted again. "I saw you desert your post, Mondragon!"

The butchered dancers bled and died in my head, a flashing series of vivid images. Without Alvarado's command to kill them I would not be the contemptible man standing on this balcony, accused by him of the least of my sins. I leaned far out over the stone rail, pointing my finger down at him as his sword pointed up at me. "Lunatic!" I howled. "Fool! Assassin!"

In the silence that fell I knew I had sealed my fate, and I did not care a *toston*, not a brass peso. I stood there in an arrogant pose, fists on hips, waiting to be seized and jailed, which shortly followed.

In leg irons and manacles in a room with three soldiers doing penance for milder crimes, I was suddenly famished, and asked one of the two soldiers who had arrested me for some food. He reminded me that our food supplies were running low due in part to a severe shortage of maize after a drought, or so Moctezuma had said; they themselves had had no breakfast yet. Hollow, echoing hunger made me curse my mad bravado and deep dejection followed. I saw, in a dim way, that I had, by insulting Alvarado, contrived this punishment, if not for the crime of which he had accused me. It was Juan Morla who came in and shared with me his ration of half a liter of boiled beans and two tortillas. He advised me to drink a lot of water to make the beans swell up and better fill the belly. To my surprise, I found that last night's slaughter had dismayed even this hardened soldier. "I only killed one," he said, "and I did it clean, right through the heart."

With food, my own heart rose slightly. I closed my eyes and sailed out of my prison on memories of love, and then into a lovely daydream, that somehow she would find that she no longer loved Cortés, that somehow she and I would sail to Cuba, man and wife, to live in blissful serenity. I placed our home on the cliff where I first glimpsed Cortés' flagship, never dreaming then to come back with a treasure more precious than even gold or gems: my love, my only love.

How totally I, his mistress and his tongue, had underestimated Hernán Cortés! That the trusted Pizarro went over to Narváez must have evoked great anger; Cortés transformed it into a greater will to win. But Alvarado gave way to secret terror that burst forth in the mass murder of innocent Aztec dancers. I saw that horror, helpless with the shock of it. I was fortunate that Cortés had assigned a soldier to protect me, even though I do not now think that the Aztecs watching the dance would have fallen on me then and there as Arturo Mondragon believed. Our sanctuary was the secret treasure room of Axayacatl. When I saw again the crystal skull, I became as certain as Arturo that every Spaniard in the city was sure to be killed by outraged Aztecs bent on swift vengeance. His hope that I might be spared I did not share; I knew that to the Aztecs I would be surrogate for the absent Cortés, who had promised Moctezuma that the Spaniards left in the city would cause no harm.

That long night I spent sealed as if within our tomb was the strangest I had ever known, and it taught me once again how wrong it is harshly to judge another. I came to understand my mother's hasty bedding with my uncle after my father died: in women Death's near presence can arouse a deep need to perform that act that gives life.

Arturo and I left the treasure room the next morning to learn that Cortés had defeated Narváez: no slaughter of Spaniards had ever taken place. Watching jubilant Spanish soldiers in the main courtyard as they capered around the mounted Alvarado, who looked as innocent of last night's bloodshed as Arturo, I began to shake inwardly, a trembling I could not control. My body had resigned itself to dying and now knew it would live. I wanted to be in some quiet place where I could collect myself; my footsteps took me to the room I had shared with Cortés. I fell across the canopied pallet where he had last held me in his arms and a storm of sobbing shook me. I wept for my frailty, for the sin of despair that had led to a greater sin. At last I knelt before the same small Virgin that had been my weapon in San Juan Ulua. She brought me clarity of mind. Remorse had not told me by what miracle Cortés had emerged the victor, nor why, even so, there had been no retaliation against at least those Spaniards who had bloodily proven what fifty well-armed soldiers can achieve in minutes against half-naked unsuspecting victims.

I made myself presentable and went to Moctezuma's chamber, but was told by an attendant that he was still at the temple with his gods. I returned to Cortés' room and sent a servant for Orteguilla, who might know enough to enlighten me. He appeared quickly, still carrying his guitar.

Moctezuma's forbearance was swiftly explained. The news of Cortés' stunning and absolute victory had reached him by courier the evening before, a little too late to be imparted to Alvarado in time to assuage his fears, for he had already left with his fifty soldiers for the harvest dance. Moctezuma had not attended, Orteguilla said. He had been under such great tension as to the outcome for Cortés that the abrupt good news had left him weak with relief. He had taken to his bed a little after sundown, ordering his attendants not to allow any visitors to awaken him, for he had slept badly for many weeks. He had assumed that if he informed Alvarado of the good news early in the morning, that would be well and good.

"Cortés has a gift for good luck, and no one can deny it," Orteguilla said. "Although it was also his knowledge of the climate of Vera Cruz that turned the tide for us. On the morning of that final large-scale battle while Narváez boasted of surely winning, a violent rainstorm from the north swept in. Cortés, of course, had correctly read the sky the night before and was prepared for the deluge. But torrents of rain soaked the enemy's unprotected powder supplies and rendered all their artillery useless. By this time Cortés had got a good number of Narváez's soldiers to defect to our side: mercenaries aren't too particular as to causes, and gold is a good persuader." The dwarf grinned up at me. "In short, it is victory, total victory, against overwhelming odds! Narváez is now in chains in Vera Cruz with a pike wound replacing one eye. Not only has Cortés' triumph saved us here, but it is sure to draw the attention of the Council of the Indies to the justice of Cortés' cause and the injustice of his persecution by Velásquez, a former conqueror now old and fat and jealous of our greater accomplishments in this land!"

He had not answered one question: "But by now Moctezuma must know about the slaughtered dancers, and yet has taken no action against Alvarado. Has he decided to wait until Cortés returns?"

Orteguilla shrugged. "I don't know."

As he spoke, the drum atop the war god's temple began to throb, answered by other drums. Shrill cries and howls arose from across the square, and I ran to the window to look out at the first close-packed rush of Aztec warriors flowing into the Zocalo in full battle dress. They came in from each avenue leading to the causeways, from each quarter of the city, the banners of the war chiefs raised high. I could not see how even the cannons and artillery Cortés had so strategically mounted before he left would possibly stop them for long. Instead of at once storming the palace they massed themselves in the square, confronting it with jeers, with the imposing spectacle of their multitude.

In a frightened voice that tried for nonchalance Orteguilla said, "It would appear that Cortés' victory has not greatly impressed Moctezuma's subjects."

Through the curtained doorway ran one of Moctezuma's attendants to tell me that the First Speaker required my services to translate for Alvarado's ears an important communication.

On his golden chair in his chamber, surrounded by somber-faced nobles, Moctezuma looked like a man who had received a sentence of death. He wore a panache and spoke slowly, solemnly. The powerful Council of Four, representing all the thirty clan chiefs, had just come to him to say that with or without his royal permission the clans had determined that the dead dancers must be avenged. Such a mandate to the First Speaker was unprecedented. "There is nothing I can do to avert this siege," he said without emotion. "Nothing. The Council of Four chose me as First Speaker. This uprising tells me they now regret that choice." His cold, reproachful eyes met Alvarado's. "You have yourself to blame, Tonatiuh, that things have come to this pass. Leave me now."

The child of the sun now looked like the child of the moon; his voice was also pale. "Ask him if he will send a courier to Cortés so I can write and tell him of this siege we face."

Moctezuma nodded, wearily. Alvarado looked more relieved than I felt; even if his letter reached Cortés, what could he do to help us in time? His men would be exhausted from weeks of battle; even with the Narváez defectors his army would be small compared to the Aztecs'; the long march back to Tenochtitlán would take many days.

When Alvarado and I left, he said, "The Devil take these crazy Aztecs! Going against their monarch like this! It's a crime against the very principle of monarchy!"

As he strode off I called to him sharply, and he paused in irritation. I said, "When Arturo Mondragon rescued me from that slaughterhouse last night he was acting on an order from Cortés to protect me."

"Even if he didn't, I can't afford to lose one man. Jesus Christ, woman, I have to man a siege with only a hundred and forty Spaniards to hold the fort!"

They and those brave Tlascalans held the besieged palace for twelve days. Our food supply was cut off overnight. Our Aztec servants disappeared. The conduit bringing water into our palace was severed. The market was closed, so instead of throngs buying and selling I saw only empty stalls, squadrons of Aztec warriors massed down there to kill us, however long it might take. Soon everyone was hungry all the time, such food supplies as we had being doled out scantily. The water in the garden pools made some of the soldiers sick, but then they had a little luck when a well they dug gave fresh water. Seven Spaniards were killed by arrows, spears, or stones that rained in on us over the walls. But Cortés' placement of the cannons he left and other artillery had been shrewd; gunfire kept the Aztecs at bay.

For my part, I coped with constant hunger by weaving the feather tapestry I had begun; on the third day I found a box of camote candy I had forgotten. There were ten pieces left, and I ate one each day for four days, then shared the rest with Doña Luisa, who had become very weak and pale. On the twelfth day I awoke ravenous without any hope for survival, but then became aware of the silence in the great square.

Dazed, I went to the window and tried to move the heavy screen I had placed against it after an Aztec javelin arched in through it, narrowly missing me. I was so weakened by hunger and despair that it was hard to push it aside even a handspan. I stared down at an empty plaza. The Aztec warriors were gone. Over all that vast expanse not a living creature stirred except one small fat dog who ran into the square from the avenue leading to the Tacuba causeway, paused to look around, then turned and waddled back again.

It was hard to believe what I saw, but the little dog made it real and not a scene from a hopeful dream. Why this sudden cessation of hostilities, just at the point when the hollow-eyed Spaniards could scarcely have lasted another day?

Moctezuma soon told Alvarado, through me. Cortés had been on the march to Tenochtitlán for days. This news had reached the capital only the night before. Moctezuma had sent word to the Council of Four that the invincible envoy of the god was soon returning: the siege must be ended at once. So unnatural had it been for the clans to act against their ruler's orders that they now agreed to do as he wished, their worst anger against the Spaniards spent.

The soldiers' shouts of joy when Alvarado told them of Cortés' return were more like hoarse croaks, so weak were the men from hunger and thirst. But although the aqueduct was repaired and fresh water flowed into the palace cistern, the Aztec marketplace stayed closed and bare. Moctezuma had drawn heavily on the royal store-rooms, I knew, considering that the many people in his own palace had to eat. The ending of the siege made hunger more bearable; the soldiers assured one another that as soon as Cortés got back they would feast as bountifully as before.

The front rampart was thick with soldiers watching for Cortés. Arturo Mondragon looked older, so gaunt that his green eyes seemed to have enlarged. I nodded to him but did not speak. It was a beautiful day, the June sun benevolent, but the square looked like one in a deserted city. As I stood there, the recollection of a dream I had just before waking troubled me. In it Cortés had returned and seemed fatherly. Like a good daughter I told him what had happened in the treasure room. He was at first kind and seemed to take it as a natural thing of no great importance, but then grew more severe and said it must never happen again or I would no longer be his Amazon. Feeling shamed and ready to cry, I promised him never again to be unfaithful.

"Listen!" I heard a soldier say. I heard the distant cluttered staccato of hoofbeats on stone paving. It came from the direction of the Tacuba causeway. My blood began to race and I realized that soon I would see him again. The welcome sound came nearer.

Into that vast and silent square rode Cortés. Behind him floated his worn banner. His black stallion plodded, head down. The mounts of the captains who rode behind him looked as spent. As Cortés neared the center of the square the following hoofbeats became a sustained roll of muffled thunder, and I stared down at the dozens of horsemen pouring in, as though those beasts had multiplied in battle, budding as plants do. As Cortés neared our palace, the first of hundreds of foot soldiers followed the horsemen. Not a single Aztec lined the way to watch this triumphant return: Narváez had come to take over and swallow Cortés' expedition, but instead Cortés had swallowed his.

When he reached a point some fifteen paces from the palace gate the soldiers were all cheering him. Among their voices I did not think mine would be heard, but found myself calling his name. To my surprise, he tipped back his head and looked straight at me. His face was grim, but his arm went up in a salute and I raised mine in answer. A wave of true thankfulness that he was still alive lifted me on its crest, and my hand went up to my rosary. It touched only cloth, and I remembered that I had taken off Arturo's gift twelve days before.

Now the soldiers were jostling and crowding each other on the stone steps leading down to the courtyard, all eager to be there when Cortés entered. I could not make my way down to him, for although several soldiers at the top of the stairs made way for me, those below were blind and deaf. The gates were opened and Cortés rode into the courtyard, met by a solid wall of soldiers, and their cheers and shouts of welcome.

And then, on the balcony where Arturo and I had heard of his triumph, I saw Moctezuma, the little figure of Orteguilla beside him. The soldiers parted to let Cortés pass. Unsmiling, he looked up at the Aztec ruler. It was the dwarf's voice, not mine, that offered Cortés Moctezuma's words of greeting: "Welcome back, my lord! We are glad to see you victorious over your enemies."

To my astonishment, Cortés answered in a hard, cold voice: "I have with me ninety-eight horses and thirteen hundred Spanish soldiers. And eighty crossbowmen and as many musketeers. This is not a bad result from a battle you believed would be my death!''

When Orteguilla translated this in halting Nahuatl, Moctezuma seemed stunned, but answered: "Your triumph confirms my faith in you, for which I am glad."

Without an answer, Cortés turned his horse and passed by in disdain. For a moment Moctezuma stared after him, then turned and went back into the palace, Orteguilla trotting after.

I was as shocked as Moctezuma. And I knew that Alvarado in the letter of twelve days earlier when he told Cortés of the siege and asked assistance had distorted the truth to excuse himself. Cortés had to be told at once the facts about the slaughter of the dancers! His contempt of Moctezuma could only mean that he thought an act of Aztec violence had provoked it. This public humiliation of the ruler must be amended, and quickly.

By now the steps to the courtyard were clear, and I ran down and hurried to the far end where Cortés now smiled down at the solid mass of soldiers crowding around the stallion. "Cortés!" I shouted as I I neared. "We must talk!"

He turned a little in the saddle and nodded. "Soon, Doña Marina. Soon. First I must talk with my captains."

His smile was echoed on several soldiers' faces. I felt naked. It seemed to me that he had assumed that my desire for him was such that I had lost all pride and propriety. Anger quenched humiliation; I turned and went to the room I had shared with three women during my estrangement from Cortés. I now felt almost as alienated. Let someone else tell him the truth he was blind to!

Sobbing met me. Chu-Chu, considerably thinner, knelt on her pallet, rocking and sobbing. Doña Luisa and Ixlan, standing over her, were trying to comfort her. She turned toward me her cross-eyed face, tear-wet. "They killed him! That nice young soldier who said he loved me! Dead down in Vera Cruz. He was ugly, but good, and he's dead, and he said he loved me!"

I thought of all the other soldiers dead. I knew that if Cortés' insult to Moctezuma proved a last and final straw all of us would join them. My pique vanished. I turned and ran to find Cortés, learned from his groom that he had gone to his headquarters.

All his captains were there with him. It was soon clear that someone had already exposed Alvarado's lie. He and Cortés stood beard to beard, and Cortés was clearly holding down his fury with great effort. "Again I will ask it: What made you order the slaughter of the dancers?"

"Our trouble with the Aztecs started when you went up and smashed the idols in the temple." Alvarado glanced hopefully around at his fellow captains for support; their faces stayed severe and accusing.

"Why did you kill those dancers?" Cortés asked again.

"I knew the Aztecs would attack us as soon as the dance was over."

"And how did you know this?"

Alvarado's eyes sought the ceiling as though the answer might be carved in its cedar. "I think I heard it from an Aztec priest who was talking with two of Moctezuma's nobles when I went to pay my respects."

"You don't understand three words of their tongue! Who translated this for you?"

"I think it was the dwarf."

Cortés turned to Captain Lugo. "Bring Orteguilla here."

"Wait!" Alvarado said. "It wasn't the dwarf. I don't remember who it was."

"What a bad liar you are!" Cortés' rage burst out. "The fact is that the sight of some half-naked heathens capering in their jewels and feathers made you go crazy! You gave into impulse, mere impulse!"

Head down, face red, Alvarado muttered, "You didn't see those pagan devils."

"It was ill done! This terrible error of judgment is something I may never be able to rectify! I can never trust you in a position of authority again!" Cortés turned his back on Alvarado, who stared down at the floor as if he saw his own grave opening there.

Cortés saw me standing near the doorway. He came toward me holding out his hand. When mine came to rest on his palm he bent and kissed it, an elegant gesture which showed respect. "Captain Lugo says you witnessed a part of what happened in the ball court and appeared horrified."

"Yes."

"Could a reasonable man have thought it a war dance?"

"No. The Aztecs had no weapons. They were defenseless."

Alvarado cried, "A woman is no judge! They see things differently! And she left at the very start of the fight!"

I said to Cortés, "I saw enough! Arturo Mondragon got me away, for which I thank God. The paving of the ball court was red blood; blood splashed on me as I ran."

"Mondragon deserted his post," Alvarado cried, eager to deflect attention to another culprit. "If it hadn't been for the siege, when I needed every man, he'd be swinging from a rope for vultures to eat!"

Cortés threw him a look of contempt. "He obeyed my orders. You did not."

As Alvarado wilted, I said to Cortés, "Now you see how wrong you were to blame Moctezuma for the siege. You must go to him at once and tell him so."

The anger at Alvarado was turned on me. "Must? Do not command the commander! It ill becomes a woman!"

As I flinched at his harshness and stepped back from him, two Aztec nobles entered, solemn-faced. In contrast to the steel-armed Spanish captains they looked very vulnerable. "Moctezuma wishes to speak at once with Cortés in his chamber," one told me.

"He can go to Hell," Cortés said when I told him this. "I will not stir one foot to see a dog who won't keep the market open or order food for my starving men!"

I gave the Aztecs a diplomatic excuse, but they had heard the harsh sound of his voice. They looked at each other in consternation; I risked his further wrath. "Moctezuma is behaving very well, considering your insulting response to his speech of welcome!"

"He can open the market! I have to get food for my men!"

It was Captain Olid who said, "Señor! Moderate your anger."

Sandoval added, "Yes, think how good Moctezuma has been to us. How patient. He ordered the siege stopped, Lugo tells me. Except for him, all of those who remained here might now be dead and eaten!"

As though he had not heard, Cortés demanded, "Why should I answer this summons from a dog who was probably treating secretly with Narváez?"

Captain Sandoval lisped, "I think it was the other way around. Narváez tried to treat covertly with him and to convince him that we are no better than felons. But Moctezuma did not believe him, and the proof is that we stand here alive. You were wrong to humiliate Moctezuma. You are wrong now if you refuse to talk with him as he asks."

Cortés turned to me. "Have them tell Moctezuma that I will visit him after he provides food for my men. He must open the market at once. I will give him until midday tomorrow."

I said to them, "Cortés asks only that his hungry men be fed. As you can see, he is very weary. Perhaps by midday tomorrow, after the market is open, he and Moctezuma can come to a better understanding." But the two nobles had twice heard the angry arrogance in Cortés' voice. Without further comment or any farewell, they turned and left.

The captains were aware that they were offended, and Captain Velásquez said to Cortés, "You are very weary, and you should rest now."

He shook his head, but the other captains all came forward to agree. Even Alvarado, looking slightly reassured since Cortés had done nothing worse than censure him, urged Cortés not to push himself further and got a withering look for it. "I have to find quarters for the new recruits. All the new horses have to be stabled and fed. And I want to check the palace defenses, for who can say how long this peace will last?"

I saw, with stunning clarity, that Cortés would busy himself with these things to escape from giving further consideration to the gravity of Alvarado's offence or to the punishment it merited. I saw too the cause of his unreasonable anger toward Moctezuma: he was deflecting toward the Aztec ruler some of his rage at Alvarado, whom he did not want to punish for his rash cruelty, knowing that it would not have occurred except for his own grave error of judgment in leaving him in command. In other words, to judge and punish Alvarado, he would have to judge himself too. He was not prepared to do this.

Moctezuma's reply came swiftly, brought by the same two nobles. "As your prisoner here I can do nothing. But if you will release my brother Cuitlahuac I will order him to do as you wish and provide food for your soldiers."

Again I was aware of Cortés' weariness. He closed his eyes and covered them with one hand as he thought over this offer. He dropped his hand with a sigh. His gaze roved over his captains' faces. "We have no choice. We have to eat." He turned to me. "Tell Moctezuma I will release Cuitlahuac."

I must have gasped; he gave me a dark and warning look. Having excoriated Alvarado for his rashness, he now made this rash decision as though he had forgotten that Cuitlahuac had been one of the few supporters of Cacama in his rebellion.

He and the captains then left to reorganize the logistics of the entire palace, now packed with the new recruits, horses whinnying in every courtyard.

It was late that night when he finally came into the room where I awaited him. My uneasiness about the release of Cuitlahuac and another more personal matter melted into nothing when I saw him. He moved stiffly, like a man whom only great willpower kept upright. He gave me a ghastly grin out of a gray-white face in which his eyes flashed as if with a fever. "I fell asleep too soon when I left you, Marina. And now it looks as if I'll do it again."

His valet arrived on the run to help him out of his armor, and he gave a groan of relief as the breastplate was removed, sank into his chair for the greaves to be unbuckled. He dismissed the valet, stood, kept his shoulders straight as he walked in smallclothes to the bed, then fell onto it, eyes already shut. I covered him with a blanket, and as if he felt my presence, one eye partly opened. "My Amazon," he whispered, and reached an arm toward me. It dropped like lead to the bed. He was asleep.

I lay awake for a long time beside him, remembering the woman of such a short time ago who had lain here filled with longing. The only desire that filled me now was somehow to prevent him from releasing Cuitlahuac; as far as I could learn he had not yet committed that mistake. Not only did Cuitlahuac hate Spaniards; not only had he already rebelled against his ruler, but he had once been, according to Moctezuma, a contender for the throne. I knew it would be hard to reach Cortés; I had seen tonight a new or earlier-hidden side to his nature: an arrogant resistance to the truth that actions have consequences. Or perhaps he had come to believe that for him this was not true. A hero had come back from Vera Cruz. A hero who knew himself to be one. It would take all his powers to remedy matters here in the city he had managed to hold for a thankless Spanish king. It would also take a touch of humility.

Against all this, my remorse over what happened by chance in a dead king's treasure room seemed trivial indeed.

I said my prayers and told myself that tomorrow, when Cortés was rested and more reasonable, I would express my deep anxiety about Cuitlahuac.

Tomorrow proved, as it so often does, too late. Cortés' last act before he came to bed had been to set Cuitlahuac free.

32

All during the siege with its misery, hunger, and terror I had an inner battle with the recurring fear that my friend El Galán would die fighting the overwhelming Narváez forces: the odds meant to me that Death had about four chances at El Galán for one chance at each of those four enemies. So while other soldiers swarmed around the victorious Cortés as he rode his black stallion into the palace courtyard, I stationed myself by the entrance gate, watching for El Galán. Captains known and horsemen strange to me had passed in before I saw him drooping with fatigue atop a somewhat swaybacked piebald horse. His left leg was swathed in a bandage caked with dried blood, and he looked like his own older brother.

When I ran to him calling his name he looked down at me from eyes set in dark hollows and croaked, "God, what a miserable campaign. We fought the last battle in torrents of rain, but it ruined the enemy's powder supplies and rendered their cavalry less useful, I'll say that for it." With slow care he dismounted, wincing as he tried to stand on his bandaged leg. He put an arm around my shoulders and I felt the dead weight of his weary body. "I am very tired, old friend, and I will sleep a long time now, I think. Will you stable and feed my mare?" He gave her a wry, affectionate glance. "I got her from a Narváez captain who suddenly lost any need for a mount." I went with him to his old pallet next to mine, where he shed his helmet and breastplate and stretched out with a sigh of relief.

After I stabled the horse and found her some straw to eat, which was all the fodder we had, I went back to my friend. He was not asleep, probably due to his pain, so I asked him about that final battle that had saved me from extinction. "Narváez planned to defeat us on a plain near Zempoalla with all his horsemen, crossbowmen, musketeers, and cannons except for two he left in the town, mounted on the first level of the main pyramid where our cross stands. The rainstorm rendered all but the crossbowmen ineffectual. So he ordered a retreat to the town, where the horses would not be slipping and sliding in the mud. What Cortés wanted was the capture or death of Narváez himself. So Sandoval led the charge to take over the cannons on the pyramid where he was, we captains right behind, the fifes and drums beating the charge, soldiers with pikes and crossbows backing us up. And Narváez got a pike in the eye. How he yelled! 'Holy Mary protect me! They killed me and destroyed my eye!' Our soldiers shouted, 'Victory for Cortés! Narváez has fallen, Narváez is dead!' And that began the turn of the tide in our favor, although we had to battle on for a long while after this, and captured Diego Velásquez, the son of the governor, and other important fellows.''

"And did Narváez die?''

"No, he was just half-blind and bleeding. With the capture of the other captains, Cortés proclaimed to the Narváez soldiers that they should all join him in victory, surrender themselves to the rightful Captain-General and Chief Justice of Vera Cruz, founded in the name of their sovereign. And this, at last, is what they did. Narváez behaved surprisingly well in defeat; he had asked Sandoval to let his surgeon treat his wound and those of the other imprisoned captains, and Sandoval did. While Narváez was being doctored, Cortés came into the room. Narváez said, 'Señor Captain Cortés, you must consider it a great feat, this victory over me and the capture of my person.' '' El Galán smiled. "And Cortés said, 'It was one of the least things I have done in New Spain.' ''

"How did you get wounded?'' I asked. "Capturing Narváez?''

"After he was captured. There were skirmishes most of that night with those of the enemy too stubborn to recognize defeat. And I got a pike in the leg, but better than the eye. The rain had stopped and there were millions of fireflies, and by their light I saw the whoreson who did it, and I got him. And a captain, too, and commandeered his mare. She doesn't look like much but she's good-natured and plucky.''

"It must have been a great day, though, when they all surrendered.''

"It was! First the drummers and other musicians Narváez brought all marched into our camp beating their drums and playing their fifes and tambourines and calling '*Viva, viva* the few brave men who conquered Narváez and his soldiers.' A giant Negro beating on a big bass drum roared 'Even the Romans never did a feat like this!' Then Sandoval, Olid, and Ordas rode in at the head of the captured captains. Cortés looked like a king in the long orange robe he wore over his armor. The captains, including the son of Velásquez, all passed before him and bent and kissed his hand.''

Now El Galán's eyelids were closing, but he roused himself. "Then Cortés sent soldiers to the port where Narváez's ships were anchored and ordered the mates and masters to remove all sails, rudders, and compasses to keep them from sailing back to Cuba and told them to come to him and surrender, and they did.''

"And then on top of a victory like that came Alvarado's letter about the trouble here in Tenochtitlán.''

"Three days later. Cortés was furious when he learned that Alvarado was besieged after some Aztec war dance in which some Spaniards were killed.'' El Galán's weary lids closed.

The falsity of Alvarado's report stunned me. "But that's not how it was!'' A snore answered me. I jumped to my feet. Cortés had to be told the truth!

He strode out of his council chamber just as I reached the door; inside, his captains, Malinche, and a chastened Alvarado stood staring after him. I could see that a momentous scene had taken place while I was with El Galán. Cortés paused to say to me "I know that seven Spaniards were killed during the siege. I am glad you were not one of them, Arturo." He turned to call back over his shoulder to his captains, "Do you plan to stand there the rest of the day?'' They thudded past me and I stood looking in at Malinche, now alone. I saw, with a pang, that she no longer wore my rosary.

I went no closer, but called from the doorway, "Does Cortés know the truth about Alvarado?''

"Yes.''

"What is the punishment to be?''

"None!''

"I don't believe it!'' Our eyes met and I imagined that our thoughts were the same: we had been victims of that crime of Alvarado; our lapse from virtue would not have happened without it.

Yet a wave of guilt and self-despising washed over my stinking body, for we had had no water to waste in bathing. She looked so sad, standing alone in that big room. I knew what remorse she must have suffered. I turned and went silently away, the seducer of this woman whom great fear had made vulnerable to my lust. Cortés' kind words to me of a few minutes earlier now stabbed my conscience like darts.

Yet so perverse was that part of me the Devil uses to his delight and our later pain that it had stirred in excitement at the sight of her, and now stirred again as I despised my own lust. As I pushed my way along a corridor crowded with disgruntled Narváez men asking one another when they would get some food, I fiercely commanded my impish part to get used to relative chastity again.

The next day dawned warm and beautiful and I woke on my straw pallet grateful that El Galán was alive on his. I was sure that with Cortés back I would soon eat a real meal again, not just thin maize gruel or watery bean soup. I went to the front wall to look out and see if perhaps the market might already be open, but no food had appeared on the skeletal permanent stalls that stood as empty as I was, waiting for the abundance of produce that my jaws yearned to crunch, that my belly wailed for.

And then, across the square, I saw a figure come running toward the palace from the street that led to the Tacuba causeway. As it neared I saw that it was a Spaniard and that blood ran down one side of his face. Not until he was at the door below did I recognize Yago the acrobat. I ran down to the courtyard and reached it just after the sentries let him in. "For God's sake, what happened to you?" I asked.

He could only shake his head, panting for breath, and I saw that his eyes were glazed with terror. I went with him to Cortés' headquarters, where we found the general looking more like himself after some hours of sleep. When he saw Yago's bloody face, dismay showed on his.

He poured a cup of water and while Yago drank, Cortés told me that before dawn he had dispatched Yago and several other soldiers to Vera Cruz with news of our safe arrival. Yago put down the cup and told the rest. They had got nearly as far as Tacuba on the shortest of the causeways when they saw ahead a horde of Aztec warriors marching from that town to Tenochtitlán. They had let loose a flight of spears and arrows, one of which had grazed Yago's cheek. He turned and ran for his life. Tears of terror sprang to his eyes. "The causeways to the city are full of those warriors! Thousands and thousands! Spotted like jaguars, hissing like snakes, and with the heads of eagles, or helmets that are great toothed jaws, their own faces peering out. Cuitlahuac is leading them."

Almost before Yago finished speaking, Cortés sent his crier to summon the captains. They conferred only briefly. It was decided that Diego de Ordas, with four hundred foot soldiers and a dozen crossbowmen and musketeers, would go out to reconnoiter. Ordas was ordered to remain calm and avoid any battle if he could.

Moctezuma was still our hostage, but if those approaching warriors any longer intended to obey his command that the siege be ended, would they now be marching on the city? Could he still manage to save us from the wrath of his people?

Ordas and his men were not gone long. They had to retreat almost at once to the main square and fight their way past the Aztec warriors beginning to fill it—and who soon were attacking our fortress with arrows, javelins, and slings. But our cannons, placed by Cortés to command the square from the rampart and roof garden, soon cleared a way for Ordas and his force to enter, although he and almost all his men were wounded, and they left fourteen Spaniards lying dead in the Zocalo.

The battle raged all day. With sunset the attack ceased, but we had to spend part of the night repairing and reorganizing our defenses. At least eighty of our men had been wounded.

At dawn Cortés mounted a counterattack, two forces of a hundred men each. Covered by our cannons and artillery, we forced the Aztecs back across the square, but then we were trapped among the houses and had to retreat under the barrage of stones and weapons hurled down on us from those flowering rooftops we had so admired. Whistling, shouting Aztecs hounded us back across the central plaza. That day we lost another dozen men.

Cortés then conceived a plan of building mobile wooden towers on wheels, horse-drawn and each holding some twenty men. From the tops musketeers and crossbowmen could shoot out at the warriors on the rooftops as they passed, the cavalry meanwhile clearing the street below. It took a day and a night to build them of wood gotten by taking down a ceiling, but they proved nearly useless because the Aztecs put up street barricades to impede our horses. The towers had to lumber back to our palace, damaged by hurled javelins, although no one inside them was wounded.

On the third day of the siege, Cortés decided that if we could get to the top of the war god's temple and destroy all the idols there and set it afire, this might have the effect of subduing our superstitious foes. So at dawn of the fourth day, after commending our souls to God, we carried forth those wooden towers again. With cannons, muskets, and crossbows clearing a way for us, we pushed through fresh squadrons of Aztec warriors to the forecourt of the great pyramid. I was inside one of the towers, which already smelled of sweat and fear. Beside me a Narváez man steadily cursed Cortés, Narváez, and the day he left Cuba. Outside, Aztecs yelled and whistled and screamed, and stones, spears, and arrows rattled against the wood of the tower with fearsome thuds.

Peeping through one of the narrow slits in the tower I saw those thousands of skulls grinning down at our misfortune. A night rain had wetted the smooth paving stones so that our horses slipped and stumbled amid a scramble of attacking Aztecs. Had they massed at the top of the pyramid they could have shot down arrows at us very effectively, but religious scruples evidently kept them from using this elevated battleground. Hundreds of them were massed on the two lower levels, however.

It took all my courage to emerge at the prearranged signal from the safety of that huge shield when it reached the bottom of the pyramid steps. With Cortés himself leading us, we began to fight our way to the top. "Santiago and upward!" he cried to us, and this new version of our old battle cry had the power to move us after him, slashing and stabbing at the Aztecs who hoped to stop us. The angry Narváez man fell dead beside me at the first terrace. Cortés seemed more than human, a figure out of legend, as he hacked his way upward with flashing sword. As I rose behind him, step by step, I saw each enemy through the red blood lust that had come upon me and felt only joy as my sword pierced the throat of an eagle warrior, the bird beak of his helmet framing his final grimace.

We reached the top, toppled lesser idols and set fire to the chamber where the hideous war god stood. Some fresh human hearts laid at his feet began to cook and to send out a greasy smoke, then flames enveloped him. Our damage done, we had to fight our way down again, but now had the advantage that we could shoot down on the Aztecs, and we did away with enough of them to get across the pyramid's forecourt past the wreckage of one of our towers. The cannons and artillery on our rampart cleared a path through the yelling warriors in the main plaza so that we could make our way back into the palace, bringing with us two Aztec priests we had captured.

The grim night was spent in dressing our wounds and burying our dead. We knew that we had done our utmost. If the destruction of their principal gods and the burning of their main temple did not subdue these Aztecs, then all we could do was to surrender, sue for peace, and hope to God to be allowed to leave the city alive.

The idea of surrender roused in me two strong emotions: a yearning to continue living, on whatever terms, but also sorrow at the thought that sixteen months of toil, danger, and battles against great odds would be set at naught.

I was lying on my pallet; El Galán on his beside me was unwrapping the bandage from his leg wound. Despite it he had taken over that day for a wounded crossbowman, being versed in using that weapon.

NIGHT OF DANCERS, NIGHT OF TEARS

Standing for several hours at the rampart had caused his wound to open. I gasped when I saw it, for the pike had entered behind the greave and gouged a big hole in his calf. He winced as he cleaned it with sherry from his flask. "Wine is good for wounds and seems to keep them from getting pus," he remarked and began to wrap it with a strip torn from a cotton mantle. I helped, holding the lower end in place.

"It's surrender, isn't it?" I asked.

He frowned. "That will come hard for Cortés."

"What choice does he have?"

"To fight on."

"In God's name, how? The food Cuitlahuac sent us is nearly gone; I know that for a fact. The cistern is nearly empty. What happens when our ammunition is gone?"

He shrugged and tied his bandage. "Cortés' victory over Narváez was good and yet bad. It may have gone to his head. Diego Velásquez kissed his hand. The Council of the Indies seems to be on his side now. He expects any day to hear from King Carlos that a mighty force is on its way to aid him. He may believe that he can continue to inspire us to keep at it here until we're all skeletons, fed only by the courage he pumps into us."

I dreamed that night of a fortress full of desiccated cadavers pulling bows and shooting muskets at Aztecs in the square who laughed in derision while Cortés on a skeletal black stallion shouted brave words to inspire his obedient marionettes.

Morning showed the square filling with Aztec warriors fresh and well-fed and yelling for our hearts. Mine sank as my belly rumbled its demand for food. The drum atop the war god's pyramid began to throb and I guessed that another dripping heart was being held aloft to the morning sun. The thought of rebellion crept into my mind. If we all refused to fight, Cortés would have to forget his swollen pride and sue for peace.

Drearily I got up to take my post and draw my sword and hack at any Aztec who might today be boosted to the top of our wall or climb one of the ladders they used. They were very persistent in these attempts; now one looked just like another to me except for the differences between their strange helmets.

But that day El Galán and I were replaced at the wall by two soldiers who had been guarding Moctezuma. Standing as sentries outside the door to his apartment, El Galán and I could hear the sounds of battle, yet could take no part. I thought then of Malinche, probably busy at her tapestry, hearing the same sounds, able to do nothing but await the outcome.

The thought took me back once more to my early childhood with my mother in Medellín, those years when she waited while my father fought Caribs in Cuba. The lot of women seemed a sad and hard one, their fate forever determined by the acts of a man to whose destiny their own was bound.

33

When I found that Cortés had released Cuitlahuac, I could only hope that my fears were wrong. He kept his promise to Moctezuma and supplied us with maize, beans, and tomatoes, but the price was high: renewed hostilities. After an attack on Huitzilopotchli's temple failed to subdue the Aztecs besieging us, Cortés began to have trouble sleeping nights. I would wake from an uneasy doze to find him pacing around the room in a long orange robe given him by the cacique of Zempoalla. I knew that those captains who counseled surrender were right. On the third night of waking and finding him prowling the room, I sat up in bed and said, "Make your peace with Moctezuma. Tell him you are willing now to leave the city. Plead with him to announce this at once to Cuitlahuac."

He came and stood over me like a tower of flame. "We are not defeated yet!"

"Is that what you are waiting for? Defeat? How much ammunition is left? How much food have your soldiers eaten today? My heart aches for them!"

"Women's hearts were made to ache. Men's were not. I know Moctezuma could have gotten more provisions out of Cuitlahuac if he had tried! Or else he could give us some of the food stored over there in his own palace. The dog has two faces, two hearts! With one he trembles in fear of me and with the other he wants me dead! I will make no peace with him!"

"Why should he let the people in his palace go hungry to feed us?"

"Let these sycophants feel the nip of hunger!"

"Would you take from your soldiers to feed them?"

He glared down at me. "Stop all this sophistry!"

"I don't know what that means."

"It means I am weary of listening to you! Don't get above yourself. And let me think, for God's sake! Let me think!"

I dared a few more words. "Your victory at Vera Cruz may cause your defeat here. It did not make you invincible."

To my surprise, that barb struck home. He stared down at me, then gave a crooked grin. "Pride goes before a fall? Is that what you are trying to convey?"

"With all my heart."

"Do you happen to know that the soldiers of Hamilcar drank their own urine to stay alive?"

"I do not know who Hamilcar is."

"Alexander of Macedon. . ."

"All I do know is that a great leader of men can rise above pride when the lives of men who trust him are in the balance."

He rolled his eyes toward heaven. "May God save and defend me against a woman with little knowledge and a clever brain!"

"God save me from a general who is unwilling to use the good brain God gave him!" By now I was trembling with the intensity of my feelings. I lay back on the bed and crossed my hands on my breast and closed my eyes.

"What now?" he asked.

I did not answer.

He came to the side of the bed, seized my arm and shook it. "What is this? Out of words at last?"

"I am going to die soon. I am trying to ready myself with prayer."

He tossed my arm from him. "By my conscience, for the first time in my life I want to hit a woman!" I opened my eyes to see him looming above me, fist raised above his head, the arm trembling as he held back the blow.

"That will be easier than asking Moctezuma's pardon for insulting him."

The fist was slowly lowered. He turned abruptly to kneel where the Virgin Mary stood. I prayed that She would move Cortés, since I had failed.

In the morning I found that my prayer had been answered. Cortés, armed from top to toe, shook my arm to wake me. "I need your voice. I want you to go to Moctezuma and tell him that I ask his pardon if I was hasty in suspecting him. I want an immediate interview with him."

I was now wide awake. "To what purpose?"

"To tell him I wish my entire army to leave the city peaceably."

I dressed in a beautiful tunic Moctezuma had given me and wore the necklace of gold and turquoise he had also given. Sandoval and Father Olmedo, of whom he was fond, were waiting in the corridor to escort me. Sandoval was cheerful. "All will be well now, I think. I'm sorry to surrender, but also glad to have the chance to do so."

We reached Moctezuma's quarters to be met at the doorway by a solid wall of nobles. I said, "We have come to offer Moctezuma Cortés' apology for his great rudeness. He was misinformed about the true cause of the siege. He wants an interview."

A noble left the group and went toward a high screen of gilded fretwork at the room's far end and returned to say "Moctezuma will speak to Malinche." I followed him; he halted before the screen. Through the small openings in the elaborate carving I could see someone sitting behind it. Moctezuma's voice was dull and cold. "I refuse to see Cortés. Fate has brought me to such an evil pass because of him that I never want to see his face or hear his voice again."

Hiding my shock, I said: "He wishes to leave the city."

There was no response. I knew further words were useless. I bowed low to the screen and retreated.

Cortés was astonished that Moctezuma, always so amenable, had dared this defiance. "We are the ones brought to an evil pass! And he will see me! Now!" He took my arm and pulled me with him to the doorway.

At Moctezuma's door the same nobles barred the way, but Cortés called loudly above their heads: "Lord Moctezuma! Is this how you treat me when I come in all humility to offer an ending to your troubles and mine? Please, ask your nobles to let me enter!"

In a moment Moctezuma's faint voice said "Enter."

But the screen remained between them as Cortés said, "All I ask is that you go out to the front rampart and address your people. Tell them that this war must cease. All I want is to leave your city in peace."

There was a long silence. Moctezuma said: "I do not believe I can obtain an end to this war. My people listen to Cuitlahuac now. They have made up their minds not to let you leave here alive. I believe that all of you must die.''

Cortés' power to force Moctezuma to do his will had failed this last and crucial time! But Cortés, in an urgent yet humble tone, said, ''I beg you to speak to your people as I have asked. They have revered you for seventeen years. That will prove a stronger loyalty than any they may feel toward an upstart like Cuitlahuac. Speak to them!''

There was a long pause. Moctezuma spoke wearily. ''I will do this one last thing you ask of me.''

Cortés thanked Moctezuma and left, after bowing respectfully to the gilded screen. ''Thank God,'' he said as soon as we were in the corridor. His face was bright with relief, and I thanked Him too for Cortés' overnight change in perception of our situation, and I marveled at God's power to move intractable human hearts. Or perhaps it had been the Sainted Virgin to whom he had knelt the night before who had made him see that our only hope for survival was a swift exodus.

Within the hour, Moctezuma, Cortés, and I, escorted by the captains and the ruler's Spanish bodyguard, made our way to the front rampart. Moctezuma, thinner than before and with a sadder face, walked slowly to the crenellated wall splashed with patches of dry brown blood, and mounted the platform placed there so he could be well seen from the square below. I stood at one side, Cortés at the other, but lower than he. Moctezuma stood there in silence, arrayed in the great green headdress of quetzal feathers he had worn when he came to meet us. As the Aztecs looked up and saw him their derisive cries ceased and the conches and drums fell silent. Aztec chieftains called sharp commands, and I saw bows lowered and raised lances slowly fall. The Council of Four came forward and stood just below Moctezuma, looking up. He addressed them in a firm, gentle tone, saying what Cortés had asked: that they must now desist from further warfare, for we would at once leave the city and go back to our own land.

The oldest member of the Council of Four came forward and bowed to his ruler. I heard his words with disbelief, while putting them into Spanish as they fell from his lips slowly and with deep sorrow. ''Oh, Great Lord Moctezuma, all your misfortune and injury afflicts us. But now we make it known to you that we have raised up one of your kinsmen to be our lord in your place. It is your brother Cuitlahuac.'' And Cuitlahuac came forward to stand beside him, looking up at his former ruler impassively, wearing a royal green headdress.

I saw Moctezuma's body stiffen. He stood looking out at the faces of the people who had deposed him. Such a thing had never happened before in all the long history of the Aztecs. This moment must have been a strange and terrible one to bear—and not only for him, to judge by the awed and absolute silence of the Aztecs in the square below.

Then Cuitlahuac spoke. His voice was very loud and had a stony quality. "The war must be carried on. We will fight until the strangers are dead. We have prayed to the gods to guard you, Moctezuma. If we succeed in defeating the strangers, we will hold you in higher regard than ever before, and you shall rule us again. We beg you to forgive us."

Thus with respectful words he had refused to obey Moctezuma's request that the war cease and we be allowed to depart. There was a beat of silence, then a high, mocking voice shouted: "Moctezuma has been turned into a woman by Cortés!" So abruptly that we could not move fast enough to shield our hostage, a shower of stones and darts were hurled at Moctezuma. They came from a little group of warriors surrounding a tall, bold-faced Aztec. He was Cuauhtemoc, the other prime contender for the throne. Three of the stones hit Moctezuma in rapid succession, one on the head. Then Cortés and Sandoval quickly pulled him down from the battlement; he seemed unable to move of his own volition. As they did this, more stones banged against Cortés' casque and breastplate with brutal, ringing thuds.

Either the stone that struck Moctezuma's head or the shock of the attack or both had paralyzed him, for his legs suddenly crumpled beneath him; I reached out to hold him upright. The flesh of the bare arm I grasped was as cold as a dead man's. He stared straight ahead, and I saw a trickle of blood run down one side of his face like a red tear. He smelled of flowers.

We brought him to his private quarters and I told his servants there that he should rest quietly in his bed for a while, and Cortés sent in a Padre de Merced to put salve on his head wound and bandage it. Moctezuma lay immobile while his wound was dressed, then tore the bandage off and turned his face to the wall.

Whenever I looked in, that was how he lay, unmoving. Little Orteguilla, with the tears sometimes running down his face, sat crouched at the foot of the pallet and never left him. He told me that Moctezuma would take no food brought him, or even drink water. He asked that his children and wives be cared for. He never spoke again. On the third day he died.

When I looked down at him my compassion bewildered me. He lay on his wide pallet, raised on a dais and richly canopied. Beside him the great green panache stood on its golden crown, discarded symbol of past glory. His face was pure and serene and untouched by human anguish. Tears dimmed my eyes, for I knew that in his own fashion he had given greater reverence to a merciful deity than to an evil one and had paid a terrible price for having mistaken a man for a god.

Then my heart seemed to become as still as Moctezuma's as I realized that I might soon join him in death, though mine would not be this unbutchered repose that looked so like a deep sleep with no dreams.

"There lies our hope of life" a voice behind me said. I turned; the Spanish bodyguards stood there. Arturo Mondragon had spoken in a voice husky with emotion. El Galán, beside him, removed his helmet. "Heathen he may have been, and dreadful his idols, but he was still a gentleman of great nobility of mind, and I wish to God he might have died a Christian."

Cortés strode in then, with several captains; he was amazed to find Moctezuma dead. They all agreed that the head wound was not enough to kill him. I said it was not the size of the wound that mattered but the source of the stone that had made it, thrown at him by one of his subjects out of hatred and contempt.

"Are you going to tell me he willed his own death?" Cortés demanded.

"He had no people any more. Does a head want to live with its body cut off?"

His own pride let him understand this. He stood staring down at Moctezuma's corpse, shaking his head in amazement that the Aztec's will had proved in its own strange way as powerful as his own. He turned away saying, "However he died, I must find a way to use this misfortune to our advantage."

Misfortune! It was disaster. Total, final, and irretrievable. He knew it. I knew it. Soon all the soldiers would know it. And then the Aztecs.

The priests arrived then to decide what rites should be administered to this infidel who was doomed to burn in Hell for all eternity. They decided to commit his spirit to God's mercy. I looked again at

Moctezuma, at those feet pointing outward in their golden sandals, never again to tread this earth. I remembered my father lying like that before his burial. Whatever happened to Moctezuma's spirit, this husk that had contained it merited some gesture of respect. I brought the feather tapestry I had just finished. I had intended it for the wall of the chapel. I covered Moctezuma's body with it instead. It was a nativity scene showing the Three Kings looking down at Mary holding in her arms the infant Jesus, made with tiny flesh-colored feathers, His halo the yellow of ripe maize.

And I told myself that God's mercy would protect this Aztec's spirit as tenderly, knowing as He did how close Moctezuma had come to accepting Him on the night of the auto-da-fé.

After consultation with his captains, Cortés decided on a bold stroke: to lay the blame for Moctezuma's death on his own people. He had me instruct the two Aztec priests he had taken prisoner to go to Cuitlahuac and inform him that Moctezuma had died of the head wound sustained when he was stoned three days before.

The two black-robed Aztec priests, devastated to learn of his death, were brought out of their cell and I solemnly spoke to them Cortés' words: "I will return to his own subjects the body of Moctezuma. He is to be buried like the great king he was. And tell Cuitlahuac, raised to kingly power that was not his by right, to remember and obey Moctezuma's last words to his people: that a peace should be made so we can leave Tenochtitlán." But then Cortés' bravado took command of him. "And say that if this is not done, we will destroy this city which so far we have spared out of respect for the king who is dead." This threat was of course impossible to carry out, but served to remind Cuitlahuac of the supernatural authority Moctezuma had credited him with.

During the time since Moctezuma's ill-fated speech on the rampart hostilities had been sporadic. The deposing of their ruler had subdued the Aztecs' spirits; they had also learned that their attempts to storm the palace were futile because of Spanish artillery. There was a total lull in the fighting when the two docile Aztec priests left to bring Cortés' message to Cuitlahuac. Following them came six captured Aztec warriors who carried Moctezuma lying on his palanquin, the cascading feathers of his green panache trailing in the dust. Cortés had the drummers beat a dead march in slow tempo, and all the Spanish soldiers and captains stood with heads bowed in respectful silence.

NIGHT OF DANCERS, NIGHT OF TEARS

Minutes later we heard cries and shrieks and groans of distress arise in the Zocalo, intensifying as word of the death of Moctezuma spread among the Aztecs there. We waited tensely for Cuitlahuac's answer to Cortés' plea for peace and a safe retreat. Within the hour one of the warriors who had left with the dead king came back to say to Cortés: "Now you will pay for the death of our King and Lord, and for the dishonor to our gods. The new king we have chosen is not faint-hearted like the good Moctezuma, and you cannot deceive him with false promises. So do not trouble about how and where we bury Moctezuma. Worry for your own lives, for within two days you will all be dead."

I felt my lips blanch with fear as I translated this devastating response. Cortés stared at the Aztec warrior who had delivered it; his face was stark. He pointed silently to the gate. Walking slowly to deny any fear, the messenger departed.

The sounds of lamentation turned to the whistles and jeers of warfare; a shower of arrows, lances, and stones came over the palace wall. The siege had recommenced. I knew that even if with his superior weaponry Cortés killed twenty thousand Aztecs, another twenty thousand would take their places. And the day was coming when his ammunition would run out. Food, already scant, would be gone even sooner.

I had seen Cortés in many moods and lights, but never before had I seen him as I did then, for standing white-faced in his armor he seemed helpless and immensely vulnerable. As all his army was trapped inside the palace walls, so he was trapped in steel, a walking coffin in which he could die untouched by any weapon except slow starvation. When he spoke I heard only an echo of his old assurance. "Within two days we will not be dead. Nor within twenty days. Cuitlahuac does not realize that he is fighting Castilians."

That night I learned of the decision his captains had all agreed with out of desperation or conviction. Cortés had learned from Xicotencatl's son that there was a little-used route to Tlascala that bypassed the steep sierra of Ahualco and Cholula too. And he had determined that his only strategy lay in leaving the city at night by the short Tacuba causeway in the hope that once we were out of the city itself the Aztecs' fury would be largely dissipated. He sounded grimly confident as he said, "This way I utilize their Achilles' heel: they never fight at night. Darkness becomes our ally, their foe."

Into our room came a soldier named Botello. Small, wise-eyed, and earnest, he was a practitioner of a science he called judicial astrology.

"Several of his predictions in the past have indeed come true," Cortés said. "I have told him I need a night with no moon, and he has offered to read his own horoscope in hopes of also telling me which moonless night will prove most favorable for our exodus."

Botello solemnly stated that the night of the thirtieth of June and first of July was by far the most favorable. "Even though," he smiled sadly, "there are indications that I may then perish."

"And the rest of us?" Cortés asked, smiling a little to show that his credence was not total.

"A triumphant departure," Botello assured him.

The day after the death of Moctezuma Cortés launched a foray with towers, cannons, and cavalry to battle his way to the Tacuba causeway, setting fires to houses on the way and razing some to fill in canals that crossed the avenue leading to it. He found that the Aztecs had already removed the first causeway bridge. He fought his way back to the palace again, which took so long that the rumor went among the soldiers that he had been killed. I would not believe this and denied the possibility to the frightened woman who had heard this whisper. For I knew that whether the astrologer had been right or wrong about the auspicious night, only Cortés could lead us all from certain doom here to possible safety on the other side of the wide lake.

When he returned he was grim. "Our route is now prepared," he announced to the men. "There are not many roofs left for the Aztecs to attack us from, due to the useful fires we set today." He ordered the shipwright Martín Llopez and Nuñez the carpenter to construct a large movable bridge sturdy enough to bear the cannons and horsemen that could be carried forward with us by soldiers and put down to cross the causeway gaps.

The army took well to this plan when he announced it. Even though in such a departure it was likely that some would be killed, each man held the comforting notion that it would not be he. The prospect of decisive action after having been so long pent up enlivened their spirits.

My own stayed at a low ebb. Ever since the night I had in desperation attacked Cortés for the sin of pride he had been distant and cool. To live close to a hero, I had found, is to either risk losing his affection or pretend not to see his flaws, and this I had been unable to do. He took time to advise me carefully to select those possessions of greatest value and leave the rest behind. He found no moment in which to let me understand that he still loved me.

Thus we approached the last day of June and the moonless night of stars said to be propitious. The season of rains had begun. In summer in the Valley of Anahuac they come quite regularly in the early afternoon, last an hour or two, and cease abruptly, leaving a clean and sparkling world for the descending sun to set aglow. But as the sun set and the Aztecs began to leave the square I saw from my window the sullen gray cloud bank rolling in from the northeast and already hiding the crests of the mountains. I knew that Nature was making one of her exceptions. The moonless night would be starless too, and rain would surely fall.

In Cuba we have storms called hurricanes, but none of these was ever so alarming to me as the storm that broke on the night all of us who lived through it will always call the *noche triste*. The rain began not long after dark, just a stealthy pattering of large drops, but you could smell all the moisture gathered in the low heavy clouds, dark and dull by last light as unburnished armor. My mother once said that no one enjoys the details of battles so much as the soldiers who fought in them. But even if I wanted to tell all that happened on that sad night, I could not endure the task. It pains me to remember even the small part I witnessed.

On the afternoon of June thirtieth, to confuse the Aztecs, Cortés sent out to Cuitlahuac one of their captured warriors with the message that we were readying ourselves to leave in a week and would leave behind all the gold and treasure Moctezuma had given us if he would allow us free passage from the city. But this was done to put them off guard, for we had readied ourselves to leave that very night, after dark. At sundown the Aztecs regularly evacuated the Zocalo to camp elsewhere, having learned that darkness did not deter us and that they were not safe there from our cannons and muskets and crossbows. A stealthy exodus seemed possible.

Our plan was that four hundred Tlascalans and a hundred fifty Spaniards would protect the *tamanes* carrying the bridge we had made and defend it after it was placed in that first gap of the Tacuba causeway, guarding it until the rest of the army and all of our baggage had crossed. Two hundred Tlascalans and fifty Spaniards were in charge of protecting the cannons. Four captains and a hundred fifty Spaniards were chosen to go forward first in case our way was opposed by any Aztecs from the mainland. After them would ride Cortés and a dozen mounted captains to fight to the forward or rear, whichever group might be in most need of help. Pedro de Alvarado and another captain led the rear guard, to protect our *tamanes* with our baggage. Between this rear guard and Cortés' group were to march the soldiers of Narváez, several hundred Tlascalans, and thirty Spanish soldiers charged with the protection of Malinche, the other Indian women, and our prisoner Cacama. I was one of these thirty soldiers, and Cortés said to me: "Guard Doña Marina well."

"I will," I answered fervently, and felt my face go hot as I remembered how I had guarded her before.

Before we left, Cortés had a great amount of gold and silver and precious objects brought and piled high in the greatest hall of the palace. The King's Fifth he placed in charge of two men named as king's officers, who were given half a dozen horses no good for fighting. He then had his secretary and the royal notary bear witness to the fact that he could do nothing about the removal of the rest of the gold. "Since it cannot be placed in safety, I now give it to any soldiers who care to take it. Otherwise, it will be left for these dogs of Aztecs."

I could guess his double intention: to reward us in a way that would raise our spirits vastly and also to satisfy his animosity toward Velásquez by letting his share of gold augment this gift to us.

The soldiers of Narváez were wild with joy, having given up any hope of the rewards Cortés had enticed them with, and swarmed to the great heap of ingots. I went, too, and picked one up. It was very heavy. El Galán cried, "No, no, Arturo! Look!" And he held out to me the wooden box he had, containing six of the green *chalchihuites* that the Indians prized far above gold. "Look for these," he whispered, "or any other gems Cortés and the captains may have missed." I saw his wisdom and at once found two more *chalchihuites*. Juan Morla had apparently found another trove of them, for I saw him secrete something green in the top of his helmet, which he then strapped firmly under his chin. But I could not entirely resist the heavy gold when I found three wide bracelets; I fastened them on my left arm. My gold necklace from Cortés was already around my neck. I went pawing feverishly through the rapidly diminishing mound of wealth hoping to find more *chalchihuites,* but came upon something even better lying beside a gold ingot. It was an emerald bigger than my thumbnail. Thrilling with joy at this find, I tucked it into my pocket along with the two pieces of carved jade. As I did, a body shoved me aside and a hand reached down for the ingot. I heard a grunt and turned and saw one of the Narváez recruits add it to the stack of ingots he clasped against his chest; he was bent slightly forward by their weight. "Don't be a fool," I said. "We've got miles to march tonight. You won't even make it as far as the causeway if you load yourself up like a burro." But he only gave me an idiot's grin and asked me if I were jealous of his luck. A big, burly fellow, he evidently counted on his bull strength to get him through. Later I saw that he had put the gold in two cloth sacks attached by a rope slung around the back of his neck and hanging down like panniers at either side. This left both hands free, but with the weight of his armor and the gold he moved no faster than a giant snail, burdened by a fortune that only speed and a good sword arm would permit him ever to enjoy.

When we set out after dark for the Tacuba causeway it seemed to me that the weather was conspiring with us. The sky had clouded over entirely and the moonless, starless night was black, hiding the glint of our steel. Our horses' hooves were padded. No one spoke above a whisper. Malinche was wrapped in her black hooded cloak, and little Orteguilla sat on the rump of her gray mare; thinking he might be called upon to guard her life, he showed me a dirk that he wore in his belt like a sword. I marched directly ahead of them, my more adequate blade ready to serve in the same cause.

When we were halfway across the great deserted square a heavier rain began to fall. We moved in careful silence along the deserted street whose houses Cortés had earlier burned. The Tlascalans with the bridge reached the causeway first, as planned, and put our bridge in place, and the first detachment crossed over safely. Cortés and a dozen captains followed. Suddenly, far behind us, an Aztec conch horn sounded. I had just crossed the bridge, Malinche and the dwarf behind me, when I heard many shrill cries like squadrons of Aztec warriors bearing down on us from the rear. Looking back, I saw that Malinche's gray mare was safely over the bridge. My pace quickened to a run and my heart began to pound. How glad I was not to be burdened by much gold! This race for life would go to the lightest laden. But a rift in the clouds let the moon gleam through for a moment to show me a terrible sight. The lake was alive with the dark shapes of dugout canoes closing in on the causeway from both sides. Then I heard piercing Aztec battle cries on the causeway ahead. We were surrounded.

All we could do was to thrust ourselves ahead toward where the soldiers of the van, led by Cortés and his captains, were battling their way through the oncoming Aztecs. Soon I was slashing out with my sword at the long lances prodding up at us from the canoes.

The moon had been swiftly swallowed by thick clouds. The rain began to fall more heavily, then lightning flared and a clap of thunder sounded in the sky directly above my head. Through these sounds came the mocking cries of the Aztecs and screams of pain from the wounded behind us. As I reached an open gap in the causeway where the Aztecs had removed the bridge, I realized it would be foolish to wait for our movable one, which Tlascalans and Spaniards to the rear were defending against the enemy and over which our forces were still passing. With some horror I looked down and saw that a sort of bridge existed in the gap ahead: the body of a horse, still floundering feebly, a number of bundles and boxes, and two dead men, gold-laden. I turned to tell Malinche she would have to abandon her mare, which could not make this crossing. A shock of horror hit me like a blow. Only the dwarf now rode on the animal's back, flattened forward to escape the arrows now being loosed at us from the canoes. "Where is she?" I howled at him over the increasing din.

"Here," she said, and came forward from the other side of the mare.

"No bridge!" I pointed ahead.

"I saw. What about Orteguilla?" She had to scream the query over the sounds from the enemy and our own soldiers: groans, prayers, curses.

"We'll pull him along between us, but hurry!" In a wave of energy, those behind us were surging forward, away from the pursuing Aztecs. I rushed back and lifted the dwarf off the mare. With Malinche holding one of his hands and I the other, we ran to the edge of the gap, where I let myself down onto the body of the dead or dying horse—which sank beneath my weight but then held firm, so that the water came only to my knees. I lifted down the dwarf and she followed and the three of us blundered forward across the horse, the bundles and boxes, and one of the dead men. The other had sunk, perhaps from the weight of his armor and his gold. At the other side I lifted Malinche and the dwarf up ahead of me and, just as I followed, a prodding lance from a canoe that had closed in on our right grazed my bottom. Once up, I slashed out at it with my sword and it fell in halves that lay on the belly of the dead horse.

As we three hurried forward, pushed from the rear by the others who had crossed the gap after us and stepping on the heels of the ones ahead, the rain came down heavier and thunder rolled our death knell; at last we reached the third gap in the causeway. In this one there were the bodies of many men, Tlascalans and Spaniards, and to step on them like rocks in a river was terrible to do but my fear was so great that I did, pulling the dwarf and Malinche after me. But the bodies of the men did not give the support the horse had; one tilted under me and I plunged into the water, regretting every ounce of gold and every gem on my person. I found that the fundament of the causeway made the water in the gap less than four feet deep, so my head and shoulders were not submerged. I remembered to pull the dwarf up by one limp hand, and he bobbed to the surface gasping, his cap gone, his hair plastered to his head and his face like a frightened child's. But Malinche had vanished. I heaved the dwarf up onto the causeway and then waded back, calling her name. I submerged to feel about for her underwater, but all I felt was the breastplate of a sunken Spanish soldier. As I emerged for air, a heavy weight suddenly struck my upper back and pressed me forward and under the water again. It was the prow of a dugout canoe that had darted into the gap. I got my feet under me, standing on the drowned soldier, and, gathering all my strength into the pit of my abdomen, I straightened my body suddenly, tipped the canoe off my back and heard cries and splashing as it overturned, which gave me just enough time to wade to the shoreward side of the causeway and haul myself up, gasping and coughing up water. The dwarf was not there, vanished into the jumbled horde ahead. But I stayed where I was, calling her name, jostled by the men who waded the gap as I had, their faces set and eyes blank. But there was no sign of her. Still I tipped my head back and screamed her name out into the rain, again and again. Then a mass of frantic soldiers scrambled up from the water where I had last seen her and pressed me onward with their bodies and their terror, and I stumbled forward streaming rain and tears. I damned the dwarf, for if I had held onto Malinche's hand instead of his, she would have been the one saved.

A fork of lightning glared in the sky and I saw some Aztecs in a dugout canoe carrying off a Spanish soldier with them. As thunder crashed I realized that this is what might have happened to Malinche, and I damned God.

After that I do not remember anything very well, just pressing forward and hacking with my sword at the long Indian lances prodding up over the causeway's wall from the canoes massed below, blindly probing for flesh. My teeth chattered from fear and the cold rain. The next bridge we came to had not been removed, I suppose to give Aztecs on the mainland the chance to get at us. Many of their bodies clogged the causeway, twined curiously with those of fallen Spaniards.

Somehow I finally made it to shore. Just beyond the end of the causeway Cortés and some captains and soldiers were massed together under the dubious shelter offered by large trees. As I plodded toward them through the mud, Captain Olid cried out to Cortés that they must not abandon the foot soldiers still struggling to cross the causeway.

"It's a miracle that any of us escaped," Cortés said in a hollow voice.

My tongue was unable to tell him that Malinche had not. Agony seared through me. I reached the shelter of the trees and sank down onto the muddy ground, gasping. I did not care much at that moment that I was alive.

"Well, come on then, on to the damned causeway," I heard Cortés say, and he and some horsemen galloped down the slope to that accursed place to aid any survivors. I found I was thirsty and tipped my head back and opened my mouth and walked out from under the trees and let the rain fall into my gullet as if it might ease my grief as well as my thirst.

In a very short time Cortés and the captains returned with what was left of the rear guard: Alvarado and four Spaniards and nine Tlascalans. Alvarado was on foot, his sorrel mare having been killed under him by lance thrusts stabbing up into its belly from the canoes. He carried with him a long spear he had wrested from one of the Aztecs and had used to vault over the last gap in the causeway. "He flew right over my head," said one of the soldiers with him, "as if he had wings, and landed on the other side." Blood flowed down his face and Alvarado's was bloodied, too.

"Now," Alvarado said, "the gaps in the causeway are choked with bodies. And gold. And the body of Juan Velásquez de Leon, and many other men from my own company."

"And Malinche," I said, walking toward where he stood looking up at Cortés, still mounted.

"Malinche?" Alvarado said. "Doña Marina? Doña Marina is dead?"

"Drowned, or captured by the Aztecs." As I choked out the words, tears sprang to my eyes. Cortés was staring down at me. Rain streamed down his face. "Let us hope she drowned," he said in a drear, heavy voice. I knew he meant that this fate was to be preferred to her capture, for what would lie in store for the woman who had been his tongue was beyond imagination. Stoically I waited for his wrath to strike me, charged as I had been with her protection. His left hand, wrapped in a bloodsoaked rag, drew up as though to slash back-handed across my upturned face, but then fell. Knowing as he did the horror of our escape, it was beyond him to fix blame. There writhed through my head, straight from Satan's hell, hideous images of Malinche strapped to a sacrificial altar and waiting the descent of a stone knife, her body perhaps then flayed in honor of the idol called Xipe, and her lithe young being all dismembered, legs here, arms there, later to be eaten by the priests and their favorites. "God forgive me!" I cried aloud. "God help me!" Without any forethought I turned and ran back toward the causeway, as if by traversing its length to where I had last seen her I might find her alive.

As I reached it I saw something crawling toward me. I ran toward it and knelt down. Juan Morla, his face nearly severed in half by a gash that had taken out one eye, had somehow made it to shore. He inched closer and with a sigh rolled onto one side and rested his bleeding head on my thigh.

"Helmet," he croaked. "Take off." A flash of lightning showed me his one eye looking up just as it froze in the sudden vacant stare of death I had come to know so well. His mouth dropped open, there was a rattling in his throat, and blood came out. "Poor Juan," I said aloud in a voice like a little boy's. Mechanically I obeyed his last request and undid the strap of his helmet and pulled it free from under his dropped bloody chin and the thick black beard that seemed to cling to it. As I removed the helmet I heard something clink inside it and remembered when he had put it there. I reached in and felt something large, cold, and very hard. Another glare of lightning showed me what I held in my palm. It was too clear for jade. It was an emerald, nearly as broad as my hand, carved into the shape of a squatting frog. As thunder crashed I closed my hand around it, numb with awe. I knew I held a king's ransom. Malinche was dead, and God knew how many Spaniards and Tlascalans, and probably my friend El Galán. But I held in my hand a thing of much more value than all the gold I had dreamed about in Cuba.

Kneeling there in the rain, I cried like a little child.

With a dead man's head on my lap I heard a voice from the tomb and saw El Galán limping toward me, bare-headed and streaming rain. I had just put on my helmet, Juan Morla's emerald inside it. I went to embrace my friend, filled with such joy at seeing him alive that it was hard to believe I had been weeping only moments before. He went to where Juan lay, looked down at him sadly, crossed himself, bent, and picked up Juan's helmet and put it on.

The voice of Cortés called us then to form ranks to begin the long march to Tlascala. He had dismounted and stood under one of the dark trees by the lakeshore. We straggled past him, the pitiful remnant of his army, lighted intermittently by those flares of malevolent brilliance the sky provided between rumblings of thunder. He stood stoic at first. But then, just as El Galán and I reached him, my limping friend stumbled on a stone and pitched forward, going down on his hands with one knee in the mud and letting out a groan of pain. I helped him to his feet, and then saw Cortés standing with one mailed arm covering his eyes, his body leaning against the tree trunk, and I heard his sobs.

It made me fearful to see him weep, but in a moment he mastered his emotion. He straightened and came several steps toward us. Lightning glared on his gaunt face streaming with rain and tears, white as if carved from marble, with terrible burning eyes. His voice was loud and hollow. "It appears that evil has triumphed this night, but we must still have faith in God's power." Then meat and blood and hope came back into his voice. "Satan will not have the final victory!" I heard it as a promise he was making to himself and God.

We sent up a ragged cheer; he called to one of the captains and said that El Galán was to ride a lamed horse that was no good for fighting. As I marched through mud with the tatters of our army I could feel the weight of the emerald frog atop my head and tried to comfort myself with visions of future wealth and power, although any future at all seemed very uncertain.

Our Tlascalans led us along the little-traveled route they knew, avoiding the main road where our enemies might look for us. We marched several weary miles along a muddy footpath and at last came to a hill with a huddle of empty houses at its base and atop it a sizable deserted temple. Exhausted as we were, we halted there to rest and care for our many wounded. Climbing the stone stairs, I remembered all the previous temple stairs we had mounted and all the idols we had destroyed. But here there were none. A thick layer of dust showed that for reasons unknown deities, priests, and people had left this place a long time before. In the empty buildings below, our Tlascalans found some stacks of wood and in the spacious room atop the pyramid Sandoval made a good fire in the central hollow of the sacrificial altar. Even if we had had food we could not have eaten, for we had all reached that point beyond exhaustion where the belly's wants do not matter. Kneeling, we wept for our dead and prayed for their souls. I secretly prayed that whatever happened to Malinche, she would not be sacrificed to pagan gods, she who had so sweetly and sincerely turned from them to Jesus.

It was then that the awful reality of her death struck me as it had not before. I remembered her face as I first saw it in the sunlight at Tabasco, saw again the terror in her eyes when I captured her, and the gentle look as she cleansed my shoulder wound. Once again in rags of seaweed she stood like Aphrodite risen from the sea, and then I saw her barbaric figure below the white cross on the dune. In the tent of Cortés she denied betrayal in an impassive voice. I closed my eyes to recapture that sweet passion in the treasure room we thought our tomb, but the pain of that memory was too great and I groaned aloud. To deny the truth that her warm flesh was cold or soon would be, I created a future: again she returned to Cuba with me as my bride, and I imagined a house for us on the cliff by the sea where she slept beside me in my bed and woke me mornings saying, as my mother always did, "God has sent us another sunny day, that we may do His work and ours."

I was roused from this waking dream by the wan voice of Padre Olmedo. He stood at the far end of the room with the friar Casas and Aguilar and several other churchmen looking sadly out over our huddled and recumbent bodies, and he read from the sheet of paper in his hands the names of some of the dead and captured: Juan Velásquez de Leon, Francisco Saucedo, and Sedeño, in whose caravel I had sailed, and Francisco de Morla, Juan Morla, and Gonzalo the traitor, and Yago the acrobat, and the Three Moors, and Orteguilla the page, and Cacama, our prisoner, and the other prisoners with him, and Botello the astrologer, and all the Indian women; oh, the list was long. "And, most sadly, the excellent Doña Marina, who has been of such great help to us." Aguilar, who was standing with clasped hands and downcast eyes, raised his head then to look at me with sorrow.

The pallid secretary of Cortés, shaking like an old man with the palsy, estimated the Spanish dead at nine hundred forty and the Tlascalan dead at two thousand. Of the soldiers who had come with Narváez, almost all had lost their lives on the causeway or been captured, weighted down with too much gold. Of our ninety-eight horses, only twenty-three were left us, some of them wounded. The cannons and artillery and all ammunition were gone. We had a dozen sound crossbows, though not many arrows. These were the conditions under which we had to try to make our way to Tlascala. Even if we managed to, we did not know how we would be received there. They had admired us as victors; now we were the vanquished.

As night paled to dawn additional sentinels were posted on the upper level of the pyramid to watch for Aztecs. I was one. A few clouds to the east flushed to a pale pink. As the orb of the sun rose above the mountains I was thinking how clever I had been to hide my two emeralds inside the leather padding of my breastplate. The frog was pressing hard against my chest, reassuring me that if I managed to stay alive I would go home rich.

A faint sound distracted me from this pleasant thought. It was the insistent throbbing of a distant drum. It came from the direction of Tenochtitlán. I stared at the risen sun in horror. If Malinche had not drowned or been killed, then she would surely walk up the steps of the war god's pyramid. At this very moment her heart could be cupped in the bloody upraised hands of an Aztec priest. This morning sunlight would shine down on it and her dead face just as it was shining on me. I closed my eyes and covered my ears, but still I heard that slow drum beating, beating.

PART VII

THE VANQUISHED AND VICTORIOUS
July 1, 1520–December 25, 1520

35

Of the *noche triste* escape on the causeway I saw little. At the second gap of water where the Aztecs had removed the bridge, our makeshift one was still behind us. I had to abandon the gray mare on which Orteguilla was riding with me, and Arturo took one of the dwarf's hands and I the other. He leaped down onto the wreckage clogging the shallow water, taking Orteguilla with him. I stared down at two dead Spanish soldiers and a dead horse, my steppingstones to safety. But at the third gap as I jumped down I felt the black cloak I was wearing wrenched tight around my throat, choking me, and knew that someone following close behind had stepped on its hem in the instant it lay on the causeway behind me. The hard tug threw me off balance. In the same second I unclasped the cloak, missed my footing, and plunged into the black water. I had glimpsed an Aztec canoe nosing into the gap from the other side, a warrior in it with spear raised. So I swam under water, away from the causeway, for as long as I could. When I surfaced, I saw by the glare of lightning a *chinampa* floating nearby.

Clinging to its edge with my head only far enough out of the water to breathe, I was grateful for its chance presence, but then realized that it might just as well drift back to Tenochtitlán as to the Tacuba shore I hoped to reach. For a long while I was deaf to the Aztec war cries and the screams of wounded Spaniards, desperately scanning both shores to see which seemed to be getting closer. The rain worsened, big drops pockmarking the black water around me and finally agitating it to a frenzy like the one inside me as the *chinampa* drifted away from the causeway but no nearer either side of the lake.

Because of the cold the strength finally left my hands, so I held onto the coarse basketry *chinampa* rim with my teeth, tasting wet earth, smelling green plants growing just above my head. I reached

311

up one numb hand, found a stem and plucked it, a green onion, very cold and strong. I ate it all; it was life I ate, the promise of survival. When I looked again toward the Tacuba shore, it seemed closer.

I lost all sense of time, clinging with numb hands or my teeth. Finally one of my feet brushed lake bottom. Ahead was a thicket of reeds out of which a duck paddled toward me, then veered away. The *chinampa* glided in among the reeds. I was safe.

Pushing my way through the reeds in water up to my hips, I stood at last on firm wet earth, hidden by canes nearly as tall as I. The causeway was a long distance to my right. I did not know how many Aztecs might be rounding up strays between. Their war cries were few and faint. The rain had stopped. In the rifts between moving clouds a few stars gleamed.

Avoiding the lakeshore road above me I made my slow way through the reeds toward Tacuba. After an hour or so I heard, in the thicket ahead, voices speaking Nahuatl with the accent peculiar to Tlascalans. As I neared I distinguished, to my joy, the voice of Doña Luisa praying aloud that God would continue to save them from the Aztecs. When she saw me she screamed; a Tlascalan warrior put his hand over her mouth. She and a few other of the women had been brought safely over the causeway, and the Tlascalans had decided to hide themselves rather than search for those Spaniards who had managed to get across alive. A scout had just returned from the Tacuba end of the causeway to report that there was no sign of any living Spaniard. Certainly the captains had been able to get across before all the bridges were removed by the Aztecs, and some foot soldiers too, but where were they now?

My mind was not working well, but I reminded them that Cortés intended to march back to Tlascala, and not through Cholula; they decided on the route he would have taken. And so we set forth, a straggling band of refugees, fearful of being fallen upon at any moment by Aztecs still lurking along the shore. Just before sunrise we saw ahead a small hillside town. The first rays of the sun glinted on the armor of the Spanish sentinels patrolling the upper level of its temple. Was Cortés alive? Arturo? Orteguilla? Aguilar? It suddenly seemed to me that if I found them to be dead or prisoners of the Aztecs, the life God had chosen to spare would have little worth to me. My past anger at Cortés, my criticism of him, now seemed childish: this night had proved that he had dealt with a people so bloodthirsty that even as the Spaniards had obeyed the request of the Aztec priests to leave the city, the warriors had been unable to resist the urge to kill and to get prisoners for their war god.

The Tlascalans had one of their white crane banners and held it aloft so the Spaniards might not take us for Aztecs and shoot down on us. As we reached the town wall I heard the faint booming of a distant drum telling me the grim destiny of prisoners the Aztecs had taken. Then one of the sentries shouted "Let them enter! They're Tlascalans!"

As we crossed the plaza to the foot of the pyramid I looked down at my mud-caked skirt, my tunic smelling of lakewater and sweat. "Malinche!" a glad voice called. Arturo Mondragon was leaping down the steep stone steps, his face alight. "You're alive!" he whispered in a choked voice.

"And Cortés?" I asked.

"Alive."

My heart beat again. "And Orteguilla? Did you manage to save him?"

"No better than I saved you," he said bitterly.

"God did that." I told him about the *chinampa* as we went up the steps of the temple. At the top the sun's rays lighted his face; the drum, which had briefly stopped, began its throbbing again. "Poor little Orteguilla," I said. In spite of his clever mind his tiny body had doomed him to die.

Arturo saw my grief. "If he was taken prisoner, maybe Cuitlahuac will pardon him since he was Moctezuma's friend."

False hope. The dwarf had had little chance to survive that frenzied rout on the causeway amid men blind with terror. And a Spaniard was a Spaniard to Cuitlahuac.

Behind me a crow squawked "Madonna!" I whirled. Cortés had emerged from the doorway of the temple. "My Doña Marina!" he cried again in a voice choked with emotion. His face spoke of a miracle and he came toward me, arms outspread. I ran to him. They closed around me. That embrace of cold steel was more thrilling than if his naked body had pressed close to mine. "Thank Jesus and the saints for giving you back to me!" He held me away and his eyes drank in my face as if it were not taut with exhaustion. His hand came up to touch my cheek. He arrested the motion in midair and swiftly lowered it, but I saw the gory bandage and its shape. He had lost two fingers, the smallest and the one next. It was his left hand, his sword hand.

313

I gasped. Smiling down he said, "A small matter. I can learn to use the other."

By then captains and soldiers had poured out to surround us. With his arm around me Cortés told them, "Doña Marina has been returned to us, and that augurs well for the immediate future. Now I will be able to parlay intelligently with the Tlascalans."

I suffered a flicker of doubt that his joy at seeing me alive had been untainted by practical considerations, then scorned myself for the thought. Of course he needed to use anything he could to encourage the men left alive! Proof of his affection soon followed: he delayed the march, risking discovery by Aztec scouts, so that I and the rest who had had no sleep at all the night before could recover somewhat from our exhaustion before setting out. A bundle of mantles and robes had somehow been brought across the causeway by a dogged *tamane,* and Cortés had a bucket of water brought from the town's cistern so I could wash the mud from my body. When I was clean and dressed in dry clothes I felt less weary. The other women and I curled up on mantles in a corner of the inner temple to rest an hour, and Cortés himself came to wake me, bending to whisper in my ear "In Tlascala we will take our joy together, and what an end to the journey ahead!" I opened my eyes and looked up into his and knew that the last shred of alienation from him was gone forever, a feather in the wind.

Before we left the temple a small band of Aztecs besieged it, but the dozen crossbowmen made every arrow tell; those Aztecs who were not killed ran off in fear.

The march to Tlascala took one frightful week. Cortés gave me one of the horses to ride, though telling me that in case any battle threatened I would have to give it to one of the captains. It was a stallion, strong-mouthed and large, and I regretted the loss of my mare and ached to think of the poor thing abandoned by me on the causeway. I told myself that the Aztecs would not kill her but would keep her alive as a curiosity and imagined a pleasant future for her as a new member of the garden zoo.

That first day we marched until sundown, then camped and slept with no incident to wake us. The next day we were harassed by warriors from a town we had to pass, but this happened on open land where the cavalry could move freely, and at sight of the horses our attackers gave up and ran away. A dozen soldiers were sent out to scavenge for food and found a field of ripe melons and one of maize, so that night everyone had food, if not much. The next day Cortés easily captured a small Indian town, its inhabitants fleeing as we approached, and we rested there a full day and ate well. But the next day our Tlascalan guides kept losing the trail we followed, so we made slow progress, camping that night in the hills at the edge of a wide plain. In the morning we saw some Indians atop a nearby hill; seeing us they quickly vanished. Cortés and several horsemen reconnoitered to see what lay beyond. A large city stood in the plain ahead; Indians were swarming out of it toward us. A Tlascalan said the name of the city was Otumba, long loyal to the Aztecs.

"Oh Tomb?" said Cortés. "But not ours!"

As I watched from a hilltop the encounter that followed, I felt that he was wrong. The approaching warriors had slingshots, which they used very well, wounding Cortés on the face. How could so few Spanish and Tlascalan soldiers, so many of them already injured, hope to battle a whole city full of fresh enemies? Yet I knew we could not go back. Our route to Tlascala lay across that open plain.

Fortunately, the sight of the horses alarmed the first group of warriors enough so that they withdrew, but they first killed one of the horses. Cortés had some soldiers drag it back to our camp, where it was butchered, cooked, and eaten that night. The meat and broth seemed to give the soldiers new strength to face what we saw the next morning. The enemy had decided on a pitched battle there on the plain. Thousands of them were massed around their various caciques, each marked by an elaborate headdress and by a standard carried high behind him.

They had never seen a Spanish cavalry charge.

Cortés had no cannons or muskets, but he had twenty unwounded horses and ordered them prepared for battle. His plan was simple: charge and return, charge and return. Prime targets: the caciques.

I know that the soldiers must have felt that they had come to their last day on earth on seeing that enormous array of warriors, like bees defending their hive, and heard their derisive whistles and cries. But their very numbers told against them. They hemmed themselves in by their sprawling mass so that they could neither maneuver nor readily flee. The Spanish cavalry seemed to believe it was immortal. As the caciques fell, one after the other, under remorseless charges, I saw the ranks that had followed them begin to waver and break. The Spanish foot soldiers at first fought as only the doomed can, defensively, but when they saw Cortés' strategy begin to turn the tide, they seemed to become strong and filled with fresh spirit. They knew that every blow they struck was just and fulfilled God's desire that their dead and cruelly sacrificed Christian comrades should now be avenged. Does not the Bible tell us that God can be a God of wrath?

The Tlascalans also fought like avenging angels, but the son of Xicotencatl the Elder fell that morning; he obeyed Cortés' order and wore no plumes that would distinguish him to the enemy, but he fell anyway. Doña Luisa wept for her brother. As I comforted her she told me that her father would be very sad. "He loved my brother who is dead much better than the son who bears his name." My mood, raised by the extraordinary spectacle of the Spanish triumph over the Otumbans, plummeted. How would Xicotencatl, over ninety and too old to beget more sons, feel toward Cortés on learning of the death of this one? Our only hope was his continued friendship.

But this mood passed in my admiration for Cortés. Even though I learned that the Otumba warriors had been joined that day by others from the nearby town of Tepeyac, Cortés defeated them that July seventh, although he left on the battlefield the blood and bodies of many Spaniards, so that his army was reduced to four hundred once again. After the enemy retreated across the plain the soldiers and all of us knelt and gave thanks to God. But it was clear to me, having observed the whole battle as I did, spread out like a great chessboard, that much though our Saviour had surely aided Cortés, it was the horses that had made so few able to conquer so many. Those brave, magnificent beasts merited all the awe I ever felt for them. To the defeated Otumbans they must have seemed creatures out of the apocalypse long foretold.

The next day, hungry and limping, we reached Tlascala.

My relief was great when three minor Tlascalan caciques came out to meet us and offer food and shelter in a nearby town. The people there received us well enough, but then demanded payment of the soldiers for food and shelter. Cortés was disturbed to learn that El Galán paid one of his *chalchihuites* to their hosts, Arturo giving him a gold bracelet to pay for his share. But they were so glad to have a comfortable place to sleep and bathe and food to eat that they did not complain, and said that the women of the house were washing their clothing and had given them *nequen* robes to wear. Arturo Mondragon, for some reason, had on his breastplate over his, which Cortés said, smiling, made him look like a Roman soldier. But even as he joked I knew he was wondering about the feelings of Xicotencatl the Elder.

How would he treat us when he learned that his beloved son was among the devastating list of other dead compatriots? We already knew that the avarice of these townspeople showed that they saw Cortés as no returning hero, which meant that news of the *noche triste* had already filtered over the Tlascalan wall.

When several soldiers ran up to say that Xicotencatl the Elder was approaching the town with his retinue, I took a deep breath and readied myself for the interview that would decide our fate. Cortés looked grim as he and I followed the soldiers to the edge of town to meet the man most revered in all Tlascala.

As he approached us, gray head high, sunlight on his closed sunken eyelids, I marveled at his dignity. Although two nobles walked at either side, they did not support him. He walked alone, a long staff reaching out occasionally to touch the ground lightly. On his spare but still muscular body the simple straw-colored *nequen* toga looked as regal as any of Moctezuma's rich garments had.

His attendants told him that Cortés and I stood before him. Behind us were massed the Spanish soldiers and captains who had followed; I knew they were holding their breaths. The blind ruler spoke.

"How grieved I am at your misfortune, Cortés, and for the death of your men, and for our many Tlascalan soldiers killed with yours! But we do not hold it a small thing that you have escaped with your lives from that impregnable Aztec city. We always knew you were brave, but now we think you even more valiant. And though many women in Tlascala will weep for the deaths of their sons, husbands, brothers, and kinsmen, that is not for you to trouble about. Now you must rest, for you are home. Soon you will come to my city, where we will find you comfortable quarters and where you are welcome as long as you want to stay."

Cortés embraced and thanked him, deeply moved. But then he had to be told about the death of his son. "Tell him he died fighting bravely," Cortés reminded me.

When I did, the old ruler nodded. "I know that."

As the captains and soldiers cheered him, I began to wonder where the younger Xicotencatl was. Once he had sworn to Cortés his lifelong friendship, yet now did not bother to greet him.

The next day we went to the capital where the warm welcome of the citizens showed beyond any doubt that these Tlascalans were truly Cortés' allies and friends. We were housed in the same buildings as before, where sleeping mats were already provided for every soldier.

The only sadness that marked our return was the death of the four most severely wounded soldiers, who did not recover from Otumba. "Oh, Tomb for them," Cortés said sadly, "and God rest their souls." But soon he was less sad. Our bone-deep exhaustion had passed and that night we found again the joy we had not known for so long. I knew that God meant us to be together always, for why else would such ecstasy lift us beyond mere earth, mere flesh?

The night after our arrival was a beautiful one, a full moon and a splendor of stars. Cortés and I went walking together, celebrating the unaccustomed peace that surrounded us here. We happened to pass a group of soldiers sprawled under a tree in a small garden or park. Unseen, Cortés paused to listen to them. It was a pepper tree, and its long fronds were like a screen. I heard Arturo's voice say "Cortés will let us rest here a while, and then we'll march to Vera Cruz. I have hopes of returning soon to Cuba."

El Galán said, "You're hoping for the impossible. Cortés is not going to leave for Cuba until he hears from Carlos. Not a word of thanks for that treasure ship! In my opinion we can blame Fonseca. He rules the Council of the Indies, and he's a friend of Velásquez. I admit it angers me that all we have done and suffered does not seem to have moved our monarch to regard us favorably, but then who can hope to understand kings?"

Arturo said, "Well, at any rate, we will not soon be forgotten in Tenochtitlán. Their remote descendants will hear legends about the time we came and nearly conquered them."

"To me that is worth exactly the dung of a sick duck," another soldier said in disgust.

"Less to me," Cortés whispered. He was staring at nothing. His bitter tone made me momentarily uneasy. I think that was when he began to conceive his incredible plan.

"You should be glad you're alive, Rafael," Arturo said.

"You didn't lose half an ear," Rafael answered.

Another voice I did not recognize spoke of a more crucial loss, and hearing the blunt language Cortés hurried me away. I smiled to myself. After what I had seen and lived through, how could he believe me so delicate as to be offended by a word referring to male anatomy? But I knew then that he wished to believe I was; Spaniards like to endow their women with a Madonna's purity while requiring them to bear children and otherwise accommodate male desires.

"But failure is not a permanent state," Cortés said, more to himself than to me.

36

During the next three weeks I learned that nothing in this life is to be surely counted on, people least of all. The younger Xicotencatl, who had sworn eternal friendship and had helped raise up an army of thousands to march with us, was now going about saying that the Tlascalans should kill us and make friends with Cuitlahuac, the victor. Hearing of this, his old father rebuked him and said it was infamous to scheme against us when we had come back so sorely defeated, but even worse to set at naught the nation's century of independence from the Aztecs. But his son defied him, insisting that the shrewd move was to make friends with them. Then, old and blind though he was, the elder Xicotencatl went to his son and tore his mantle from his shoulder, a great disgrace. The other nobles and caciques present seized Xicotencatl the Younger and threw him down the steps of the palace and would have killed him except that his father forbade this.

Thus it was that Tlascala remained loyal to us, which was fortunate in view of what Cortés now had in mind.

With sleep and good food, the soldiers' wounds healed well in that clear mountain air. After the men had enjoyed three weeks of comfort and abundance, Cortés had his crier call them all together in the main square of the city, and from the steps of a temple he told his plan: to march against the Aztec garrison of Tepeyac to the southeast of us. "For their ruler Moctezuma swore an oath of allegiance to King Carlos of Spain, but they sent soldiers against us at Otumba, and therefore they are traitors and shall be punished."

I could not believe my ears. He had three hundred ninety-six defeated Spaniards—fewer, counting the maimed. Take a town?

"I have already sent back to Vera Cruz for powder, crossbows, a cannon there, and some muskets, as well as the crews of the Narváez ships there," Cortés said robustly. "And Xicotencatl the Elder promises me a strong fighting force." Cries of dissension arose; he waited them out. "But such is the spirit and heroism of my Old Guard, you who have been with me from the start, that I do not have any doubt of the outcome of this little foray. The enemy will meet us in numbers on open ground as at Otumba, and our cavalry will carve up their chiefs, and our staunch foot soldiers will let light into their bellies, and we will have a triumph on our hands.'' It was Alvarado, face rosy from the summer sun, who sent up a cheer, only faintly echoed.

"And we need this victory," Cortés said urgently. "We need it for the sake of our consciences, our very souls. I cannot feel that Otumba alone has sufficiently avenged our dear comrades whom the Aztecs killed and sacrificed and cannibalized."

I saw that as always he had hit on the right note to move his men as he wished. Any soldier who had lived through what they had could not help but be gnawed by a degree of guilt concerning the dead.

I watched them set out for Tepeyac and was heartened by the turnout of four thousand fresh Tlascalan warriors marching twenty abreast in white and red, drums beating, conch shells blowing, white crane banners bright in the sun. Crossbows and a good supply of arrows had arrived from Vera Cruz, though no cannon. The Narváez mariners Cortés had promised his men were only six in number.

The dismal feeling that Cortés might not come back to me kept recurring as I waited the outcome of the Tepeyac assault. It had seemed particularly sinister that Cortés had opted not to take me with him, saying that Sandoval would serve well enough as interpreter. This told me that he knew the danger was very great. Doña Luisa's effort to comfort me only revealed her secret certainty that Cortés' ambition had led him astray; she assured me that I was like a sister to her, and that even if the worst happened I would have a home in Tlascala to the end of my days. But this was not to be my destiny.

As Cortés had foreseen, the defenders of Tepeyac repeated the mistake of the warriors at Otumba and came out in great numbers to fight on open ground. Even with only seventeen horses, the cavalry cut their leaders down, and the foot soldiers attacked the demoralized rank and file. Only four Spaniards were seriously wounded and only three Tlascalans were killed. Cortés took the town and named it Villa de Segura de la Frontera. By way of example to other towns loyal to Cuitlahuac, Cortés had all the conquered inhabitants branded on the arm with a G for *guerra,* meaning that they were war prisoners and the property of King Carlos of Spain. They were then sold as slaves to the soldiers, the money thus raised intended to be offered to the Spanish monarch as proof of yet another victory.

The auction had the effect of informing Cortés that almost all the soldiers had managed to get some gold out of Tenochtitlán, though not in the greedy and foolish amounts attempted by too many of the Narváez men. And so he had a proclamation read to the effect that all gold must be turned over to him and that three-fifths of it would be returned to each owner after the King's Fifth and his own had been subtracted. I knew that he was deeply upset that a great portion of the share due the king had been lost on the *noche triste,* but still I was incredulous at his daring this. I decided he must be playing a game with himself to see how far he could take advantage of his men and still command their devotion.

Naturally this request aroused the anger of the soldiers. They protested that since Cortés had told them to take the gold on the *noche triste,* any they had was a free gift. Since the captains all had taken gold too, they took the soldiers' side. The proclamation was ignored, and Cortés dropped the matter. He was philosophical, even somewhat amused. "I'm glad to see they've got their spirit back. It proves that Tepeyac had just the effect on them I wanted."

It was as though that triumph had turned the tide of Cortés' luck. He soon learned that two ships had put into Vera Cruz loaded with arms, gunpowder, and other stores intended for the Narváez expedition, its fate being still unknown in Cuba as a result of Cortés' prompt dismantling of all its fleet. The captain in charge at Vera Cruz went aboard one, lured the captain ashore, then arrested him in the name of Cortés. He took the matter gracefully and was brought to Cortés along with his men. It turned out he was an old friend, Pedro Barba, the commandant of Habana. The governor had commanded his services; he seemed not unhappy at this outcome. Cortés embraced him and made him captain of the crossbowmen, a considerable honor. On learning his identity, Arturo Mondragon came to our palace to see him and to ask about his family in Havana. Don Pedro was very much surprised at the change in him and said his own mother would not know him now. The news of Arturo's family was good, I was glad to know.

But Barba brought other news that was alarming; smallpox had been brought to Vera Cruz by a big Negro who had arrived with Narváez and who had died of it. Now it was spreading rapidly, a real plague. Indians, he said, seemed particularly affected by this disease, apparently carried from person to person by some mysterious means. A good many of our friendly Totonacs had died of it in both Zempoalla and Quiahuiztlán. And it was now rampant also among the Aztecs of the coast. "A fair return," he said, "for the syphillis Spaniards got from the Indians of Hispaniola and Cuba." Cortés debated this point, saying he thought it was the other way around.

The arrival of the smallpox proved another piece of good luck for Cortés. He soon learned that it had reached Tenochtitlán, perhaps with one or more of the captured Narváez men. The reign of Cuitlahuac proved a very short one: he died of it. The new Aztec ruler was Cuauhtemoc.

This meant little to me, for I thought that the triumph at Tepeyac had assuaged Cortés' bitter humiliation of the *noche triste*. He had struck a last blow at the forces of Satan, and when he next wrote to the Spanish monarch, as I was sure he would, he could report a victory wrenched from total defeat.

For the first time since I had known Cortés, our life was without immediate stress. No danger surrounded us on all sides, unacknowledged yet omnipresent. Used as I had been to that dark ambiance, the sunlit present as honored guests of admirable people found me creating a worry to replace the past ones I evidently missed.

That worry was that Cortés would grow weary of waiting for word from King Carlos and would decide to return to the West Indies and present his case in person to the Royal Audience at Santo Domingo. This soon extended itself to the idea that he might even decide to cross the ocean to Spain itself, seek out his ungrateful sovereign, convince him of the great value of the new colony he had founded in his name. But whether he went to the one place or the other, was it likely that he would take me with him?

I was sure now that he loved me well, that my usefulness as interpreter took second place to my importance to him as a woman. On the rare occasions when I thought of that one strange night in the treasure vault, I could recall it only dimly, like a dream that has nearly faded away. My strongest feeling concerning it was gratitude that the urgent matter of his dangerous insult to Moctezuma had taken immediate precedence over some possible selfish desire to clear my conscience by confession, forcing him to share the burden of my sin. I knew that it was not likely that he had always been faithful to me, either. During the Narváez campaign he might well have eased himself with one of the Indian women the fat cacique had given him, for—as I knew—danger always aroused his desire. But these were small matters now. All we had been through together had made us very easy with one another, as a husband and wife can be, I thought.

His actual wife in Cuba was unreal to me. I knew by then that like many Spanish husbands he viewed her as a bond he could not shed but which need not too much inhibit him. But with my hidden fear that he would decide to leave New Spain, Doña Catalina assumed larger proportions in my mind. I did not believe that he would choose to bring back with him to the West Indies an Indian mistress. My nagging worry that he might soon leave me, and for a long, unendurable time, began to invade my dreams: I, like a luckless *soltera* no man had ever loved, draped in a black rebozo like Doña Luisa's, walked in the marketplace and bought food I would eat alone. Or awaiting Cortés in Tlascala I learned from a sad-faced Doña Luisa that he was never going to return.

On the day I revealed to Cortés my secret fear, he and I were alone in the garden of the palace where we lived, I with my embroidery, which he liked to see me do because that was what Spanish ladies like his mother did. He had on one of the *nequen* robes Xicotencatl had given him. We were taking our ease before our afternoon siesta, a Spanish custom in which he could now indulge. I was kneeling on the grass, which he did not like but which was more comfortable for me than the stone bench on which he sat. We had spoken idly of a number of small matters, but for all his appearance of indolence, I knew he was preoccupied; at such times his left leg, crossed over the right, would swing in small impatient jerks, while his eyes roved over objects around him, not really seeing them but rather his own inner visions. With the forefinger of his maimed left hand he began to smooth one of the lines across his forehead again and again, as if to erase both it and all memory of the past anxieties that had put it there, and which might, if remembered, overload him with caution.

All these signs made me sure he was planning to leave me, and suddenly I could not contain my anxiety any longer. I pushed the bone needle through the square of cotton cloth, completing the last stitch in the blue wing of a bird. "When you go, will you take me with you?" I raised my eyes to catch his surprise that I had guessed his thoughts.

"Of course," he said, surprised. "I will need you there."

"In the West Indies, or in Spain?" I was filled with a sweet relief, yet pleased to let him know how well I knew what he had been thinking.

"Spain? The West Indies? What are you talking about?" He straightened and made a sweeping gesture toward the west. "I'm going to Tenochtitlán."

The needle stabbed my finger; I dropped the embroidery to the ground. And then I learned his ambitious plan: to send Barba to Jamaica to buy more horses. And to send to Spain yet another letter, pleading for Carlos' belated support. And to march once more to the Valley of Anahuac. And to build there a fleet of a dozen shallow-draft sloops to use on the lakes when he attempted to conquer Tenochtitlán!

The horror I felt was like pain. I gaped up; he smiled down as if he could already taste that triumph. He had gone mad! All virtues in excess become vices and can destroy: his excess of courage would now kill him. I stood up. "Do you want another *noche triste?* Or worse?"

He stood too, his smile gone. "With those ships I can dominate the lakes and besiege the city. I can cut the aqueduct."

"What ships? Ships of air? Do you think the Aztecs will stand by and let you build a fleet on their lakeside?"

"First we will dominate one of the lakeside towns."

"Oh, a simple matter! And reeds are abundant. Reed ships? *Chinampas* with sails?"

"Xicotencatl will supply all the wood I need, and thousands of Indians to haul it to Anahuac. I have safely stored in Vera Cruz all the ironwork, sails, rigging, even nails from the fleet I sank there. Martín Llopez is an admirable shipwright. I have talked with him at length. He can train enough soldiers to turn out a dozen hulls, given the wood and the time." My resistance aroused his resentment. "Why am I justifying my plan to you? It's going to be done!"

"You cannot do it. No one could. The Aztecs are too powerful. You will have to fight your way there. You will not be able to hold one lakeside town against the might of all the rest."

"Listen to me! The Aztecs up there and the towns they have dominated, such as Texcoco, are undergoing upheavals they have not known in two centuries! The deposing and death of Moctezuma began it; the repercussions from such a momentous event don't die down in a few months or even years. Then their Cuitlahuac died of smallpox. To a superstitious people two such events are shattering. Omens! God knows what prophecies now abound. I tell you, those Aztecs are afraid they have slaughtered and driven out godlike beings: us!"

"All four hundred of you!" I cried derisively.

"Three hundred ninety-three. But I can count on Xicotencatl for thousands of Tlascalans, and they are brave men!"

"But why? Why? Even if you should succeed, do you imagine that even that would nudge awake your stupid, ungrateful king?"

He smiled at me coldly. "I did not conceive this idea to please Carlos. I am doing it to please Cortés! Defeat is defeat only if it is acknowledged as final. That is why the sun rises: to remind men that each day is new and full of promise if they will forget the night. *Noche triste* is now months in the past. And I swear to you that God's Holy Cross is going to stand atop that Aztec temple of sacrifice, and God's sun shine down on it!"

I knew that nothing human would stop him. Moving slowly and without conscious knowledge of where my steps were taking me, I found myself kneeling before the simple wooden cross on the wall of our sleeping room. The little Virgin I had often prayed before had been a casualty of the departure Cortés was now determined to redress. But I closed my eyes and imagined Her there, and prayed that Cortés might be restored to sanity. "Do not let him attempt this! Do not let his courage kill him!"

"Praying, Doña Marina?" His hard voice spoke behind me. "For me? Better pray for the Aztecs. Even better, come to bed."

His hand fell on my shoulder. I looked up at him. He raised me to my feet and enfolded me, burying his lips in my throat. To be taken so suddenly from pain of mind and prayer to the edge of ecstasy numbed my protests and soon my fear. I remember how, after he was sleeping, I lay looking at the ray of sunlight that slanted into the room from a window and saw how motes of dust danced in it. I knew I had no more volition than one of those specks. My destiny was not mine any longer, and would never be again.

When we left for Tenochtitlán on the twenty-fifth of December I was all but certain that I was going to bear his child. I did not tell him this. I feared that he would insist that I stay safely behind in Tlascala. I preferred to face with him the dangers ahead. I knew I would endure those better than long months of waiting for word of his triumph or his death.

he would remind us of terrible marches of Alexander or Hannibal or Caesar to make us less depressed by our own difficulties.

One day an excited soldier descended from his treetop observation post to tell Cortés there was a city only a few hundred paces ahead. A large one, he guessed, because the *teocalli* atop its sacred pyramid stood even taller than the treetops. The prospect of reaching civilization made us all cheerful, for by this time our supplies of food were used up and we had been subsisting for days on roots, nuts, and berries scantily supplied by our imprisoning forest. But when we reached that city, cheer vanished. We found it deserted of all but snakes and lizards. Forest vines and creepers hid whole buildings and crawled up the pyramid the soldier had seen, only its summit still free of this green shroud. We had found not a city but a tomb, deserted by all its people and left to crumble away. I wondered if it might have been the home of my remote ancestors and whether others had later followed their lead in leaving forever behind them the corruption of the noble and priestly classes. The clown at that point managed a sort of joke: "Small wonder the people left a climate like this one!" His painted smile was trickling down his face along with his sweat; in addition to our other troubles the air had become even more humid; moisture from our own bodies ran down to mingle with the marshwater that soaked our feet.

Lacking Indian guides now, Cortés had only the map Nan Chan had sent us and a compass. After a long day's march before reaching a place dry enough for a night's slumber, he decided to give the army a full day's rest and time to gather enough roots and berries to make a meal that would really fill the stomach. By now a number of the Indian warriors and *tamanes* had died from hunger and from the heat, humidity, and low altitude to which a lifetime high up in the mountains had not accustomed them. One of the pages had also perished. After a supper of hot water, Cortés tried to conceal his gloom and disappointment as he spread out the map by the campfire and studied it. Sandoval, El Galán, and the other captains crowded around him, peering down in search of some landmark that would inspire hope. "Although this chart won't tell us if a town's still standing," El Galán remarked.

Cortés lifted the compass from the chart and nodded. "I can't forget those damned burned villages," he said. "I have to fight the suspicion that even if we come to a place of human habitation it will be only chars and cinders. By God, there has to be a malign unifying force behind this kind of warfare!'' He turned to me, for I had joined the group, unable to sleep for hunger. "Tell me, Doña Marina, could it be Nan Chan? Could he have deceived me with pretenses of friendship? Could this chart be false and designed to lead us into this wilderness of trees and muck where at last we'll leave our bones?''

I did not have to ponder. "What would that gain him? He is in a good position as your friend and first ally on this continent. That is what keeps him in power in Xicalanco, his friendship with Cortés.''

Cortés stared down at the point of the compass, turning it in his fingers. "What about Cuauhtemoc?''

"Cuauhtemoc?'' His old suspicion had reclaimed him; the compass had become the spear of an Aztec assassin in a nightmare he once had.

He frowned. "Could Cuauhtemoc have managed to communicate with a chieftain of these parts, perhaps by night when we thought him sleeping? Could he have suggested to them this sabotage of my venture?''

"Not without an interpreter,'' I reminded him. "He does not speak or understand any dialect of the Mayan language.''

Cortés gave an abrupt laugh. "I forgot that.''

Sandoval offered his theory. "Maybe the natives here all went crazy in unison, having heard that we defeated the Aztecs and were marching toward their own villages.''

El Galán rubbed his old leg wound and shook his head. "No. I think Cortés is right. A clever leader could have risen among these Indians of Yucatán. He realizes that we were counting on living off the towns and villages of this miserable land.''

The compass in Cortés' hand stabbed down into the center of the chart. "But who? Who is this enemy? Who?''

"That is something we may never learn,'' El Galán said. "So for my part I think we had better study the chart and figure how much farther we have to travel before we come, by God's sweet mercy, to another town.''

"Four months of this!'' Cortés announced without any need, for we all knew that. "I planned in this length of time to reach Honduras, hang Olid, and return to the city of Mexico!''

With gallows cheer El Galán said, "Well, since we cannot hope to live through another four months like these last, let us assume that the end of our journey is near.''

At this point Don Juan Jamarillo joined Cortés and the captains somewhat tentatively. "When Hamilcar's soldiers were trapped in a desert pass after a grueling march . . . ,'' he began.

"They drank their own pith," lisped Sandoval, "but lack of water is not our problem."

"Aculán!" Cortés announced, pointing to the map. "It's a large province, directly ahead, apparently not more than a week's march. Or ten days, allowing for fatigue, hunger, and this hellish forest. Nan Chan indicates its capital city, called Petén. A smaller trade city is still closer." He pointed to the chart, and we all looked at the X on the map he pointed to and tried to imagine a town with a bursting marketplace and a friendly cacique eager to feed us everything in it.

The days somehow passed. Spirits sank as if the swamp pulled them down into slimy depths. In lofty branches above our heads parrots screeched and unseen birds sang mockingly.

By now I was thinner than I had been even after the first siege at Tenochtitlán, and thought of it as providential that I had eaten so well after losing my second child. We had discovered that a certain bark, boiled, was edible.

When at last the trees about us grew more sparse so that real daylight filtered down upon our faces, I scarcely dared to hope we had reached the forest's end.

We ran out from under the last trees, spirits soaring. We found ourselves on the bank of a river far wider and swifter than any we had passed, or any I had ever seen. Dizzy, I looked out over the rushing waters.

Louder than the river's steady muted roar was the great groan that rose from the throats of the foot soldiers. Many of the horsemen echoed it as they realized no horse could swim that mighty flood. I heard one say "This is the end of our journey! That river cannot be crossed. All that's left us is to try to return the way we came or find a better route back to Tabasco."

"Yes, another route!" a soldier cried. "And here I sit until Cortés decides on one!" In total agreement, the foot soldiers all sat down along the narrow beach.

Ignoring this, if indeed he had heard, Cortés continued to eye the sweep of water. He turned. "We can build a bridge," he said matter-of-factly, as if the feat were of no great difficulty. He waved an arm toward the lowering forest we had left. "Plenty of wood. Lianas for ropes. A floating bridge is what we'll build, anchored to this shore and extending outward, log after log, until it touches the other."

The soldiers' earlier groans turned to shouts of disbelief. "We're done in, Cortés," one rose to yell. "You might as well ask us to build a Spanish galleon! Or the city of Madrid to camp in while we do it!"

"A bridge can be built," Cortés told him. "And will be, if not by you." He asked El Galán to bring Cuauhtemoc and the cacique of Tacuba to him. The Spanish soldiers waited alertly. Cuauhtemoc listened patiently as I explained what Cortés wanted. He said he would urge the nine hundred Indian warriors to volunteer their aid.

"I can do no more than ask them; I cannot command, having no more power over them," he said.

"Then add to your persuasion the fact that Cortés commands this of them," Cortés ordered. "And point out that it will be to their great advantage to reach Aculán, since many more Indians have died than Spaniards."

The response of the Indians was swift; within the hour came the sound of a hundred hand axes attacking the nearest trees of the forest. "Those Indians respect Cuauhtemoc, whatever he may say," Cortés remarked to his captains. "I doubt if they would have responded to me any better than my Spanish soldiers did, yet Cuauhtemoc could persuade them."

"And lucky that he could," Sandoval nodded.

Shamed by the good spirit with which the Indians had fallen to the task, the Spaniards soon joined them. For three days the thudding of axes on wood drowned out the river's sound. The bridge Cortés had conceived ultimately required a thousand trees, each log of wood as thick as a man's body. When after four days the bridge was done, I had to marvel at it. So did the men who had chopped and hauled the trees and labored to lash log to log. "Nothing but fire can destroy it!" Cortés exulted. It was a monument to his refusal to acknowledge defeat. That tough, undaunted spirit of his had communicated itself to his soldiers, who now showed each other their raw blistered hands with jaunty pride.

It was devastating to discover, with that river finally crossed, the river which had seemed the final barrier before we saw ahead the towers of the first trade city of Aculán, that still another swamp had to be crossed, worse than any yet. Horses floundered ahead up to their bellies in muddy water. Sometimes, whinnying with terror, they sank into deep quagmires from which the soldiers and riders got them out only with great effort, covering the muck around these treacherous pits with the boughs of trees onto which the poor muddy beasts desperately floundered.

But when at last we struggled through this enormous swamp we came to solid ground that rose in a gentle slope upward. At the top we could see the first cultivated fields of Aculán, the tall ripe maize, hundreds of yucca plants, many pepper trees. It seemed to the padres a very good sign that we had reached this land of plenty on the first day of the Lenten season.

That night when we camped the air was full of the good smell of roasting ears of maize or baking cassava roots, for Cortés could not forbid the starved men from plundering these wide fields. After food, everyone became cheerful. The musicians, listless for some time, began to play their tunes, and soon some of the Spanish soldiers were singing. The Indian camp, apart from ours, was silent, but they went to sleep earlier than the Spaniards.

Cortés had lost his look of constant anxiety and was laughing at his juggler, who skillfully kept four gnawed maize cobs in the air at once. But his merriment was short-lived—and mine. A converted Aztec wearing a silver cross on his bare chest came to Cortés' campfire outside his tent to whisper an accusation of Cuauhtemoc.

I, of course, served as translator. The accusation was that a conspiracy had been set afoot by Cuauhtemoc and that the cacique of Tacuba and other Indian nobles were privy to it. Cuauhtemoc had decided that before we reached Honduras, at some moment when the army was again bogged down in a morass or handicapped by some other obstacle, the Indians, greatly outnumbering the Spaniards, would suddenly fall on them and kill them all. Then Cuauhtemoc would lead the Indians to Olid's settlement, conquer it, and take command. News of this successful revolt would be sent to the capital. It would foster an Indian uprising there, and after that in other Spanish colonies. Vessels in the ports would be seized by Indian rebels to prevent news of this general insurrection from crossing the sea to Cuba or Spain. The Spaniards' overlordship would thus be ended forever.

While the informer narrated this wild plot his eyes roved crazily and his voice became higher and higher, finally only a squeak. He seemed to me to be a man impelled to tell some nightmare he had dreamed, or some fantasy of his own, and so rid himself of its baneful effect.

Knowing Cortés' slumbering suspicion of Cuauhtemoc, I volunteered this opinion, and others. "Would any sane man dream of such a scheme? A venture certain to fail? Even if Olid's settlement fell, even if this provoked a general uprising, which is very doubtful, any intelligent mind can see that if just one Spanish ship escaped eastward, the entire might of the Spanish Empire would be flung against him!"

"Let Cuauhtemoc defend himself," Cortés said brusquely, the two frown lines between his eyes deep and harsh. "If he is innocent, he does not need your help, and if he's guilty you're wasting your breath." He turned to Sandoval and El Galán. "Get a complement of soldiers and bring Cuauhtemoc and the Tacuban cacique and those other Indian nobles here to me."

While we waited in silence, I noted that his face, like my own, was very thin from the hunger we had undergone. I said, "You are weary. That makes you impatient. But remember, Cuauhtemoc is weary too. If he shows anger at this accusation, or is sullen and refuses to defend himself, remember how he got the Indians to help you build the bridge."

He ignored me, staring into the fire. "I think my famed luck may have run out in this accursed land. Lachesis seems to have taken a hand in my affairs of late."

"Lachesis?"

"The Greeks of long ago believed there were three Fates. One spun the thread of a man's destiny. One cut the thread. One wove the shroud. Lachesis was the Fate who cut the thread. Yes, that great whore Lachesis is clicking her shears and laughing at me."

His face as he spoke looked flushed by more than the firelight. Two patches of red glared on his cheekbones. I reached out and put my hand on his forehead. It nearly burned me. "You have caught that fever that killed so many in the swamps," I said.

He put a hand to his own head and nodded. "Yes, I am ailing. Just one more way my luck has turned bad."

"Luck never made Cortés. Luck won't break him," I said.

"Your faith is touching, but I still hear Lachesis laughing."

Cuauhtemoc and the Tacuban cacique appeared, the latter looking up at the former as usual. Behind them were half a dozen nobles of their two cities. "Tell him what the informer said," Cortés ordered me.

I did so, but added that I myself believed this accusation to be untrue.

What happened then was most unfortunate. Several of the noble Tacubans, eager to ingratiate themselves with Cortés out of fear of him, came forward and admitted that, yes, they had indeed heard Cuauhtemoc speak of some sort of uprising against the Spaniards, but they had refused to take any part in it. Reluctantly I conveyed this information to Cortés.

"Well?" he asked Cuauhtemoc, standing up to face him. "What do you say to that?"

Cuauhtemoc showed no fear. He tossed those Tacubans a look of contempt and drew himself taller, staring at Cortés without anger. "I was a fool not to have taken my own life before surrendering to you. I was perhaps also foolish to have told you where you could find a quantity of gold after you saved me from having my feet burned off, for that made you think the pain had cowed me. But I am not such a fool as to imagine I could succeed in fomenting such an uprising. Even if every warrior with me joined in such a conspiracy, I would have to reach Honduras without any idea where it is. Even if I reached it, I would not be likely to succeed against Spanish weaponry; but even if I did, this could not cause a general uprising of native people from sea to sea. But even if that came about, there remains the final impossibility—that every Spanish vessel in every port could be kept from sailing to your ruler Carlos with news of this uprising. And what that would bring down on the heads of all the native people of my land of Anahuac and elsewhere does not even bear thinking about. Can you really believe that I would subject my race to a second conquest even more terrible than the first? I am not a fool. I am not a madman."

By now Cortés was nodding, unable even in his feverish state to resist the logical progression of Cuauhtemoc's defense. He caught himself in this silent act of agreement and turned sharply to me. "He argues well. Or did you put the words into his mouth?"

"You have admitted in the past that I have some powers of logic. I merely said what any rational mind would conclude."

Cortés turned to Cuauhtemoc. "Then these Tacubans who said they heard you conspiring are all liars? And the informer—a liar too?"

Cuauhtemoc stared straight ahead. "One of them brought up the idea of a rebellion against Spaniards. I said this idea was foolish, and why. The informer may have eavesdropped and heard only part of what I said, and so assumed I was outlining the plan of a rebellion instead of denying its feasibility. He may therefore have believed what he told you. But as for my planning any uprising, the Tacubans who said so are liars and cowards."

Cortés' maimed hand was pressed to his burning forehead. "What it comes down to is that I can believe them or you."

"According to the code I live by my surrender was absolute, final for all time. I cannot take it back or change it. I have given myself over to you as conquered. No rebellion could ever change that act of

407

mine. The last Aztec ruler was Cuauhtemoc. He now rules only himself. He is not a foolish king.''

Seeing him standing there immobile as a tower on his scarred feet, I felt admiration and great compassion. The rock he once hurled at Moctezuma had rebounded against him a thousandfold, but he was not broken and would never be.

Cortés' face showed that he, too, had not been unmoved by those words. ''I am impressed by what you say, Cuauhtemoc. I also respect the former cacique of Tacuba, who did not shelter himself from my anger by turning against you.''

''When two have burned together side by side it creates a close bond,'' Cuauhtemoc said.

Cortés blinked. I could see he did not like being reminded that he had not prevented that act of torture. But he said: ''Then I hope that the perils of this journey may have the same effect on you and me'' and dismissed Cuauhtemoc and the others with him.

His fever grew worse that night; unable to sleep, he left his tent to prowl through the camp—looking, he said, for spies sent by the cacique whose borders we had reached. He returned in an excited state, woke me from my half-doze to whisper that the truth about why those towns had been burned had dawned on him. ''You remember I said this clever schemer had to know something of our ways? Who could this devil be but a Spaniard? Eh? Yes, a Spaniard. He learned somehow the route I planned to take and moved ahead of us, inspiring the natives to burn their towns. But what Spaniard, I asked myself? An answer came to me: Guerrero!''

''Guerrero?''

''The Spanish priest who was with Aguilar in Yucatán! The one who would not leave because he had an Indian wife and sons. He has turned on his own countrymen!''

I sat up. ''But the town where he lived was a great distance from here, on the west shore near Cozumel!''

He ignored geography. ''Yes, Guerrero has become an Indian, but one who knows our methods and our ways. He can think as we do. Oh, if I had guessed such a thing would happen, I'd have hauled him out of there myself by the hair of his head! I'd have laid him dead at the feet of his Indian wife!''

This fantasy frightened me more than I dared to show. ''It's only your fever talking. And even if you had such an enemy, he failed to stop you, because here we are at Aculán.''

His eyes burned below his burning forehead. "But a long way yet from the north shore of Honduras. The Spaniards who first found it called it the Golfo Dulce. I wonder if the seawater is sweet there? Could such a thing be?" As his mind wandered from sweet seawater to the existence of mermaids, I knew how sick he was and went for cool water to bathe his head, urging him like a mother to go to his bed, to rest, to sleep. As I sponged his hot body as well, he suddenly seized my arm in a steel grip, but spoke gently. "You are a good Indian, my proof that such exist."

He fell asleep then, and slept heavily until dawn. I waited by the tent for his valet, to tell him not to wake Cortés. When he woke and dressed he seemed better. The flush was gone from his face and his words seemed normal and rational. The captains were by then waiting to confer with him, and I left them talking of the day's march while eating boiled maize the quartermaster had cooked.

Don Juan Jamarillo surprised me with a present: he had been very kind to me during that long and terrible journey, bringing me berries he had found, and once some orchids, apologizing that they were not edible. The gift he brought me that morning was a baby parrot; he had found it on the ground, one of its wings lamed or broken. He had made a little cage for it out of a basket. I named it Orteguilla because its bright coloring and way of cocking its head to one side reminded me of my dwarf friend.

Because the morning was a lovely one, less warm than usual, Don Juan and I walked a little distance from the camp together, enjoying the sun and the pretty landscape with its pepper trees. There were some ceibas too; a large one marked the beginning of the wide roadway that would lead us toward Petén. When we reached one of the pepper trees, the spot where he had found the parrot, he pushed aside the dangling feathery branches to point to where it had lain on the ground. I looked up into the tree for the nest from which it might have fallen, for it was very young. Seeing the clumps of small red pepper berries, I wondered if parrots ate them. I tasted one. Only the black seed had a strong flavor; the red hull was tasteless. But should such a young bird eat pepper berries, even if older ones did?

The dangling leaves beside me were suddenly parted. I stared at El Galán's bearded face, the skin pale and beaded with sweat. His eyes were anguished. "For God's sake, come with me. Cortés is going to hang Cuauhtemoc! You must try to stop this thing!"

I thrust the parrot cage at Jamarillo and ran down the road beside

THE CEIBA TREE

El Galán toward the great ceiba tree I had seen earlier, around it a great clot of Spanish and Indian soldiers, their backs toward me. "Let us through!" he commanded. I stopped dead at the inner edge of the crowd, staring up in shock.

From a great dark branch of the ceiba tree Cuauhtemoc was hanging, head tilted sharply to one side, neck stretched long by the rope around it. His body dangled limp and dejected, the morning sun burnishing his dead flesh, his golden necklace and bracelets. Near him, on a lower bough, swung the cacique of Tacuba.

I could not scream, I could not weep, I could only stare at the last Aztec king. I closed my eyes, opened them, and only then was aware that Cortés stood directly opposite me across a short space of dusty roadway. He raised his maimed hand and with a sudden slashing gesture indicated that the bodies were to be cut down. A soldier's sword severed the rope that had hanged Cuauhtemoc, and his limp body fell with a thud onto the dust of the road.

I think I made some sound; Cortés turned his head and saw me. Our eyes met like those of strangers above the corpse of the man he had promised to treat with all honor.

Into his came a startled look, as if he had read mine and seen my deep revulsion. We stared at each other for an instant longer and then I turned and ran down the road, away from the disillusionment I knew I would never outdistance or forget.

I had slowed to a walk when I heard the voice of El Galán behind me; turning, I saw that he and Sandoval had also left the group around the hanging tree. As they fell into step at either side of me Sandoval said in a troubled voice, "I can't forget Cuauhtemoc's last words. When the noose was put around his neck."

"What were they?" El Galán asked.

" 'I knew I was wrong to trust in your false promise to honor me, Cortés. I knew I was destined for a fate like this at the moment I surrendered instead of taking my own life.' " There was a pause. "And then he said, 'Your God will demand to know why you kill me so unjustly.' "

"Unjustly," El Galán repeated, somberly.

"And then the cacique of Tacuba looked up at Cuauhtemoc and said, 'I ask no better fate than to die beside my Lord Cuauhtemoc.' "

"Is Cortés going mad?" El Galán asked. No one replied. The three of us who had admired Cortés and loved him continued in silence away from the murder of two brave men. The last words of Cuauhtemoc haunted me: if he had known that Cortés would surely kill him, why had he endured this perilous journey to the final moment when a noose snapped his neck? He could have escaped a hundred times. Did his code of absolute surrender prevent him? Was it his belief that his gods had deserted him? Was it his razed city, gone forever? But all these were just ideas: it seemed to me that he had not valued life enough, just life itself, the sunrises and sunsets, the starred nights, the beauty of trees or the sea, and the little daily pleasures of food to eat, a friend to talk with, the sound of music, a child's smile. Why had he remained a docile prisoner of Cortés, his nemesis? Such fatalism was beyond my understanding. "I knew you had destined me for a fate like this . . . ."

I was shivering in the warm sunlight. I knew that my life with Cortés had come to an end under that ceiba tree. We were six years from the day I first saw him and thought him a god.

46

All the rest of that day I was like a woman suffering from a fatal illness. When the march to Aculán began I could not mount my mare, told the groom to ride her, and took to the litter. Despite the heat I began to shiver with a chill and hid under a blanket. The sun hurt even my closed eyes; I covered them with my bent arms. The pat-pat of the litter-bearers' broad feet made me drift back in time; I thought of myself as going not toward Petén but toward Tabasco. In fantasy I escaped the Spaniards by staying hidden among the mangroves until darkness fell and I stole out late at night and found Kukul, who hid me until the gods had sailed away forever.

I found I was very thirsty and again remembered an earlier journey on a litter much like this. I heard the slow clop-clop of a horse's hooves. A shadow fell across my covered body; I felt the sun's heat leave me. I stiffened under the blanket. Cortés?

"Doña Marina?" a gentle voice said. I lowered my arms from my face and looked up at Don Juan Jamarillo. He held the horse's reins in one hand, in the other the little parrot in its cage. His expression was compassionate. "That was a terrible sight for a woman's eyes," he said. "Is there anything I can do to bring you comfort?"

"Yes. Get me some water."

"Water? Surely." He fumbled a bit at the other side of his saddle, then bent to offer down his flask. I drank. The water was cool. Some spilled. I did not care. Water is life, I thought. I am drinking life. I am not like Cuauhtemoc.

Those few words shocked me with the deeper meaning implicit in them. Don Juan Jamarillo became determinedly cheerful. "This poor little parrot seems to miss you. Look how eagerly he is watching you now." He lowered the cage, smiling in his neat blond beard.

I looked. The parrot's yellow round eye met mine. The caged bird seemed a symbol for Cuauhtemoc. And me. I sat up and reached for the cage. As soon as the parrot's wing is healed, I thought, I will set it free. "Thank you," I said.

Jamarillo nodded. Pleased and believing he had somewhat cheered me, he spurred his mount and rode forward to rejoin the other horsemen.

I lay back. Holding the parrot cage in the curve of one arm, I put together the meaning of the fragments of thoughts and feelings I had just experienced. I knew I had to escape Cortés. Not because I feared for my life; because I feared for my soul. Painfully, I went back to the beginning of our time together, and I saw with utmost clarity that while Cortés had been busy creating a new colony for Spain he had also been creating a new Cortés. He had overcome every obstacle that stood between him and the achievement of his ambition, and in doing so he had turned from a man of unusual courage into a monster with new ambitions yet unsatisfied.

That one single act, the hanging of Cuauhtemoc had opened my eyes to what I had been willfully blind to before. Every other action he had been able to justify to a woman who yearned to continue to love him. But this act he could never justify. I knew the fear that had inspired it, a fear that had waited only for the moment to spring like an adder on its victim. "Below the green panache of power bad dreams dwell." The conqueror hates the conquered, however much he tells himself his own cause was just. Humans do not become the greater by subduing others, but by serving them with love.

As to how I could manage to leave Cortés if he did not wish me to, I did not know. Nor did I see how I could also manage to claim my son in doing this. All I knew was that I would. Somehow. Someday. In time.

From the day of Cuauhtemoc's execution, Cortés was moody, irritable, and unlike his former self. His fever continued, burning like a low fire, although his mind became clear of fantasy. Our friendly welcome at the large trade city of Aculán, which we reached late that day, did not seem to remove from his mind the shadow of that dark ceiba tree. We were given pleasant quarters and ample food, yet he slept scarcely at all. His tossing and turning gave me an excuse to ask for a separate room. "This terrible journey has wearied and weakened me very much. I am only a woman, after all, and am suffering great anxiety about my child whom I have not seen for so long."

He gave me a hard, probing look as if he half-suspected my aversion. That maimed left hand, the claw with which he had signaled the cutting down of Cuauhtemoc's body, had become particularly horrible to me. I could scarcely believe that on the morning of our reunion after the *noche triste* the blood-soaked bandage that covered it had filled me with compassion so that I ached for him and his pain and the loss of his fingers.

"Very well," he said. "You can sleep in the antechamber to this room if you wish. I admit this fever keeps me restless."

The next day I learned, with horror, that Cuauhtemoc had not been buried beside the cacique of Tacuba as I had assumed. Cortés had brought the body with him, slung in a great sack which two of the soldiers carried on a pole. "His reason was strange," El Galán told me, troubled. "He said he did not want Guerrero to find the grave and know our hostage was dead. He has told the cacique there that the last Aztec monarch is still with him, though unwilling for company, which God knows is true. Cortés did a wrong and terrible thing in hanging him. He should have cherished him like a precious jewel, proof of his victory over the Aztecs and his noble treatment of a vanquished foe."

I did not trust even El Galán, in my desperate state of mind, and did not tell him I agreed. I shrugged. "Cortés was ill with fever. Perhaps in his right mind he would have behaved differently." But I knew that the fever Cortés suffered from was no passing one caught in the swamps; it was a fever that would burn in him until he died or had explored and conquered all the unknown lands of the world and then, perhaps, would have him eyeing the cold far moon and wondering if it might be made of silver.

A few nights after we reached the city of Aculán, when Cortés went out to walk on the upper level of the temple near our dwelling place, perhaps to see if any spies or other interlopers were skulking in the garden of our palace, he slipped and fell many spans to a stone paving on which he injured his head. When he came into the anteroom where I slept, I screamed on seeing the fierce face pinched with pain, one glaring eye staring at me, the other hidden by a curtain of blood. For an instant I thought one of the Aztec soldiers with us might have tried to kill him in revenge for Cuauhtemoc's death. But as I dutifully wiped away the blood and bandaged the wound I learned of his misstep on a high place, and I knew his enemy within had caused the fall: that conscience by which he so often swore had risen up against him and seized the chance to hurl him down to the earth.

But remorse he would not admit, and insisted to me and others and later, in a letter to King Carlos, that the former monarch of Mexico, by the ascendance of his character and his former high station, had maintained an influence over his countrymen that would have enabled him at any instant to rouse their smothered animosity into open rebellion against Spanish rule.

I did not try to reason with him; even if I had wished to it would have been fruitless, for it soon became plain to me that he was not in his right mind. One evidence of this was his great sensitivity about the fall he had and the head wound it had left him with. He tried to conceal this injury from his soldiers, a futile effort since the gash refused to heal firmly and would suddenly open and let blood run down his face. But I knew his reason for wanting to preserve the illusion among the men that he was all but invincible against common injury. We were still a long way from the Honduras colony where Olid maintained his stolen authority, unaware that his nemesis was inching closer.

From that first Aculán town we went to Petén, a pretty city built on islands in a lake and so reminding me of Tenochtitlán on a much smaller scale. There again we were well received, and there the priests introduced Christianity and again the ruler of Spain attained another vassal. There, too, Cortés' smoldering fever abated at last, leaving him gaunt and somewhat yellow, the lines at each side of his mouth gashed very deep. He soon regained something of his old assurance.

This was fortunate, because after we left Petén, further hardship and peril confronted us. Instead of sucking swamps we had to make our way over a mountain of flints some nine leagues across. It took twelve days; the flints cut the horses' feet to pieces, and so many slipped suddenly down into deep crevasses that when we reached the other side there were only thirty-two mounts left out of more than a hundred. There, at last, Cuauhtemoc was buried; by then the stench was so terrible that no soldier would carry the sack containing his corpse.

The flints left behind, the season of rains began to deluge us, swelling rivers to torrents that we crossed with great danger and further loss. For my part, I marveled that I had once considered the first journey to Tenochtitlán an arduous one; now it seemed like a holiday. My clothing was shabby and travel-stained except for that one Spanish gown of green velvet, which I had worn only once—in Petén—to impress the cacique there. It had dressed a marionette who stood beside Cortés and performed her well-known duty.

But at last we neared the Golfo Dulce and Olid's colony at the eastern end of the north coast of Honduras. The salt smell of the sea first told us our journey was nearly over; from a thickly forested hill we looked down at the distant little town, surrounded by a wooden stockade, poor and shabby-looking under the glare of the tropic sun. Weary and shatttered as we were, the only hope was to take the colony by surprise. Camped amid trees that hid us from his objective, Cortés was in consultation with his captains about the strategy to be employed when the hand of tragic irony struck him.

Scouts sent ahead to sniff out the terrain and the strength and weakness of the fort came running back with grins and the astounding news that they encountered some people from the settlement who were friendly and talkative. "Olid is dead!" the flushed soldier said. "It seems that Casas was not drowned in that shipwreck you learned about. The mariners who reported the wreck to you saw the vessel on the rocks and assumed the worst. But the fact is that Casas and most of the others got safely ashore. Armed with his orders from you, they marched right into Olid's settlement, got the majority of the Spaniards there on the side of the law. And then they hanged Olid!"

Looking at Cortés' stricken face, all I could think was that our terrible journey had been for nothing. All for nothing! "Then God is good to have saved me from that disagreeable duty," Cortés managed to say.

I saw then the great irony: he had set out to hang Olid; instead he had hanged Cuauhtemoc. Punishing a traitor like Olid would have gained him only respect. Hanging Cuauhtemoc had already brought him reproach from such men as El Galán and would surely bring him more, elsewhere. And it had lost him the admiration of his Amazon. His talisman. His tongue.

Cortés entered the little settlement at the head of his dispirited army, and at once sent for de las Casas to demand why word had not at once been sent to him of Olid's capture and execution.

"It was!" de las Casas protested. "I dispatched a small troop overland to Coetzacoalcos. They either died en route from the dangers of the journey or else were killed by hostile natives. You cannot blame me for that."

Cortés indeed could not, remembering the obstacles our large expedition had barely survived. But then he said one word which chilled me: "Guerrero!"

De las Casas did not understand, and Cortés explained to him his theory of the renegade Spaniard.

A terrible despondency settled over me, for I knew that it was hopeless to try to appeal to Cortés' kinder side, to try to make him understand how desperately I yearned to see the son I had thought I was leaving for only a few months at most. This dreadful expedition with its ending that had turned all the pain and loss into a grim joke Cortés was unable to deal with except to believe that an unforeseeable enemy accounted in part for the great fiasco. If I showed him my true feelings, would he decide I had been in league with Guerrero?

My low spirits were not helped by the fact that the little colony was in a state of near famine so that even the modest comfort of sufficient food was denied us. Having no other challenge to face at the moment, Cortés took this as one. Since the land offered nothing, he said, the sea would have to be made to feed us. Finding that on the rocks of a natural jetty near the town there was an abundance of crabs, he inspired the making of dozens of crab nets out of lianas plucked down in the jungle and woven into a mesh tied to hoops of wood. Of crabs there seemed no end, large juicy ones, and in a few days simmering kettlesful had turned the tide of listless near-starvation. We had some fishhooks with us, dugout canoes were made, fish were hauled up in quantities ample enough to lead to merriment.

Hunger coped with, Cortés and a party of soldiers set out to explore the area farther than the desperate colonists had, but reported only dismal swamps and venomous insects. There were also alligators; he brought a dead one back as a trophy, hopeful that it might taste somewhat like iguana, but it did not.

For my part, I disliked the ugly little settlement, which felt too much like a prison with its surrounding stockade, and took to wandering along the beach near it. There I would gather seashells, of which there were some pretty ones. It became almost a passion with me, and when

I found a shell unlike any other it seemed like a piece of great luck that betokened good fortune in the future. This inane occupation temporarily assuaged my feeling of being forlorn and friendless. This was merely self-pity; I deeply hurt poor Don Juan Jamarillo when I refused his offer to accompany me on one of my walks.

One day I wandered farther from the town than I ever had before; it was out of sight behind dunes of brownish sand. I stood there with a seashell in my hand gazing southward. I knew that somewhere beyond the ocean before me lay the vast continent of South America, and on its western side the fabled mountain cities of the Incas. Somewhere to the west, perhaps, was the secret strait to the Pacific Cortés hoped to discover for King Carlos. Would I find myself one day ascending high mountains toward the Inca cities? Or would I sail through that strait to the great ocean to the west? Was I fated to journey with my captor endlessly? I looked back in wonder at the self I had once been, filled with pleasure when Cortés told me he wanted me with him in Honduras.

Alone on that beach, I was the first to see the Spanish ship and ran back to the town to spread the news. Very soon two brigantines arrived, stopping off en route to the principal Spanish colony on the Nicaraguan coast, Trujillo.

With something like his old enthusiasm, Cortés told me he had decided to embark with the major part of his force on those ships. "From Trujillo I will plan and launch a new expedition, to search for the strait to the Pacific. I also intend to explore and subdue the entire province of Nicaragua. The emperor, I know, will look on this with favor and send the needed vessels and supplies." He smiled down at me. "In Trujillo you will find things more to your liking, Marina. It's a large colony now. There are some women there for company, and other pleasures and conveniences."

I could not speak, only nodded mutely. I turned and went out to my lonely refuge, the seashore. Another expedition, and after that another. And I the faithful Indian mistress at his side, his good-luck piece, his comfort on some nights, his possession, as useful as his horse. With an infinitely somber sound waves broke and slid back into the sea, dragging pebbles after.

Cortés spoke behind me. "Why do you wander out here alone? What is wrong with you, Marina? Why do you look so sad, now that our troubles are over at last? Oh, it was a hard journey for you, and I admit it. Had I guessed the misfortunes ahead, you would have remained safe in the city of Mexico with Martín. But here we are, alive after it all, at a new beginning. For my part, I am looking forward to the journey ahead.'' He gestured toward the wide blue sea. ''If that strait exists I'll find it! That will please our sovereign more than all the gold and silver I've sent him from Mexico!''

I felt no response. Not pride in his renewed spirit, not fear for the dangers he would face: nothing. It was like being partly dead. Perhaps this is how dying feels, I thought.

His smile vanished. ''What do you want of me, Marina? Tell me. What?''

''I want to go home to Martín.''

''I do not intend to retrace my steps to Mexico. It's a waste of time. The new project begins in Trujillo.''

''Then let me go to Martín alone.''

''That's absurd. You'll like it in Trujillo. You'll sail there on a fine ship!'' He tried a smile.

I took a deep breath, and risked everything. ''I want to leave you, Cortés.''

He stepped back, gave me a cool, probing look. It told me that he knew and would always know that I had seen him at his worst, knew that I would never forget Cuauhtemoc hanging from that ceiba tree.

He turned his back abruptly and walked away from me to stand some distance off, staring out over the sea. At last he faced me, keeping that distance between us. His voice was calm and resolute. ''This life of mine is a hard one for any woman to share. She must live in safety without me or else stay at my side to endure great privations and dangers. And my life will never change. Ahead of me I see a secret strait, an Inca city, the wide Pacific, the South Seas. Before I go there, I want to explore the Pacific coast of Mexico northward. I'll build another fleet at Zacatula.''

''Your life will never change,'' I agreed, holding my breath.

He straightened, looking at me kindly. ''And so it seems, Doña Marina, that we have come to the parting of our ways.''

''Yes, to our parting,'' I managed to whisper.

He nodded, took one step closer, paused. ''There remains the matter of your future. I have given it some thought. I do not intend you to live it alone, a woman abandoned. You need a husband. I suggest Don Juan Jamarillo.''

This abrupt arranging of my future left me numb. I said that I needed no husband, only my son.

"For the sake of that son, as well as your own, I prefer that you marry a Spaniard. Don Juan is of a fine old family, which would give you the status you well merit. Martín would benefit from a stepfather able to set him an example of the manners and morals of a Castilian of high category."

I found my voice, even tried to smile. "But surely Don Juan has something to say about this arrangement?"

"It has not escaped me that he is in love with you. He will say yes and thank me from the bottom of his heart. As a wedding gift I intend to endow him with a handsome grant of land. You I will also endow, and to a much greater degree. I intend that you shall have an estate encompassing your little town of Paynala and many leagues of land around it."

"You are very generous."

"I wish also to make you a gift of a number of jewels beyond those I have already given you. Despite the heavy financial cost of this failed expedition to Honduras, I have the faith that I can retrieve the loss elsewhere, and so I will be able to muster up some gold as well."

Our eyes locked. In his I thought I saw a yearning, as if perhaps he hoped that I would run to him across the space of sand between us and tell him that no grant of land, no jewels, no gold, no Castilian husband could ever compensate me for the privilege of continuing at his side. I said, "Then Martín will live with me?"

He nodded. "With you and Don Juan Jamarillo. As for Martín's future, he is my son and heir. The plans I have made for him will remain unchanged except for the better, depending on what capacities he develops as he grows older."

"May I request one thing more?"

He nodded. I pointed to the brigantines anchored offshore.

"Could you have one of those ships take me to Mexico at once?"

He shook his head. "No. I need them both to take me and my men to Trujillo. I will see to it that another ship is sent here for your passage to Vera Cruz." He smiled. "And that will allow time for your wedding to Don Juan."

Thinking only of returning to my son, I had considered this marriage a future event. "Surely the marriage can wait."

He frowned. "No. I intend to embark for Nicaragua knowing that you are the legal wife of a knight of Castile and that this much of my arrangement for your future well-being has been complied with." Now he had struck his most arrogant pose, head high, one fist on his hip.

419

It occurred to me then that his enthusiasm for Don Juan Jamarillo concealed a fear that his son might end with an Indian stepfather.

Looking at him there, backed by blue sea, I remembered Cortés as I had first seen him in Tabasco. It seemed to me that just as I had been wrong then in thinking him a god, so I might have been wrong now in thinking him a monster. Yet I knew that since escaping him meant marrying Don Juan Jamarillo, marry him I would. Perhaps in the green velvet Spanish gown, if that was what Cortés desired.

I bowed my head in assent. "He is a kind gentleman and will be good to Martín."

He nodded, relieved at my compliance, and came toward me. He held out his hand, not the three-fingered claw but his right whole hand, and seeing what he wished I rested mine upon it. He bent and kissed it as he would the hand of some fine Spanish lady. He straightened and looked deep into my eyes and his face assumed an expression combined of affection and regret. He pressed my hand, then released it; it slipped from his. "Know this: Cortés will never forget you."

"Nor I Cortés," I said, truthfully, and saw Cuauhtemoc hanging. In that instant I knew he was the symbol to me of all the native people of Mexico. The promises Cortés had made concerning them had all been broken too.

And so we parted, Cortés and I, and the only sound of mourning was the cry of a seagull passing overhead toward another shore. That cry, and the hollow crash of a breaking wave. We turned and walked sedately toward the crude buildings of the little town and my wedding day.

Cortés kept his promises to me. And so because of him I became not only the caciqua of Paynala but also the entitled owner of the land on which it stood, and even of the great cave, ancient refuge of my people. It was in Paynala that I chose to live, Don Juan being graciously anxious to please me in this as in all things. For Martín the change seemed for the better; he ceased having the colds and fevers that had sometimes plagued him in the drafty stone governor's palace at that high altitude, and as his tutor formed part of our household, his education did not suffer. His beloved Doña Luisa also joined me there. At first we lived in the stone palace where I had spent my childhood, my mother and her son having long since been removed by the clan heads to a more modest dwelling, but soon Don Juan became engrossed in the project of building us a Spanish house of adobe bricks on the corner of the plaza opposite the site chosen by Aguilar for the mission his Franciscan order was constructing there.

On the day Don Juan declared our new home finished to his satisfaction and took me proudly through its rooms, I learned that Cortés had not been wholly mistaken in his wild fantasy concerning Guerrero, the Spanish renegade. A letter came to me from Orteguilla, who sometimes wrote to me, although he could not bring himself to leave forever the aura of pomp and prestige enjoyed by a page of the governor, chief justice, and captain-general of New Spain.

Captain Montejo had been sent to Yucatán by Cortés to carry out the subjugation of all Yucatán, which proved a hard task. The various caciques there, already bound together by the same traditions of more than a thousand years' duration, had been formed into a strong coalition against Spanish conquest, inspired by Guerrero, whose knowledge of the Spanish mind and whose great personal valor offered Montejo a challenge he had not expected. "Imagine this renegade turning against his own people in such a fashion!" Orteguilla wrote indignantly. "What will history say of such a traitor? How could he betray the land that nursed him in order to aid another, inferior race?"

That night I dreamed I met Guerrero, and in my dream he looked like an Indian warrior and was the age my father would have been if he had lived. His tall, well-muscled body seemed to glow as he emerged from among the trees around us, for I was going along a trail through a deep jungle. He spoke to me in Spanish, with that mournful intensity that people in dreams sometimes have. "I am Guerrero, that Spaniard who went over to the Indians, and whom my former countrymen call traitor and hold in contempt. You are Malinche, an Indian who went over to the Spaniards. Will you, too, face contempt from the people you were born among?"

I said, "Still, I will live in Paynala."

"That is either very brave or else a great folly."

I became angry with him, in this dream. "My people will never hold me in contempt!"

He looked at me with pity. "That is what I once thought," he told me, and turned and vanished among the trees.

Most dreams fade, but this one has remained with me, for I already knew when I dreamed it that many millions of Indians had come to hate Cortés, and that with him they must hate me. There are those who call me *La Chingada,* as if I were a whore. But a whore sells her body and I gave mine. There are those who call me a traitoress. Liars, too. The Aztecs were never my people, but their oppressors, and it was the Aztecs Cortés set himself against and fought and conquered. And so I betrayed no one, I who had once been so monstrously betrayed, so cruelly betrayed, and by the woman who bore me. If there was a betrayal on my part, then the one person I betrayed has been myself. I knew long before I acknowledged it that Cortés was ruthless but I called it courage. I knew he was cunning but called it cleverness. And I knew that shedding Indian blood did not seem to him like murder, but I assured myself that the many souls he would save could wash it all away. Passion against reason was the battle that I lost. And if I call passion love, it does not change defeat to victory.

But there is a Power greater than Cortés. And so I believe that wrongs done by him will be made right at last. This I must believe. I must trust in God, walk humbly, and do whatever good I can.

PART
XII

THE FIST OF SATAN
January 1, 1530–June 30, 1530

47

At the start of the year 1530, my twenty-ninth birthday just ahead, I was able to look upon myself with satisfaction and to consider the past eight years of my adulthood well-employed. I was the most important man in Havana, nor was the name of Don Arturo Mondragon unknown in Santiago, even Spain. If anyone had told me that within a few months my life would be abruptly changed forever, I would have laughed and denied the possibility.

The decisions I made as a veteran of twenty-one who had just acquired a modest fortune from the sale of two emeralds and some gold proved wise ones. I had to weigh three alternatives. My father took up my mother's cry of "Salamanca!" He told me that wealth and the study of law go hand in hand. Cousin Enrique had other plans for me. He owned a fleet of vessels and now was eyeing New Spain with avarice, enthralled by what he had learned from me of the many products aside from gold and silver which could be imported into Europe at good profit: chocolate, vanilla, cochineal, tobacco, tomatoes, potatoes both white and sweet, cotton cloth, and even *guajolotes,* that large delicious fowl, unknown in Europe, which soon came to be called "turkey birds." A partnership was what he saw: my knowledge of New Spain and his ships. But my marriage to his daughter of sixteen, Amalia, was also in his mind. It would have been an advantageous marriage, since she would one day inherit the bulk of his fortune, but having known with every fiber of my being what real love felt like, I could not imagine myself embracing that pale thin little body, and for the rest of my life at that. But how to get the partnership without getting a wife I did not want?

A third alternative faced me: should I use a portion of my money to exploit better the Mondragon land adjacent to Havana, which was clearly destined to become the major port of the Caribbean? I had learned that sugar cane throve in a tropic climate with heavy rainfall, and sugar in Europe was worth almost its weight in gold, a luxury enjoyed only by the rich. It was this project that lured me most; my old fantasy of bringing Malinche to Cuba as my bride had not perished, for I knew Cortés could never marry her. I wanted to create a small self-contained world where a boyhood dream could come true.

Among these three choices I vacillated. The hard benches and drafty lecture halls at Salamanca did not appeal to me, yet I suspected that any future dealings with the shrewd Enrique would make some knowledge of the law a necessity. But a huge plantation of sugar cane with some Negroes who knew how to plant, harvest, and mill had such allure that I made a trip to the south of Spain and the meager cane fields there to get the plans for constructing a sugar mill. I learned to my delight that canes planted horizontally and watered well produce plants that tower to three times a man's height or more within eight months. I imagined Enrique's ships' holds bursting with ingots of Mondragon sugar.

On my twenty-first birthday I was still vacillating at Enrique's villa, honored by a fiesta. Amalia, as usual, was beside me. Her father, in conversation with a plump widow in black, glanced fondly at the two of us, and the widow, seeing this, smiled and nodded her approval of the pair we made, Amalia and I. "Happy birthday, dear cousin," Amalia said, and stood on tiptoes to place on my cheek her impulsive, girlish kiss.

I had been thinking of sugar cane, and she took me by surprise. Her lips were as cool as her gray eyes; a moth's wing might have brushed my cheek for all the response I felt. On second thought, the kiss did not seem to me impulsive but rather calculated; with it she claimed a right to that tiny sector of my body. And, strangely, it evoked a memory of Malinche, by contrast. Amalia's pale, adoring presence was a mere shadow; Malinche's dark and vital beauty remembered seemed more tangible. Amalia represented life's reality: an advantageous marriage. Malinche stood for the dreams men live by, which inspire heights of effort merely practical considerations do not.

"What are you thinking of?" Amalia asked—one of her more annoying habits.

"An Indian princess."

She hid annoyance with a look of innocent amazement. "A princess? Really? A real Indian princess?"

"As real as dreams," I said, to her confusion. And then my mind seemed to brighten. I saw with immense clarity that I did not have to choose among three alternatives; I had to embrace all three! I would learn enough law so Enrique could not cheat me; I would get his ships without getting his daughter; I would plant sugar cane in Cuba. All three were possible; all three I would accomplish. By shrewdness and hard work I would use my small fortune to attain in time a much greater one. And so the Indian princess as real as dreams ruled the realities of my existence, dictated a life shaped as though by getting richer I would get her too.

It was fortunate that I did not know that Doña Catalina was destined to die in less than a year, leaving Cortés free to marry Malinche. By the time I learned of this, I was well embarked on my triple plan: my brain was stuffed with a year of law; the canes to plant my first field were en route to Cuba in one of Enrique's vessels, which would return to Spain loaded with goods from Mexico; and Amalia was destined to meet on my return to Valladolid a young veteran named Rafael, whom I had reencountered in Vera Cruz and who was more than willing to marry an heiress.

It was he who told me that Doña Catalina had died of a lung congestion in the city of Mexico. I concealed from him the shock I felt at the news; how cruel of Fate to deal the one blow I had never expected! With gloom I watched Rafael's meeting with Amalia a month later, saw the round O of her mouth pointed toward him, not me, by the evening's end. My not marrying Amalia cost me a land grant in Mexico; Cortés wanted only colonists who would remain there and bring wives.

I decided that Cortés would not marry Malinche for at least a year after Doña Catalina's death, but after that I expected to learn at any moment that Malinche was his. By now she was somewhat famous. A history of the conquest of Mexico, written by one who had taken no part in it, had made the name of the beautiful young Indian woman who so nobly served the Spanish cause almost as widely known as that of Cortés himself. It was as Doña Marina that she had been so honored; the lavish description of her raven tresses and form divine rivaled for banality the poem I once wrote to her. This portrait bore little resemblance to the Malinche I had loved, nor was her past life before she encountered Spaniards even touched upon. Full-grown, she arrived in our midst to graciously aid us, a goddesslike aborigine without a past worth note. Since fame always stirs some to malice, there was a counter image as false: she was the enamored Indian female of whom a virile and clever Cortés had taken every advantage, to Spain's benefit and his own.

So I knew that their marriage would be no secret long and after a time got used to the idea that I had lost her. But the good thing about ambitious plans is that they have their own momentum and carry one along to new concepts; I decided that I wanted to possess a ship of my own, for in this way I could make a number of short trips to Mexico and stockpile in my Havana warehouse nonperishable goods which Enrique's vessels could then pick up when they brought to Havana the European goods I would later sell in Mexico. I returned from Spain to Cuba in my own caravel, as proud as if it were a galleon, only to find that I had missed seeing El Galán.

On his way back to Mexico from Cortés' disastrous campaign to Honduras and Nicaragua, a storm had struck and his ship was driven clear to Cuba—in fact, to Havana, and so he had decided to visit me. He had acquired, my mother said, a new scar, a recurrent fever, a hatred of lush green forests, and little else. Moreover, Cortés' intention to search for a strait to the Pacific had been abruptly terminated when he learned that his funeral services had been held in the city of Mexico, word having arrived and been spread wide by his enemies there that he and all the other members of his expedition were dead. There had been no choice for Cortés but to return and prove he was very much alive, if battered, fever-ridden, and impoverished.

"I must say I like your friend Bernal Diaz del Castillo," my mother said. "He stayed here for several days, but then could wait for you no longer as his ship was repaired by then."

"Did he happen to mention Doña Marina?" I asked.

"That Indian woman? Yes. He said she is married."

I had known that this was inevitable, but still the words brought a pang. "Yes, I was sure Cortés would marry her at last," I said with admirable calm.

"Cortés?" My mother was astounded. "Why would a man of his fame, a man any number of rich and noble women would give their hope of heaven to get, why would he marry a penniless Indian woman?"

Her lengthy rhetorical query had left me confused. "Cortés didn't marry her?"

"Of course not. She married quite well, though. A Castilian gentleman named—let me think—named Don Juan Jamarillo. In Honduras, it was. Or Yucatán."

Jamarillo? Who was this Jamarillo?

"What is wrong with you?" my mother asked. "Your face is white as cotton."

I turned away, saying I was going to the cane fields. Staring up at those green lofty stalks that towered above me, I saw instead the green forests of Yucatán which El Galán had told my mother he hated. If I had gone there with Cortés, would I now be in lucky Jamarillo's shoes? The thought was unbearable; that night I got very drunk.

In the morning, sad and sober, Malinche's marriage continued to puzzle me. I thought of the years she and Cortés had spent together, the child she bore him. Had Cortés really turned his back on his faithful Indian mistress so as to marry some noble and wealthy lady? But, even so, why had she married this upstart, this Castilian gentleman who came galloping to Cortés' banner after the conquest had been won by braver men? Where were they now? In Spain? In the city of Mexico? Where?

It was El Galán who at last told me. A letter from him said he was for a time in Santiago, where he had married the woman he told me of when we first met. I sailed there in my caravel with a wedding gift.

In the eight years since I had last seen him his brown hair had receded; the look of youth had quite vanished. His wife was buxom and pretty and left us to talk while she went to see to our evening meal; they were living in a modest house belonging to her parents. He was full of information about Cortés.

"After we returned to Mexico in twenty-six, pretty well battered by that damned Honduras campaign and knowing we had been declared dead, things looked up for him. In the towns where we stopped on the way to the capital the colonists entertained us royally, and since word of our resurrection had preceded us we got a wonderful welcome to the city of Mexico: flower-decked canoes on the lake and a big feast at the convent of St. Francis, built just about where Moctezuma's palace was. In a few days, Cortés had his hands firmly on the reins of government once more.

"But would you believe that within a month the Court at Madrid sent over a resident justice to take over the actual governing of Mexico? It seems that Cortés' enemies got Carlos to believe that Cortés intended to establish himself as an independent sovereign, cutting Mexico off from Spain. This was a bitter blow to Cortés, but he took it in stride and welcomed the resident justice, named Ponce de Leon. He turned out to be a fair-minded fellow and he and Cortés got on well. But then he died in a month of the same lung congestion that killed Doña Catalina. On his deathbed he appoined the Royal Treasurer to succeed him. This Estrada happened to hate Cortés, inflicting on him and his friends every annoyance a petty mind could think of and ignoring all his recommendations. When Cortés finally protested the theft of some land from one of Sandoval's men, Estrada ordered Cortés to leave the city. Think of it!''

"But did Cortés go?''

"He didn't want to be the cause of a civil war that would have Spanish blood flowing in the streets. He was bitter at heart, but he and his loyal followers left for Texcoco where we stayed until another blow fell. Cortés learned that a Royal Audience planned to examine a large number of charges against him—charges made, of course, by Estrada and his cohorts. This Audience would have the power to send Cortés to Spain for sentencing and punishment.''

"Punishment for what, in God's name?''

"Lies and calumnies, mostly. And a few misfortunes and mistakes, to be sure. This final blow was too much for Cortés. He left at once for Spain to plead his cause in person with the King. He took quite a retinue; it included Sandoval, now his closest friend, myself, a son of the elder Xicotencatl, Orteguilla and his wife Blanca, and four amusing Indian jugglers. He also brought two hundred thousand gold pesos and some jewels of great value; I myself saw some emeralds of remarkable size.'' He winked. "No frog among them.''

"I guess he was wise not to meet the King looking poor.''

"Face, face; he had to save face!'' He frowned then. "But for all this pomp, he crossed the Atlantic very much saddened, for en route, in Vera Cruz, he got word that his father had died. We landed at Palos—the port, you remember, where Columbus returned thirty-seven years ago after discovering a new world for Isabel, only to die at last in poverty and neglect. 'And I may end no better,' Cortés said to me. Only a week later, in Rabida, Sandoval died in Cortés' arms of the disease he contracted on that Honduras march, a recurrent fever. And in that same town, as if to prove that loyalty dies and treachery flourishes, Cortés encountered Francisco Pizarro. With an abominable aplomb, Pizarro flatly denied any past betrayal of Cortés, then boasted that he had high hopes of soliciting royal financing for an expedition to the land of the Incas.'' He grinned. "I said to him that I wished him soldiers as loyal as he had been to our commander in Mexico, and the look he gave me would have felled an oak.''

In spite of the questions I had come here to ask about Malinche, Jamarillo, and their whereabouts, I found that I wanted to know how Cortés had fared with the King, and asked El Galán about that.

"In spite of his sorrow and bitterness, Cortés wrote a brilliant letter to Carlos, denying all charges against him. It brought an invitation to Court. The magnificent welcome surprised us, and the King was very gracious, and appeared at Cortés' side on all public occasions. In other words, he accepted Cortés' appraisal of himself. I must say that I enjoyed the flattery and attention of a number of ladies of the court, having been long estranged from women in silk and velvet and perfume." He smiled blandly, "Although I was truthful and told them I had lost my heart to a certain faithful young woman in Santiago."

As one who had also lost his heart to a certain young woman, I asked about Malinche. "I know of her marriage to this Jamarillo fellow. But where is she now? What has happened to her? Do you know?"

"Still living in peaceful obscurity in Paynala, I believe."

"Paynala? The place where she was born?"

"After their marriage in Honduras she returned to the city of Mexico with her new husband to reclaim her son, and they left shortly for this little town; Cortés gave it to her. After all, in the course of her years with Cortés she had endured several lifetimes of excitements and danger, quite enough for a mere woman."

"Mere she was not."

"Agreed. But still a woman. Now, after such perils, she has attained what most women want most: a nest. She has her son to raise, an adoring husband, and, for all I know, other children by him."

"But why this Jamarillo? What happened between her and Cortés?"

He was silent for a moment; I could see loyalty to Cortés struggling with candor. He gave me a long look. "Well, as to precisely what passed between them, I do not know, of course. But I must admit that Cortés showed a very strange side of his nature during that long march across Yucatán. For one thing, he hanged Cuauhtemoc, you know." I nodded. "This seemed to affect Malinche very deeply. And then, for a time, Cortés was somewhat crazed. I would guess that she could not bear the change in him. Women, you know, like to look up to their men. And there was Jamarillo, very handsome, very loving— and, I must admit, very brave though mostly out of a certain innocence of the fact that heroes can die. To give Cortés his due, after he recovered his senses I think he realized that since he had no intention of marrying Doña Marina, it was unfair to keep her from a decent life with a very worthy husband."

Stricken, I saw again that if only I had been there in Honduras, my boyhood dream might have come true. That night I dreamed of my emerald frog, the proud possession that had more than anything else inspired me to return to Cuba while I still had it. It was of giant size, and hopped toward me, mouth open as if to swallow me, but it had very sad eyes.

The next day as I was leaving I thanked El Galán for having shared with me his wealth of information. "You seem to know so much more than I about the destinies of these people who once shared ours."

He smiled ruefully. "I have a peculiar quirk, Arturo. People and events in themselves seem to fascinate me much more than whatever wealth I might extract from them. My fear, now that I have started a family, is that I may depart this earth with nothing more to leave my wife and children than a thousand tales of the Conquest which they will have already heard."

Memories of Malinche haunted me on the journey home, and I relived those days of romantic idealism when I could see a Madonna in an Indian girl's face and could feel more ecstasy in dreams of her than any flesh under mine has brought me since. But I would not have voyaged to Paynala had it not been for what I learned from Cortés when he stopped at Havana on his way back to Mexico with his bride.

48

"A welcome must be arranged at once," the commandant of the port of Havana told me, having arrived at my door in a state of great excitement. The news had just reached him that Cortés, his new wife, his old widowed mother, and a large retinue had stopped in Hispaniola on their way from Spain to Mexico and would undoubtedly come to

Havana when they continued westward. A small, excitable man with a wispy beard, he was in all ways opposite to Pedro Barba. "We must plan a reception of style and elegance, worthy of the Marques of the Valley of Oaxaca. That is the newest of Cortés' titles, conferred by the sovereign personally."

It seemed to me that in raising Cortés to the height of titled nobility with one hand, King Carlos had pushed him downstairs with the other when he appointed someone else to govern Mexico. I said as much.

"Still, Cortés is overlord of more than twenty large Indian towns and has something like twenty-five thousand Indian vassals," the commandant said. "This is in addition to his large estates in the city of Mexico and Cuernavaca. And he's still captain-general of New Spain. Wealth, high honor, and none of the hard work of governing a huge territory. Do you think a mere reception will seem an adequate welcome? I think a procession and a band should meet him at the dock, with pretty children to present him with bouquets, that sort of thing."

"Do as you will."

The real reason for the visit to me then emerged. Would I be willing to defray some of the expense? "There must be a barbecue for the whole town. The wine must be the best we can get. There is not just Cortés to consider, but his noble wife. Doña Juana de Zuñiega is the niece of the Duke of Bejar, who defended Cortés so well at Court. We don't want her to think that Havana is just a rude, backward colony, do we?"

I agreed to pay half the costs, for the sake of the honor of Havana. Week after week passed with no word of Cortés' imminent arrival. The news that finally reached Havana was almost unbelievable. The Royal Audience in the city of Mexico had attacked Cortés again. A lengthy document charged him with many crimes and malfeasances. A copy of this Secret Inquiry had been delivered to him in Hispaniola, another had been sent to the king.

I told the commandant that we might as well shelve the idea of a splendid reception: before a royal investigation of these charges could be completed, the wine bought to toast Cortés in Havana would have turned to vinegar, the plump pigs for the barbecue would be ancient sows. He glumly agreed.

My disappointment was keener than his; because their son Martín was with Malinche I believed I could learn more about her from Cortés than El Galán had known. Was her marriage a happy one? Did she have other children now? Was she still living in Paynala? Or had her Castilian husband taken her to Spain? And so the Secret Inquiry that had prevented Cortés from coming to Havana had a personal significance to me. Would he be pardoned or found guilty? If guilty, he would probably be arrested and taken to Spain for punishment or reprimand by Carlos. But if the charges against him were refuted, then he would most likely continue the journey westward from Hispaniola as he had planned.

A privateer arrived from Hispaniola to tease me with half-news. Just before he had sailed, a galleon had arrived from Spain, flying the royal banner. He thought it might have brought to Cortés the king's decision as to the Secret Inquiry. But what it was, the stupid fellow had not waited to learn.

The humid heat of early summer had settled over Havana. On a sweltering afternoon in late May I was standing on the cliff where I had sighted Cortés' flagship more than eleven years before. But now I was watching for my partner Enrique's brigantine from Spain, long overdue. I saw instead a splendid galleon sailing grandly toward Habana's harbor, sails full and white against the lowering cloudbank that promised the rain my sugar cane needed. As the ship came closer I saw that it flew the royal banner. By the time it dropped anchor within the protective arms of the bay, I was on my horse headed for town, the first raindrops pelting me.

But no boat left the galleon for shore. Sailors climbed the rigging, furling the sails. The ship floated serenely on dark emerald water, prepared to wait out the storm. Was Cortés on the vessel? And if so, did he plan to come ashore or merely take refuge in the harbor until the tempest had passed?

Impatience seized me; I went to the cantina and there found a fisherman willing to row me out to the galleon.

The ship's hull loomed as high above me as a palace. The rain was heavier by now, and a crash of thunder drowned out my first hail. But then a mariner peered over the rail far above. He confirmed that Cortés was indeed on the vessel, lowered a wide rope ladder and took me to the aft cabin. As I neared it, the wind blowing my cloak wide, excitement gripped me at the realization that in moments I would see again that hero of my youth who last wished me godspeed in the dismal ruins of Tenochtitlán.

Cortés, his hair and beard grizzled, was pondering the chessboard on a small table between him and a fair young lady who wore on a gold chain around her neck a large emerald carved in the shape of a flower. Her little white hand fondled the jewel as Cortés played his knight and then looked up. The grooves in his cheeks were very deep, like old wounds. Seeing me, he was at first blank-faced, but then smiled as gladly as though I were an invited guest. He came to me, embraced me, and presented me to his wife. "Doña Juana is inclined to seasickness," he said then, smiling down at her. "This harbor was a welcome sight."

She had an exaggerated Castilian lisp, like the late Sandoval. "Thith ocean ith much bigger than I guethed."

Cortés gazed down at her as fondly as though she had quoted Aristotle. He clapped for a servant, ordered wine brought, and himself drew up a chair for me so we were three around the little table. When I told him how the commandant and I hoped that a proper reception could be arranged in the morning, he said he had already planned to sleep aboard and glanced with satisfaction around the cabin, quite sumptuously appointed, with walls of polished teak, bedcover of dark red velvet, and even a carpet on the floor. "Now tell me, what can I do for you, Arturo? If this visit concerns claiming land in Mexico, I stand firm about the need for permanent colonists."

Although I knew he must be often pressed for favors by the greedy or the needy, I was still annoyed. "My visit lacks so practical a motive, Cortés. Does your arrival in this fine ship mean that you stand cleared of the charges made against you by the Royal Audience?"

His face darkened. "Can you believe that those knaves hatched a document a hundred folio pages in length?" I saw the old signal of his anger, that distended vein throbbing in his temple. "I read it with astonishment and disgust. The testimony was vague and contradictory. The witnesses to the crimes attributed to me were either obscure persons who could have had no firsthand knowledge of anything I did or else were known enemies of mine." The vein had subsided; he shrugged. "The same old charges: that I withheld revenues due the Crown, hid Aztec gold, and so on. For novelty, two new crimes were added." He smiled crookedly. "But then, fame always attracts human maggots looking for a corpse to inhabit."

"What were the two new accusations?" I asked.

His eyes met mine levelly. "That I murdered Ponce de Leon, the first resident justice of Mexico. And that I murdered my first wife, Doña Catalina."

Astonished, I cried, "But what motive could they find?"

THE FIST OF SATAN

His sharp glance accused me of feigning innocence. "Of Leon, that I resented his power. Of Doña Catalina, that I loved Doña Marina and wished to marry her." He reached for Doña Juana's hand, which left her emerald pendant. "Since I did not do so, one would think this a poor motive, but such limping logic was typical of the whole absurd and venomous document. After my first anger abated, I saw that it had no legal weight whatever. I chose to scorn it as a momument to the petty malice of my enemies. I so wrote to the king." He smiled. "Did you happen to hear that when I fell ill in Madrid last year he personally visited my bedside and remained more than an hour?"

Doña Juana nodded solemnly. Blonde, gray-eyed, and lipped like a cupid, she lisped, "And then he thent a jugged hare hith own cook prepared, and a thoup!"

I said to Cortés, "And yet you will no longer govern Mexico."

His graying beard jutted toward me as his head went back, proudly. "Our sovereign told me he was removing that burden from me so as to throw open the door to my ambition for new conquests. I will soon explore and map the entire western coast of Mexico, and perhaps the shore of the great continent I believe lies to the north. I will later journey to the South Seas that Magellan found, where the king has promised me I will personally rule over any lands I conquer." He leaned toward me, his dazzling eyes fixed on mine. "First I will go to the north of Mexico, sailing up the west coast to that narrow sea where the great pearls are. I intend to circumnavigate it, find if the land mass to its west is an island or peninsula. You should come with me! How would you like to bring a bucket of pearls home to your wife?"

"I have no wife."

"Well, to your pretty mother, then."

"I have a sugar plantation and a small thriving enterprise which I cannot abandon to go looking for pearls." I smiled.

"Small enterprises do not interest me." He leaned back. "To complete our interrupted discussion of that Secret Inquiry, on writing Carlos that I did not deign to defend myself against accusations so scurrilous and false, I also said that I would not sail one league westward or embark on any new venture until the charges against me were dropped, my name cleared. I also asked that the present Royal Audience be dismissed and another appointed. I said that I would wait in Hispaniola for his assurance that this was being done." He smiled shrewdly. "Only three days ago he so informed me, and placed this galleon at my disposal. So now I will take my bride and my mother to my new governor's palace in Cuernavaca, where the weather is mild and pleasant. There I will begin to make arrangements for my expedition to the Sea of Pearls.'' His eyes evaluated me. ''Did you know there's an Indian legend that says that to the north of that sea there is a city with walls of gold? El Dorado! The land to the west is located more or less where the legendary Isle of California is supposed to lie, rich in gems of all kinds. You should join me, Arturo! I'll buy you a horse and make you a captain.''

''I have a horse.''

He warmed. ''What has happened to your spirit of adventure? Where is that brave young man who would have gone with me to Mexico against his parents' wishes and in only the clothes he stood in?''

''He was seventeen. A city of silver could lure him. But I am older now, and golden cities do not. The less so since I have learned all about your disastrous and unrewarding campaign in Yucatán and Honduras.''

He leaned back from me, looking older. ''I finally sent Montejo down there, with a fourth expedition. He had some severe difficulties before his ultimate success. Do you know who his worst enemy was? Guerrero, that Spaniard who chose to stay behind when I rescued Aguilar. He became an Indian in mind and body. Under his leadership, those Yucatán Indians nearly won.'' Anger heated his voice, and then he shrugged. ''But who can read the future? It is always a dark land toward which we must march with courage, expecting triumph.''

I saw the gray adoring eyes of Doña Juana gazing up at him, and I remembered midnight eyes that had once looked up with just such admiration. ''I am told that Malinche is now married to a gentleman called Jamarillo,'' I said.

The abruptness of this remark, for he could not know the thought which had prompted it, took him off guard and erased his smile. ''She was.''

''Was?''

''Jamarillo is dead.''

My heart stopped beating. ''When?''

''Last December. In Spain, where he went to visit his ailing parents.'' Cortés shrugged. ''A foolish duel. He was never much of a swordsman—''

''And Malinche? Where is she?''

"In Paynala. She has a large estate there, my wedding gift to her. She preferred that place to any other, although I consider it a wretched area—heat, humidity, storms, and earthquakes. Only last week a mariner I talked with in Hispaniola said he had just come from that area and had experienced three temblors in as many days. Slight ones, he said, but still I am beginning to wonder if Paynala is where my son should live."

His indifference to Malinche jarred me. "What about the boy's mother? How slight were those temblors?"

"No one was injured, or so I was told."

But I had to know this for myself. Jamarillo's death had filled me with wild hope. Yet anxiety for Malinche tore at my heart. I asked if a ship's boat might row me ashore.

"But the storm's not over yet," Cortés said, glancing at the aft window streaming with rain.

"No matter."

Crossing the dark and agitated waters of the harbor, I whispered a prayer for Malinche's well-being. Twice I had lost her. But now, at last, my chance had come.

Cortés was welcomed to Havana, but not by me. I alerted my pilot and crew that night and sailed with the early morning tide.

49

A winding river road led from the port to Paynala. Five leagues had never seemed so endless by the time I reached the town in the late afternoon. On the south side of the paved central plaza stood a Christian church of whitewashed adobe, buttressed and boasting a belltower. To the north loomed a gray-stone pyramid to the ancient gods. They faced each other like adversaries. All around the square were thatched stone Indian houses, except at the southeast corner, where a flat-roofed adobe dwelling in the Spanish style held shadow in its arcade. The enormous poinciana tree beside it flaunted brilliant orange blossoms, as if proclaiming the triumph of local verdure over the alien dwelling.

Evidently Spanish visitors were few. In the middle of the plaza an old Indian woman with a basket on her arm stopped to stare. Several dark little boys in loincloths came toward me to look up shyly, ready to flee. I smiled down at them and pointed toward the Spanish house. "Señora Jamarillo?" One of them, after a pause, pointed in the other direction, toward the church. My relief vanished when I saw the small cemetery to his left, behind a black iron fence. But surely the child would have told me if she were dead. On my ship I had dressed with care to look affluent but not pretentious: hose of indigo, doublet of pale blue, the sleeves lined with ruby silk. Hope had made me dress for celebration, to deny anxiety. As I took off my flat velvet cap to wipe sweat from my forehead, a choir of young voices sounded from the open door of the church as piercingly sweet as though a flock of the Pope's castrati had been magically transported to this backwater Indian town on the Isthmus of Tehuantepec.

My black mare's hoofbeats were loud on the paving as I headed for the cemetery fence to tether her. I had just reached it when the voices ceased and in a minute more Indians began to trickle out onto the steps and down, the women with shawls over their heads, the men in loincloths and some in shirts of unbleached cotton cut full-sleeved in the Spanish mode. At the sight of me they all stared, but no one greeted me or smiled. I walked toward the church steps, eyes on the entrance for first sight of Malinche in her widow's black. The steps were empty, the Indians making their ways home across the plaza.

Then from the dark mouth of the wide doorway she came into the sunlight. She wore a mantilla of black lace but her cotton skirt and loose chemise were like those she had when I first saw her, only of a deeper, richer turquoise. Beside her was a little boy in a ruffled white shirt and short dark pantaloons, Indian sandals on his bare feet. She paused to speak to him and to drop the shawl back onto her shoulders. Her black hair was dressed high on her head and the strong column of her neck was the color of honey. When she saw me, her face lighted up with the beacon of her smile. She held out her arms to me. I ran to her, and our outstretched hands clasped. We were both laughing. "Arturo! My dear Arturo."

"Malinche!" As we briefly embraced, no moment I could remember had ever contained the joy of this one. My head was light with it. Why had I tormented myself with foolish anxiety, lost the pleasure of anticipating this reunion?

"Mother, who is he?" The boy at her side was looking up at me with dark, unsmiling eyes.

439

She stepped away from me to put one arm around his shoulder. "This is Martín," she said to me. And to him: "This is Don Arturo, a dear friend of mine from long ago."

I smiled at him, "When I last saw you you were only three months old."

"Only three months old?" He looked up at me dubiously. "Then that is why I don't remember you." Above his head I saw a tall, thin priest in the brown robe of a Franciscan, and recognized Jeronimo Aguilar.

He stared at me intently. Nodding and smiling, he came to where we stood. He carried a little more flesh now, but his eyes were still cavernous. "You have been often in my thoughts and prayers, Arturo." His eyes went to something behind me and I turned and near the steps saw a group of Indians watching us. "Come inside and let me show you our church." I looked at Malinche, one eyebrow raised. I did not wish a church tour moments after our reunion, but she turned toward the door she had just left and I obediently fell into step, telling myself it would be good to get out of the hot sun.

High in the wall above the altar was a stained-glass window of the Virgin holding Jesus. Aguilar pointed up. "That was made in Europe, and to pay for it Doña Marina gave jewels that a vain woman would have kept to adorn her own body." In the soft light falling on her face from the holy scene she glowed with such loveliness that she needed no gems. When would I kiss those lips?

Aguilar was indefatigable. "She also built a school behind the church proper. The children learn to speak Spanish and to read and write. Doña Marina teaches them, aided by my young acolytes." He must have seen that the school did not interest me, for he smiled and changed the subject. "But you have had a long journey. Come, I will take you to your room where you can rest and refresh yourself."

A bed at the church, like any casual wayfarer? I glanced at Malinche, expecting that she would insist that I be a guest in her home, but she only asked us both to take an early supper with her at seven and hurried out, the boy beside her.

I was being offered everything I did not want—a bed, a nap, a good supper, instead of what I desired above all else: an uninterrupted private hour with Malinche. No boy, no Aguilar, no observant Indians. As I followed Aguilar to a monkish cell overlooking the church's inner patio with its central fountain, a slight resentment nagged. I had the feeling that he had guessed that Malinche was about to invite me to her home and had deliberately interposed his own invitation. But why had she so passively permitted this? Her house was quite large, so there could have been no lack of room for a guest. And she had been overjoyed at my sudden appearance. Of that I was sure.

I turned to Aguilar. "I would welcome a glass of wine, after my horse has been watered and fed."

He must have caught the cool undertone, but ignored it. "Yes, I must see to your horse. It must not be left unguarded in the plaza a moment longer."

He hurried out and I followed. "Surely you do not mean it could be stolen? In such a Christian town?"

"Paynala is only half Christian. You will understand that the old pagan influences have not been eradicated in only the few years since this church was built. There is a faction here that resents Spaniards and everything Spanish, including our Faith." He turned his head to regard me severely. "You were foolish to make the journey from Coetzacoalcos alone."

"I hired two Indian guides in the port."

"Well, your horse is all right." He sounded relieved. From the church steps I saw that it had drawn a modest crowd of a dozen children and as many adults, among these a tall, muscular Indian of perhaps thirty-five, dressed with ostentatious simplicity in a loincloth that reached only to his knees and was made of brown leather, perhaps deerskin. He wore a snakeskin band around his head and a necklace of dark green jadeite and silver. As I passed him to untether my mount he made a harsh remark in his native tongue, staring at me with beetle-black hostile eyes.

"Guilliermo is the leader of the unregenerate heathens here," Aguilar told me as we led my mare through the cemetery gate and around the church to a small stable at the rear. "He prefers his pagan name, Na Chel Cuy. He is a thorn in my heart, an obdurate creature whom the grace of God has not yet touched. It was his hope, apparently, to take Doña Marina as his wife after she returned and became cacique. In his rage when she came back from Honduras as Señora Jamarillo he has done all he could to undermine our efforts to Christianize this town wholly."

We were crossing the patio toward the front wing of the church. As he finished speaking, I felt the ground under my feet shift, a very slight, uneasy motion that seemed to arouse a tremor inside my body. "Did the earth move just then?" My voice sounded less calm than I would have liked.

"These temblors began again recently after many years of calm.

441

The old exiled priest Ah Tok tells people they are signs of the anger of the ancient gods of this land. He was banished half a dozen years ago and lives now in the depths of a cave in the hills, where I know he holds secret heathen rites to which some of the townspeople steal away, out of their superstitious fear of their old deities.'' He must have seen that my interest in these two thorns of his was not intense, and forced a smile. ''But now I must offer you the refreshment I promised. It is a wine made here at the mission, from our own grapes.'' As he poured it I saw a few broken veins on his cheeks and noted that he drank with eagerness.

The dim refectory with its long dark table and benches was pleasantly cool, and the wine was welcome, yet I would infinitely have preferred to be drinking plain water with the woman I had come here to see. I decided to speak bluntly. ''I feel that in offering me a bed here you discouraged Malinche from inviting me to stay at her home. Why?''

He refilled his glass. ''Perhaps she also preferred that you sleep here. She is recently widowed, still young, still beautiful, and the caciqua of Paynala. Her every action is scrutinized by many eyes. A male guest . . .''

I put down my goblet with a crash. ''I came here to marry her!''

He stared. ''Then you already knew of Jamarillo's tragic death?''

''I sailed from Havana as soon as I learned of it.''

''You are widowed too?''

''I never married.''

In their caverns his eyes left mine to glance at nothing, or the past. Was he remembering a heartbroken youth with a borrowed guitar, serenade unsung? He surprised me then by saying, ''I would not be sorry to see her leave Paynala. She does not owe these people here her whole life. God understands all she did, and forgives it all. But she must now forgive herself.''

''For what, in God's name?''

He reached for the wine carafe, saw my half-empty glass, filled it and then his own. ''You are a Spaniard, and you see her with Spanish eyes. But can you for a moment imagine yourself an Indian of this land—freed from the Aztecs only to find yourself a serf under the heavy yoke of Spanish rule? I tell you, hers is a heavy cross. To thousands—no, to millions—of Indians in New Spain, Doña Marina is their betrayer. What matter that in Paynala there has been no slave labor for an unfeeling Spanish landowner? These Paynalans know that she rules them not just as a hereditary caciqua but as a sworn vassal of Carlos of Spain. And they have heard what Spaniards have done to Indians in other places. Oh, they have heard! And so she is hated by hundreds of her Paynalans. And feels guilt, at times, as though she had indeed betrayed her own kind instead of having helped Christians to overthrow the cruel Aztecs and so bring Christ to pagans.'' His rhetoric had so moved him that tears stood in his eyes.

I was dumbfounded. "But surely the Catholic Indians here must respect and love her?"

"To more than half her people she is almost a saint. But to perhaps a third she is merely Cortés' former mistress who then took another Spaniard as husband. And as this town is split, so is she. Only her faith holds her together. She knows herself to have been God's servant when she aided Cortés, yet at times she suffers dark hours because of much cruelty the people of this land have suffered at the hands of Spaniards. With great courage she stands firm against acts of enmity done to her and hers, and continues with her Christian duty here. Of late, she has begun to worry about Martín's well-being. Only yesterday, she spoke to me about Cortés' promise to educate the boy . . ."

"She deserves a better life than this!"

He nodded. "But does she think so?"

When I went with Aguilar at seven to the Jamarillo house, all that he had told me of local hatred did not prepare me for what met my eyes as I stepped under the arcade. Beside the front door, bold against the white wall, the vile epithet was smeared with what looked like brown excrement: *LA CHINGADA*. The whore, the degraded victim, rumped and left in the dust to crawl away or die!

Stunned by anger and outrage, I bent my arm and tried to erase the words with my sleeve. The stink told me what had been used to print them. The stuff was dry. Some rubbed off but the whitewash below was stained brown. Aguilar took my arm and stopped me. "I'll see that this is scrubbed clean. You go in. Say I'll be a little late."

"Who did this filthy thing?"

"Na Chel Cuy, probably, or one of his bravos. I was afraid your presence in her home would bring on some act of malice. Now it seems that your mere presence in town has sufficed."

"An Indian did this?"

"I told you we've taught some of them to read and write."

"How can you be so calm?" I cried.

THE FIST OF SATAN

"This is not the first time, nor the worst."

"What could be worse than this?"

"A poisonous viper. Twice these have been found in the patio of her house. They are quite rare here. Once might have been chance. Two, no."

"Then her life is in danger here!"

"So I have told her. Knock and go in." He turned away.

The door was opened by a figure both familiar and strange. All in black relieved only by a large silver crucifix, the woman had a sad, serene face and looked like a Spanish widow until I recognized Doña Luisa, the daughter of the cacique of Tlaxcala. She greeted me pleasantly, with an apprehensive glance at the thickening twilight outside, but did not see the words on the wall. "Welcome, Don Arturo, to our house of sorrow." She closed the door, slid in place a large bolt, led the way to the *sala,* and said that my hostess would join me immediately.

Against whitewashed walls stood dark carved furniture from Spain. A lighted candelabrum on the table relieved the dimness. Shutters at the two small windows were closed and the air was hot and still. A vase of roses caught candlelight. There seemed too many empty chairs.

I felt Malinche's presence before she spoke and turned. She seemed to light the room. Now she wore earrings of gold filigree; a few small ornaments gleamed in the dark crown of her braided hair. I suddenly wonder if my stained sleeve stank. Would I still smell to her like young grass? "Aguilar will be a little late," I said.

"Sit down, my dear Arturo. There are so many things I want to ask you about your life now." As she gestured toward an armchair with her left hand I noted for the first time the absence of any ring. This, and the simple blue-green native dress instead of black intrigued me. Had El Galán been wrong in supposing a blissful domestic life with Jamarillo? She sat in a chair angled toward mine, the curve of the table with the candlelit roses between us. Suddenly her head turned and she glanced toward the arched doorway that led to the small entrance hall. "What is that sound? Do you hear it?"

I did, though barely: a mere whisper from the other side of the dark paneled front door. I knew what made it: a scrubbing brush cleaning the filth from the wall just outside. "I hear nothing," I lied. If the faithful Aguilar wished to protect her from such a sight, so did I. "As for my life, I am a sugar planter and a trader and own a caravel, and without much doubt will be the next alcalde of Havana."

She nodded. "Are you happy? Do you have children? What brought you here to Paynala?"

"I came here to see you. I have no children. Because I have no wife. As for happiness, I would say that I am busy rather than happy." It was the first time I had put my condition into these words: they sounded true.

"You mean you lost your wife?" Her eyes were wells of sympathy.

"I never had one to lose." I leaned toward her. "I never wanted a wife, because . . ."

The door knocker hammered. Doña Luisa admitted Aguilar. The tatters of interrupted intimacy hung on the air, but he did not notice them as he apologized for his tardiness with the grim look of satisfaction that attends a dirty job well done. Her eyes kept straying to my face, and I was sure my long bachelorhood was the reason. Good! Before this night was over I was going to spend time alone with Malinche, and in the meanwhile she could puzzle about my single state and perhaps come to the right conclusion.

At supper she sat at the head of the table, I at the foot. Aguilar was on one side, Martín and Doña Luisa at the other. Bowls of soup were placed before us by an Indian servant girl. The bowls were of red-brown clay but the spoons were silver. "As you can see, Don Arturo, we are a house of women now," Doña Luisa said, and cooled her spoonful of soup with her sigh.

"Except for me," Martín said.

"Except for you," Malinche agreed. I saw the motherly pride as she looked at him. The absence of other children told me that Jamarillo had given her none, for which I was deeply grateful. I wondered then about Malinche's absent mother and half-brother, and asked if her mother were still living. "She and her son Lazaro live in the little palace where I grew up." Her tone was cool. "Both are Christians. Her baptismal name is Marta."

Doña Luisa sounded even cooler. "Marta tries to seem devout, but she does not convince me. And why is she still friendly with Na Chel Cuy after he spat upon . . . ?"

"Enough!" Aguilar was firm. "I know your fondness for the late Don Juan, but we must be patient with Marta and Lazaro. They lead sad lives and have few friends."

"She is very nice with me," Martín said. "And she gives me camote candy."

"She is very fond of you," Malinche said.

445

"But Lazaro is stupid," Martín offered. "He thinks Spain is a city in Madrid. He thinks some god named Tlaloc brings rain to make the maize grow."

"But his Spanish vocabulary has improved greatly this past year," Malinche said.

The front door knocker sounded, a loud repeated battering, but no one showed interest and in a moment the Indian servant girl appeared to say "No one. Again."

I had become aware of a peculiar atmosphere, hard to put into words. It was as though a plague raged outside in the town, all over Mexico, and the people around this table were aware of it but chose to act as if it were not there. It was very hot and I wished the windows were open for the sake of whatever evening breeze might be astir, but knew enough not to suggest it. The yearning I felt to be alone with Malinche made me less appreciative than I should have been of the fine supper. At last it was over and Aguilar left and Doña Luisa took the boy to his bed. When I remarked on the authentically Spanish ambiance the house had, Malinche showed me through it in a truly Spanish gesture of intimacy.

The sala and dining room occupied the front or main building. In the right wing were her bedroom, Martín's, and a third which had been, she said, Jamarillo's. Malinche's bed had four tall carved posts but no canopy or curtains because of the heat here. When I remarked on the contrast between her Spanish home and her Indian clothing, she smiled. "I have some Spanish dresses Don Juan gave me, but they are very warm for this climate." Her rejection of that clothing, however practical the reason, pleased me. I found that I felt more kindly toward Jamarillo. Many hints had suggested that theirs had been a companionable but not ardent marriage. "But perhaps the contrast you mention tells a truth about me. I am a spiritual *mestizo*. Part Spanish, and part what I was born," she said.

We had returned to the *sala*; the heat within that shuttered room was now nearly intolerable, and I wished that I had chosen comfort above elegance when I had dressed that morning on the ship for this reunion. Worse than physical discomfort was the dismaying fact that since dinner my brain had grown torpid; I could find no words with which to make my way back to that moment of intimacy Aguilar had interrupted. "Might it be cooler in the patio?" I asked.

A cautious look reminded me of two vipers found there. I would have faced two dragons for fresh air. She nodded and rose.

Outside I was at once struck by the immense silence of the night. Even the cicadas were quiet now, although they had been chirping their lulling chorus loudly enough when I had crossed the plaza with Aguilar at sundown. In Cuba such a humid calm precedes a storm, but the sun had set in a clear sky, an orange orb that had slowly disappeared behind the high hills to the west of the town. Now a humpbacked moon shone down from a sky of stars. I found that I was nervous as we sat on the wide rim of the fountain. We both started to talk at once, laughed and broke off, and waited politely for the other to speak. I had to break the constraint between us.

I leaned toward her. "You were wearing this same color when I first saw you in Tabasco and fell in love with you." I was surprised that my voice trembled and tried to read her face, lighted by the gibbous moon. "Before supper I had started to tell you why I never married . . ."

A harsh scream cut off my words. I started, flesh prickling, and looked wildly about. A caged parrot hung from a hook on the patio wall. "Santiago and onward!" it cackled.

Malinche stood and went toward it. "When Orteguilla says that he wants to be let out of his cage." She opened the little door, and the parrot hopped to her wrist, wings wide to attain balance. Even by moonlight I could see its vivid coloring. It walked up her arm and settled on her shoulder, turning its head to regard me with a round eye. A malevolent eye; a possessive eye, its bright body brushing her hair. Was I jealous of a parrot? "I see the likeness to our dwarf friend," I said. "Who taught him Cortés' battle cry?"

"Don Juan. He gave me Orteguilla in Yucatán." The sorrow in her voice, the haunted look on her moon-paled face transferred my jealousy from a parrot to a dead man.

"Mother?" Martín, naked except for a small pale loincloth, emerged to stand beside his mother and to regard me with sleepy dislike.

"It's late, and you should be asleep, Martín."

"I just came to get Orteguilla. He likes it in my room."

"But you must put him back into his cage."

The parrot had other ideas, fluttered from Malinche's shoulder to the rim of the fountain. Martín stalked him halfway around it. The mother watched him fondly. I watched her. At last the boy and the parrot departed. By then I had the desperate idea that at any instant another interruption would occur: Doña Luisa would emerge to admire

447

the hunchbacked moon; the servant girl would decide to water the plants; Aguilar would return on some pretext. Malinche had seated herself on the fountain's rim; I reached for her hand and held it firmly. "May God forgive me for it, but I envy a dead man. If I had been in Yucatán, maybe it would have been me you married. Lucky Jamarillo!" The laugh I attempted was a mistake.

She stared as if at a cruel idiot. "Lucky? You think he was lucky?"

Confusion made me hate my tongue, which stuttered. "F–forgive me! That was an outrageous remark. May God rest him, poor fellow." The last sounded false as a brass gold piece.

"Don't you know how he died?"

"A duel, Cortés told me. Last January. In Madrid."

"Yes. He went there on the pretext of his mother's ill health. It enabled him to escape for a time from his existence here."

"The Castilian gentleman grew bored with life in a backwater Indian town?"

The remark made her back go rigid. Her voice was both hard and sad. "Did Aguilar tell you nothing of his life in Paynala? That Castilian gentleman endured three years of misery, of contempt, of malice. He was an alien even to the true Christians here. His blondness, his clothing, his home, his language, all these marked him as a Spaniard and set him forever apart. To the heathens, to Na Chel Cuy and his followers, he was the little husband of the whore of Cortés. And knew it. So do not speak of him with contempt again."

"But why in God's name did you stay in this place?"

"Where were we to go? To Spain? He knew that to return to his family with an Indian wife would put me in the same position as his here. Our hope was that time would prove our friend, that as the Christian faith prevailed in Paynala, the enmity would diminish and fade away. Here our home was, here my people were, and here we stayed. I cannot blame him that he took to drinking too much, and badly. I concealed this fault as best I could from Martín; Don Juan was good to him and Martín loved him. I was glad when he decided on the trip to Spain. I believed that being there and surrounded by his family and by people who respected him would be good for him and restore his self-esteem." Her voice broke; she bowed her head, I think to hide tears.

"Poor Don Juan Jamarillo," I said softly, and reached for her hand again.

She snatched it from mine, raised her head. "He died in a cantina—in a swordfight with a man who called me *La Chingada*."

The church bell began to toll the hour; ten iron tones. "But you are not to blame for that!"

"His mother told me the way he died in a short, cold letter. And said I had taken ruthless advantage of her son's romantic nature when I married him." The last iron note died away. She stood up. "Forgive me for speaking of such sad and bitter things. I did not mean to ruin our reunion. Now we must say good night."

I stood too. "Do you really think that I will allow this night to end on the dismal misfortune of your late husband? Or his mother's cruelty in her grief? Guess again, my dear. You have had enough of sorrow. I came here with one intention: to ask you to marry me. In Havana, as my wife, you will be treated with respect. This I can promise you."

"Your wife?" Her eyes were wide. "In Havana?"

"Why do you think I never married? I wanted no one but you!" I went to her and took her in my arms. At last, after so long! The sudden warm aroma of her body enveloped me, and with it the past we once shared. I kissed her mouth, and after the first amazing instant of feeling her lips melt into mine, the man I now was excelled the fumbling young Arturo. My hands caressed and fondled her and my shuddering sighs breathed my passion into her mouth, and we stood locked together, one ardent creature. I will swear that there was never a kiss like that before on earth. It stopped time; a little eternity passed like an instant; I was carried up into a realm where there was only us.

When at last we parted we stood staring into each other's eyes and I knew that not just our lips but our souls had kissed. Joy brimmed in me. "We belong together," I whispered, holding her hands tightly, kissing the back of each one. "Everything else that happened was just a mistake. Marry me! Tomorrow! Yes, tomorrow morning!"

Her eyes longed; her voice was desperate. "You cannot live here. I cannot live in Cuba."

"Marry me tonight! Aguilar can perform the ceremony."

"No."

"I do not hear no! I can only hear yes! I give you a choice. Tonight? Or tomorrow morning? Which?"

"No, Arturo. No." She tried to pull her hands away. I clung. "You do not understand. I will not desert the faithful Christians here. And I must stand firm and hope to help the others, no matter how they hate me!"

"They have Aguilar!"

"I will not desert my people!"

The desperate inflexibility and all that Aguilar had told me of her

449

made me realize I was now on risky ground. I spoke calmly. "Then I have the perfect solution. We will live part of the year here and part in Cuba. I own a ship, so transportation is a simple matter. You will not desert your people here, and I will not abandon my obligations there." I secretly believed that her pleasant existence in Havana would soon make her see how foolish it was to immolate herself in this place.

But she was shaking her head as though at a dense child. "Do you really think I would let you live here after what Jamarillo faced? Do you really think I would be regarded any differently in Havana than in Madrid? Do you think there is any place we can escape what I am? Do you imagine that I want you shamed as he was? Harmed, as he was? He died because of me!"

"I am not Jamarillo!"

"Neither was he, at the start!"

Again I remembered what Aguilar had told me of her. Only she seemed in a more extreme condition than he had believed. I took her shoulders in my hands and gently shook her. "Listen to me! You are not responsible for what he became, or for how he died! Or for what Cortés has done to Indians! You cannot punish yourself any longer. I won't let you! And I will not let you punish me by refusing the happy life I know I can give you."

She spoke as primly as a saint. "My happiness concerns me less than your future misery."

"For the love of God, stop confusing me with Jamarillo! I am not a fragile Castilian knight with my head in the clouds! I've worked, and schemed, and been clever. I am Don Arturo of Havana. I can offer you another world, my world, where you will forget the petty local conflicts here in Paynala!"

"The conflict would always be in my heart. We cannot change that."

"We can, and we will! The fact is, you love your misery! It is your penance. You act as if you are here by God's will. It is your own will that keeps you here. But my will is the stronger. And I tell you, you will marry me!"

She surprised me by saying "You have a ship."

"Yes!"

"Then when you leave here, take Martín with you. To Cortés. He wants to educate his son. It is time. I must not keep him here with me any longer."

She had astounded me. "Are you saying you would give up the son you love before you will leave this place?"

"He has a certain destiny as the son of Cortés. I will not cheat him of it. That is not love."

"And what will that leave you with, other than martyrdom? I see it now. You are unbalanced. You have had more grief than any woman could bear. You must rely on other judgment than your own. On mine. On Aguilar's. He wants you to leave this place."

She nodded. "He thinks my life may be in danger. I do not believe that. But even if I did, I would stay."

"I am taking you to Havana. To safety. Martín too."

She smiled at me tenderly. "I wish I did not know what I know. I wish I were not as I am. I wish I could share your life in Cuba. But . . ."

I flung my arms around her, pressed her tight against me, silenced her refusal with my lips on hers. The last words between us this night were going to be hers, just spoken. She would sleep with them echoing in her head. I took her hand and kissed it, back and palm. I broke my resolve and whispered, "I will never leave Paynala without you."

The household was asleep as we walked through dark rooms to the front door, our way lighted by the candle I carried. "Until morning," I said as I left her in her doorway. I looked back as I reached the arcade and she stood in the dark doorway beside the white wall cleaned of its ugly epithet, and I saw her as one standing on the threshold of a new life, her life with me.

Crossing the moonlit silent plaza to the church, I knew that this reunion with Malinche had given meaning to all my striving life since I last left her in Texcoco. In my cell on my boardlike cot I stared up at the darkness, smiling. I knew I would rescue her from this troubled place. For if God wanted her here, I would never have learned about Jamarillo's death, would never have come to Paynala. As He had shaped her path so it crossed ours in Tabasco, so He had shaped mine so it had brought me here. On this serene and heartening thought I let sleep close over me, deep, dark and dreamless. . . .

. . . To awaken and sit bolt upright to the sound of the world ending. Under me the earth stirred and heaved in slow waves to a low, grinding roar. Nausea trembled in the pit of my stomach. I tried to cross to the door but was flung to my knees. I heard the water ewer crash down and shatter, and the water ran to where I knelt on hands and knees like

451

a dumb animal. There was a last small shuddering under me, and then uneasy quiet. I got to my feet and ran through the church, past Aguilar who emerged from another doorway, shielding a lighted candle with one hand, his face elongated with shock. Far above our heads the temblor had set the church bell ringing wildly. I hurled myself out of the church and down the steps. Across the plaza the Jamarillo house stood serene in the moonlight. I started toward it.

The second temblor was worse than the first. I struggled for footing as though on a pitching ship. The terrible underground noise was louder, and to my horror I saw a chasm open the paving only a few paces ahead of me; first a small crack, it yawned jaggedly to a width of nearly an arm's span. I told myself this was earth's last hour. It was splitting into fragments, and next would come Judgment Day. I was flung to my knees and began to pray: "Be with us now in the hour of our death . . ."

The crevasse started to close with a great grinding noise from below. Ahead, the Jamarillo house began to shudder in the moonlight. The front arcade fell slowly forward; the crash as it struck earth and broke into rubble was unheard in the rumble of the earthquake itself. The entire front wall fell outward and added itself to the broken arches, while at the same time the right wall fell to the north side of the house. By now the earth had stopped groaning and so I heard the awful thud as the roof of the right wing dropped to the floor. Dust arose, silvery in the moonlight. I got to my feet and ran across the seam where the crevasse had just yawned and to the edge of the fallen rubble of Malinche's house. Now I could hear moans, cries, and screams from all around the plaza. The great church bell was still tolling crazily: the church still stood.

I climbed over the jumble of adobe bricks and looked down at the broken roof of the right wing, the wing where Malinche and the boy slept. The water had splashed out of the patio fountain, leaving the basin empty. The servants' wing still stood. Someone was screaming within. I struggled over wreckage to the place where I thought Malinche's bedroom was and saw jutting from the rubble a dark bedpost, broken off jaggedly. I frantically lifted and heaved aside broken chunks of mud brick that had paved the flat Moorish roof.

By the time Aguilar and some others arrived to help me, I had excavated down to the corner of her bed, my hands already scraped and bleeding, my lips repeating my litany: "Let her be alive!" When we got the rest of the roof off the bed, she was not in it. I paused, panting, full of a wan gratitude.

I uncovered her bare foot a little later. We all worked silently and grimly to lift a fallen roof beam and found the rest of her on the floor between bed and door. She lay on her side, profile toward me, legs wide like a runner's, one arm reaching forward. She had slept naked and the sight of that body pierced me with a longing even as I became aware that the thick dark tendrils across her cheek were her blood.

I touched her shoulder. It was warm. Aguilar said we should carry her to the church, in case another quake leveled the rest of her house. We carried her on a litter we made from a blanket one of the stunned, tearful servants brought, and we laid her on the cot of a monk's cell like mine, and covered her nakedness. Her eyes were closed and she was breathing faintly. One side of her head was badly injured, crushed. For the rest of the night I stayed by her cot, dozing briefly. Sometimes I poured water, drops at a time, through her parted lips. Her closed lids had the same look of mystery as a statue's orbed blind eyes. I kept touching her hand, and it was cold, but not with the chill of death. Sometimes I softly kissed her unwounded cheek and whispered that I would always be with her and that she would heal and be well again and come with me to Cuba. Once I lifted the sheet and looked at that brave body, so finely made, so generously breasted. I prayed, and prayed, and prayed that she would live. At dawn a troubled Aguilar came in to say that the body of Martín had not been found. This seemed a strange but unimportant piece of news.

The sun had risen when I nodded off to sleep, but I awoke with a start, looking all about for the strange presence I felt in that room. What I had felt was the absence of life in her. I touched her hand. She was gone.

50

"Her spirit is with God and all the angels of heaven," Aguilar said.

But I had yearned for her flesh on earth.

"God's ways are mysterious, and as a good Christian, you must bravely accept this loss."

But what of her loss, the loss of her life? What kind of God would permit an earthquake to kill a woman who had brought so many souls to worship Him?

"Remember that she has now attained life everlasting."

And a grave. In my heart the worm of heresy gnawed and became a serpent.

I was scarcely moved when Aguilar told me that Martín was alive. "It seems that he was eavesdropping and heard his mother ask you to take him with you when you left. So he ran to the garden of his grandmother's house, carrying his parrot with him, and he was hiding there when the earthquake struck. One could say that his mother's concern for his future saved him from a death like hers."

The serpent within me stared at him with cold eyes. It coiled cold as a stone at the Mass held for her soul, and when I stood in the churchyard while her coffin was lowered into the grave, and while earth was spaded onto it. The simple stone cross did not please me, and I told Aguilar "I want an angel in white marble, wings half spread, and it should have her face." I made a sketch of the angel. "Is there a stone cutter here who is enough of an artist to carve this?"

He nodded, and I gave him money to pay for it. His sorrowful face was more cadaverous than ever now, and in a remote way I recognized that his loss had also been great. He said, "This earthquake has been more than a physical disaster to Paynala, even though twelve died in it. The most terrible effect has been on the minds of the Christians here, because it killed Malinche."

"There is nothing I can do to stop that, or you either, perhaps."

"But I will try."

"I wish you well. For myself, I cannot bear to stay in this hellish place another day."

"You are thinking only of yourself and your own grief. What about Martín? The grandmother has taken him to live with her, a fact you would know if you had not been so preoccupied with your own suffering. Should a Christian boy, half Spanish in blood, be left to live among Indians of dubious faith? But Marta is possessive of her grandson and says she has the right to him now. And it is true that she is his closest living relative, except for one."

"Cortés."

He nodded. "Martín may not wish to go, but it's the best solution."

"All right. I'll take him to Cortés."

"Do you know which house is his grandmother's? Come, I'll point it out to you. I'm sure you can persuade him."

"Why should I persuade him? You're the one he loves and trusts."

He spoke gently. "My task here will be hard enough without Marta wailing to everyone who will listen that I kidnapped her grandson from her."

I grinned. "You devious men of God!"

Seeing the steep thatch roof of the palace where Malinche's mother lived, the thought occurred to me that if Malinche had been sleeping in such a house on the night of the earthquake she might still be alive. Her Spanish house had buried her. I went up the stone steps, calling Martín's name.

For minutes there was only silence, and then in the doorway there appeared a short, stolid aging Indian woman in old and ragged clothes, her hair hanging in two braids. She looked like a madwoman or a beggar, and then I realized she was mourning in the ancient Indian way. On her stony face hints of a savage beauty still lingered. "What does the Spaniard want?" she asked in heavily accented Castilian, standing in the doorway as if to bar me from entering her home.

"To speak to Martín."

"He plays in the garden."

"Then find him and bring him here."

"He will not want to see you."

"Bring him." Under my hard glance she wavered.

"Enter, then."

The walls of the main room were decorated with faded, bizarre figures that marched in endless procession, some with high headdresses, some carrying spears. A small green lizard sitting very still on the shoulder of a warrior sped suddenly across the wall and vanished.

Marta returned with Martín beside her. He wore only a loincloth. On his bare chest lay a necklace of large flat turquoises set in silver. When I asked him if he would walk outside with me, he nodded. Marta started to follow us, but I told her sharply I wished to speak with the boy alone.

In the shade of the ceiba tree was a stone bench, and it was far enough from the doorway where Marta stared out at us so she could not hear my low voice. "Are you happy here with your grandmother?"

Martín looked up from under thick black lashes. "I am happy nowhere."

"Forgive me. I did not mean 'happy.' I mean, are you contented living here?"

"I am not contented, either." He bent his leg, knee to chest, and picked at a scab intently.

"Would you like to go to live with your natural father?"

455

THE FIST OF SATAN

"With Cortés?"

"Yes. Do you remember him?"

"I think not. Maybe so." He removed the scab from his knee. A little trickle of blood ran down his shin. He spit on it and rubbed it away with his palm. "Why should I live with him?"

"Because that is what your mother wanted for you." To my horror, with those words a lump of pain filled my throat and tears blurred Martín's sullen face.

"Well, don't cry," he said.

I tried to deny that I was crying. No words would edge through my throat. I turned my head away from him, staring across the plaza until I had mastered my emotion. His face was gentler when I looked back at him to say, "I have a ship anchored in the harbor at Coetzacoalcos."

"Martín!" called a woman's voice, seductive. It was Marta, still in the doorway.

He looked at her and stood up. She beckoned him toward her, smiling. He faced me. "Let's go, then. To Cortés."

As we started side by side toward the church, Marta called his name again, her voice sharp now and imperious. He turned and looked back and gave her a very Spanish salute of farewell.

Enough of his clothing had been retrieved by the servants so that he could be outfitted in Spanish garments for the journey. A mournful Doña Luisa trimmed and combed his hair while he assured her that he would come and see her, something she clearly doubted. Against my arguments, he pleaded to bring his parrot, so I contrived a cloth pannier to hold the birdcage which would hang by his left foot when he rode behind me. In the other pannier I put the small flat locked chest Aguilar gave me just before we parted. It was beautifully inlaid with various woods and a design in mother-of-pearl. He said, "This contains a document I wish Martín to have, and which you may read at your leisure. I will leave it to your discretion whether to give it to the boy now or at some later time." He gave me the tiny key that unlocked the chest.

I left him on the steps of the church, standing where I had seen Malinche after so many years. Turning in the saddle to offer a last wave to that indomitable robed figure, it seemed to me that if any churchman could keep the Indians of Paynala from the dark cave into which the old high priest was trying to lure them, it was he. And I knew it would be not only a duty to his God, but an expression of the love he had felt for the woman now lost to both of us.

Martín was delighted with my ship, and I saw his sullen sorrow lift for a moment when he saw his first dolphin. We had fine weather for the run to Havana, where I would outfit myself and get money for the long journey to Cuernavaca and Cortés. I had intended to read on shipboard the document Aguilar had given me, but found that I had lost the key to the chest that held it. Rather than mar the wood by prying it open, I decided to wait until we reached Havana, where a key could be found to fit.

My mother welcomed Martín kindly, although even after I explained his presence she seemed perpetually astonished to find the bastard son of Cortés sleeping in her home. Martín was as astonished at our six Negroes, for he had never seen a black man or woman before. Rubén took him to see the sugar plantation and the mill, and my father showed him the site of his last mine up in the hills and told lies about the gold he would extract from it. The night before we left for Vera Cruz, Martín came into my room and asked "If Cortés doesn't want me, can I live here with you?"

Somewhat touched, I said, "What man would not be pleased to have such a fine son?" But I lay in bed debating in my mind the wisdom of this venture. How would Doña Juana behave, finding herself suddenly confronted with his natural son, and half Indian at that? How would Cortés feel about this fruit of a liaison now so many years in the past? It was one thing to have promised the mother that Martín would be given a position of importance when he was adult, but another to rear him. Lying sleepless, I suddenly made up my mind that if I saw that the boy was not welcome, I would raise him myself. More and more I had seen in him sweet traces of Malinche. Their smiles, now that he sometimes smiled, were almost identical. The very fate that had wrenched her from my arms might well have given me her son, the flesh of her flesh. This was not the flesh I had yearned for, but I had learned of late that destiny is a hard bargainer, and to snatch back any small portion of the lion's share it demands is not a small feat.

How strange was that journey to the plateau of Anahuac, which we had to cross to get to Cuernavaca! I passed along the same route I had traveled long before, but now the child of the woman I had loved then rode behind me. We were part of a caravan that included several mounted Spanish soldiers from the garrison at Vera Cruz and a coach full of Spaniards with business in the capital. We passed the edge of Lake Texcoco and I saw the new city of Mexico on its isle, and though many buildings had risen, they were not to be compared to those that once had gleamed like pale silver. I had no curiosity to enter this city.

The mountain trail to Cuernavaca led us so high that for a time we rode through clouds, but then we descended into a pleasant valley, much lower in altitude than the vast one we had left. The town was small, but the new governor's palace was built as for all time of dark gray volcanic stone and overlooked a park shaded by trees and lighted by flowers. The anteroom to which an Indian serving woman admitted us showed signs of very recent residency: several large wooden crates stood as yet unpacked, and the room was furnished with only a rude bench by the door. Martín and I sat side by side, the parrot cage on his lap, while the servant went to tell Cortés that Don Arturo awaited him.

He entered smiling, a smile that dimmed to a look of puzzlement as he saw the boy beside me. I rose and Martín followed suit, putting his parrot down on the bench. I said, "Cortés, allow me to present to you your son, Martín."

Flicking me a question with his eyes, Cortés looked down at Martín and said pleasantly, "It's been a good many years since last I saw you, Martín. Do you remember me at all?"

"No, Father." Martín looked up calmly.

"And how is your mother?"

"Dead."

The smile vanished. Cortés looked suddenly old and hollow-cheeked. Lifeless eyes met mine. "Now I understand the reason for this visit."

A pretty little voice called "Hernán?"

He did not seem to hear it. "How did she die?" he asked me.

"An earthquake."

"Hernán?" Into the anteroom came Doña Juana, dressed in pale blue and her emerald. She stopped to stare at Martín, then at me, then back at Martín again.

Cortés went to the boy's side and dropped a casual hand onto his shoulder. "This is my son, Martín. He will live with us now."

And that young gentlewoman smiled down at the boy without the flicker of an eyelid; she might have been anticipating this visit for weeks. "You are motht welcome, my dear, though I muthst warn you, things are in a meth. We only got here yethterday."

I found it in my heart to be glad that no rejection faced him here, yet at the same time a feeling of loss cast its fleeting shadow.

We supped very well and afterward Cortés declined to play a game of cards, of which his old mother was very fond, and he and I walked together into the garden, sweet with the smell of flowers. I admired the naked white marble nymph he had unpacked and set in place only that morning. He had bought it in Rome, where he went to bring the Pope a gift of four Indian jugglers, pleasing him greatly. Faintly from within the house came the voices of Martín and Doña Juana and Señora Cortés, playing their card game with a childish amount of delight at a win, loud moans at a loss. "Santiago and onward!" the parrot called, to laughter.

Suddenly realizing that I had not seen Orteguilla the dwarf among the household, I asked what had happened to him. "He and Blanca are enjoying an extended visit at the home of the Duke of Bejar, my wife's father. The pair created quite a stir at Court. The elegance of his wardrobe dazzled all beholders. He now wears two-inch *chopines,* like an actor, and towers as tall as Martín." The smile left his face as he mentioned the boy, and he thanked me for my kindness in bringing his son to him. "I will of course repay you for the costs of the journey."

I spoke rather brusquely. "I can well afford what it cost. It was a kindness I did in memory of his mother, and because the boy could not be left to be reared by the Indian grandmother who had treated her own daughter so cruelly."

"Your good qualities showed themselves to me when you were a green youth, and they seem to have grown with the years," he said politely. There was a silence in which crickets chirped their cheery yet lonely a capella chorus. "An earthquake," he mused. "I gave her that town to reward her, and in it she died. Sad. Very sad."

"Sadder for me. If she had lived, we would have married." I remembered her refusal, her renunciation, but I brushed them aside. I would have won her!

He was looking at me with amazement. "Married?" For all his praise of a moment before, he sounded as if he did not believe it.

Fury gripped me. "Married! To me, Cortés! Me! You were the first, I don't deny that. First in her heart. But I would have been the last, if she had only lived! Because she loved me, too. Didn't you ever understand that?''

"I knew she was fond of you," he said calmly. "But with you she would have been nothing more than a little foot soldier's camp follower. I made her a legend. You cannot argue the truth of that, nor will history.''

I could not argue with that. As Doña Marina and as La Chingada she would be remembered as long as there were Spaniards and Indians. But he had had her and I had not, except for one brief night. My voice was cold as I said "I think a chill is falling, and I confess to being weary. Perhaps you will forgive me if I retire early. I wish to leave early in the morning for Cuba.'' I moved toward the lighted doorway.

His laugh after my coldness astonished me. "Cuba again? Always Cuba! Why not stay here as my welcome guest and go with me to the Sea of Cortés?''

I turned. "Where?''

"That northern sea I told you of where the pearls are found. Surely there is someone you can entrust to manage those little enterprises of yours? My God, you're not yet thirty! You're too young to tie yourself to sugar cane and trade and miss the chance to meet an Amazon.'' He nudged me, full of good cheer. "Remember those tales of the big-breasted wild women, laden with gold and gems and hot for love?''

"Having already tempted me with a golden city, you now offer Amazons. What else among your wares? Don't mention fame or glory, and for the love of God don't talk of the salvation of heathen souls, for in my present doubt of either a heaven or a hell I consider the heathens well enough off as they are.''

In the sudden silence I decided I had shocked him, and cursed myself for revealing my heresy. I must learn to keep my present state of mind to myself, for the Inquisition was busy and widespread, and for words like mine men died in flames.

He spoke softly. "I offer you something else. Not glory or fame or riches or saved souls. Something else. Something that you want more than you ever wanted any of these, something you secretly yearn for, something you have missed, something you need without knowing that you need it.''

"What?''

"Danger.''

"Danger?''

"Great peril. The whisper of Death's black robe passing you by

460

inches. The full taste of the mystery which is being alive, alive and far out on the edge of the known, all that lies ahead a vast surprise.''

There was a sudden pang inside my chest as though a gong made of my own flesh had been struck there and still reverberated. I knew that he knew me, and that we were alike. We had been forged by conquest into other creatures than most men are. A wild urge filled me to abandon caution, leave the gains of the years, follow him once more. With an effort I shook my head. ''No.''

''Danger,'' he whispered again. We had reached the lighted doorway; our faces were no longer shadowy masks. His eyes were fixed on mine, gleaming, glittering, a wizard's eyes, or a siren's. I saw that for all his fame and glory and wealth and noble wife and fine bastard son, he needed to know he had not lost his old touch, could still lure men to follow him to an unknown sea.

But it was as important to me to know he could not lure me. I smiled. ''Danger is a whore I no longer frequent.''

He blinked, recoiled slightly. The luster faded in his eyes. I doubted that any other man had ever implied that he was a whoremaster, his trulls Danger and Death, Gold and Glory, and felt a kind of elation at my daring as we entered an empty *sala*, cards still scattered on a polished table. Cortés went to a sideboard and poured a glass of wine for himself and another for me. He watched me over the rim of his glass as we drank. In a gentle voice with just a tinge of mockery under it he said, ''On second thought, I wonder if I want you with me after all. You're reasonably brave, and you're clever. But one thing about you puzzles me. A certain lack of awareness, shall we say? Yes, a tendency to take matters at face value.''

''I don't understand what you mean.'' Pretending to sip wine casually, I felt myself grow tense.

''Has it never occurred to you to wonder why I always treated you differently from the rest? With particular kindness and concern? Why I made you my spy, my confidant, my secretary on occasion, giving you knowledge of privy matters?''

''How many of your soldiers could read and write?'' But my voice sounded unsure.

He shook his head slowly from side to side. A smile parted his grizzled beard and his eyes pierced mine. ''You could have been my son.''

After a stunned instant, I knew he was not my father. My resemblance to Francisco Mondragon was too great. But he had not

461

claimed that. He had only said he might have been. I remembered the blush on my mother's cheeks when I had asked her at seventeen if she had known Cortés intimately, and I recalled her vehemence in denouncing him as a womanizer. Had hers been the married woman's balcony he had climbed, falling from the wall on the way down? Or had he seduced her before she knew my father, when she was a very young girl and he a stripling? I would never know, but I knew what he was telling me with his cruel hint. He had seduced her.

"Ah, now I think you are aware," he said, eyeing my face as his earlier words echoed in my head: you could have been my son.

An answer to his attack rose in my throat like a scream: and Martín could have been mine! Oh, that would tent him, prick him deep in, rob him forever of his faithful Indian mistress who had loved no other man until their last farewell in Honduras. I felt the veins in my temples throbbing as his used to, and I clenched one fist, but I throttled the gush of words in my throat before I told him I had cuckolded him in the treasure room of a dead Aztec king. I could not be so faithless to my dead love.

So his was the last thrust. But mine was the victory. For as my anger ebbed I knew that his need to hurt me was a weakness and my silence a strength.

He had a servant come to lead me to my bed, and in going I passed the open door to the garden and saw the white marble nymph chastely covering her private parts with a spill of stylized drapery. I wondered if my white angel yet graced Malinche's tomb.

In Cuba I at last opened the little carved chest Aguilar had entrusted to me, which I had put away in the rush of preparation for my departure to Cuernavaca. A small key to a chest where I kept private documents fitted the lock, and on a stormy night in the privacy of my room I read the story of Malinche's life until her parting from Cortés. Sometimes it seemed as if I could hear her voice speaking, and I looked wildly around the room. Sometimes I felt her presence. I marveled at her ability to remember the very words people had said.

It was after midnight when I sat beside a last guttering candle, shaken by the power of her mind, the depth of her feelings, she, one of those Indians Europeans had regarded from the first as an inferior race. The senseless waste of that mind to death now aroused in me an anger as great as that I had felt at the waste of her beautiful body. The candle flickered out and I went to bed. The wind was howling around the house, and for me the universe reverberated with the shrieking, mocking laughter of a dark power that might be Satan but surely was not God.

There might be a God somewhere out there amid the distant spheres of the planets of this universe, but he had never been with us on our march to Tenochtitlán, nor had we ever been the fist with which He had smashed idols and killed men to save heathen souls. Where men kill in God's name, there God is not. That is true whether the weapon is a Spanish sword or an obsidian sacrificial knife.

During the next month this island of Cuba shrank to a paltry place, and my sugar mill and my ship turned into toys for a child. All my enterprising years seemed just a silly game played for petty stakes, and if a hurricane had flattened my cotton and young cane and the house with me in it, it would have been all the same to me. For hope a man must have, however unlikely, however much it is a secret, unacknowledged except in dream or reverie. And the source of mine lay in earth below a marble angel.

I wrote to my partner, Don Enrique, charged my faithful Rubén with the care of all my property when my father was indisposed, and told my parents I was leaving them for a time. Then I went to the storeroom and got out my old breastplate and the gilded helmet with the centaurs.

I might encounter pearls, perhaps, or Amazons, or the rediscovery of my old faith in God, or the bone-faced gentleman in black with the lipless grin, or even the golden city of El Dorado. But very surely I would find what Cortés had last promised me.

ACKNOWLEDGEMENT

The author wishes to express her indebtedness
to the works of Bernal Diaz del Castillo and
William Prescott and the many Mexican
histories which were rich sources of fact and
inspiration; her gratitude to Ellis St. Joseph for
criticism, suggestions, and encouragement, to
her friends Vera Caspary, Irving and Susan
Niemy, Wolfgang Nebmaier and Ramona
Stewart, and to her agent, Jay Garon, and her
editor, Beverly Jane Loo.

ABOUT THE AUTHOR

A third-generation Californian, Jane Lewis Brandt was raised in Los Angeles, the daughter of a noted painter. Until her first year at the University of Southern California, it was her aspiration to follow in her father's footsteps, but under the influence of a distinguished English professor she decided to dedicate herself to becoming a writer. Her first novel was published under the pen name Lange Lewis shortly after she graduated magna cum laude and Phi Beta Kappa, with the Bovard Award for top grades. Since then she has published seven other novels, as well as a number of short stories and novellas.

It was while teaching English in Mexico City (where her former husband studied medicine) that Ms. Brandt became fascinated with the subject of the Mexican conquest, especially the mysterious figure named Malinche, and began research for *La Chingada*, her first historical novel.

Ms. Brandt, an anthropology buff who also enjoys swimming and creative sewing, has one daughter, Haven, and now lives in Sherman Oaks, California.

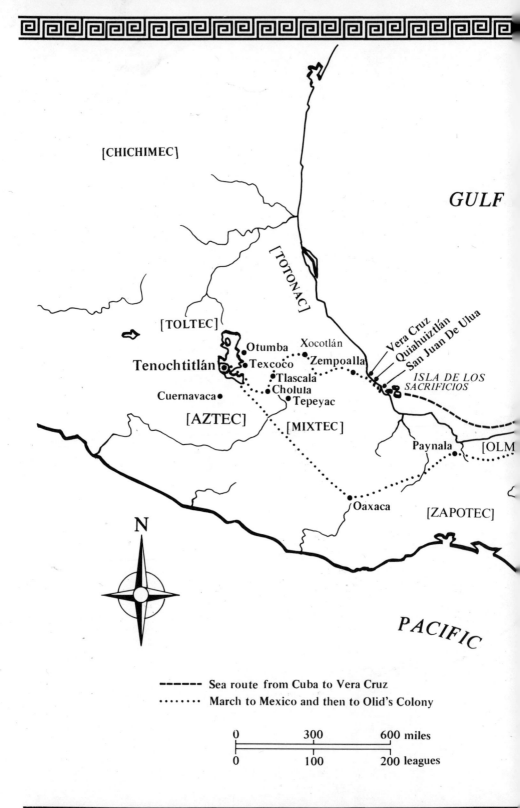

[CHICHIMEC]

GULF

[TOTONAC]

[TOLTEC]

Otumba   Xocotlán   Vera Cruz
                                  Quiahuiztlán
Tenochtitlán   Texcoco   Zempoalla   San Juan De Ulua

Tlascala   ISLA DE LOS
Cuernavaca   Cholula   SACRIFICIOS
                Tepeyac

[AZTEC]   [MIXTEC]

                                  Paynala   [OLM

                Oaxaca   [ZAPOTEC]

N

PACIFIC

------- Sea route from Cuba to Vera Cruz
······· March to Mexico and then to Olid's Colony

0   300   600 miles
0   100   200 leagues